AESTHETIC REVELATION

AESTHETIC REVELATION

Reading Ancient and Medieval Texts after Hans Urs von Balthasar

OLEG V. BYCHKOV

The Catholic University of America Press

Washington, D.C.

Copyright © 2010
The Catholic University of America Press
All rights reserved

Library of Congress Cataloging-in-Publication Data
Bychkov, O. V.
Aesthetic revelation : reading ancient and medieval texts after
Hans Urs von Balthasar / Oleg V. Bychkov.
   p. cm.
Includes bibliographical references and index.
ISBN 978-0-8132-3645-2 (pbk)   1. Balthasar,
Hans Urs von, 1905–1988.   2. Aesthetics—Religious aspects
—Catholic Church.   3. Aesthetics, Ancient.
4. Aesthetics, Medieval.   I. Title.
BX1795.A78B93 2010
230'.201—dc22   2009052772

Родителям моим Виктору и Людмиле посвящаю

To my parents, Victor and Lyudmila

CONTENTS

Preface and Acknowledgments ix

Abbreviations xvii

Introduction *The Hermeneutical Problem* 1

Part One: The Contemporary Horizon

1. The Modern Philosophical Concept of the Aesthetic 15
2. The Aesthetic in Theology *Hans Urs von Balthasar* 51
3. Hans Urs von Balthasar *The Aesthete and the Hermeneute* 78
4. Retreading von Balthasar's Path 101

Part Two: The Ancient & Medieval Horizons

5. The Platonic Tradition 129
6. The Stoic Tradition 176
7. The Augustinian Tradition 212
8. Bonaventure and the Late Medieval Tradition 268

Conclusion 323

Bibliography 335

Index 345

PREFACE AND
ACKNOWLEDGMENTS

In this age of interpretation it is all but impossible to make a credible claim without laying out the entire hermeneutic process of arriving at it, which often means going back to the roots. This task becomes increasingly difficult as the postmodern critique subverts the traditional modern rationalist techniques of interpretation, as well as the modern systems of thought: hence our renewed interest in retrieving our premodern roots. Our condition is also characterized by two great losses. We suffer from the loss of the aesthetic element, which has been stifled by science, technology, and formal logic. Our longing for the lost element of beauty renews interest in aesthetics. The equally profound loss of the divine dimension of reality once again generates interest in theological topics. The present study combines all these areas of contemporary interest by reanalyzing the retrieval of theological aesthetics from premodern thought by Hans Urs von Balthasar.

No such project has previously been undertaken, because scholars who possess the linguistic skills to tackle ancient and medieval material—classicists and medievalists—rarely are interested in, or possess an extensive knowledge of, contemporary philosophical, hermeneutic, and theological issues. On the other hand, the scholars who possess the latter rarely have the linguistic skills required to carry out a detailed analysis of ancient and medieval texts in original languages. The current project acquired its present shape gradually, starting with the classicist-medievalist approach of textual analysis and extending into contemporary theoretical areas as the deficiencies of the interpretive techniques practiced in present-day classicist and medievalist circles became obvious.

More specifically, this project started as an attempt to disentangle the conceptual issue of ancient and medieval "aesthetics." An interest in the premodern history of aesthetics was generated at the beginning of the twentieth century in view of the importance of the academic discipline of aesthetics at that time. Presently, it continues to be fueled by the nostalgia for our premodern roots that follows the deconstruction of modern rationalism. However, studies on ancient and medieval aesthetics available at the inception of the project seemed to lack conceptual coherence and to many appeared anachronistic, given the modern origin of the discipline. One of the most coherent approaches to the question of aesthetics in ancient and medieval traditions, surprisingly, came from Hans Urs von Balthasar, who examined the issue not as part of an academic study of aesthetics, but in the context of his discussion of philosophical and systematic theology. In their quest for ancient and medieval aesthetics, earlier academic studies had tried to pull together scattered ancient and medieval philosophical theories and to find unity among them based on the unified structure of the modern discipline, which includes art, beauty, and the mechanism of sense perception as its necessary components. Often these areas do not belong together in Antiquity and the Middle Ages, and such contemporary studies become discordant collections of notes on ancient psychology, theory of art, and definitions of beauty. Von Balthasar, by contrast, attempted to find the "unifying center" for ancient and medieval theories that would naturally emerge from the tradition itself. The ancient and medieval insight that the origin of the world is divine became, for him, that unifying center: the insight that reality is based on certain eternal principles, and that we can directly perceive these principles, or the divine, that radiate from its depth. It is the radiation of these eternal principles, as well as our ability to perceive them directly, that the ancients and medievals associated with the type of experience we now call aesthetic (the beautiful, the sublime, etc.). The study of ancient and medieval texts, moreover, reveals that even the terms used by the ancients and medievals for this type of experience were much broader than their modern counterparts and extended into areas other than aesthetic. Thus what we call the aesthetic (for example, the beautiful) to the ancient and medieval mind represented some universal aspect of different types of human experience, rather than forming an area of its own, as it does in many recent aesthetic theories. It was thus logical to follow von Balthasar's lead and approach the question from this direction.

The renewed interest in the question of theological aesthetics as a whole added to the appeal of this direction. In part because of von

Balthasar's efforts, theological aesthetics has become an important contemporary discipline. Whether or not the authors themselves who write on the topic are fully aware of this, a surge in the interest in theological aesthetics can be interpreted as a response to the post-modern thrust to subvert the traditional conceptual framework of truth and value by attacking the claim to "truth" by rational discourse. In post-modern circles, "truth" claims of rational discourse appear to have no more foundation than the convincingness of well-constructed rhetoric, and traditional ethical principles have no more value than the aesthetic appeal of an artwork. However, in contrast to Nietzsche's solution—to assume that the aesthetic point of view is the only possible one (the ultimate expression of the "will to power")—theological aesthetics, at its core, takes a different approach. By demonstrating an analogy, and in the case of some thinkers even an essential unity, between aesthetic and other types of experience, theological aesthetics attempts to show the reverse, that is, that the aesthetic is actually indicative of some sort of core "truth." At its foundation, the source of all human experience is of the same nature, and instead of reducing all traditional truths and ethics to aesthetics, one could just as well show how all aesthetic experiences point to some basic truths and ethical principles, even though one may not be able to define such principles with absolute precision. Theological aesthetics, thus, can be seen as an attempt to arrive at, or to show that one arrives at, some core principles by aesthetic means—by demonstrating the essential unity, or at the very least an analogy, between aesthetic, cognitive, and ethical principles.

Another common trend opposed by theological aesthetics is the idea, developed in the nineteenth century, that aesthetics, even if it is not the only viable discipline, is at least an autonomous area independent of either ethics or metaphysics. While the initial reaction of theologians was to banish aesthetics from theology, theological aesthetics realizes that viewing aesthetics as an autonomous discipline is damaging to both aesthetics and theology. Having become disconnected from the true and the good, aesthetics loses its roots as a philosophical discipline. At the same time, theology loses a vital area of human experience that has always been a way of connecting with the divine, and a most attractive and appealing way at that! Indeed, visual and auditory experience is a major part of being human, and a large part of human perception of reality comes in non-conceptualizable form. According to some scholars, certain truths, especially those of religion, are "wedded" to their aesthetic form. Although it is possible to restate them otherwise, doing so would be similar to trying to "restate" a musical ratio of 2 to 1 by means of an architectural proportion of 2 to 1. Both seem to convey the same basic concept, but the experience of this ratio in music will never be the same as the experience of it in the visual medium. In fact, it appears that conceptual-verbal form is not even the best medium for conveying certain types of truth. Language and conceptual patterns originally developed as a social tool, for the purposes of communication in order to coordinate group efforts to achieve concrete practical tasks. Therefore, it is precisely this collective functional-technical part of human experience that can be articulated most clearly by the linguistic-conceptual part of the human consciousness. When it comes to the more speculative realm of individual consciousness, which is where much philosophical and religious reflection belongs, one may not find language all that suitable. In this light it seems untenable to single out language and concept as an exclusive area of engagement, and the discipline of aesthetics, especially in theology, becomes especially significant. Human aesthetic activity in the form of artistic creations is also the most obvious way of demonstrating another important trend in contemporary theology: the contextual nature of human religious experience, the fact that forms of experience differ from culture to culture. Thus theological aesthetics rediscovers the power of the aesthetic and attempts to reabsorb aesthetics based on the "engaged," rather than autonomous, model for interpreting aesthetic experience.

Theological aesthetics also becomes important in the discussion of theological method. According to von Balthasar's account, the Catholic tradition, unlike the Protestant, never severed its ties with aesthetics. However, although formally preserving aesthetic concepts such as beauty, it "eliminated aesthetics" in a different way: by eliminating all attempts to *look* for the form of revelation and replacing all aesthetic insight by the "historico-critical" approach, which is meant to make theology more "scientific." Theological aesthetics restores the balance in this area as well, through an alliance with contemporary hermeneutic theory, which, unlike the historico-critical "method," sees the process of interpretation, in particular in theology, as creative, more akin to our aesthetic experience and interaction with artworks than to scientific research or "exact science."

It is important at this point to determine the precise role of von Balthasar and his project within this general scheme. Von Balthasar, of course, did not invent the discipline of theological aesthetics, nor is he the only contemporary writer to address the topic. Furthermore, the study of theological aesthetics is by no means confined to the Roman Catholic tradition, but thrives outside of it, as bibliographical references in the following chapters will show. It is undeniable, however, that von Balthasar's study, like no other, has reinvigorated the discussion and left a lasting impression on generations of theologians and philosophers. Also, no equally extensive contemporary study of theological aesthetics in the Western tradition exists, and von Balthasar is certainly unique in his attempt to retrieve some foundational insights for his theological aesthetics from the Western ancient and medieval tradition by engaging the texts to such an extent.

The current study has been thought out as a dialogue with von Balthasar. His perspective bears many distinctive features of a typically Roman Catholic approach to aesthetics, with its emphasis on analogy in comparing aesthetic experience with revelation, as well as its particular attention to the revelatory aspects of the aesthetic, and hence to the ideas of "seeing" (or an analogy of seeing) and aesthetic form, or perceiving a certain regular pattern. Some of these features, such as the revelatory nature of the aesthetic and the special place of aesthetic experience in mediating the divine, are shared by Catholic and some Protestant thinkers, such as Karl Barth or Paul Tillich. To this extent the current discussion will reflect some universal patterns in theological aesthetics. However, some other features of his thought, such as the analogy or the crucial role of form-beauty, are more distinctly Catholic, and thus we will necessarily emphasize certain themes typical of the Catholic tradition. At the same time, some features that are more typical for Protestant theologians, such as the emphasis on the emotive, affective, and transformative sides of aesthetic experience, as well as on the "non-beautiful" aspects of the aesthetic, will unfortunately be neglected. The limitations of this study require that we focus on the more speculative issues that have to do with the ways something is manifested or "seen" in the cognitive sphere. It will thus be about the phenomenological and cognitive value of aesthetic experience, rather than about the role of the arts in theology in general. One can see how this study would naturally call out for another, one that would re-examine ancient and medieval texts from the point of view of the aforesaid trends typical for the Protestant tradition.

Another important observation is that my own textual and terminological study of ancient and medieval texts revealed certain shortcomings of von Balthasar's approach and thus called for a more extended analysis of, and possible modifications to, von Balthasar's picture. And so, building upon and in some sense going beyond his work, this book attempts to answer the following question: can a more rigorous hermeneutics of the same types of ancient and medieval textual material, based on precise philology, knowledge of context, and maintaining certain principles of historicity, support von Balthasar's claims? Of course, the reader may ask why such historical, textual and terminological fine points are important for the budding discipline of theological aesthetics. Contemporary hermeneutic theory, whose insights von Balthasar intuitively followed in his own efforts, shows that all current ideas are rooted in the past and cannot be adequately understood without their historical horizon. No term or concept can be taken without its prehistory, which is all somehow present in it at any point. In fact, certain inherent meanings of a term or an idea cannot even be explained without turning to its origins. This is precisely why, in this hermeneutic age, elucidating the history of the conceptual framework of a discipline at its developing stage becomes a methodological necessity.

Since the problem with the studies of ancient and medieval aesthetics has always been their methodology—and the main accusation, anachronism—this study will start precisely with a discussion of how feasible it is, from a hermeneutic perspective, to look for modern ideas in ancient and medieval texts. Another crucial issue which still plagues many a study of "aesthetics" is what "aesthetic" actually means. Thus the study will continue with an analysis of the meaning of this term, starting from the inception of the modern discipline of aesthetics. Since this book is envisioned as a dialogue with von Balthasar's study of ancient and medieval aesthetics that will either confirm or critique his analysis, the next two chapters (namely, Chapters 2 and 3) will outline his idea of theological aesthetics and his approach to the hermeneutics of ancient and medieval texts. The introductory part will conclude with an outline of my own approach: the definition of aesthetics suitable for the analysis of ancient and medieval traditions in a historically acceptable and unified way, the principles of selecting the texts, and the main hermeneutic principles of approaching the texts.

The second part of the study will cover several major ancient and medieval authors for whom aesthetic experience plays a key role. Each chapter will present the current state of research in the area of the history of aesthetics, von Balthasar's assessment of the text or author, and then my own detailed reading and analysis of relevant ancient and medieval texts on aesthetics, in original languages, based on the principles outlined in Chapter 4. Some reflections on the essence of aesthetic experience and on the discipline of aesthetics, the fruits of the analysis of ancient and medieval texts in dialogue with von Balthasar's work, will conclude the study.

This project would never have materialized in its present form without the help and support I received from several individuals and organizations. First of all I need to thank my former academic advisor, Brian Stock, for his continued support of my project through the years. I owe my understanding of modern aesthetics in part to Calin Mihailescu, who took great interest in my project and was very helpful during its formative stages. Critical comments from Richard Viladesau and Frank Burch Brown, who read and commented on the manuscript more than once, have vastly improved the final shape of the book. My wife, Paula Valley, offered invaluable advice on the style of the manuscript, which further greatly benefited from the diligent work of CUA Press copy editor Susan Barnes. Finally, the project was supported by several research and travel grants funded by the Martine and Keenan Foundations affiliated with St. Bonaventure University, and the book owes some of its research quality to the opportunities provided by these grants.

ABBREVIATIONS

AB	Riches, J., ed. *The Analogy of Beauty: The Theology of Hans Urs von Balthasar.* Edinburgh: T&T Clark, 1986.
BEM	Gardner, L., D. Moss, B. Quash, and G. Ward, eds. *Balthasar at the End of Modernity.* Edinburgh: T&T Clark, 1999.
CCCM	Corpus Christianorum, Continuatio Mediaevalis
CCSL	Corpus Christianorum, Series Latina
CD II/1	Barth, K. *Church Dogmatics.* Edited by G. W. Bromiley and T. F. Torrance. Vol. 2/1. Edinburgh: T&T Clark, 1964.
CSEL	Corpus Scriptorum Ecclesiasticorum Latinorum
GL1–GL5	Balthasar, H. U. von. *The Glory of the Lord: A Theological Aesthetics.* Translated by E. Leiva-Merikakis et al. Edited by J. Riches et al. Vols. 1–5. San Francisco/Edinburgh: Ignatius Press/T&T Clark, 1982, 1984, 1986, 1989, 1991.
GPFA	Boudouris, K., ed. *Greek Philosophy and the Fine Arts.* 2 vols. Athens: International Center for Greek Philosophy and Culture, 2000.
GW	Lehmann, K., and W. Kasper, eds. *Hans Urs von Balthasar: Gestalt und Werk.* Cologne: Communio, 1989.
LS	Long, A. A., and D. N. Sedley. *The Hellenistic Philosophers.* Vols. 1–2. Cambridge: Cambridge University Press, 1987.
NA	Olejniczak Lobsien, V., and C. Olk, eds. *Neuplatonismus und Ästhetik: Zur Transformationsgeschichte des Schönen, Transformationen der Antike 2.* Berlin, New York: Walter de Gruyter, 2007.
OCT	Oxford Classical Texts
PL	Patrologia Latina
SB	Spicilegium Bonaventurianum
SVF	Arnim, I. von, ed. *Stoicorum veterum fragmenta.* 3 vols. Lipsiae: B. G. Teubner, 1921.
TM	Gadamer, H.-G. *Truth and Method.* Translated by J. Weinsheimer and D. G. Marshall. New York: Continuum, 1999.

Introduction
The Hermeneutical Problem

Ancient and medieval texts have been a continuous source of inspiration for contemporary philosophers and theologians who explore the area of the aesthetic, in particular the idea that aesthetic experience somehow reveals, and connects us to, the transcendent or divine: the work of Hans Urs von Balthasar, one of the most prominent figures in the area, can serve as an example. It is apparent that von Balthasar and many other scholars freely draw on ancient and medieval texts, as if they constituted a certain prehistory to their own ideas, and assume that the understanding of aesthetic experience as revelatory goes far back in time. Scholars such as von Balthasar who explore revelatory aesthetics by engaging in a dialogue with traditional ancient and medieval texts have themselves attracted considerable interest in recent literature.[1] As a result, because of the importance of some ancient and medieval authors for contemporary theological and philosophical discussions of aesthetics, there is also a growing interest in these authors, whose texts are often freely interpreted in terms of contemporary aesthetic ideas.[2] It is thus extremely important to provide a theoretical ba-

---

1. See bibliography on von Balthasar in the appendix to Chapter 2. The growing interest in theological aesthetics is clear from the number of recent studies, some of which have an extensive discussion of von Balthasar (such as the volume by Viladesau cited just below): F. Burch Brown, *Religious Aesthetics: A Theological Study of Making and Meaning* (Princeton: Princeton University Press, 1989); R. Viladesau, *Theological Aesthetics: God in Imagination, Beauty, and Art* (New York/Oxford: Oxford University Press, 1999); A. García-Rivera, *The Community of the Beautiful: A Theological Aesthetics* (Collegeville, Minn.: The Liturgical Press, 1999); G. E. Thiessen, ed., *Theological Aesthetics: A Reader* (Grand Rapids, Mich./Cambridge, UK: W. B. Eerdmans, 2004); O. Bychkov and J. Fodor, eds., *Theological Aesthetics after von Balthasar* (Aldershot: Ashgate, 2008). Numerous other titles exist.

2. There is a plethora of studies and interpretations that discuss ancient and medieval texts in terms of modern and contemporary aesthetic theories: some will be cited and dis-

2 ⮕ The Hermeneutical Problem

sis for the contemporary use of such texts: Are they still relevant? Can they still be successfully engaged and bring about a deeper understanding of aesthetic ideas in a contemporary context?[3]

This task becomes even more important in view of the following problem. The tendency to interpret ancient and medieval texts in terms of contemporary aesthetic ideas generates skepticism among textual scholars, who for the most part practice "historically accurate" and rationalistic approaches to traditional texts and who question the very possibility of a constructive dialogue between such texts and contemporary thought and dismiss contemporary interpretations as "non-scientific."[4] The main challenge, for a medievalist or classicist interested in contemporary interpretations, comes precisely from those scholars of medieval and ancient texts—and they are a vast majority—who use the "historicist" approach inherited from the eighteenth- and nineteenth-century hermeneutics of the Romantic school. One such recent historicist approach that exemplifies all makes the claim that in order to understand the works of ancient (and, one can add, medieval) authors, "we must take account of all

---

cussed later in this volume. A rather complete bibliography of the studies of ancient aesthetics can be found in: A. Sheppard and O. Bychkov, *Greek and Roman Aesthetics* (Cambridge: Cambridge University Press, 2010). Also cf. S. Büttner, *Antike Ästhetik: Eine Einführung in die Prinzipien des Schönen* (Munich: C. H. Beck, 2006). An extensive bibliography on the subject of medieval aesthetics can be found in: O. Bychkov, "A Propos of Medieval Aesthetics: A Historical Study of Terminology, Sources, and Textual Traditions of Commenting on Beauty in the Thirteenth Century" (Ph.D. thesis, University of Toronto, 1999), 4–10. Cf. also idem, "The Reflection of Some Traditional Stoic Ideas in the Thirteenth-Century Scholastic Theories of Beauty," *Vivarium* 34, no. 2 (1996): 141–60; "*Decor ex praesentia mali*: Aesthetic Explanation of Evil in the Thirteenth-Century Franciscan Thought," *Recherches de Théologie et Philosophie médiévales* 68, no. 2 (2001): 245–69.

3. Despite the great number of general studies on theological aesthetics, in his *Theological Aesthetics*, x and 11, R. Viladesau admits that the subject is too broad for one book and that new, more focused studies on theological aesthetics are needed that would provide "more detailed and adequate treatments" of the subject "to complement and advance" his "introductory and schematic study." The present monograph is one such focused study. The lack of a theoretical basis for the interpretation of traditional texts in terms of aesthetics is apparent both in the existing philosophical studies on medieval aesthetics (see O. V. Bychkov, "A Propos of Medieval Aesthetics"), and in studies of theological aesthetics, including the one by von Balthasar: see below in Chapter 3.

4. It is true that many studies of "medieval aesthetics," indeed, lack any consistent approach and cannot stand up to such critique. E. de Bruyne's *Études d'esthétique médiévale*, 3 vols. (Bruges: De Tempel, 1946), for example, lacks almost any method in selecting "aesthetic" texts; G. Pöltner's *Schönheit: eine Untersuchung zum Ursprung des Denkens bei Thomas von Aquin* (Vienna/Freiburg/Basel: Herder, 1978) often overinterprets without a clear textual basis (see O. V. Bychkov, "A Propos of Medieval Aesthetics," 4–6, 8). However, the question raised here is a general one and should not be affected by the fact that particular studies failed to address it properly.

the concrete conditions in which they wrote" including the "framework of the school," contemporary rhetorical rules, etc.[5] "One cannot read an ancient author the way one does a contemporary author ... " because "works of antiquity are produced under entirely different conditions."[6] The most important rules of the suggested "method" of interpretation are "placing it [the text] in the group from which it emanates, in the tradition of its dogmas," "understanding its goals," attempting to "distinguish what the author ... could or could not say, and, above all, what he meant to say" (p. 64), working hard "at discerning the original meanings of the formulae" (p. 68). This approach reduces the texts to their "historically accurate" meanings that can be understood only in the "true historical context," that is, after studying all the surrounding circumstances under which they were created: contemporary school systems, debates, etc. The ancient or medieval tradition is viewed as a number of rigid individual "systems" of thought and school affiliations, the "true" meaning of which can be discovered. Thus only one particular historical period or a particular "system of thought" is allowed to be studied that is totally separated from, and has little in common with the present-day theoretical reflection.

There is certainly nothing wrong with good philology and knowledge of contemporary practices. In fact, the present study will attempt to make a good use of the tools developed by the historico-critical method that seem to be lacking in some present-day interpreters of the past traditions in aesthetics. However, a narrow-minded approach to the historico-critical method creates an extremely limiting system of views on interpretation. From this limited point of view, if one assumes the standpoint of a medieval or ancient thinker, many present-day issues in theology and philosophy, including aesthetics, become nonexistent, and, therefore, one cannot legitimately look for them in earlier texts. Several scholars claim that to address the question of aesthetics as medieval is a historical impossibility. Unlike in the modern period, they maintain, there is no conceptually unified aesthetic theory in the

---

5. P. Hadot, *Philosophy as a Way of Life: Spiritual Exercises from Socrates to Foucault*, edited by A. I. Davidson, translated by M. Chase (Oxford: Blackwell, 1995), 61. Hadot's approach is favored by many medievalists, as exemplified by a reference in J. McEvoy, "Does Augustinian *Memoria* Depend on Plotinus?" in *The Perennial Tradition of Neoplatonism*, edited by J. J. Cleary, Ancient and Medieval Philosophy 1.24 (Louvain: Leuven University Press, 1997), 393–94.

6. Hadot, *Philosophy as a Way of Life*, 61.

Middle Ages, and modern aesthetic categories are, strictly speaking, inapplicable to earlier periods, since an exclusively aesthetic understanding of certain types of experience does not come until the appearance of bourgeois theories of taste.[7] The historicist approach also presupposes a precise methodology, which must help the scholar to arrive at that "correct" historical knowledge that is the goal of a historicist. Such methodology, naturally, calls for the exclusion of any possible modern or contemporary influence.

Now even if the task of discovering the "correct" meaning of texts were possible, the above approach would relegate ancient and medieval texts to their limited historical value: they would have meaning and value only in the context of contemporary medieval debates, but not of our present-day thought and tradition. However, this type of approach immediately runs into a major methodological problem. On the one hand, it rightly acknowledges the historicity of medieval texts and affirms that

---

7. Thus, J. A. Aertsen ("Beauty: Medieval Concepts," in vol. 1 of *Encyclopedia of Aesthetics*, edited by M. Kelly [New York/Oxford: Oxford University Press, 1998], 249–51, here 251), after acknowledging that Aquinas's statements are "not intended as an aesthetic theory," adds that it is "misleading to speak of a 'medieval aesthetics' or the 'aesthetics of Thomas Aquinas.'" According to him, "only after the Middle Ages is a philosophical aesthetics established in which beauty is given an independent place beside truth and goodness." A. Speer, in his article "Aquinas, Thomas" in the same volume (76–79), contends that a modern understanding of aesthetics "is not to be found in the Middle Ages," and the "statements of Thomas Aquinas about 'art' and 'beauty' must not be taken in this sense" (78). According to Speer, the "multiple meanings of artistic activity in the Middle Ages, each deriving from particular and diverse conceptions of beauty, can only be understood if read with respect to a general hermeneutical reservation." See Aertsen, "Beauty: Medieval Concepts," in vol. 1 of *Encyclopedia of Aesthetics*, edited by M. Kelly, 249–51 (New York/Oxford: Oxford University Press, 1998); cf. idem, "Beauty in the Middle Ages: A Forgotten Transcendental?" *Medieval Philosophy and Theology* 1 (1991): 68–97; A. Speer, "Aquinas, Thomas," in vol. 1 of *Encyclopedia of Aesthetics*, edited by M. Kelly, 76–79 (New York/Oxford: Oxford University Press, 1998). Cf. L. Müller, "Das 'Schöne' im Denken des Thomas von Aquin," *Theologie und Philosophie* 57 (1982): 423, according to whom the "problem of aesthetics is alien to the Middle Ages." Regarding the bourgeois theories of taste see: P. Bürger, *Theory of the Avant-garde*, translated by M. Shaw (Minneapolis: University of Minnesota Press, 1984); A. Bowie, *Aesthetics and Subjectivity: From Kant to Nietzsche* (Manchester: Manchester University Press, 1990); L. Ferry, *Homo Aestheticus: The Invention of Taste in the Democratic Age*, translated by R. de Loaiza (Chicago/London: University of Chicago Press, 1993). Some studies provide a more balanced approach—without, however, extensively engaging contemporary hermeneutic thought. Cf. V. Olejniczak Lobsien, "Neuplatonismus und Ästhetik: Eine Einleitung," in *Neuplatonismus und Ästhetik: Zur Transformationsgeschichte des Schönen*, Transformationen der Antike 2, edited by V. Olejniczak Lobsien and C. Olk, 3–4 (Berlin/New York: Walter de Gruyter, 2007; henceforth abbreviated as *NA*). Although she points out that there was no unified discipline of aesthetics in premodern times, Lobsien still thinks that some aspects of premodern aesthetic thought are relevant today and sees a possibility of a constructive dialogue between ancients and moderns.

the historical difference between the contemporary standpoint and the historical time period cannot be dismissed. It proclaims that a medieval text is enclosed in its historical period and is essentially removed from contemporary mentality. On the other hand, the rationalistic-historical approach sets the impossible task of discovering the "true meaning" of medieval texts!

Given this seeming impasse, theoretical reflection on the process of recovering the meaning of ancient and medieval texts in our time becomes crucial. In order to claim legitimacy for any particular way of reading a traditional text, one must first become fully aware of the hermeneutical approach that will be used to address a number of theoretical questions: Is it at all possible to retrieve the meaning of ancient and medieval theological and philosophical texts? What sort of meaning can we hope to recover? And, finally, how should one proceed to recover this meaning? Thus, before turning to the interpretation of ancient and medieval texts in terms of the idea of aesthetic experience as revealing, we must first of all answer, in a consistent way, the question whether traditional texts can be successfully engaged in a dialogue involving an essentially modern topic of aesthetics.

At the theoretical level, two major questions arise: first, how to bridge the temporal distance between the present and the ancient/medieval tradition, and, second, whether there can be a precise methodology of interpreting traditional texts in contemporary terms. We will approach these questions using Gadamer's discussion of hermeneutics.[8]

First of all, Gadamer sharply criticizes the position that "an age should be understood in terms of itself" (Dilthey), and the presumption that "one can overcome the fact that the historical observer is tied to time and place."[9] He regards as "absurd" the claim that a "correct" interpretation of a historical text can be obtained by a present-day interpreter (*TM* 120). Because of the historicity of our position, the temporal

---

8. My understanding of the theory of hermeneutics, as laid out in the following account, was greatly enriched by the international conference "Between the Human and the Divine: Philosophical and Theological Hermeneutics," which was held on May 5–10, 2002, at St. Bonaventure University, N.Y., in particular by the papers presented by M. Westphal, R. Palmer, and F. Schüssler-Fiorenza. Some of the material on Gadamer presented below was used in my own paper presented at that conference, as well as in the paper "The Hermeneutics and Retrieval of the Aesthetic Meaning of Traditional Texts" presented earlier at the 15th International Congress of Aesthetics at Kanda University, Makuhari, Japan (Aug. 27–31, 2001).

9. H.-G. Gadamer, *Truth and Method*, translated by J. Weinsheimer and D. G. Marshall (New York: Continuum, 1999), 231. This translation will henceforth be referred to as *TM*.

distance between the present-day interpreter and the past can never be fully overcome. Although it seems natural to try to determine what the "actual" intention of the author was, as well as the way the text was "actually" perceived by a contemporary reader, in fact such an approach "is full of unexamined idealization" (*TM* 395). The past that is reconstructed by a present-day interpreter will always be historically conditioned by the present position of the interpreter (although such reconstruction, of course, can be achieved to some degree, depending on the mastery of the interpreter). Still, despite the claims of the "historical" method, it can never overcome its own historicity (*TM* 300–301).[10]

Given the fact that one cannot fully overcome the temporal distance between the present and a traditional text, how is any interpretation of texts from the past at all possible for a present-day scholar? The phenomenological tradition of Husserl and Heidegger provides an important insight into the mode of being of ideas and their understanding, which might just show the way out of this perplexity. All our conscious experience is open to the historical horizons of the past and future. However, these horizons are fused into a unified flow of continuous temporal experience that underlies all other particular experiences.[11] Heidegger insists on the crucial role of the historical temporality and finitude of our experience. This temporality is also the "mode of being of understanding itself . . . " (*TM* 121). All understanding is temporal: just as one cannot ignore the "historical layer" of understanding, one cannot exclude its present-day framework, which has undergone a significant change in the course of history. Although no "correct" historical

---

10. Cf.: "Ultimately, this view of hermeneutics is as nonsensical as all restitution and restoration of past life. Reconstructing the original circumstances, like all restoration, is a futile undertaking in view of the historicity of our being" (*TM* 167). The same holds true for trying to reconstruct the "intention of the author," or the author's experience and meaning. This feature of Romantic hermeneutics was already abandoned by Heidegger. Following N. Wolterstorff, one can say that what the reader of a text wants to know is not what the author intended to say, but what the author actually said about something: cf. N. Wolterstorff, *Divine Discourse: Philosophical Reflections on the Claim That God Speaks* (New York: Cambridge University Press, 1995), 93.

11. "[T]he discreteness of experience . . . is not an ultimate phenomenological datum. Rather, every such intentional experience always implies a twofold empty horizon of what is not actually meant in it, but toward which an actual meaning can, of its nature, be directed; and the unity of the flow of experience obviously includes the whole of all experiences that can be thematized in this way" (*TM* 245). This observation is certainly reminiscent of Husserl's assessment in *Cartesian Meditations*: cf. E. Husserl, *Cartesian Meditations: An Introduction to Phenomenology*, translated by D. Cairns (The Hague: Martinus Nijhoff, 1960), 43 (Meditation 2), 60–61 (Meditation 3).

understanding of the past is possible "from the point of view of that period," one must bear in mind that any present understanding is always historically conditioned: so there is no such thing as the "present meaning" of something, either. The understanding of any concept or text always includes its "temporal extension": the tradition of its interpretation is part of it. Our understanding of a particular phenomenon is a product of a historical development, and so contains all the past "layers." There is thus a sort of a reciprocal relationship between the past and present in any process of understanding/interpretation.[12] This "historical extension" of concepts or texts, which is always included in the process of understanding/interpretation, is paralleled in the historical being of artworks and becomes one of the major features of Gadamer's view of hermeneutics.[13]

We arrive, then, at a viable solution to the problem of interpreting the past. First, it is not entirely impossible to overcome the temporal distance between the past and the present, since we are part of that past tradition, and so there is always some continuity. The fact that we, too, belong to the tradition, that is, have our "temporal extension," combined with the observation that our temporal experience of the past and present forms a continuous whole, creates the necessary connection between the past tradition and our present perception of it. The fact that "understanding in the human sciences . . . lets itself be addressed by tradition" (*TM* 282–83) removes the antithesis between tradition and our understanding of it. Since tradition affects the human sciences, despite all attempts to "purify" the methodological procedures of these sciences, the element of tradition must be recognized and made productive, instead of being viewed as an impediment to knowledge. Because of the continuity of our temporal experience, Gadamer writes, "time is no longer primarily a gulf to be bridged because it separates; it is actually the supportive ground of the course of events in which the present is rooted. Hence temporal distance is not something that must be overcome. . . . In fact the important thing is to recognize temporal distance

---

12. "But understanding it will always involve more than merely historically reconstructing the past 'world' to which the work belongs. Our understanding will always retain the consciousness that we too belong to that world, and correlatively that the work too belongs to our world" (*TM* 290).

13. According to Gadamer, the unity and identity of a text or a work of art includes all the history of its interpretation: all its historical dimensions are contained in it contemporaneously (*TM* 120–21).

as a positive and productive condition enabling understanding. It is . . . filled with the continuity of custom and tradition, in the light of which everything handed down presents itself to us" (TM 297). In fact, all that a medieval or classical scholar needs is a sharp sense of the historicity of ideas. In order to engage a contemporary idea in the context of a traditional text, one can trace the continuity of the idea back to the earlier tradition, thereby highlighting its "historical extension."

Second, the goal of overcoming this temporal distance in an unbiased and "historically correct" way—as historicists want—is not even particularly desirable. Gadamer uses the example of the "classical" to show that only the tradition that is relevant to the present—that is, that can be interpreted by it (thus becoming "timeless")—is preserved.[14] Traditional texts become intelligible to us only if a present-day "living" meaning is retrieved.[15] Gadamer's idea that a classic is both historical and a-historical at the same time, and that the truth that it discloses somehow transcends history and remains relevant is extremely important, for example, for the sort of interpretation that occurs in systematic theology.[16] It is quite remarkable that the seemingly "uncritical" approach—predating the "historical school"—that dealt with traditional texts as if they were contemporary and tried to retrieve only relevant meanings, now acquires critical validity! Gadamer describes the process of such historical understanding, which combines the horizons of the past and present, continuously influencing each other, as the "fusion of horizons" (TM 306). The true "historical consciousness" does not attempt to transpose itself from one horizon to another, but constantly moves toward convergence of the two horizons, broadening the horizon of the present so as to include the historical dimension (TM 304).[17]

---

14. "[T]he classical preserves itself precisely because it is significant in itself and interprets itself; i.e., speaks in such a way that it is not a statement about what is past . . . rather, it says something to the present as if it were said specifically to it. What we call 'classical' does not first require the overcoming of historical distance, for in its own constant mediation it overcomes this distance by itself. The classical, then, is certainly 'timeless,' but this timelessness is a mode of historical being" (TM 289–90).

15. "it is universally true of texts that only in the process of understanding them is the dead trace of meaning transformed back into living meaning" (TM 164).

16. E.g., cf. D. Tracy, *The Analogical Imagination: Christian Theology and the Culture of Pluralism* (New York: Crossroad, 1981), 102. As an example of the continuing relevance of traditional texts Tracy mentions (103) the retrieval of Aristotle's notions of φρόνησις and 'truth of poetry' in contemporary thought by Gadamer and others.

17. Cf.: "In fact the horizon of the present is continually in the process of being formed because we are continually having to test all our prejudices. An important part of this test-

Turning to the question of method, Gadamer has serious doubts about the "precise" scientific methods of the historical school that preclude any interpretation of traditional texts in contemporary terms.[18] In fact, he questions the general applicability of such methods to the human sciences.[19] But if no precise "scientific" methods of approaching historical texts can be found, what is the appropriate way of engaging a historical text? In this case, the model of a dialogue or conversation becomes very productive.[20] According to Gadamer, the hermeneutics of a traditional text "... implies the primacy of dialogue and the structure of question and answer": the text also puts a question to the interpreter (*TM* 369). The "highest" type of hermeneutic experience, according to Gadamer, includes maintaining an "openness to tradition" (*TM* 361), allowing oneself to be "addressed by tradition" (*TM* 377), being able to "listen" to tradition: in other words, treating tradition as another person or a partner in a living conversation. As a result of such a dialogue, the aforementioned "fusion of the horizons of understanding" is achieved (*TM* 378): in the process of understanding, the interpreter bends the

---

ing occurs in encountering the past and in understanding the tradition from which we come" (*TM* 306).

18. A prominent feature of Romantic hermeneutics already repudiated by Heidegger is exactly such methodological "objectivism," described by W. Dilthey in "The Rise of Hermeneutics," in *Hermeneutics and the Study of History*, vol. 4 of *Selected Works*, edited by R. A. Makkreel and F. Rodi (Princeton: Princeton University Press, 1985), 235–58. Thus according to Dilthey, there could be a "complete and objective interpretation" (238) of a literary or philosophical work that would glean the intention of the author, provided that it follows a "rule-guided procedure" or methodology (237).

19. Following Gadamer, Tracy (*Analogical Imagination*) gives an excellent account of the problems that arise from a historicist approach that applies "scientific" methods to traditional texts. The advocates of "scientific" methods, according to Tracy (105), assume "that the past is irrevocably strange and has no more than spectator interest for us now"; that "the real meaning of a text may be uncovered by a deciphering, via some new method or technique . . . , the mind of the author, the social circumstances, the life-world of the text, or the reception of the text by its original addressees." As a result, he continues, "the meaning of the text becomes an object for our insatiable curiosity as to the strange possibilities of the human spirit. The text itself has simply nothing to say to us any longer, for its questions and answers, its subject matter, are now merely historical curiosities. The text is simply a clue to the mind of the author or to a particular social and historical situation. And neither of these realities, we assume, has any more to say to us than the text which articulates them." Such scholars understand interpretation "as only the exercise of those objective, critical controls provided by historical and social-scientific methods" (106).

20. On the importance of the dialogue and "listening" in *Truth and Method*, see: J. Risser, *Hermeneutics and the Voice of the Other* (Albany: SUNY Press, 1997). Tracy follows Gadamer closely in applying to theology the model of the "back-and-forth movement" of conversation, where one must listen, reflect, and "allow the question to take over" (*Analogical Imagination*, 101, and notes to pp. 135–36).

text, and the text, in return, bends the interpreter; as a result, like two people in a dialogue, text and interpreter arrive at common ground.

However, a dialogue with a traditional text is unlike a dialogue between two people, because the text is historial and the author no longer accessible. Thus the principle "nothing should be put into a text that the writer or the reader could not have intended" simply does not work and "cannot define the limits of a text's meaning" (*TM* 395). First of all, in any process of understanding or interpretation, as Gadamer stresses, after Heidegger, certain fore-structures of understanding are always present.[21] Certain meanings are constantly being projected and "put to the test" in the text as it is being read and understood (*TM* 267). One might add that this is usually more evident in theology than in philosophy. Since one cannot escape these projections, they must be acknowledged and consciously included into the hermeneutic process. The same is true of interpreting traditional texts. "To try to escape from one's own concepts in interpretation is not only impossible but manifestly absurd" (*TM* 397). A truly historical consciousness does not exclude the contemporary "layer" but instead tries to mediate between past ideas and one's own thinking. As a result of such "fusion of horizons," the interpreter's thoughts "re-awaken" the meaning of the text and bring it to life (*TM* 369). A creative interpretation of tradition extends the tradition's inherent possibilities (*TM* 462).

Gadamer suggests several approaches to intuitive interpretation, at the same time warning against the fiction of a "correct" method. Taking into account the dialogical nature of interpretation of texts, he suggests simply allowing this dialogue to happen, to unfold, and guide the interpreter (*TM* 464). According to Gadamer, the only "rule" of true interpretation is to listen to the text and observe what "consistently follows from the subject matter itself" (*TM* 464). Thus, radical interpretations and strong prejudices should be rejected: a true dialogue with tradition presupposes some sort of a "discipline" or "ethics" of interpretation.[22]

---

21. On the importance of the fore-structures of understanding see M. Heidegger, *Being and Time*, translated by J. Macquarrie and E. Robinson (New York: Harper and Row, 1962), 191–93. According to Heidegger, in every case our interpretation is grounded in something we have, see, and grasp in advance (*Vorhabe, Vorsicht, Vorgriff*).

22. Tracy, *Analogical Imagination*, 104, follows Gadamer in this respect, listing several "requirements" for an appropriate retrieval of the classics: e.g., such retrieval must be "controlled by subject matter" and "possess a tact, a common (as communal) sense in a genuinely critical manner."

In its "passion-like" nature, which makes it akin to dialectic (*TM* 465), the hermeneutics of texts differs greatly from the method of natural sciences. Textual interpretation is not a method but a creative, ingenuous process (*TM* 474). The most important conclusion that follows from Gadamer's analysis of hermeneutics is that it is only through hermeneutic dialogue that one can understand the meaning that "comes into language." Traditional texts have no "objective" meaning as such: the only meaning they have is the one that appears in a particular act of understanding/interpretation, and it is a "fusion" of the past and present horizons (*TM* 474–75).[23]

What are the implications of Gadamer's view of hermeneutics for the present-day interpretation of ancient and medieval texts? At the more general level of the history of ideas, the notion of the continuity of a particular concept in its "historical extension" is most productive. One would take an idea that currently exists in our minds and analyze how it extends in history, through various stages of its formation. During this process, one must remember that, because of the fusion of the horizons of the past and present, one will, in fact, analyze particular aspects of this idea, not in an abstract "historical" way, but in the way they exist at the present time in one's mind through the mediation of traditional texts with which one has come in contact. After engaging in a dialogue with traditional and modern texts, one would have a more complete picture of how one has arrived at this contemporary conceptual framework, and what texts were used in this process, despite the fact that, for the authors of those texts, the framework might not have been fully and deliberately articulated.

At the more particular and practical level of textual scholarship, Gadamer's hermeneutics provides a general theoretical background that makes possible an interpretation of ancient and medieval texts that is not necessarily bound by some "scientific" or technical approach. The basis for the understanding and interpretation of such texts, ultimately, is their present-day meaning and significance.

---

23. A good example of this type of hermeneutics is von Balthasar's interpretation of medieval texts in terms of theological aesthetics: see a detailed discussion in Chapter 3.

Part One
The Contemporary Horizon

CHAPTER 1

The Modern Philosophical Concept of the Aesthetic

The approach based on engaging ancient or medieval texts using the modern notion of aesthetics as a starting point of the dialogue still faces a challenge: in order to proceed with a dialogue, one must delimit the field, which, in the case of aesthetics, has been traditionally extremely broad. Is it possible to establish certain common characteristics of the concept of the aesthetic that have developed in the Western European philosophical tradition since the time when the principles of aesthetics as a separate discipline were formulated in the eighteenth century by Alexander Baumgarten?[1] Aesthetics as a separate discipline appears against the general intellectual background of its time: the increased significance of the human point of view over the divine (the "withdrawal of the divine") and greater value accorded to sensibility.[2] Still retaining an earlier bias that favors the rational element, in the introductory chapter to his *Aesthetics*, Baumgarten discusses the position of aesthetics in relation to rationality and truth. In order for aesthetics to be justified as a separate science, it must be in some way concerned with cognition or truth.[3] Following this train of thought, aesthetics is defined as a "lower-

---

1. Although the following sketch of the formation and development of aesthetic thought was developed independently from any consideration of von Balthasar's work, the latter discusses most of the same authors in his account in *Glory of the Lord*, vol. 5 (GL5; see Appendix to Chapter 2). In particular, he notes the importance of Schelling's view of aesthetics to his own project in GL1 in GL5 566–67. A recent study examines much the same list of authors, and also explains why it is important to look at the German tradition in aesthetics: K. Hammermeister, *The German Aesthetic Tradition* (Cambridge: Cambridge University Press, 2002).

2. Cf. Ferry, *Homo Aestheticus*; my understanding of eighteenth- and nineteenth-century aesthetics is greatly influenced by his account. Also cf. Bürger, *Theory of the Avant-garde*.

3. Truth in this case is understood without doubt as "correctness" or "correspondence":

level epistemology" (*gnoseologia inferior*),[4] "art of the analogue of reason" (*ars analogi rationis*), or "science of sensory cognition" (*scientia cognitionis sensitivae*).[5] Baumgarten tries to avoid presenting the subject of his science, which he describes as "sensible things, phantasms, fables, perturbations of affections," as unworthy of a philosopher's attention on account of its concern with the "lower" region of the human faculties (§6, p. 4). The task of the new science, he says, is to "extend correct knowledge even beyond the boundaries of things clearly known to us" (§ 3, p. 3). The "analogue of reason," central to Baumgarten, implies not inferiority to reason but similarity to it. Aesthetics must strive for the "perfection of sensory cognition," which is beauty (*pulchritudo*, §14, p. 10), and avoid its imperfection, which is ugliness (*deformitas*). Baumgarten is anxious to assign to aesthetics its own separate area: it will occupy a middle position between proper cognition (rationality) on the one hand and sense impulses on the other.[6]

In accordance with the task of elevating aesthetics to the level of science, Baumgarten tries to show that aesthetics, too, possesses its own "truth," which he calls "aesthetic truth" (*veritas aesthetica*). "Metaphysical truth" (the most general category) sometimes presents itself to the "intellect"—in the case "when it resides in the things clearly perceived by the soul"—and then it appears as logical, and "sometimes—to the analogue of reason and the lower faculties of cognition," and then it appears as aesthetic (§424, p. 54). While "logical meditations," he writes, "aspire to the clear and intellectual perception of things," aesthetic meditations, "subsisting below the horizon of the former, try to intuit the same things in an elegant way by means of the senses and the analogue of

---

see a discussion of the meanings of the term "truth" in M. Heidegger, "The Origin of the Work of Art," in *Poetry, Language, Thought*, translated by A. Hofstadter (New York: Harper & Row, 1971), 50–52. Heidegger does not understand truth in art and aesthetics in this way (see the end of this chapter). Cf. the discussion of the various meanings of truth below in Chapter 4.

4. "Lower-level" here is simply a reference to the "lower" realm of the senses with which it deals, not to the lower status of aesthetics as a science.

5. A. G. Baumgarten, *Theoretische Ästhetik: Die grundlegenden Abschnitte aus der "Aesthetica"* (1750/58), translated and edited by H. R. Schweizer (Hamburg: F. Meiner, 1983), §1, p. 3; in what follows, paragraph and page numbers are provided in brackets according to this edition. All translations from the Latin, Greek, and modern languages in this volume are my own, unless otherwise specified.

6. "The beauty of *sensory cognition* . . . must be distinguished, on the one hand from the beauty of *cognition*, of which it is the initial . . . part, and on the other hand from the beauty of matter and [material] objects" (my italics) (§18, p. 12).

reason" (§426, p. 56). Baumgarten, again, stresses that the aesthetic way of perception is analogous, not inferior, to reason. The beautiful (the result of aesthetic perception) is, then, a linkage of sensible (particular) representations that is analogous to intellectual structures (linkage of concepts) and belongs to "metaphysical truth": "aesthetic truth requires a joining of objects of thinking-in-a-beautiful-way [i.e., aesthetics] with reasoning and objects of reason, to the extent that this [joining] is to be sensibly cognized" (§437, pp. 64–66). The realm of the "analogue of reason," then, will be constituted by relations among sensations.

The need for such "quasi-knowledge," in addition to clear cognition, must be clarified. In order to justify the creation of its own separate field for aesthetics, Baumgarten claims that aesthetic representations possess specific unity and wholeness (a certain "charm") which clear conceptual knowledge can never achieve.[7] Aesthetics thus has a double advantage over "rational" sciences. First, aesthetics is especially interested in the particular as something that possesses the highest degree of wholeness and integrity.[8] According to Baumgarten, abstraction is accomplished at the expense of a considerable loss of material, and therefore the highest "aesthetic truth" dwells at the level of the most concrete things: "the aesthetician, aspiring to the highest truth he can perceive, prefers, as much as he can, more specific, less general, and less abstract truths to general, most abstract, and most universal truths, as well as the singular to all general" (§440, p. 68; cf. §441, p. 70). The first advantage is thus the ability to accommodate the particular that is lost in the movement toward the universal. Second, aesthetic truth can refer both to real and to hypothetical objects—as long as their sensible unity, perception, and beauty are preserved (§439, pp. 66–68). This means that, as long as aesthetic objects satisfy the criteria of "aesthetic truth" (that is, unity and beauty of emotion created by the aesthetic feeling), they do not have to be "true" in the sense of corresponding to some objective reality: this distinctive feature of aesthetic truth explains the possibility of using fiction in art. "But at times," Baumgarten writes, "a certain necessity may arise for the thinker-in-a-beautiful-way [i.e., the aestheti-

---

7. "Only those general aesthetico-logical truths are [truly] aesthetic, which can be . . . represented in a sensory way to the analog of reason with their charm remaining intact" (§443, p. 72; cf. §439).

8. Cf. Heidegger, "Origin of the Work of Art," in *Poetry, Language, Thought*, 46–47: things and artworks "resist" attempts to break them up.

cian], as a result of which he will not be able to remain in this world any longer without a detriment to the beauty of the whole, [in which case] his spirit should rather extend itself into other possible worlds."[9] Thus the second advantage of aesthetics over rational sciences is its ability to encompass a richer field of human experience.

Perhaps, the most fundamental achievement in elaborating the concept of the aesthetic belongs to Immanuel Kant, who greatly influenced European aesthetic thought. Unlike Baumgarten, Kant no longer tries to present aesthetic experience as a process similar to rationality. For him it is clearly a separate area. This position of Kant later generates the idea of aesthetics as an autonomous discipline, which is prevalent in academic aesthetics in the late nineteenth and the twentieth centuries. Kant himself, though, was far from restricting himself to studying aesthetics as an autonomous field: in his philosophical system, aesthetics fulfills a very specific role, and is not examined as such "for its own sake."

Aesthetics appears in the *Critique of Judgment* within the framework of Kant's transcendental philosophy, which postulates the existence of certain principles that are situated beyond the reach of our cognitive faculties (that is, these principles "transcend" our cognitive faculties) but still have a regulatory effect on thinking and action. His aesthetic theory plays a crucial role in working out how this can be thought in a coherent way. What attracts Kant's attention is the revelatory quality of aesthetic experience, or its ability to manifest or reveal something that seems to transcend the understanding. As Kant's task is to sort out the relationship between the immanent and the transcendent, the idea of the possible manifestation or appearance of the transcendent in the realm of the immanent becomes very attractive. As Kant generally favors any possibility of a direct intuition or insight,[10] in the third *Critique* he attempts to ground the principles of his philosophy—although

---

9. §475, p. 106; cf. §476: things that are false from the point of view of correspondence to objective reality do not have to be false aesthetically. Baumgarten here introduces the category of "verisimilar": one can reproduce, analogically, "true" archetypal relations between sensible representations even by means of "false" (i.e., non-existent in reality) material, such as artistic fiction. Cf. the discussion of various types of truth below in Chapter 4.

10. A good analysis of Kant's aesthetics that underscores the idea of aesthetic experience as "presenting" or mediating can be found in D. W. Crawford, *Kant's Aesthetic Theory* (Madison: University of Wisconsin Press, 1974), and in Ferry, *Homo Aestheticus*. Despite his opposition to the transcendental scheme of the "Kantians," von Balthasar appreciates Kant's attentiveness to actual aesthetic experience, or direct "seeing": see discussion below.

they are traditionally viewed as being a priori—in aesthetic experience understood precisely as immediate perception of something evident and manifest. In Kant's system aesthetic experience is called upon to manifest the unity of the supersensible ground of all experience, including the moral. This insight allows him to ground his moral theory through the realm of the sensible.[11]

A short explanation of the term "transcendental aesthetics"—the way Kant's aesthetics is usually described—will be appropriate at this point, since the term "aesthetics" has now almost lost its original meaning and stopped being transparent. What Kant (not unlike Baumgarten) understands under "aesthetic" is really close to the Greek αἴσθησις: sensitivity or sensibility, something that has to do with sense perception. "Transcendental aesthetics" then means something like *"trans-*sensitivity" or *"trans-*sensibility," that is, an ability to sense something from the transcendent realm (the "beyond," "across the divide") directly, as if it were given as sense data from the world around us. This ability to sense something transcendent, the "transcendentally sensible" or "sensible across the horizon," is thus seen as analogical to the "directly sensible" by our senses.[12] We must also note that while the present-day understanding has deviated from the original eighteenth-century concept, which consistently maintained a connection to sensibility (the *aisthetic*), it is the original Kantian sense of "aesthetics" that we are reviving here to be used as our working definition.

Kant starts his *Critique of Judgment* by outlining the general *aporia* which needs to be resolved. On the one hand, there is an "immeasurable gulf ... between the sensible realm of the concept of nature" which is given in intuition (as phenomena), but not as a thing-in-itself (*Ding an sich*), "and the supersensible realm of the concept of freedom," which is given as a thing-in-itself but of which there can be no intuition. Although no transition by means of theoretical reason between these two worlds is possible, they are "meant to have an influence" upon each

---

11. Already in his *Lectures on the History of Philosophy,* Hegel acknowledges Kant's attempt to ground his supposedly a priori principles in concrete experience: "Noch ist die dritte Seite in der Kantischen Philosophie übrig, dass auch hier die Forderung des Konkreten eintritt, worin die Idee dieser Einheit nicht als ein Jenseits, sondern als ein Gegenwärtiges gesetzt ist—die Idee der Urteilskraft" (G. F. Hegel, *Werke,* edited by E. Moldenhauer and K. Markus Michel, vol. 20 [Frankfurt am Main: Suhrkamp Verlag, 1971], 372).

12. Such an understanding of transcendental aesthetics is confirmed, e.g., by Husserl, who uses this concept to designate one of the stages of his phenomenological analysis that has to do with direct intuition: cf. *Cartesian Meditations,* 146.

other: since we are perfectly able to use our will in the realm of nature, there must be some sort of a connection between the two worlds. "The concept of freedom," Kant writes, "is meant to actualize in the world of sense the purpose proposed by its laws, and consequently nature must be so thought that the conformity to law of its form at least harmonizes with the possibility of the purposes to be effected in it according to laws of freedom."[13]

The only explanation of this *aporia* is that such a connection exists but necessarily escapes our notice, and therefore must a priori be placed in the supersensible.[14] "There must," says Kant, making his most important statement, "therefore, be a ground of the unity of the supersensible, which lies at the basis of nature, with that which the concept of freedom practically contains; and the concept of this ground, although it does not attain either theoretically or practically to a knowledge of the same, and hence has no peculiar realm, nevertheless makes possible the transition from the mode of thought according to the principles of the one to that according to the principles of the other."[15]

Kant does not, however, confine himself merely to postulating the supersensible character of such a connection between natural concepts and morals; he tries to find some indication of the unity of our experience in experience itself. Certain phenomena that seem to point to our immediate perception of the connection attract his attention: the feelings of beauty and sublimity. Since the connection between morality (reason) and natural concepts (understanding) is obscure, Kant tries to resolve the problem through the seemingly more obvious connection between sensation and the faculty of understanding. It is here that aesthetic experience (and especially, although not exclusively, the phenomenon of beauty) is particularly revealing. On the one hand, aesthetic reaction is a judgment (the aesthetic judgment, or the judgment of taste), but on the other hand, this judgment is not based on a concept, but im-

---

13. I. Kant, *Critique of Judgement*, translated by J. H. Bernard (New York: Hafner Publishing Company, 1951), 12 (KS 175–76). I will quote Kant according to Bernard's English translation (providing paragraph numbers, page numbers, and German terms in brackets). If his translation departs significantly from the German original, I will adjust the text according to the German edition (I. Kant, *Werke*, edited by W. Weischedel, vol. 10 [Frankfurt am Main: Suhrkamp Verlag, 1957], abbreviated *W*) and will provide the relevant page number from the German. References to the Introduction, which is not contained in *W*, will be given according to the older edition, *Kants gesammelte Schriften*, vol. 5 (Berlin: G. Reimer, 1913), abbreviated *KS*.
14. The transcendental manner of solving aporias: see below.
15. Kant, *Critique of Judgement*, 12; KS 176.

The Modern Concept of the Aesthetic ⟡ 21

mediately follows the representation of an aesthetic object, which brings it closer to sensibility. In this paradoxical nature of aesthetic judgment there looms a solution to the problem of the connection between the phenomenal world and the understanding (and, ultimately, of the connection between nature and freedom). Kant resolves this antinomy (the "antinomy of taste," which is applicable to both beauty and sublimity) in his transcendental manner.[16]

Since the judgment of taste is supposed to have validity for everyone (it has a certain "touch" of a concept) and yet is not based on any determinate concept, it must be based on an indeterminable (for us) concept whose "determining ground lies perhaps in the concept of that which may be regarded as the supersensible substrate of humanity" (§57, p. 185). "The subjective principle," Kant continues, "viz. the indefinite idea of the supersensible in us, can only be put forward as the sole key to the puzzle of this [i.e., aesthetic] faculty whose sources are hidden from us" (§57, p. 186, W 446).

How does the transcendental connection work in the experience of beauty? For Kant, the faculty that is responsible for the production of sensible representations (phenomena) for the faculty of understanding is the imagination. Kant's analysis of representations that result in the experience of beauty leads him to conclude that such representations produce a state similar to that which precedes the formation of concepts—although no concept is formed—and thus induces a certain type of intellectual pleasure (aesthetic). To experience the beautiful is to "perceive the accordance of the representation with the harmonious . . . activity of both cognitive faculties [i.e., the imagination and the understanding] in their freedom, that is, to feel with pleasure the mental state" produced by the representation (§39, p. 135, W 388). This state of the "free play" of imagination and understanding is thus "subjectively purposive," since it usually accompanies the transition from sensible in-

---

16. The nature of Kant's transcendental solution of *aporiae* or antinomies can be outlined as follows: the very existence of an intellectual problem indicates that its solution must lie beyond the reach of the intellect, and one of the contradictory terms must be taken in its "transcendental" meaning. The solution of an antinomy consists in showing that "two apparently contradictory propositions do not contradict each other in fact, but that they may be consistent, although the explanation of the possibility of their concept may transcend our cognitive faculties" (§57, p. 185, W 445), and "the antinomies force us against our will to look beyond the sensible and to seek a priori in the supersensible the point of union for all our faculties" (§57, p. 187, W 447).

tuitions to concepts, that is, it appears as if for a certain purpose.[17] It is also disconnected from any interest (is disinterested, or pleasing *per se*), but still possesses a compelling sense of universal validity: beauty is a phenomenon of reacting in a certain way that is assumed in everyone.[18] In sum, beauty may be considered perfectly contingent, but the mere fact that it can so coincide that a harmonious interplay of our faculties results from the observation of (contingent) natural phenomena (that is, natural phenomena show subjective purposiveness, or certain organization which harmonizes with one of our inner faculties) means that there is (because of such a possibility) an internal kinship between our faculties and the phenomenal world. However, this correspondence, which becomes manifest to us in aesthetic experience, cannot be explained conceptually by our faculty of understanding. Therefore the experience of beauty immediately hints at some transcendent ground that makes this harmony possible.

In other words, in the experience of beauty our aesthetic judgment is completely disinterested and cannot be explained conceptually by our faculty of understanding. Yet, it creates an impression of purposiveness and possesses a compelling sense of universal validity, which means that beauty has the ability to "present," or make us immediately *aware* of, the subjective purposiveness of nature or certain organization in nature that harmonizes with our inner essence. Such ability of aesthetic experience to present or make us aware of something directly, without a concept, is even more evident in our experience of the sublime, which, according to Kant, creates a more immediate "bridge" to the "ideas of reason" (and the realm of morals).

The most important aspect of Kant's theory of presentation[19] is that

---

17. "Only where the imagination in its freedom awakens the understanding and is put by it into regular play, without the aid of concepts, does the representation communicate itself, not as a thought, but as an internal feeling of a purposive state of the mind" (§40, p. 138, W 392).

18. It is not possible here to discuss at length Kantian reflections concerning the basis of such communicability of aesthetic sense; in brief, it is the presupposition of "ordinary sound understanding" in everyone as a subjective condition of aesthetic perception (§39, p. 135, W 388).

19. There is a certain inconsistency in Kantian terminology (Hegel criticized this inconsistency) concerning the terms "presentation" (*Darstellung*) and "representation" (*Vorstellung*). However, in general, to "present" means, for Kant, to provide a "sensible illustration" or some other palpable demonstration of a thing (*hypotyposis, subjectio sub adspectum*, §59, p. 197, W 459). The term *Vorstellung* is almost synonymous with "phenomenon," i.e., anything that becomes part of our experience. This Kantian meaning of *Darstellung* as 'presentation' must be kept in mind for the rest of this chapter, as well as for reading von Balthasar. Many English

concepts (of understanding) can be presented (their "reality" is "established") by "intuitions" or sensible images (for empirical concepts, it is examples, for the pure concepts of understanding, *schemata* [§59, p. 196, W 458]). The ideas of reason, on the other hand, cannot be presented (their objective reality cannot be established), for there is no intuition that is adequate to them (§59, p. 197, W 459). The experience of beauty points to the supersensible realm of ideas by making us aware of certain processes which we cannot explain on our own, but it falls short of presenting ideas. In the experience of the sublime the human mind approaches the presentation of ideas as closely as it can. The essence of this experience (using the example of the "mathematically sublime") is as follows. Whenever our faculties of sensation come in contact with an object of nature that is so great that they fail to comprehend it—although we know that any size can be thought conceptually—we catch a certain glimpse of a faculty that transcends all sense, and, being above our conceptual activity (which can be "illustrated" with sensible images) and unattainable to it, is able to command even extremely great magnitudes.[20] In brief, the "sublime is that, the mere ability to think which shows a faculty of the mind surpassing every standard of sense" (§25, p. 89, W 336). In the experience of beauty we can dwell on a perception of a certain harmonious state; the sublime, by contrast, provides a more immediate connection between sensible experience and transcendental ideas (of reason). The feeling of the sublime comes rather as a momentary revelation, shock, and the feeling of awe that arises from our immediate intuition of the impossibility of presentation. The closest that one can approach the presentation of an idea by means of sensible images is in the experience of the "dynamically sublime": when the feeling of the sublime is produced by the perception of might in nature, for example, by the stormy ocean. It is important to bear in mind that the sublime is, in fact, a negative presentation of the ideas. The feeling of the sublime arises from our immediate intuition of the impossibility of presentation; it makes one aware of the utter impossibility of the senses grasping

---

translations miss this important nuance and translate *Darstellung* as 'representation,' whereas what is meant is 'presentation.'

20. "But because there is in our imagination a striving toward infinite progress and in our reason a claim for absolute totality, regarded as a real idea, therefore this very inadequateness for that idea in our faculty for estimating the magnitude of things of sense excites in us the feeling of a supersensible faculty" (§25, p. 88, W 336).

the ideas, and thus is absolutely contrary to the nature of our senses.[21]

At this point, the crucial role the aesthetic plays in Kant's program to establish a connection between the realm of natural concepts and morality becomes clear. First of all, aesthetic experience confirms the possibility of such a connection by pointing to the common supersensible ground of all our experience. The "interplay" of faculties in aesthetic experience, which is immediately perceived, demonstrates the agreement of the phenomenal world with the understanding, the source of which (the supersensible realm) escapes us. However, Kant goes beyond establishing the mere possibility of the unified transcendental ground of our experience that is intuited from the affinity between the aesthetic and the realm of natural concepts. In order to complete the main task of the third *Critique*, the relation of natural concepts to morality also needs to be demonstrated. A demonstrated connection between the aesthetic and the moral disposition would allow one, via the aesthetic, to bridge the realms of natural concepts and morality. Kant attempts to make such a connection by presenting aesthetic experience as analogical to moral.

According to Kant, the kinship between moral and aesthetic judgments rests on the following observation: both judgments occur spontaneously, "without any clear, subtle, and premeditated reflection" (§42, p. 143, W 398). Yet, despite the fact that aesthetic judgments are not based on any reasoning, they have "compelling" and necessary character. This

---

21. Kant describes the sublime as an "object (of nature) the representation of which determines the mind to think the unattainability of nature" (for the senses) "as a presentation of ideas" (for the intellect; §29, *General remark*, p. 108). Thus the feeling of the sublime marks an unsuccessful effort to present the unpresentable ideas. "This effort," Kant continues, "—and the feeling of the unattainability of the idea by means of the imagination—is itself a presentation of the subjective purposiveness of our mind in the employment of the imagination for its supersensible destination and forces us, subjectively, to *think* nature itself in its totality as a presentation of something supersensible, without being able objectively to arrive at this presentation" (ibid.). What we have then is a positive presentation through a negative phenomenon: "For in the very inadequacy of nature to these latter [i.e., ideas], and thus only by presupposing them and by straining the imagination to use nature as a schema for them, is to be found that which is terrible to sensibility and yet is attractive" (§29, p. 104). The sublime deals with abstractions (infinite magnitudes, powers, etc.) and therefore it is "quite negative in respect to what is sensible" (§29, *Gen. r.*, p. 115). However, since the imagination finds nothing beyond the sensible to which it can attach itself, it feels unbounded "and thus that very abstraction is a presentation of the Infinite, which can be nothing but a mere negative presentation, but which yet expands the soul" (p. 115). "Thus the satisfaction on the aesthetical side (in relation to sensibility)," Kant continues, "is negative, i.e. against this interest, but regarded from the intellectual side it is positive and combined with an interest" (§29, *Gen. r.*, p. 112).

means that they come from a source beyond our understanding, that is, are based on an a priori principle.[22] But so does morality, or the morally good, which is the "representation of an absolutely compelling law" and is characterized by necessity that "rests *a priori* upon concepts."[23] The resemblance between the "formal conditions" of action according to the principle of duty, on the one hand, and aesthetic judgment, on the other, is so strong that morality can be described in aesthetic terms.[24] Moreover, the aesthetic (the sublime in nature) "cannot well be thought without combining therewith a mental disposition which is akin to the moral (*zum Moralischen ähnlich*)."[25] The beautiful and sublime, Kant remarks, "united in the same subject, are purposive in reference to the moral feeling. The beautiful prepares us to love disinterestedly something, even nature itself; the sublime [prepares us] to esteem something highly even in opposition to our own (sensible) interest" (§29, Gen. r., p. 108, W 357). This crucial remark refers to our readiness to sacrifice usefulness to moral principles, and sacrificial action can be detrimental to our physical well-being. Both the disinterested character of the beautiful and the negative perception of the capacity of the senses in the sublime, being nevertheless pleasing, serve as a kind of "teaching mechanism" through the enticement and bait of pleasure. While in moral judgments we experience only the power of the abstract compelling law with no sense of its correspondence with nature, in aesthetic judgments we actually feel immediately and very vividly such correspondence or noncorrespondence between the laws given by the spirit and the laws that we see in nature.[26] "Now I say," Kant summarizes, "that the beautiful is the symbol of the

---

22. "In this modality of aesthetical judgments, viz. in the necessity claimed for them, lies the main point (*Hauptmoment*) in the critique of judgment. For it enables us to recognize in them an *a priori* principle, and raises them out of empirical psychology" (§29, p. 106, W 355).

23. "The absolutely good, subjectively judged according to the feeling that it inspires . . . , as capable of determining the powers of the subject through the representation of an absolutely compelling law, is specially distinguished by the modality of a necessity that rests *a priori* upon concepts. This necessity involves, not merely a claim, but a command for the assent of everyone" (§29, Gen. r., p. 107, W 356).

24. "But the determinability of the subject by means of this idea [moral law] . . . i.e. the moral feeling, is yet so far cognate to the aesthetical judgment and its formal conditions that it can serve to represent the conformity to law of action from duty as aesthetical, i.e., as sublime or even as beautiful" (§29, Gen. r., p. 107, W 356–57).

25. §29, Gen. r., p. 109, W 358; cf. §39, p. 134, W 387: "Pleasure in the sublime in nature . . . presupposes . . . a different feeling, viz. that of our supersensible destination, which, however obscurely, has a moral foundation."

26. The connection between the aesthetic and morality is most clearly expressed (al-

morally good, and that it is only in this respect . . . that it gives pleasure with a claim for the agreement of everyone else. By this the mind is made conscious of a certain ennoblement [*Veredlung*] and elevation [*Erhebung*] above the mere sensibility to pleasure received through sense."[27]

The desired demonstration of the connection between the areas of natural concepts and morality is thus achieved. On the one hand, aesthetic (sensible, natural) experience is in harmony with the faculty of natural concepts (understanding): the harmony that has a supersensible ground. On the other hand, aesthetic experience is analogous to the moral feeling, the possibility of such an analogy also arising from a supersensible ground. Since there is an area of experience (the aesthetic) that can conform to both natural concepts and morality, the supersensible ground that underlies all these areas of experience must be common to all, that is, also common to the understanding (faculty of natural concepts) and reason (morality). "Hence," Kant writes, "both on account of this inner possibility in the subject and of the external possibility of nature that agrees with it, it[28] finds itself to be referred to something within the subject as well as without him, something which is neither nature nor freedom, but which yet is connected with the ground of the latter, that is, the supersensible. In this supersensible ground the theoretical faculty is bound together in unity with the practical in a way which is common and [yet] unknown."[29] "Taste makes possible the transition," Kant concludes, "without any violent leap, from the charm

---

though not so clearly argued) in the following passage: "But this interest is akin to moral (*der Verwandtschaft nach moralisch*), and he who takes such an interest in the beauties of nature can do so only in so far as he previously has firmly established his interest in the morally good. If, therefore, the beauty of nature interests a man immediately, we have reason for attributing to him at least a basis for a good moral disposition. . . . In that case the analogy between the pure judgment of taste which, independently of any interest, causes us to feel a satisfaction and also represents it *a priori* as suitable to humanity in general, and the moral judgment that does the same thing from concepts without any clear, subtle, and premeditated reflection—this analogy leads to a similar immediate interest in the objects of the former as in those of the latter" (§42, p. 143, W 398).

27. §59, pp. 198–99, W 461. The Kantian understanding of the symbol and analogy lies outside the scope of the present study. A good discussion of this subject, as well as of the statement "the beautiful is the symbol of the morally good," can be found in: G. Felicitas Munzel, "'The Beautiful Is the Symbol of the Morally-Good': Kant's Philosophical Basis of Proof for the Idea of the Morally-Good," *Journal of the History of Philosophy* 32, no. 2 (1995): 301–30.

28. I.e., the faculty of aesthetic judgment that gives a law to itself.

29. §59, p. 199, W 461. The analogy is intensified by the fact that we use moral terms when appreciating aesthetically pleasing objects—majestic, magnificent, joyful, innocent, modest, tender; therefore, these must be analogous feelings.

of sense to habitual moral interest, as it represents the imagination in its freedom as capable of purposive determination for the understanding, and so teaches us to find even in objects of sense a free satisfaction apart from any charm of sense."[30] In sum, the aesthetic feeling in Kant appears both as our natural "guide" in the world that provides us with an immediate insight into (or "presents") the connection between the areas of natural concepts and morality—which otherwise escapes our intellect—and as our "instructor" in morals that presents to us clearly the validity of the disinterested attitude.

The immediate successors of Kant in the tradition of German idealism, of whom Schelling is a good example, do not add anything radically new to his understanding of the role of aesthetic and artistic experience.[31] Thus, although in principle they view aesthetics as an autonomous area, they still use it for specific purposes to make their general philosophical systems work. Schelling's *System of Transcendental Idealism* contains a good survey of his aesthetic views.[32] Just as Kant did earlier, Schelling attempts to find a common ground between consciousness and the reality of a thing-in-itself, which requires locating an activity that is both conscious and unconscious. According to Schelling, there is only one such activity, the "aesthetic," with works of art as its products. "The ideal world of art and the real world of objects are therefore products of one and the same activity; the concurrence of the two (the conscious and the unconscious) without consciousness yields the real, and with consciousness the aesthetic world" (Introduction, §3; p. 12). Without reproducing here Schelling's deduction of the principles of transcendental idealism, we can present, in the following sketch, the essence of his system and the role of aesthetic experience in it.

In order to find the common ground between the ideal and the real, Schelling chooses to focus on something that demonstrably comes from the same ground, but includes the elements of both consciousness

---

30. §59, p. 200, W 462–63. For more information on the issue of the relation of aesthetics to morals in Kant see: P. Guyer, *Kant and the Experience of Freedom: Essays on Aesthetics and Morality* (Cambridge: Cambridge University Press, 1993), 27–47.

31. They do, however, modify his position and subtract certain elements: e.g., Schelling does not uphold Kant's connection between the aesthetic and the ethical.

32. The translation used here is F. W. J. Schelling, *System of Transcendental Idealism* (1800), translated by P. Heath (Charlottesville: University of Virginia Press, 1978). This work is greatly influenced by Fichte so it can serve as an example of both Schelling's and Fichte's systems.

and the "real object." One must thus search for the type of intuition or knowing "whose object is not independent thereof, and thus a knowing that is simultaneously a producing of its object" where the producer and product are one and the same. Since sensory intuition does not produce its own object, he calls this type of knowing "intellectual intuition" (Part I, Section 2; p. 27; as becomes clear later, a product of art qualifies precisely as such area of experience). In Part III, Section I (First Epoch, Section B) Schelling clarifies how such intuition is possible. His phenomenological description of the activities within the "self" revolves around the observation that in our experience of either sensation or thought the self is somehow limited. In sensing "real" objects its ideal activity does not extend beyond the limit, which is therefore perceived as the border of the object or "thing-in-itself." Since the self cannot "overstep" the limit created by perceiving real things of nature, one must find a phenomenological situation where the self can somehow be both "on this side" of the limit and beyond it.[33] In other words, in this experience the self as limited and the self as limiting should somehow come together.

According to Schelling, this can happen only through a "third activity . . . at once both ideal and real . . . undoubtedly the producing activity" (p. 67). Thus the situation of "internal production" of its object by the self (Schelling will eventually speak of artistic production), where the self acts as both the observing side and the object, reconciles the two realms.[34] In the process of production one can model the process of creating a thing-in-itself, except that in this case, unlike in the case with perceiving "real" things "outside," this thing-in-itself can be transparent to the self since it is entirely generated by, and located within, the self. In this one particular type of activity, one can intuit the thing-in-itself (although the self is originally ignorant of the fact that this is its own product).[35]

---

33. "[S]uppose that the self were to be limited by its mere overstepping of the limit, it would in thus overstepping, still be ideal, and hence qua ideal, or in its ideality, be real and limited" (Schelling, *Transcendental Idealism*, 66).

34. Schelling is obviously trying to break the age-old mind/reality impasse.

35. Cf.: " . . . what the ideal activity becomes fixated as? So far as it is fixated at all, it ceases to be pure activity. It becomes in the same action opposed to the activity confined within the limit, and is thus apprehended as an activity fixated but set in opposition to the real self. So far as it is apprehended as fixated, it acquires an ideal substrate; so far as it is apprehended as an activity opposed to the real self, it itself becomes—but only in this opposition—a real activity; it becomes the activity of something really opposed to the real self. But this real op-

Before we pass on to Schelling's understanding of the role of art and aesthetic experience in this scheme, we should note that his system is essentially monist; it does not presuppose, as Kant's system does, a transcendent realm that is totally inaccessible. The separation of the two realms is only an appearance; their foundational unity ensures the possibility of interpenetration of the two. Thus the separation between the ideal self and the thing-in-itself does not pose a fundamental problem that would require "transcendental mediation."[36] However, as will be clear from our subsequent discussion of von Balthasar, it does not actually matter for the current study how the system of thought itself presents the structure of reality ontologically. What is important is the actual phenomenological experience of reality (in our case, aesthetic experience) by the human consciousness, and this experience in Western thought seems to be described in similar terms no matter what the ontological position of a given system of thought is.

Adhering to his strategy of bridging the chasm between the ideal and the real, Schelling restates his task as follows: one needs (according

---

ponent to the real self is nothing other than the thing-in-itself. Thus the ideal activity, having passed the limit and now become an object, at this point disappears as such from consciousness and is transformed into the thing-in-itself. The following observation is easily made. The sole ground of the original limitation is, by the foregoing, the self's intuitant or ideal activity; but this latter is here reflected, as ground of limitation, to the self itself, though not indeed as an activity thereof, for the self is now simply real; rather, as something opposed to the self. The thing-in-itself is therefore nothing else but the shadow of the ideal activity, now over the boundary, which is thrown back to the self by intuition, and is to that extent itself a product of the self" (no. 3a, p. 68). "The deduction has now progressed to the point at which something outside the self is for the first time present to the self as such." "For the self that intuits itself as sensing, the sensed is the (previously sensing) ideal activity which has crossed the boundary, but is now no longer intuited as an activity of the self," i.e., the "limiting factor" "cannot enter consciousness" "without transforming itself into the thing-in-itself" (p. 69). "It is manifest that the self cannot intuit itself as sensing, without intuiting itself as opposed to itself, and simultaneously in limitant and delimited activity . . . this opposition in the self itself, which only the philosopher perceives, appears to his object, the self, as an opposition between itself and something outside it" (no. 3b, p. 70).

36. Thus Schelling himself, probably having Kant in mind, speaks against presenting something unknown (by "dogmatists," according to his own expression) as coming "from without" as a "revelation," without the possibility of further explanation: that is, in his opinion all can be thought through and deduced (cf. section C, Theory of productive intuition. Introductory; p. 74). In this sense, Schelling is not a "revelationist" in the sense that Kant can be (see above), and, as will become clear further on, his thought, according to von Balthasar, can support a theological aesthetics no better than the systems of other "monists" such as Hegel. Theoretically, reality itself can be deduced and explained from ideas and categories, without leaving the "split" between the immanent and the transcendent. At the same time, upon Schelling's own words (see below), the basic phenomenological observation that artistic activity is something that reveals to us the essence of reality can still hold.

to him) to explain how the self itself can become conscious of the original harmony between the subjective and the objective.[37] He assumes that objective reality is "something originally posited in harmony" with the subjective but then separating from the latter in "appearance."[38] As Kant had before him, he observes that such original harmony must be postulated: otherwise one could not explain how the realm of freedom can have an effect on the realm of nature.[39] The way of demonstrating such a unity of the activity that is originally one is by showing that the products that do not originate from conscious activity can also be purposive in character. Again, as Kant had done before him, Schelling points out that nature appears to be precisely such a purposive thing, without, however, any clearly discernible purpose. In other words, just as Kant did, Schelling comes to the question of teleology.[40]

It is clear at this point that in Schelling's system the existence of the original harmony can be proved without any reference to art or aesthetic experience. The latter two are needed, however, for the self to *become aware* of it.[41] Schelling returns to the initial idea of demonstrating the original unity of the ideal and real using the model of a "product" (see above). However, in the present case natural products are not suitable, since their principles do not lie within the self and therefore cannot be

---

37. Part Four. "System of practical philosophy according to the principles of transcendental idealism." III. "Deduction of the concept of history." Section F. The task, of course, is reminisent of that of Kant.

38. Schelling, *Transcendental Idealism*, I.2, p. 213.

39. "It would be equally hard to understand how a realization of our purposes in the external world could ever be possible through conscious and free activity, unless a susceptibility to such action were already established in the world, even before it becomes the object of a conscious act, by virtue of that original identity of the unconscious with the conscious activity" (ibid., 214).

40. "But now if all conscious activity is purposive, this coincidence of conscious and unconscious activity can evidence itself only in a product that *is purposive, without being purposively brought about*. Nature must be a product of this sort, and this, indeed, is the principle of all teleology" (ibid., 214). Cf. Part V ("Essentials of teleology according to the principles of transcendental idealism"): nature must appear "as a product that is purposive without being brought forth in accordance with a purpose"; it is produced unconsciously, but looks like a product of conscious activity (p. 215); nature is exactly what it should be, yet not consciously produced (p. 216).

41. "An intuition must therefore be exhibitable on the intelligence itself, whereby in one and the same appearance the self is at once conscious and unconscious for itself, and it is by means of such an intuition that we first bring forth the intelligence, as it were, entirely out of itself; by such an intuition, therefore, that we also first resolve the entire problem of transcendental philosophy," i.e., prove the existence of a harmony between the subjective and objective (pp. 217–18).

clearly manifested to it. The experience needed, then, "can be no other than the intuition of art" (p. 218). In other words, just as it does in Kant's system, art appears at this last crucial stage in Schelling's system and is called upon to demonstrate clearly the solution to the main problem of transcendental philosophy, which is accomplished in Part VI.[42] According to Schelling, the art-product combines the characteristics of both the product of nature and that of freedom (§1, "Deduction of the art-product as such"; p. 219); in it, freedom and necessity are united (p. 220); as in Kant, art appears natural (cf. p. 221), that is, an artist operates *like* nature. For the current discussion, the most important point is Schelling's description of the moment when the self encounters a product of art and achieves the experience of the "union" of the ideal and real. The product starts as part of the intelligence. However,

> Since production set out of freedom, that is, from an unceasing opposition of the two activities, the intelligence will be unable to attribute this absolute union of the two, in which production ends, to freedom; so as soon as the product is completed, all appearance of freedom is removed. The intelligence will feel itself *astonished and blessed* by this union, will regard it, that is, in the light of a bounty freely granted by a higher nature, by whose aid the impossible has been made possible. (p. 221, my italics)

In other words, even within this monist framework that theoretically denies that anything lies "outside" or is unknown, the actual experience of the transition is still described in almost religious terms as something coming from beyond, as a sudden awareness of a higher reality that reveals itself.[43] Schelling reinforces his view of aesthetic experience as a "revelation from beyond" as follows: "This unknown . . . whereby the objective and the conscious activities are here brought into unexpected harmony, is none other than that absolute which contains the common ground of the preestablished harmony . . . " between them (p. 221). " . . . If this absolute is reflected from out of the product, it *will appear to the intelligence as something lying above the latter,* and which, in contrast to freedom, brings an element of the unintended to that which was begun with consciousness and intention" (pp. 221–22, my italics). Again,

---

42. "Deduction of a universal organ of philosophy," or "Essentials of the philosophy of art according to the principles of transcendental idealism."

43. As the reader will realize from subsequent chapters, Schelling's phenomenological description of aesthetic experience is precisely that upon which theological aesthetics after the fashion of von Balthasar draws.

although for Schelling this "absolute" is the primordial self itself, phenomenologically, from his own words, becoming aware of it is not that different from becoming aware of "transcendental ideas" in Kant or of any other transcendent principle in more theologically oriented thinkers (see below). An art product is different precisely because, although starting with the conscious intention of the artist, it always comes to contain something beyond what one consciously tried to do. Some "dark unknown force," which is precisely artistic genius, completes the work and "radiates back from the product" (p. 222).[44]

Thus it is the product of art, or of genius that takes on the revelatory role in Schelling's system, and proves to be most convincing:

> Now every absolute concurrence of the two antithetical activities is utterly unaccountable, being simply a phenomenon which although incomprehensible,[45] yet cannot be denied; and art, therefore, is the one *everlasting revelation* which yields that concurrence, and the marvel which, had it existed but once only, *would necessarily have convinced us* of the absolute reality of that supreme event. (p. 223; my italics)

In some strong concluding statements (§3. "Corollaries. Relation of art to philosophy"), Schelling reiterates that art becomes some sort of an objectivity for intellectual intuition, which otherwise cannot be given any solid objectivity (p. 229). In fact, one could hardly proclaim the importance of art for philosophical reflection in stronger terms than Schelling: "If aesthetic intuition is merely transcendental [= intellectual] intuition become objective, it is self-evident that art is at once the only true and eternal organ and document of philosophy" (p. 231).

Romantic aesthetics, which in many ways is an heir to Kant's tradition, also does not advance much over Kant's ideas. At the same time, it contributes to the importance of the aesthetic element in nineteenth-century theology.[46] Both Romantic philosophical reflection and Ro-

---

44. One can see Schiller's view of art (see below) as very close to that of Schelling. Thus, according to Schelling, art is supposed to resolve the "uttermost contradiction in us" (p. 222), bringing together the realms of nature and freedom, precisely because "philosophy only concerns a fraction of a man, and art the whole man" ("General observation on the whole system," p. 233). Note also similarities with the Romantic aesthetic theory as a whole: according to Schelling (§2. Character of the art-product, p. 225), the artist depicts an infinity, not accessible to finite understanding; art is an expression of something infinite in something finite; and beauty is "the infinite finitely displayed."

45. Schelling's note: "from the standpoint of mere reflection."

46. See my treatment of von Balthasar's analysis and critique of the Romantic tradition in theological aesthetics below in Chapter 2.

mantic art illustrate the same basic principle already expressed in these terms in Schelling: the manifestation of the infinite (invisible) in the finite (visible) that can take the form of aesthetic experience (the feeling of the sublime or spiritual in nature) or art.[47] This Romantic idea is exemplified in Schiller's letters *On the Aesthetic Education of Man*. Schiller pictures our aesthetic and artistic experience as somehow visibly revealing the balance between reason and the senses and thus fulfilling a mediating function between the two. According to Schiller, the main opposition in human nature is between the sensible (sensitivity, emotional drives, "nature") and the rational ("culture," laws, morality). At the present time, there is no harmony between these two principles: in order to make an object intelligible, the intellect destroys it as the object of "inner sense," and the intelligible form "veils it . . . from our feeling."[48] There are presently two types of characters (neither of which is perfect) which are based on the principles of either the intellect or sensibility. The intellect tends to generalize and create laws, the sense, to judge all by the particular, "for the former stood too high to discern the particular, the latter too low to survey the Whole." Hence the abstract thinker very often has a "cold heart" and dissects his impressions that must remain whole, and a man of practical affairs has a "narrow heart," for he cannot go beyond the particular (Let. 6, p. 39). The main social task is thus to restore the harmony and wholeness of the individual, for "the keying up of individual functions of the mind can indeed produce extraordinary human beings; but only the equal tempering of them all, happy and complete human beings" (Let. 6, p. 43). In order to pass from the senses to reason, one needs to be in a perfect state of balance. According to Schiller, it is the aesthetic state that provides this sort of freedom and balance, being posited in the middle between sensation and reason and appearing when both principles are equally active. "From this twofold straying," Schiller writes, the human character "is to be brought back by means of beauty" (Let. 10.1, p. 63). "In contem-

---

47. Enormous literature exists on the subject. As an example of a primary source, see W. H. Wackenroder, L. Tieck, *Outpourings of an Art-Loving Friar*, translated by E. Mornin (New York: Ungar, 1975). As an example of a secondary source, cf. F. Apel, *Himmelssehnsucht: Die Sichtbarkeit der Engel in der romantischen Literatur und Kunst sowie bei Klee, Rilke und Benjamin* (Paderborn: Igel Verlag, 1994).

48. F. Schiller, *On the Aesthetic Education of Man in a Series of Letters*, translated and edited by E. M. Wilkinson and L. A. Willoughby (Oxford: Clarendon Press, 1967), 5 (Letter 1); further on, letter and page numbers are given in brackets.

plation of the beautiful," he continues, "the psyche finds itself in a happy medium between the realm of law and the sphere of physical exigency," for it is equally removed from both constraints (Let. 15, p. 105). Beauty thus removes both types of limitations: it "restores harmony to him who is over-tensed, and energy to him who is relaxed" (Let. 17.2, p. 117). Schiller's final statement reads that the "transition from a passive state of feeling to an active state of thinking and willing cannot, then, take place except via a middle state of aesthetic freedom.... In a word, there is no other way of making sensuous man rational except by first making him aesthetic" (Let. 23.2, p. 161).[49] Schiller thus assigns to the aesthetic an important sociological and cultural role: as in Kant, the revealing capacity of beauty allows it to educate and perfect the "natural" people and develop in them susceptibility to ethics and moral laws.

Coming from the tradition, especially Anglo-American, of the academic study of aesthetics, one might be surprised at the absence, in the discussion thus far, of "aesthetic autonomy" and the idea of "art for art's sake," a disinterested experience to be enjoyed and not to be used—a trend in aesthetics that is usually traced back precisely to Kant and his followers.[50] Instead, the picture that consistently emerges from these pages is that of aesthetics being in the service of some other area: epistemology, ethics, psychology aimed at restoring some balance within the human experience (not to mention theology, which will be discussed later). One might also wonder why this account ignores or de-emphasizes certain figures crucial to the development of nineteenth- and twentieth-century aesthetics, or "philosophy of art," as an autonomous academic discipline. Indeed, for most of the thinkers discussed here aesthetics, or philosophy of art—as beauty and the sublime gradually move to the background—is important only as part of their philosophical systems. Either it creates, structurally, an area that mediates and establishes a common ground between fundamental principles, such as "will and representation,"[51] or "morality and reason," or it functions practically, as

---

49. Cf.: "We need, then, no longer feel at a loss for a way which might lead us from our dependence upon sense towards moral freedom, since beauty offers us an instance of the latter being perfectly compatible with the former, an instance of man not needing to flee matter in order to manifest himself in spirit" (Let. 25.7, p. 189).

50. A framework explained and effectively critiqued by N. Wolterstorff in "Beyond Beauty and the Aesthetic in the Engagement of Religion with Art," in *Theological Aesthetics after von Balthasar*, edited by O. V. Bychkov and J. Fodor, 119–33 (Aldershot: Ashgate, 2008).

51. As in Schopenhauer discussed below.

part of an educational system designed to bring together various areas of human experience into a complete whole. However, it is precisely here, within these great philosophical systems, that the idea of the overall importance of aesthetics for human beings is formed. And it is from this point on that the development of aesthetics as a discipline in its own right is justified, and aesthetics moves into a prominent position in academic circles.

At the same time, in contrast to the initial insights of its founders, academic aesthetics in the end of the nineteenth and beginning of the twentieth century gradually lost its original emphasis on the revelatory and presenting power of aesthetic experience—at least in textual accounts[52]—as well as on the "engaged" aspects of aesthetics, which at the beginning was used to illuminate the continuity between the realms of the true, the good, and the beautiful. One could say that after the role of aesthetics within the system of studies was firmly established, academic aestheticians became preoccupied with intra-disciplinary issues and forgot about the initial insights that elevated aesthetics to its current important status. Thus, although the main trend in academic aesthetics parted ways with revelatory aesthetics, this main trend must rather be seen as betraying the original spirit of aesthetics by focusing on Kant's idea of aesthetic autonomy but ignoring other aspects of his aesthetic theory. A careful analysis of texts shows that such separation of aesthetics from other areas into "aesthetic autonomy" is not at all in the spirit of its eighteenth-century founders. Moreover, as this study will eventually show, this trend is at odds with how the nature of art and aesthetic experience have been perceived through most of Western thought.[53] As von Balthasar astutely points out, by departing from the original (ancient, medieval, and early modern) view of aesthetic experience as revelatory of something transcendent in the world, aesthetics gradually "relinquishes any claim to being a philosophical discipline" and "becomes an epiphenomenon of psychology."[54]

The crucial figure standing at this important junction is certainly

---

52. The question of the visual arts is quite separate and will not be discussed here. It is probably safe to say that, from the Romantic art onwards, the revelatory impulse in art remains ever-present.

53. Our assessment of the place of "aesthetic autonomy" view in the Western tradition will have to be relegated to the Conclusion.

54. GL4 324. See next chapter for a detailed discussion of von Balthasar's views.

Hegel, a major figure in academic aesthetics. Hegel marks the major point of departure from the engaged model of aesthetics, which presents aesthetics as vital to epistemology, ethics, or theology. Hegel's thought also marks the departure from the view of aesthetics as an essential link between the "transcendent" and "immanent" realms (when it reveals the latter to the former) in favor of the "monist" point of view, where the idea of the aesthetic as revealing (and thus of aesthetics as a whole) loses its importance.[55] In his Introduction to *Lectures on Aesthetics*[56] Hegel right from the beginning signals a shift from the revelatory aesthetics of the beautiful and sublime to what for all practical purposes becomes the autonomous discipline called "philosophy of art" (p. 22). In fact, the term "aesthetics," devised by its eighteenth-century founders for the "science of sensation or feeling" in general, is not even appropriate for Hegel's account. Hegel thus immediately banishes the realm of natural beauty from consideration by his discipline, leaving only "artistic beauty" (p. 23). In this sense Hegel already heralds the beginning of aesthetics as the technical discipline that deals mainly with formal and stylistic aspects of art, which makes this version of aesthetics useless for any discussion of the place of aesthetic experience in metaphysics, ethics, or theology.

Another consideration also makes Hegel's aesthetic theory rather unimportant to the discussion of revelatory or theological aesthetics, to which aesthetic experience is fundamental. To Hegel, art is not the highest mode of bringing "the mind's genuine interests into consciousness" (p. 32). It is capable of only a certain "grade" of truth, and some forms of truth, such as Christian, are incapable of being expressed through art, but can be expressed only through religion or philosophy, which are higher forms of expression. Thus "art no longer satisfies our

---

55. The trend already started by Fichte and Schelling, for whom, however, aesthetic experience still remains both crucial and revelatory. In fact, according to von Balthasar, who gives a good account of the genesis of modern aesthetics toward becoming a more formal and technical academic discipline in GL5 595–610, the two movements are directly related. Thus he links the rise of subjectivism and psychologism (and thus a degree of autonomy) in nineteenth-century aesthetics with the fact that the Absolute Spirit in German idealism coincides more and more with the human spirit (i.e., with the movement toward "monism"), a trend that is strongest in Hegel (GL5 599).

56. The text of the Introduction will be quoted according to G. W. F. Hegel, *On Art, Religion, Philosophy: Introductory Lectures to the Realm of Absolute Spirit*, edited by J. Glenn Gray (New York/Evanston: Harper & Row, 1970), with some crucial terms checked against the German original.

supreme need" (p. 32). As he puts it in his famous dictum, "art is . . . a thing of the past" (p. 34) no longer capable of mediating higher truths. The only enterprise that makes sense to Hegel is to construct a "science of art" (cf. p. 37) as a curious intellectual exercise, a post-mortem of sorts on something that has ceased to play an important role in the history of the Absolute Spirit.

Despite Hegel's departure from the "engaged" model of aesthetics, the tendencies that were predominant at the dawn of modern aesthetics are always somehow present and reemerge *en force* in the twentieth century—for example, in Heidegger.[57] Thus the present account could be seen as restoring the balance in the history of aesthetics and bringing to the forefront the element in philosophical aesthetics that was present and even crucial since its origin, but lost its prominence in the later academic tradition. The reason for emphasizing the revelatory and "engaged" aspect of aesthetics is simple. It is precisely this original understanding that is important for the theological aesthetics of von Balthasar (and, he would say, for aesthetics as a philosophical discipline as well) and his project of retrieving important aspects of ancient and medieval aesthetics.

In fact, Hegel's lack of interest in natural beauty and the lowly position he assigns to the arts notwithstanding, even he understands the basic function of aesthetic experience of art as revelatory, which places him firmly in the tradition of German Idealist aesthetics. Thus, fine art is a "mode of revealing to consciousness" (*zum Bewußtsein zu bringen*) the "divine nature, the deepest interests of humanity, and the most comprehensive truths of the mind." Art shares this capacity with religion and philosophy, except that "it represents even the highest ideas *in sensuous forms*," bringing them closer to the senses and feeling.[58] The importance of the revelatory capacity of art hinges on the view that "an appearance or show *(Schein)* . . . is essential to existence *(Wesen)*. Truth could not be if it did not appear or reveal itself *(erscheinen)*, were it not truth *for* someone or something."[59] Art has precisely this capacity to re-

---

57. A. Andreopoulos aptly expresses this loss of the need to "illuminate" or "reveal" anything by art, as well as the recovery of this function of art in some contemporary artists and their theories of art: cf. A. Andreopoulos, *Art as Theology: From the Postmodern to the Medieval* (London: Equinox, 2006).

58. *On Art, Religion, Philosophy*, 29 (Hegel's italics here and below). Later he states that artistic beauty is the "sensuous representation *(Darstellung)* of the absolute" (103).

59. Ibid., 30.

veal (*erscheinen lässt*) not false appearances but "universal powers," in a manner that is more organized than that of the senses (p. 31). Although it is the realm of thought that provides us with "truest reality," art, unlike the senses, "points beyond itself and refers us (*hinweisen*) away from itself to something spiritual" (p. 32). Thus art fulfils its mediating role: it can "heal" the "schism" created by the mind and thought between the sensuous and the "suprasensuous" by reconciling pure thought (reason) and the sensuous (nature; p. 30). Despite his critique of Kant's system as a whole, Hegel's understanding of the role of aesthetic experience is essentially the same as Kant's.[60] Thus, according to Hegel, the function of art is to reconcile the opposition between nature, or the concrete, and the moral law, or the "ought" (pp. 84–86). "Art has the vocation of revealing (*enthüllen*) the truth in the form of sensuous artistic shape, or representing (*darstellen*)[61] the reconciled antithesis just described [i.e., of nature and morals], and, therefore, has its purpose in itself, in this representation (*Darstellung*) and revelation (*Enthüllung*)" (p. 87).[62]

It is also noteworthy that even after Hegel and the rise of "scientific" aesthetics, major nineteenth-century philosophers (not academic aestheticians!) who reflected on aesthetic topics preserve the Kantian understanding of aesthetic experience as revelatory.[63] For example, Schopenhauer openly acknowledges many parallels between his thought and that of Kant,[64] which he also compares with the thought of Plato (see Chapter 5). In an attempt to reconcile Plato and Kant, Schopenhauer maintains that the two thinkers basically express the same view (which is also his own) that the world is structured as an idea, presentation, or manifestation of the will (which is the Kantian thing-in-itself).[65] With-

60. Hegel is a "monist," and so for him the whole scheme of the unity of freedom and necessity (or moral law and nature etc.) can be demonstrated, while for Kant it can only be a priori assumed, but remains inaccessible to us. (Kant, according to Hegel, only strains the antithesis of nature and the moral law, while at the same time rightly pointing it out.)

61. I.e., rather "presenting": cf. note 19 above about the Kantian terms *Darstellung* and *Vorstellung*.

62. Cf. further: artistic beauty is "one of the means which resolve and reduce to unity the above antithesis and contradiction between the abstract self-concentrated mind and actual nature" (88).

63. That is, without subscribing to his philosophical system in general. One must note, once again, that we are discussing the similarities between descriptions of the "phenomenology" of aesthetic experience, i.e., how it appears to an observing subject.

64. Again, the parallels are self-professed, not necessarily always real. However, here we are concerned only with the issue of the revelatory quality of aesthetic experience, on which issue Schopenhauer seems to be in agreement with the mainstream Idealist tradition.

65. A. Schopenhauer, *The World as Will and Idea*, vol. 1 (London: Kegan Paul, 1896); Bk. 3,

in this scheme, the proper way of considering an object is to contemplate it until one becomes one with the object. At this point, one loses individuality and becomes a "timeless subject of knowledge,"[66] that is, one could say that some objectivity of the thing comes through in an idea during this process. Now the sort of knowledge that is concerned with ideas, that is, "direct and adequate objectivity of the thing-in-itself, the will" lies precisely in the area of art and the work of genius (§36, pp. 238–39), which is "the faculty of continuing in the state of pure perception, of losing oneself in perception" (p. 240). According to Schopenhauer, all are capable of transcending themselves and knowing or intuiting the ideas in things, that is, all have an aesthetic capacity. A genius retains this sort of knowledge of ideas and then relates them to others in a work of art.[67] "The work of art is only a means of facilitating the knowledge in which this pleasure consists" (§37, p. 252). That is, there is a connection between art and the knowledge of ideas. Art and aesthetic experience reveal a kind of truth, except that this truth is transmitted through "seeing" rather than reasoning. In his analysis of a Dutch still life—strikingly similar to Heidegger's reflections on Van Gogh's image of a pair of peasant shoes[68]—Schopenhauer notices that Dutch artists directed their objective perception at quite insignificant things and elevated them to their "objective" status. The natural beauty of such objects "discloses itself suddenly to our view" and "delivers" us from subjectivity into the "objective" world (§38, p. 255), and art thereby reveals the "objective" reality of depicted things.[69]

F. Nietzsche radicalizes the position of aesthetics even further—past Schelling's high evaluation of aesthetics over conceptual knowledge, and past the view of aesthetics as an autonomous discipline—by elevating it to the status of a universal science, wherein the aesthetic view not only is worthy in itself but is the only possible one. In fact, after Nietzschean

---

"The World as Idea, Second Aspect. (The Platonic Idea: The Object of Art)." This translation will henceforth be identified by paragraph and page number.

66. Schopenhauer, *World as Will and Idea*, §34, p. 231.
67. This is, again, very close to the Kantian understanding of genius.
68. Discussed further in this chapter.
69. Similarity with Kant also extends to Schopenhauer's use of the term "sublime" as contrasted with "beautiful" (§39, p. 260). In agreement with Kant, Schopenhauer holds that in the experience of the sublime, knowledge is terrible, whereas in the experience of beauty it is gained "without struggle" (261). He even borrows Kant's terminology for the sublime: dynamical and mathematical (265), and, as Kant does, he speaks of the connection between the sublime disposition and morals (267).

developments in aesthetics, a serious philosophical or theological engagement can hardly afford to ignore the aesthetic problematic.[70] Foreshadowing the postmodern turn, Nietzsche's views developed in opposition to the traditional "Platonic" system (which Nietzsche calls the "will to truth") that features, on the one hand, the "true," universal, unified, ideal values—the true, the good, etc.—and on the other hand their inferior "appearances" in the world. Nietzschean "genealogy," which leads to the deconstruction of traditional metaphysics and ethics, attempts to demonstrate that both the true and the good are merely disguised and indirect manifestations of the primordial "will to power." According to Nietzsche, art—which is for him the manifestation of the aesthetic *par excellence*—is a much more adequate and immediate expression of life and its primordial drives (will to power) than rationality. With the loss of universal ideal values of the true and the good, the world, in the eyes of Nietzsche, becomes purely perspectival and "dispersed." It is only various individual perspectives that reflect unique individual wills to power that matter: for Nietzsche, perspective is the "basic condition of all life."[71]

In a world where no universal criteria are possible, where only individual experiential points of view matter, it is not surprising that valorization from the point of view of "truth" and morality (the good) is radically replaced by subjective aesthetic valorization, the only possibility in a perspectival world of pure "appearances."[72] Aesthetics replaces philosophy and becomes a universal science, and art acquires greater value than truth.[73] "In a universe that is now wholly perspectival, in a world once again become infinite in that it offers the possibility of an infinity of interpretations, only art presents itself authentically as what it is: an evaluation that makes no pretence of truth,"[74] that is, a more immediate

---

70. Many, of course, did, as a matter of fact, but this does not detract from the validity of this statement that reflects the ideal scenario.

71. F. Nietzsche, "Beyond Good and Evil," in *Basic Writings of Nietzsche*, edited and translated by W. Kaufmann (New York: Modern Library, 1992), 193; cf. Ferry, *Homo Aestheticus*, 171. In quoting "The Birth of Tragedy" below, all references will also be to Kaufmann's translation. The following German edition will be used: F. Nietzsche, *Die Geburt der Tragödie*, edited by G. Colli and M. Montinari, *Werke* 3/1 (Berlin, New York: 1972); henceforth abbreviated as *W*.

72. Cf. Ferry, *Homo Aestheticus*: "the liberation of the sensuous and of appearance that the genealogy of the true world brings about is just as much a liberation of art" (p. 152, cf. p. 153).

73. For Nietzsche, art should be "truer" than truth and philosophy should become an aesthetics (cf. Ferry, *Homo Aestheticus*, 183); cf. Hammermeister, *German Aesthetic Tradition*, 145–50.

74. Ferry, *Homo Aestheticus*, 167.

evaluation that has not yet been transformed by any secondary conceptual framework (e.g., the belief in the power of "truth").

To be sure, Nietzsche's aesthetics can be seen in opposition to both Baumgarten's aesthetic as a kind of truth and Kant's aesthetic as a symbol of the morally good. In a Nietzschean universe the only possible ground is aesthetic. However, despite all the differences, Nietzsche—at least in the *Birth of Tragedy*, which owes much to the previous Idealist and Romantic tradition[75]—understands the function of aesthetic experience along the same lines: as something that gives us an insight into the nature of reality, and at the same time reconciles us with, and "tames," a broader range of the phenomena and experiences that one faces at the brink of rationality. The need for art and its revelatory and redeeming power arises when at a certain point science (which operates within the framework of truth) reaches a boundary, that is, the point of contact with the beyond that transcends it. The encounter with such transcending experience destroys rationality, and the aesthetic comes as a "savior" to repair the shattered perspective. Nietzsche speaks of "such boundary points (*Grenzpunkte*) on the periphery from which one gazes into what defies illumination. They [thinkers] see to their horror how logic coils up at these boundaries and finally bites its own tail—suddenly the new form of insight breaks through, tragic insight which, merely to be endured, needs art as a protection and remedy."[76] The aesthetic serves as a necessary healing and saving principle that "tames" that which surpasses reason:

> Man now sees everywhere only the horror or absurdity of existence . . . he is nauseated. Here, when the danger to his will is greatest, art approaches as a saving (*rettende*) sorceress, expert at healing (*heilkundige*). She alone knows how to turn these nauseous thoughts about the horror or absurdity of existence into notions with which one can live: these are the sublime as the artistic taming of the horrible, and the comic as the artistic discharge of the nausea of absurdity.[77]

In line with the tradition of pre-Nietzschean aesthetics, aesthetic experience in Nietzsche somehow bridges the split between the realm of rationality and something that is beyond reason. The taming function

---

75. Cf. Hammermeister, *German Aesthetic Tradition*, 143.
76. *The Birth of Tragedy*, chap. 15, in Nietzsche, *Basic Writings*, 98.
77. Ibid., chap. 7, 60, W 53.

of the aesthetic in the face of something horrible, for example, is comparable to "negative presentation" in Kant's idea of the sublime: the aesthetic absorbs the horrible and unthinkable into the human experience by harmonizing it with the latter and turning it into something positive. The exclusive role of the aesthetic in Nietzsche allows him in general to proclaim the coming of the "aesthetic age," which should replace the era of unified systematic or dogmatic views, after which point the aesthetic justification of the world becomes unavoidable. This important idea is formulated in a famous dictum from the *Birth of Tragedy*: "For it is only as an *aesthetic phenomenon* that existence and the world are eternally justified."[78]

Despite the persistence of the academic study of aesthetics as an autonomous discipline, twentieth-century philosophy sees a re-emergence of the ways of viewing aesthetic experience that hark back to pre-Hegelian or even pre-Kantian times and once again make aesthetics relevant to metaphysics, theology, and the theory of interpretation in general. These re-emerging trends in philosophy examine, once again, not autonomous but "engaged" models for aesthetics. Aesthetic experience is once again seen as revelatory of some truth about reality. Two figures stand out, Heidegger and Gadamer, who are also responsible for shaping the revolutionary understanding of the hermeneutic process that is assumed for the present monograph.[79] Heidegger in particular can be seen as renewing the "Romantic paradigm" and returning to the tradition of German Idealism[80] by restoring both Schelling's understanding of art as revelatory of the nature of reality and Schopenhauer's view of art objects as revealing the "objective reality" of depicted things. In his early essay "The Origin of the Work of Art," Heidegger bases his account of the way aesthetic and artistic experience works on a concept of truth that is different from the traditional understanding of truth as correctness or correspondence. Heidegger claims to have revived the ancient Greek sense of truth

---

78. Ibid., chap. 5, 52, W 43. The German reads: "denn nur als *aesthetisches Phänomen* ist das Dasein und die Welt ewig *gerechtfertigt*" (Nietzsche's italics). Cf. chap. 24, 141: "Here it becomes necessary to take a bold running start and leap into a metaphysics of art, by repeating the sentence written above, that existence and the world seem justified only as an aesthetic phenomenon." See more on Nietzsche's aesthetic justification of the world in the chapter on Augustine below.

79. See Introduction.

80. On the relation of Heidegger's aesthetics to German Idealism, and specifically to Schelling, see Hammermeister, *German Aesthetic Tradition*, 173, 181–82, 185–89.

(ἀλήθεια) as disclosure or unconcealedness: "Truth is the unconcealedness of that which is as something that is. Truth is the truth of Being."[81] According to Heidegger, even the notion of truth as correspondence is ultimately reducible to something that is immediately evident (truth as the unconcealedness of being).[82] Moreover, it is not we who presuppose this unconcealedness of beings: on the contrary, this unconcealedness is a certain condition of being that puts us in such a position that we are always aware of it.

Using the term 'truth' in this sense allows Heidegger, even after Nietzsche, to assert that art can still lay claim to truth. In Heidegger's famous example of Van Gogh's painting of peasant shoes, an artwork is the "disclosure of what the equipment . . . *is* in truth. The entity emerges into the unconcealedness of its being" (p. 36). Thus in the artwork there occurs "a disclosure of a particular being, disclosing what and how it is" (that is, its truth) (p. 36). The way the truth of beings occurs in the experience of art is described using the metaphors of light, ability to shine through, and revelation: "Some particular entity . . . comes in the work to stand in the light of its being. The being of the being comes into the steadiness of its shining" (p. 36);[83] "Truth happens in Van Gogh's painting. This does not mean that something is correctly portrayed, but rather that in the revelation of the equipmental being of the shoes, that which is a whole—world and earth in their counterplay—attains to unconcealedness" (p. 56).[84] It is precisely this luminous revelation of the truth of being that, according to Heidegger, is referred to as beauty: "That is how self-concealing being is illuminated. Light of this kind joins its shining to and into the work. This shining, joined in the work, is the beautiful. *Beauty is one way in which truth occurs as unconcealedness*" (p. 56; Heidegger's italics). It is important that for Heidegger appear-

---

81. Heidegger, "Origin of the Work of Art," in *Poetry, Language, Thought*, 81. Page references given in parentheses are to the translation by Hofstadter.

82. Cf.: "naturally, in order to understand and verify the correctness (truth) of a proposition one really should go back to something that is already evident . . . this presupposition is indeed unavoidable" (52).

83. Cf.: "The art work opens up in its own way the Being of beings. This opening up, i.e., this deconcealing, i.e., the truth of beings, happens in the work" (39).

84. The reference to the "world" and "earth" comes from Heidegger's description of the function of the work of art as a certain dialectical process of concealing (the principle responsible for this is called "earth") and disclosure (as the "world" that the work of art opens up and keeps open; cf. 46–47, 53). Although the main element in the essence of the work of art remains its ability to reveal, concealment is dialectically necessary.

ance is the main feature of the aesthetic experience of beauty. The traditional "formal criteria" of beauty ultimately stem from that initial revelation of being as being (something that is): "When truth sets itself into the work, it appears. Appearance—as this being of truth in the work and as work—is beauty. Thus the beautiful belongs to the advent of truth, truth's taking of its place.... The beautiful does lie in form, but only because the *forma* once took its light from Being as the isness of what is" (p. 81). In sum, the essence of the work of art is precisely in revealing to us that something is, or is in a certain way, which is the main source of wonder in our aesthetic experience of beauty: "namely this, that unconcealedness of what is has happened here, and that as this happening it happens here for the first time; or, that such a work *is* at all rather than is not"; "this thrust, this '*that* it is' of createdness, emerges into view" (p. 65). One can see that such an understanding of aesthetic experience already has theological overtones, as does the very expression of wonder in the face of the existence of something in the world.[85]

The idea of truth as disclosure that Heidegger derives from our experience of art becomes instrumental for Gadamer's understanding of philosophical hermeneutics. Gadamer attended Heidegger's lectures on the "Origin of the Work of Art," and in his work *Truth and Method*, he takes over the idea that the general characteristic of being is its ability to be revealed, be manifested, and become evident (cf. *TM* 487 and passim). This "speculative character" of being forms the ground of hermeneutics, just as do reason or language (*TM* 477). Now beauty, following Heidegger's account in the "Origin," is precisely the name for this ability of being to be manifested and disclosed. In the concluding section of *Truth and Method*, Gadamer traces the idea of the aesthetic experience of beauty as manifestation or appearance even further back, to Plato.[86] The beautiful can be grasped immediately, its nature is to be "visibly mani-

---

85. Of course, according to von Balthasar's account of Heidegger's thought, the latter's understanding of the ontological difference in terms of "identity" precisely prevents such wonder and thus the building of a theological aesthetics (*GL5* 447). At the same time, he thinks that Heidegger's philosophy is most "fertile" for such a task (*GL5* 449). In any case, one could safely say that Heidegger's account shares at least "phenomenological" similarities with the aesthetics of revelation.

86. Cf. *TM* 477–81. The ancient idea of beauty, according to Gadamer, can be of service to contemporary hermeneutics (*TM* 477). For a more detailed discussion of Gadamer's retrieval of Plato's aesthetics, see below in Chapter 5.

fest"; it "reveals" and "presents" itself and has the ability to dispose us in its favor "immediately" by "its own radiance" (*TM* 481), which is not one of its qualities but "constitutes its actual being" (*TM* 482).[87] Light, shining, appearance belong to the "ontological structure of the beautiful" and point to the kinship between the beautiful and the Word as the principle of manifestation in the Christian tradition (*TM* 483).

Although beauty is still "in this world," its mode of appearance signals that it is something different (*TM* 482). Beauty points to something, the value of which is self-evident—namely, it points to the fact that there is a "harmony between the thing and its attendant disclosure," the disclosure (ἀλήθεια) of its being (*TM* 481). To beauty belongs "the most important ontological function: that of mediating between idea and appearance" (*TM* 481). The idea is fully present in what is beautiful in the most immediate and evident way.[88] In other words, the experience of the beautiful, in a certain symbolic and analogical way, points to one of the most fundamental structures of being: its capacity to reveal itself.

Aesthetic experience is not alone in its ability to point out the self-revealing nature of being. In this ability it is similar to the process of understanding, which is also a certain disclosure. Thus, Gadamer draws a parallel between the concept of shining forth (*Vorscheinen*) or radiance of the beautiful and the concept of the "evidentness" (*das Einleuchtende*) of the understandable (*TM* 483). Both beauty and understanding are about something that becomes evident, and what is evident, the process of seeing, "coming to light," when light is being turned on—these are always as surprising and startling as the experience of the beautiful (*TM* 486). At the same time, revelatory capacity is also one of the basic features of the hermeneutic process: the idea of "coming to light"—in both art and understanding—is what guides Gadamer's reflection on hermeneutics in *Truth and Method*. Our experience of the beautiful can illuminate two key points that, according to Gadamer, are at the core of our hermeneutic experience of the world. First, both the appearance of beauty and the "coming to light" of the understanding "have the character of an event." Second, "the hermeneutical experience, as the experience of traditionary meaning, has a share in the *immediacy* which has

---

87. Cf.: "Its being is such that it makes itself immediately evident (*einleuchtend*)" (*TM* 481).
88. Cf. Kant's presentation of the ideas in the aesthetic experience of the sublime.

always distinguished the experience of the beautiful" or the true (*TM* 484–85). Thus if in Kant aesthetic experience is analogous to the moral feeling, and in Heidegger it is analogous to the way truth appears, in Gadamer the experience of the beautiful is analogous to our hermeneutic experience. As tradition is being understood in a hermeneutic process, the latter, just like aesthetic experience or the appreciation of the arts, exhibits its capacity to reveal and bring something to light. Moreover, our aesthetic experience of an artwork can serve as an excellent hermeneutic model: indeed, in art or aesthetic experience, truth is reached not by means of a method or science, and yet in both cases truth "comes to light" clearly in an immediate and persuasive way.

Both Heidegger's and Gadamer's parallels between the aesthetic experience of a work of art and the disclosure of truth in a hermeneutic process have been taken over for contemporary theology. According to Tracy, for example,[89] in both art and religion truth is disclosed as a result of a hermeneutic process. "What we mean in naming certain texts . . . 'classics,'" Tracy writes, "is that here we recognize nothing less than the disclosure of a reality we cannot but name truth" (p. 108). Tracy thinks that traditional theories of private taste do not capture the actual experience of the work of art. In an authentic experience of art, "we find ourselves 'caught up' in its world, we are shocked, surprised, challenged by its startling beauty and its recognizable truth. . . . In the actual experience of art . . . we recognize the truth of the work's disclosure of a world of reality transforming, if only for a moment, ourselves."[90]

So is it possible, in the end, to find any common features among these various nineteenth- and twentieth-century aesthetic theories? It seems that two prominent features continuously recur in Western European philosophical reflection on aesthetics. The first is that 'aesthetic,' in line with its etymology, is something that has to do with the senses, sensing, or sense experience. In view of recent research in the areas of Gestalt psychology and neurobiology of aesthetics,[91] it is no longer appropriate, as was common earlier, to oppose sensory experience to

---

89. *Analogical Imagination*, 67–68; see Chapter 3 for more details.

90. Ibid., 110; cf. 112: "It happens, it occurs, I am 'caught up in' the disclosure of the work. I am in the presence of a truth of recognition."

91. Cf. a good survey of the state of research in these areas in I. Rentschler, B. Herzberger, and D. Epstein, eds., *Beauty and the Brain* (Basel/Boston/Berlin: Birkhäuser, 1988).

"concepts" or "rationality." It is more or less clear that sense perception and conceptualization are not radically different activities but rather are generated by similarly structured circuits of neurons that operate on similar principles, such as projection and search for preset patterns, recognition or identification, ignoring constantly repeating patterns, et cetera. (Current research also proves once and for all that some foundational aesthetic principles are indeed "objective" in the sense of being "hard-wired" into the human brain.) Therefore sense experience can no longer be characterized as something opposed to "rationality." However, it is still characterized by the very fact of *sensing*, or experiencing something from without, something outside one's consciousness. So it still makes a difference to an aesthetician, just as it did before, whether or not the source of aesthetic experience—sound, image, speech—is actually present to our perceptive activity: for example, whether we are actually looking at a painting or merely recollecting it and thinking about it. For this reason the working definition of 'aesthetic' should include the presence of the actual sense stimuli from something external to our consciousness.[92]

The second prominent feature has to do with the persistent need in modern Western thought for a direct intuition or insight (seeing, appearance, presentation) when it comes to solving key philosophical (and, as we will see later, theological) problems. This need is already evident in Kant, and it gains prominence in the phenomenological tradition (e.g., in Husserl and Heidegger). Since postmodern critique, which otherwise has many valid points, suggests that such "seeing" or intuition is either an idealist notion or simply a metaphor,[93] a short digression in defense of "seeing" would be appropriate. At a very early

---

92. The difficulty stemming from the observation that everything is really mediated through our consciousness can be resolved by performing Husserl's phenomenological analysis in order to determine what exactly in our conscious experience is part of our "egological constitution" and what consitutes the "objective world," that is, what is not, technically speaking, part of us. A different problem—what to do with cases such as imagining something visual or reciting literature or music in our mind, i.e., when the "sensory input from an aesthetic object" is actually something produced "internally" and not by an external sensory input—is not resolved by introducing this working definition. There are other contemporary views of aesthetics, e.g., that of Frank Burch Brown, which do not limit the discipline to the areas that deal with actual sense experience. However, historically this has not been the case, and the current study does not attempt to delve into this issue.

93. Cf. Derrida's discussion of the "metaphor of the sun" in his essay "White Mythology," in *Margins of Philosophy*, translated by Alan Bass (Chicago: University of Chicago Press, 1982), 207–71, but especially pp. 250ff.

stage in Western European thought, the Stoics, after an extensive discussion of the criterion of truth, determined that the criterion is a class of certain "clear perceptions" or "clear cognitions."[94] A contemporary debate with the Sceptics exposed a problem inherent in their theory: are these perceptions clear because they are true, or do we think they are true because they seem so clear? Perhaps Husserl's phenomenology, in which the ways of verification are also extremely visual,[95] provides one corrective by postulating that such perceptions must be continuously and infinitely verifiable, and not simply constitute momentary insights:[96] that is, he adds a temporal or historical criterion (cf. historical practice as the criterion of truth in Marx). Heidegger's understanding of the process of interpretation as going in a "hermeneutic circle" can further clarify the way the "criterion of truth" works. The hermeneutic process includes clarity, perhaps, as one of its stages and then proceeds to other forms of verification. We also recall Heidegger's observation in his "Origin of the Work of Art"[97] that, if one really thinks about it, all reasoning is ultimately reduced to "seeing" clearly whether something is or is not the case: for example, at the simplest level "comparing" would mean manipulating "visually" in one's imagination two elements in order to "see" if they fit.

Ultimately, the question whether such direct intuition or seeing is possible or not lies outside the scope of this study. What matters here is the fact that in Western philosophy and theology it has frequently been invoked. We will therefore simply point out when the issue of "seeing" or direct intuition appears in the history of Western thought, only occasionally remarking on the validity of particular observations in this respect. Thus as a rule the discussion of the issue of "seeing" in this study must be taken historically: that is, not as expressing the position of this author, but as a record of what has been said on the subject, so far as it is relevant to the study as a whole.

At the core of this study, however, stands the fact that aesthetic experience historically did provide an excellent analogy to such direct insight or "seeing" (whether it is actually possible or not). Indeed, in aesthetic ex-

---

94. See Chapter 6 below; in the fourteenth century Duns Scotus takes over this position: see Chapter 8.
95. Cf. the idea of "apodicticity" itself; see Husserl, *Cartesian Meditations*, 12, 14–15, 57ff.
96. Cf. ibid., 114, 127.
97. See Heidegger, *Poetry, Language, Thought*, 52.

perience there is no need to prove whether anything can be seen or presented directly—because *it is* seen; we feel and experience it directly, and it possesses utmost convincingness and persuasiveness. Now, given that the process of thinking or forming concepts is taken as some sort of seeing or direct presentation, one can transfer observations from aesthetic experience to the ways we think of such a process, or simply use aesthetic experience—as more obvious and accessible to a wider group of observers—to illustrate some philosophical and theological points. As we have seen, one of the most common observations about aesthetic experience that Western philosophers found useful is that it seems to "reveal" something and point beyond itself, or transcends itself, and it does this immediately, without reasoning or concept, and without involving any practical interest. This ability of aesthetic experience to point immediately to something beyond itself or beyond the realm of rational thought gives it a unique capacity to form analogies with a number of other basic experiences, in particular with phenomena that have to do with revelation or a "transcending" movement of thought.[98] As the reader will see, this quality has also proved useful to modern theology.

Our analysis of the history of classic philosophical aesthetics, as opposed to the academic "autonomous" discipline of aesthetics or "philosophy of art," yields another observation. What has usually interested the great philosophers who have made contributions to aesthetics (not the professional academic aestheticians) is not aesthetic experience *per se*. In fact, the issues that are most important to them are traditional philosophical questions: acquisition of truth, foundations of ethics, nature of being, etc. However, in order to discern or illustrate those issues, these great thinkers have relied on aesthetic experience to provide analogies and parallels with other philosophical problems, or have even seen some more intrinsic connection between aesthetics and other areas.[99] In

---

98. For Kant it is an analogy with morality; for Heidegger and Gadamer, with truth and understanding; for Gadamer, with the hermeneutic process. For the nineteenth-century Romantic tradition, the aesthetic also forms an analogy with the divine (as the revelation of the invisible in the visible). The analogy with the divine, of course, will be the major focus in the discussion of theological aesthetics in the rest of this monograph.

99. Some scholars, such as Frank Burch Brown or Victor Bychkov, tend to assume the latter view and present the aesthetic element as something that can be seen as integral and enriching to all other areas of human experience. If one assumes this point of view, almost any philosophical or theological enterprise would automatically turn into doing "aesthetics." This study does not, however, espouse such a broad approach and therefore uses the traditional eighteenth- and nineteenth-century definition.

other words, engaging in philosophical aesthetics means, paradoxically, not focusing on the academic discipline of aesthetics as a separate and autonomous field that deals with a particular type of enjoyment (that of aesthetic form); rather, in the hands of the masters, philosophical aesthetics is simply a certain way of resolving important philosophical issues by using insights drawn from analogies with concrete aesthetic experience. Thinkers who engage aesthetics view the processes that are at the center of traditional philosophical discussions (such as cognition, following moral laws, etc.) as happening in a manner that is *analogous* to aesthetic experience, or *as in* aesthetic experience, that is, as if by direct sensation. As the next chapter will show, this same pattern can be observed in von Balthasar's theological aesthetics. In other words, in order to locate ancient and medieval contexts that could be classified as "aesthetics" (the task addressed in full in Chapter 4) one need not have a defined academic subject of aesthetics or a consciously acknowledged treatise on aesthetics.[100] All one needs is an attempt to resolve certain philosophical or theological issues by using analogies or parallels with aesthetic experience: for this is precisely what the founders of, and some major figures in, modern aesthetics tried to accomplish.

100. As we mentioned earlier, a common objection to the study of pre-modern aesthetics points out precisely that aesthetics as an acknowledged discipline is not found in the earlier tradition.

CHAPTER 2

The Aesthetic in Theology
Hans Urs von Balthasar

In view of the general importance of the discipline of aesthetics in the nineteenth and twentieth centuries, as well as of its universalization by such thinkers as Nietzsche, it seems only logical for contemporary theology to take the aesthetic seriously. Yet the most obvious observation is that this is precisely what does not happen. Perhaps the most notable figure in contemporary thought who noticed and lamented the loss of the aesthetic dimension in theology, as well as realized the need to restore it, is Hans Urs von Balthasar.[1]

As was mentioned above, von Balthasar's project to restore the aesthetic element in theology includes retrieving foundational aesthetic insights from ancient and medieval texts—the focus of the present study. His strategy, as will become more clear from what follows, is based on his observation that the "fundamental presupposition, common to Antiquity and Christianity" (and, we can add, to modern philosophical aesthetics) is that reality and being are revelatory in nature and are capable of revealing certain higher principles (GL4 324). According to von Balthasar, modern "speculative aesthetics," from Kant on, "still for the most part appeals" to the ancient view of the revelatory nature of reality (GL4 323). This is precisely where he sees the convergence be-

---

1. For a bibliography on von Balthasar's theological aesthetics, see appendix to this chapter. It is clear (cf. GL1 50) that von Balthasar is aware of the overall importance and radicalization of aesthetics, in particular in Nietzsche, although he would most probably disagree with the idea that his own theological aesthetics is a reaction to this radicalization. However, when one puts his thought in a historical perspective, it appears that his return to aesthetics in theology can be plausibly interpreted as—perhaps a subconscious—reaction to the importance of the aesthetic point of view in modern intellectual history.

tween philosophical aesthetics (such as that of Kant), or philosophy in general (such as that of Heidegger) and theology. Now if aesthetics loses its focus on the revelatory capacity of reality, as most academic aesthetics does in the nineteenth and twentieth centuries, von Balthasar asks, "what can such an aesthetics have to say?" (GL4 324). If this revelatory capacity is removed from beauty and the world is "stripped of its radiance and worth," why is being better than non-being? (GL4 324) Forgetful of what initially set it in motion, "aesthetics then becomes an epiphenomenon of psychology and relinquishes any claim to being a philosophical discipline" (GL4 324). However, just as the loss of its revelatory or "transcendental" (or, one can even say, theological) dimension is detrimental to aesthetics, so is the loss of theology's aesthetic dimension detrimental to theology. Thus both disciplines can benefit from going to the roots of the revelatory understanding of aesthetics in Antiquity and the Middle Ages, which, as von Balthasar attempts to show later, can still be clearly seen in eighteenth- and nineteenth-century aesthetic theories.

Before moving on to von Balthasar's effort to retrieve the original aesthetic insight through a dialogue with ancient and medieval texts, it is important to understand exactly what he means by 'theological aesthetics.' In an interesting twist, his inspiration for theological aesthetics comes from the most unlikely source: the Protestant tradition which, according to his own words, almost completely eliminated the aesthetic element from its theology. In the late 1940s von Balthasar became a close friend of Karl Barth, who shared the former's love for Mozart and was inspired by his musical talent. The influence was mutual: von Balthasar, in his turn, was inspired by the section on the beauty of God from Barth's *Church Dogmatics* II, 1. In his introduction to *The Glory of the Lord* (GL1 53ff.) von Balthasar himself acknowledges that the very idea of contemplating the divine glory and of reconceiving Christian theology in the light of beauty comes from Barth.[2] Barth acknowledges (p. 651) that the Reformation and Protestant orthodoxy completely ignored the

---

2. Cf. F. Kerr, "Foreword: Assessing this 'Giddy Synthesis,'" in *Balthasar at the End of Modernity* (henceforth *BEM*), edited by L. Gardner, D. Moss, B. Quash, and G. Ward (Edinburgh: T&T Clark, 1999), 6: "the basic perspective of *Herrlichkeit* surely owes far more to Barth." On the relationship between Barth and von Balthasar see also R. Viladesau, *Theological Aesthetics*, 26–29. Some Dutch Neo-Calvinists, in particular Kuyper, anticipated Barth in his theology of divine glory: see J. S. Begbie, *Voicing Creation's Praise: Towards a Theology of the Arts* (Edinburgh: T&T Clark, 1991).

aesthetic element.³ That God is beautiful has always been an "alien" idea: theology didn't know what to make of it, and even the Catholic tradition does not come back to this idea until J. M. Scheeben.⁴ The concept of beauty was perceived as secular and considered "extremely dangerous" as bringing our contemplation of God suspiciously close to that of the world. At the same time, in a strong statement, Barth claims that too much would have to be struck out of the Bible if the concept of beauty were removed (pp. 653–54). Barth's concept of beauty is different from the classic "appearance" model accepted by von Balthasar.⁵ According to Barth's understanding (p. 653), beauty is associated mainly with the concepts of the "pleasant, desirable and enjoyable" (cf. p. 654): all familiar, but, according to the classic aesthetic theory, not constituting elements of aesthetic experience.⁶ However, beauty in Barth is linked to form; thus it still preserves the element of appearance and its ability to be immediately seen.⁷

According to Barth (p. 656) there cannot be an extended conceptual discussion of the aesthetic element in God, but only an allusion to

---

3. Barth is quoted according to the following translation: K. Barth, *The Doctrine of God*, first half-volume of vol. 2 of *Church Dogmatics*, edited by G. W. Bromiley and T. F. Torrance, 649–66 (Edinburgh: T&T Clark, 1964); henceforth abbreviated as CD II/1.

4. Cf. von Balthasar's analysis of this figure in GL1 104ff.

5. This means that, despite Barth's influence on von Balthasar, the latter's understanding of beauty comes from German philosophy, and not from Barth: see below. See some observations on the general differences between the Protestant and Catholic understanding of beauty and aesthetic experience in O. Bychkov, "Introduction" (Bychkov and Fodor, *Theological Aesthetics after von Balthasar*, xi–xviii).

6. For Protestant theological aesthetics the element of pure joy and pleasure has always been important or even central: cf. the "sheerly delightful" as an important component of F. B. Brown's "neo-aesthetics" (Brown, *Religious Aesthetics*, 11). Protestant theologians might wonder, then, why von Balthasar does not engage this aspect when he follows Barth in some other respects. The answer seems to be that pleasure or joy as such is extremely "unfocused" and irrational in nature: one can receive pleasure (as it happens at the "basic" sensory level) from things that do not necessarily fit into a certain pattern, as they do in aesthetic phenomena. One can also enjoy something that is far from "pointing in the right direction," another quality of the classic aesthetic (or τὸ καλόν: see Chapters 5–8). What is different about "aesthetic pleasure" is that in this case pleasure indicates precisely a presence of a pattern, something that can also be seen, detected, and sometimes even analyzed mathematically. At the very least, this pleasure signals the presence of something that may not be detectable (the transcendent), but is "purposive" or "pattern-like." That is, the presence of pleasure here is *not* a determining factor—but the "purposiveness" is, or a glimpse of some "truth," that establishes a pattern or a connection to something. At the same time, von Balthasar could explain, for the Protestant tradition an interest in pure, unarticulated pleasure is natural: in Protestant thought, God does not have a "form," there is nothing to be seen, and connections to pattern and cognition are not as relevant.

7. Cf. Barth, CD II/1, 654: "we are speaking only of the form and manner of His glory, of the specifically persuasive and convincing element in His relevation."

it: there is "something here which must be perceived rather than discussed" since "this insight depends too much on the presence of the necessary feeling."[8] The proof of God's beauty "can be provided neither by few nor by many words . . . but only by this beauty itself": one must see this "form or way or manner in which God is perfect . . ." that has some features that are immediately evident. Barth maintains that, despite its neglect in the Protestant tradition, it is precisely beauty, or the aesthetic element, with its ability to reveal something immediately, that is responsible for the most convincing and persuasive aspects in God. Discussing the issue of divine glory, Barth asks: to what extent does God "really convince and persuade?" What is the thing revealed and "what is the nature and form of its revealing?" (p. 649, cf. 650).[9] He comes to the conclusion that the idea of glory "contains something which is not covered by that of power" (p. 650). The concept "which may serve legitimately to describe the element in the idea of glory that we still lack, is that of beauty." We must say that God is beautiful, and "to say this is to say how He enlightens and convinces and persuades us." Since attraction and joy constitute an "inalienable form of his glory"(and for Barth these are characteristic features of the beautiful), Barth asks, "how can we dispense with the idea of the beautiful" and with the idea that God is beautiful? His glory will then be "neither persuasive nor convincing" (p. 655). However, Barth also described the convincing and revealing element as the "shape and form" of God's power that speaks for itself, wins and conquers (p. 650). This form has been "visible" to us and has made an impression on us (p. 658). The perfection of his form radiates outwards the perfection of his content: in this form the perfect content (God himself) "shines out," and "this persuasive and convincing form must necessarily be called the beauty of God" (p. 659). Finally, Barth mentions the beauty of Jesus Christ—the concept fully developed by von Balthasar—and emphasizes the importance of "seeing" the form of the event of Jesus (p. 665). Thus following the classic Western tradition of interpreting aesthetic experience, Barth sees beauty as a certain capacity to reveal and present that is immediate and convincing. These characteristics of beauty allow him to draw a parallel with immediately

---

8. Cf. von Balthasar's understanding of the aesthetic discussed below: the aesthetic remains *aesthetic* only so long as the "contact" with the immediately "visible" object is maintained, which is a classic understanding of aesthetic experience.

9. Cf. von Balthasar's discussion of these issues summarized later in this chapter.

appearing and convincing elements in God. The concept of beauty, according to Barth, shows that God is not a merely abstract idea but that something in revelation is shown and visible. God's glory is not a mere "formless and shapeless fact," effective only through his power: "it is effective because and as it is beautiful" (p. 653).

At the same time, Barth maintains that his subject is still "glory." He stresses the auxiliary nature of beauty and strongly cautions against its misuse: "We speak of God's beauty only in explanation of his glory. It is, therefore, a subordinate and auxiliary idea," used to clarify and emphasize certain aspects of glory. Barth's seeming lack of awareness of the "danger" of using aesthetic categories—a typical feature of the Protestant tradition that Barth criticizes here—is precisely due to the fact that the concept of beauty cannot be included "with the main concepts of the doctrine of God" or become a "leading concept" (p. 652). Barth concludes that the statement that God is beautiful "must not be neglected" but "it cannot claim to have any independent significance." What the statement about God's beauty explains is "how God in his glory, in his self-declaration, makes himself clear to man" (p. 666).[10]

Von Balthasar begins his overview of the history of nineteenth- and twentieth-century theological aesthetics (in *GL1*) with a concern similar to that of Barth: namely, that aesthetics has been gradually eliminated from theology: not only Protestant but also Catholic. As the aesthetic worldview gradually develops in the Romantics—following Schleiermacher and Hegel—and culminates in Schopenhauer and Nietzsche, many proclaim the aesthetic "to be the supreme value of any world-view." In reaction to this nineteenth-century radicalization of the aesthetic element, Kierkegaard declares that the aesthetic attitude is incompatible with the Christian one (*GL1* 50). The main reason for banishing the aesthetic by Kierkegaard and, more generally, by both Protestant and Catholic theologies is that aesthetics became an independent and self-sufficient field "insulated" from logic and ethics.[11] Just as the theologians eliminated the aesthetic, the "aestheticians"—for example, Nietzsche, but also most academic aestheticians—had a tendency to banish reli-

---

10. Cf. R. Viladesau, *Theological Aesthetics*, 28, who likewise notices Barth's reservation regarding the use of the beautiful in theology.
11. Cf. our observation at the end of the previous chapter that, by contrast, at its inception aesthetics always served other philosophical concerns, such as those of metaphysics, epistemology, and ethics.

gious and ethical elements. Speaking of the Protestant tradition, von Balthasar points out that it views God in such a way that we cannot touch or grasp him: everything is taken on faith and there is nothing to "see" (GL1 47). The Protestant elimination of aesthetics from theology and Christian life "meant, broadly, the expulsion of 'seeing' from 'hearing'" (GL1 70). The cautious attitude toward beauty, even in Barth, von Balthasar explains by the tendency in Protestantism to consider the nature of beauty as an event, where every sort of regularity or constant quality is considered to be a demonic corruption (GL1 67): this is why a truly great Protestant aesthetics has never been possible (GL1 68).[12] However, von Balthasar considers the total deprivation of imagery and form, such as we find in Bultmann, to be a "real dead-end" even for Protestantism (GL1 52). The elimination of aesthetics from the Catholic tradition von Balthasar sees somewhat differently. Indeed, the concept of beauty has never been officially "banished" from Catholic thought, as is evident from the numerous studies of "Thomistic aesthetics" in the 1920s and 30s.[13] What the scholar means by "elimination of aesthetics" in the Catholic tradition amounts to eliminating the "spirit of inquiring," or *looking* for the form of revelation, and replacing it by an attempt to make theology more "scientific," following in the footsteps of Protestant scholarship.[14]

It is against this background of the disappearance of aesthetics from Christian theology that von Balthasar, in the spirit of Barth's discussion of beauty in *Church Dogmatics* II, 1, announces his project to restore the aesthetic element to the theological tradition. In a strong statement, he declares that "there neither has been nor can be any intrinsically great . . . theology which has not been conceived under the constellation of the *kalon*" (GL1 10). Christian thinking is impoverished by the loss of the aes-

---

12. Cf. R. Viladesau, *Theological Aesthetics*, 30, who stresses that, according to von Balthasar, the rejection of the analogy of being by the Protestant tradition, in combination with the idea of gratuity of grace, excludes viewing beauty as some intrinsic quality, and allows one to view beauty only in terms of an event. Many contemporary Protestant thinkers, such as F. Burch Brown and J. Begbie, of course, would disagree with such an assessment. Also see: O. Bychkov, "Introduction" (Bychkov and Fodor, *Theological Aesthetics after von Balthasar*, xi–xviii).

13. U. Eco lists more than a dozen studies of the "aesthetics of Thomas Aquinas" from this period in *The Aesthetics of Thomas Aquinas*, translated by H. Bredin (Cambridge: Harvard University Press, 1988), 272–78.

14. Von Balthasar's evaluation of the "scientific method" in theology is described below in Chapter 3.

thetic perspective which "once so strongly informed theology." The task of the theologian is to restore theology to a "main artery which it has abandoned" (GL1 9).[15] It is crucial to understand that the task of reconstituting theological aesthetics does not amount to introducing existing secular aesthetic theory into theology, or to emphasizing elements that are traditionally understood as aesthetic, such as art, sensibility, beauty, et cetera. In fact, von Balthasar would side with Kierkegaard's rejection of secular aesthetics in pronouncing that aesthetics as a science also signifies a "scientific" loss of beauty and its separation from other realms (GL1 79), while the new theological aesthetics must, on the contrary, reestablish the lost unity with truth and goodness. Von Balthasar guards against any application of "worldly" aesthetics in theology (GL1 37). A theologian must "steer clear of the theological application of aesthetic concepts" (that is, those of the worldly aesthetics, GL1 38): otherwise theological aesthetics ("the attempt to do aesthetics at the level and with the methods of theology") runs the danger of turning into "aesthetic theology" (that is, doing theology by applying secular aesthetic theory), which von Balthasar views as something negative. The problem, he says, is whether, after a confrontation with Idealist and Romantic secularized aesthetics, the aesthetic element can at all "be purified and salvaged by a consideration of its historical origins" or whether it should simply be abandoned (GL1 80). Is aesthetics restricted to this world (as Kant and his followers would have it), or is the beautiful one of the transcendental attributes of being,[16] which would allow for a theological aesthetics (GL1 38)?

15. On this point von Balthasar is in agreement with Rahner: cf. K. Rahner, "Art against the Horizon of Theology and Piety," in *Final Writings*, 162–68, translated by J. F. Donceel and H. M. Riley, vol. 23 of *Theological Investigations* (New York: Crossroad, 1992). Thus Rahner speaks of the habit of reducing theology to a theology that uses words (p. 163), notes that "our times also lack a poetic theology," calls the fact that "the poetic touch is lacking" from theology a "defect" (p. 164), and outlines some theological ways of conceptualizing the role of art in theology by using the notion of human "transcendentality" (pp. 165–66). Cf. R. Viladesau's comments on this matter in *Theological Aesthetics* (pp. 6, 12). According to Viladesau, "Rahner joins in calling for a return of the aesthetic dimension to theology" (pp. 18–19).

16. The question about the "transcendental" status of beauty is a muddled one. Von Balthasar seems to believe, with the Thomists (cf. D. H. Pouillon, "La beauté, propriété transcendantale. Chez les scholastiques [1220–1270]," *Archives d'histoire doctrinale et littéraire du moyen âge* 15 [1946]: 263–329), that the beautiful was definitely a transcendental (in the Aristotelian sense of transcending all categories, or "transcategorial") already in the medieval intellectual tradition, and therefore he uses the term freely. That the beautiful was a transcendental is at least questionable, and for Thomas Aquinas most probably it was not: see J. A. Aertsen, "Beauty in the Middle Ages," and also L. Müller, "Das 'Schöne,'" 413–24. At the same time, I find at least two instances in medieval texts where the beautiful technically

Von Balthasar compiles a history of positive developments in theological aesthetics, from the Romantics (Herder) to the late-nineteenth-century Catholic thinkers (Scheeben), a history that provides him with several conceptual and hermeneutic insights. He attributes the failure of Romantic theological aesthetics, culminating in Gügler, whose theology is one of the "most significant achievements of Catholic Romanticism," to the lack of distinction between creation and revelation—"aesthetic and religious monism" (GL1 104)—as well as to the lack of an adequate account of the analogical method in theological aesthetics (GL1 103–4) that he himself would espouse. Von Balthasar's main inspiration in forming his own approach to theological aesthetics comes from Barth, from whose *Dogmatics* the scholar quotes almost all relevant passages on beauty.[17] If one adopts the Barthian insight instead of introducing extrinsic aesthetic criteria to theology, one must look for the aesthetic elements that would consistently and intrinsically emerge from revelation itself and, in spite of all the dangers, probe a possibility of a "genuine relationship" between theological beauty and the beauty

---

does have the properties of a transcendental: in a manuscript attributed to Bonaventure (see D. Halcour, "Tractatus de transcendentalibus entis condicionibus [Assisi, Biblioteca Comunale, Codex 186]," *Franziskanische Studien* 41 [1959]: 41–106, in particular on p. 65) and in Ulrich of Strassburg, *De summo bono*, lib. 2, tr. 3, cap. 4 (*De summo bono, liber II*, Corpus Philosophorum Teutonicorum Medii Aevi 1/2, edited by A. de Libera [Hamburg: F. Meiner, 1987], 57.73–77), according to whom "the beautiful, like the good, is coextensive with being as far as the underlying individual substance is concerned, but as far as its essence is concerned, it adds to it the aforesaid notion of formality." Because the issue is unclear I will mostly refrain from involving this term in this meaning in any important discussions. On transcendentals in von Balthasar, see M. Saint-Pierre's exhaustive *Beauté, bonté, vérité*. It also appears that some twentieth-century figures who are discussed in this study confuse the term 'transcendental' as 'transcategorial' and the Kantian understanding of 'transcendental' as we have explained in Chapter 1. For the purpose of clarity, then, unless expressly stated otherwise, the term 'transcendental' is used in this study only in its Kantian sense.

17. Von Balthasar mentions the "great service rendered to theology by Karl Barth" in restoring to God the "attribute of 'beauty'" (at the conclusion of his treatment of divine perfections) for the first time in Protestantism (GL1 53). Many scholars have noted that von Balthasar's project of theological aesthetics depends on Barth; according to Kerr (*BEM* 8), von Balthasar rejoices in Barth's return to pre-Reformation theology of the divine beauty: "one wonders how far Balthasar's project of writing a theological aesthetics was shaped, and even perhaps prompted, by his delight in Barth's treatise on the divine perfections." This "contemplative" quasi-Catholic trend in Barth's theology, with its return to the traditional idea of the glory and beauty of God, probably helped von Balthasar against Neoscholasticism and rationalism. *Herrlichkeit* can be seen as an expansion of Barth's reflections in *Dogmatics* II, 1. Von Balthasar confirms this himself in GL7 23 stating that Barth's theology of glory "agrees with our own overall plan" (cf. Kerr, *BEM* 9). In his treatment of Christ's form/beauty, according to Kerr (*BEM* 11), von Balthasar "could hardly be more 'Barthian.'" Cf. R. Viladesau, *Theological Aesthetics*, 30.

of the world. The important moment is precisely that Barth does not proceed from the traditional aesthetic theory, but "arrives at the content of 'beauty' in a purely theological manner," that is, by contemplating the data of Scripture, in particular the phenomenon of glory (GL1 53): the approach that paves the way for von Balthasar himself.[18]

In the Catholic tradition, it is Scheeben whom von Balthasar credits with replacing the Romantic aesthetic theology with the outlines of a "methodically founded 'theological aesthetics'" (GL1 105).[19] What attracts him in Scheeben's work is the sharp separation between nature and the supernatural: unlike in the "monism" of the Romantics, nothing naturally leads from "below" to "above." At the same time, a connection between beauty and glory eventually happens in Scheeben through some interpenetration or "marriage" of the two realms (GL1 109). In Scheeben's theology, "the vision of faith allows him to grasp certain fundamental laws of Being" in such a way that he is later able to use these laws to illumine some points in the mystery of faith (GL1 110).

The insights derived from the Romantic tradition, Barth, and Scheeben allow von Balthasar to formulate his own understanding of "theological aesthetics": "By this we mean a theology which does not primarily work with the extra-theological categories of a worldly philosophical aesthetics . . . but which develops its theory of beauty from the data of revelation itself with genuinely theological methods" (GL1 117).[20] Stressing the importance of this field, he warns that, in renouncing aesthetics, "theology would have to give up a good part—if not the best part—of itself" (GL1 117). Without beauty, the good also "loses its attractiveness, the self-evidence of why it must be carried out," and "the proofs of the truth" lose "their cogency" (GL1 19). The main division of theological aesthetics into the "theory of vision"—or "'aesthetics' in the Kantian sense as a theory about the perception of the form of God's self-revelation"—and the "theory of rapture"—or "'aesthetics' as a theory about the incarnation of God's glory" (GL1 125)[21]—implies the unity of "fundamental the-

---

18. J. O'Donnell (in *Hans Urs von Balthasar*, 20–21), mentions that von Balthasar's main hermeneutical principle is to let divine revelation set its own standards of beauty, instead of imposing existing aesthetic notions.

19. I.e., Scheeben replaces theology done aesthetically (from a secular point of view) with a systematic investigation of what kind of aesthetic can be derived from revelation itself.

20. Regarding von Balthasar's definition of theological aesthetics, also see R. Viladesau, *Theological Aesthetics*, 51.

21. Cf. Steck, *Ethical Thought*, 14, on the two aspects of von Balthasar's theological aes-

ology" and "dogmatic theology," which are inseparable.[22] Von Balthasar's stress on the elements of fundamental theology is important.[23] According to him, today's positivistic, atheistic person, blind to both theology and philosophy, needs to be confronted with the phenomenon of the beauty and glory of God.[24]

According to von Balthasar, one of the crucial strategies in making Christian faith convincing is to keep open the ontological difference between the finite and the infinite, that is, neither to reduce man to God nor to reduce God to man, as it happens in either monistic or pantheistic systems: it was this feature that attracted von Balthasar to Scheeben's approach, as opposed to the approach of the Romantics. Von Balthasar always insists on the necessity of maintaining "wonder," amazement, and tension between the two realms: any intellectual theo-

---

thetics: the theory of vision (the "objective side" of form) and the theory of rapture (a human response to form).

22. A good discussion of the differences between fundamental and systematic (or dogmatic) theology can be found in Tracy (*Analogical Imagination*, 56–57). He says that fundamental theology is aimed primarily at academic circles, while systematic is aimed primarily at the church as a community of believers. Fundamental theology uses arguments that "all reasonable persons . . . can recognize as reasonable," and systematic is "the re-presentation, the reinterpretation of what is assumed to be the ever-present disclosive and transformative power of the particular religious tradition" (p. 57). According to Tracy (p. 85, n. 31), "fundamental theology is concerned principally with the 'true' in the sense of metaphysics, systematic theology with the beautiful (and, as we shall see, the beautiful *as true*) in the sense of poetics and rhetorics." Now although it may look as if von Balthasar is developing a fundamental theology, according to him the latter is not distinct from or opposed to dogmatics. His main concern is "the confrontation of beauty and revelation in dogmatic theology" (GL1 9; cf. his remark on the unity of the two aspects in GL1 127). In fundamental theology, the "*intellectus quaerens fidem*" is nevertheless already in the "rays of divine light"; "this search may be fostered by variously showing and making visible . . . the form of God's revelation," although in dogmatic theology "*fides quaerens intellectum*" by no means develops from fundamental (as from a *praeambula fidei*; GL1 126). On the unity of fundamental and dogmatic theology in von Balthasar see J. Riches, "Balthasar and the Analysis of Faith," in *The Analogy of Beauty: The Theology of Hans Urs von Balthasar* (henceforth AB) (Edinburgh: T&T Clark, 1986), 55; R. Fisichella, "Fundamentaltheologisches bei Hans Urs von Baltahsar," in *Hans Urs von Balthasar: Gestalt und Werk* (henceforth GW), edited by K. Lehmann and W. Kasper (Cologne: Communio, 1989), 299–300.

23. Cf. H. U. von Balthasar, *Truth of the World*, vol. 1 of *Theo-Logic: Theological Logical Theory*, translated by A. J. Walker (San Francisco: Ignatius Press, 2000), 20: "Our choice, to begin with 'glory' is comparable to what was once called apologetics or . . . fundamental theology."

24. On the elements of the philosophical *preambula fidei* cf. N. O'Donaghue, "A Theology of Beauty," in *AB* 8, who acknowledges the presence of "a strong and self-sufficient philosophical structure" in *Herrlichkeit* that signals a return to philosophy and an attempt to provide the "essential prelude and principle of understanding." Also see Kerr's remarks on the relationship between philosophy and theology in *Herrlichkeit* (BEM 12).

logical schemes of mediation appear to him to be dull.²⁵ Against the general background of wonder in the face of the divine, the role assigned to the aesthetic is precisely to mediate between the two realms.²⁶ A mediation that would at the same time preserve the distance between the finite and the infinite and yet not appear dull and mechanistic, cannot be accomplished through a metaphysical principle, but only through the idea of aesthetic form. Aesthetic form is precisely the point of contact between the realms of the finite and the infinite that both unites them and keeps them apart.²⁷

Curiously, von Balthasar's aesthetics exhibits a familiar feature that we already observed in several major eighteenth-, nineteenth-, and twentieth-century philosophical aesthetic theories. "Theological aesthetics" in the Balthasarian sense is not actually aesthetics as an autonomous discipline whose final goal is to gain understanding about art, beauty, and aesthetic perception. Instead, it is a way of doing theology: its concerns are genuinely theological. However, it addresses these concerns by using analogies with aesthetic experience: a strategy based on the observation that often certain issues in theology (e.g., appearance of God in history) typologically resemble the phenomenology of aesthetic experience. In other words, the issues studied by theological aesthetics are not of themselves in the purvue of the academic discipline of aesthetics (just as neither is, e.g., manifestation of truth strictly speaking an aesthetic issue), but there is something in them that allows for an analogy with the aesthetic (just as manifestation of truth or meaning in Heidegger and

---

25. Cf. R. Williams, "Balthasar and Rahner," in *AB* 24, who notes that what was lost in post-Kantian developments is the possibility of wonder, "contemplative receptivity in the face of the world's richness." Von Balthasar is highly critical of this loss. According to him, Christians do not have the answer to Heidegger's ultimate "why is there anything at all" question. On the contrary, Christians are the only ones who are capable of the wonder of being, which is fundamental to metaphysics (Kerr, *BEM* 12). Cf. Viladesau's observation (*Theological Aesthetics*, 50) that, against the Protestant practical approach ("what God does for me"), von Balthasar suggests simply abandoning yourself to the "vision" and wonder. Henrici ("Zur Philosophie Hans Urs von Balthasars," in *GW* 254) also notes the role of wonder (*Staunen, Verwunderung*) as the basic act of philosophy for von Balthasar. A shift from perceiving worth as something "for my own sake" to worth as something disinterested and "in itself," i.e., from the classic model of the good that fulfils some need to the model of the beautiful (in the Kantian sense) that is the object of wonder, also opens up new ethical perspectives: see Steck, *Ethical Thought*, 23, and *GL*1 152.

26. E.g., in *GL*1 34 von Balthasar mentions the "transcending" ability of the beautiful and aesthetic to "cross boundaries."

27. Cf. Kant's third *Critique*, where the aesthetic (especially the sublime) always hints at the existence of the transcendent ideas, although their presentation remains impossible.

Gadamer is likened to our aesthetic experience). The meaning of theological *aesthetics*, then, as in the case of Kantian "transcendental aesthetics," can be traced back to the Greek sense of αἴσθησις as sensibility or sensitivity: sensing certain things directly in our religious experience or in theology. This means that the actual appellation "aesthetics" here is metaphorical or analogical: one can "sense" certain things in religion or theology directly, bypassing their conceptualization, just as one can in the perception of art and beauty. At the same time, the truly aesthetic examples of art and beauty (that is, when they are perceived by the senses) still play a key role in theological aesthetics as metaphors and analogies in illustrating certain theological points.[28]

What are the features of aesthetic experience that allowed von Balthasar to draw such parallels, and how do theological issues fundamentally resemble aesthetic? One must start with von Balthasar's understanding of what constitutes "aesthetics." The key to his understanding of the notions "beauty," "aesthetic," and "form" is his Heideggerian interpretation of truth as disclosure.[29] In the general movement

---

28. The question of why theological aestheticians such as von Balthasar do not turn more to the analysis of concrete examples of art to clarify certain theological points can be answered in several ways. According to Barth it is divine glory, not worldly beauty, that must take precedence in theological aesthetics, and therefore the use of actual aesthetic experience can only be tangential; its purpose is to enhance our understanding of divine glory. This is precisely why Kant, writing his aesthetics, never seriously engages concrete examples of art, and, by all indications, has neither a good knowledge of, nor taste in, art. Kant needs aesthetic experience merely in order to complete the system of his transcendental philosophy in general, and therefore generic references to aesthetic experience and how it functions suffice. (Ancient philosophers, as we will see, were not different in this respect.) The same goes for von Balthasar, again, illustrating the point that theological aesthetics is not primarily aesthetics but theology, and general examples of aesthetic phenomena are sufficient. Engaging concrete experiences and artworks, rather than merely using a broad analogy with the aesthetic, implies a very different concept of, and approach to, theological aesthetics. However, here precisely lies the "danger" perceived by both philosophical and theological aestheticians. It seems that aesthetic experience can never provide an input that would be precise enough to equal either philosophical conceptualization or theological dogmas. (This is why in German Idealism aesthetics always remains an autonomous field, despite its general importance.) For this reason, in order for the "concrete" type of theological aesthetics to be successful, it must achieve one of the two things that are currently not possible: either to show that aesthetic experience *can* convey sufficiently precise meaning on a par with concepts; or to show that no precise conceptual patterns are necessary in order to do theology.

29. According to Tracy (in *Analogical Imagination*), who outlines several models of truth (e.g., correspondence, coherence, experiential, disclosure, praxis or transformation; pp. 62–63), the Heideggerian model of disclosure is most appropriate for systematic theology; see Chapter 3 below on von Balthasar's hermeneutics. C. Lafont in *Heidegger, Language and World Disclosure* (Cambridge: Cambridge University Press, 2000) has an extensive discussion of Heidegger's notion of truth as disclosure: cf. chap. 3, p. 109ff.; cf. p. 144.

of "disclosure-concealment" (*Enthüllen-Verhüllen*) in the world, truth is the disclosure, unconcealment, revelation, or appearing of being. According to *Theo-Logic* I, 37, being can "come into appearance" and "become present"; ". . . being, precisely *as* being, can be unveiled and apprehended." "We thus have an initial description of truth," von Balthasar continues, "as the unveiledness, unconveredness, disclosedness, and unconcealment (ἀ-λήθεια) of being." "Unveiledness is, first of all, an absolute property inherent in being as such."[30] Heideggerian traits can be further seen in the fact that von Balthasar's philosophy, as primarily a "philosophy of being" (*Seinsphilosophie*)—unlike that of Rahner, which has an emphasis on the subjective side—points out the ground of the "objective visibility" of truth and being in God's revealing himself to thought as Being that can be seen and wondered at.[31] This restoration of objectivity is an important factor for von Balthasar's aesthetics, since it restores the harmony between what appears phenomenologically— the subjective *Gestalt* of faith, based on manifestation (*Erscheinung*)— and what is given ontologically, or with revelation. Thus what appears

---

30. As has been noted in scholarly literature (Henrici in *GW* 239), von Balthasar's Heideggerian understanding of truth dates back to his earlier systematic philosophical work devoted to the question of truth (*Wahrheit, I: Wahrheit der Welt* [Einsiedeln, 1947]), which was based on a dialogue between Aquinas and Heidegger; in this work, truth is already described in terms of revelation/manifestation, but also concealment ("als Offenbarung, Enthüllung, Verhüllung, aber auch als bergende Teilnahme"; Henrici in *GW* 239). Cf. O'Donnell, *Hans Urs von Balthasar*, 30, on von Balthasar's Heideggerian understanding of truth as revelation.

31. Henrici in *GW* 256; also cf. *GW* 254 and Steck, *Ethical Thought*, 17. Dependence on Heidegger is evident from direct references in *Herrlichkeit* (cf. *GL1* 59) and similarity of terminology, not only regarding the notion "truth": cf. such "catch" phrase as "facticity of historical revelation" (*GL1* 65). Many scholars notice his dependence on Heidegger (whom he studied following the advice of Przywara, cf. Henrici in *GW* 25–26). Thus, according to Steck, *Ethical Thought*, 165, an analysis of parallels between the two authors shows "just how multiple are the commonalities between himself and Heidegger," e.g., the idea of graciousness and glory of being or a response of obedience to the voice of being. According to Kerr (*BEM* 12) von Balthasar's "history of metaphysics is thoroughly imbued with Heideggerian language and insights." Heideggerian motifs are also detectible in von Balthasar's understanding of being. Thus Williams (*AB* 22) notes von Balthasar's understanding of being as somehow gratuitously given, and mentions that the analogy of being in von Balthasar "depends upon that basic sense of belonging in a world, of radical contingency" (*AB* 23). According to Williams, von Balthasar's protest against Rahner is actually directed against all the mainstream tradition of European post-Kantian (up to Heidegger) philosophy (called "the system" in his *Cordula*), his main objection being that it negates "the sense of belonging in the world" by concentrating on subjectivity, self-constitution of the subject, etc. The idea of a certain restoration of objectivity through the idea of "being-in-the-world"—where both the subject and the object are included, the "borders" between them thereby blurred—certainly brings von Balthasar closer to Heidegger and Gadamer. Cf. Steck, *Ethical Thought*, 17, who notes that von Balthasar tries to correct the emphasis on the subject in the subject-object relationship.

to our sense perception (*Wahrnehmung*) is at the same time true (*Wahrheit*), since in the self-manifestation of being, manifestation and reality (*Wirklichkeit*) coincide. That which *appears* is being itself, as it presents itself to the knowledge of the finite, historical subject; this gives especial importance to the "perception of form (*Gestalt*)."[32]

In the spirit of Heidegger, von Balthasar understands visible form as a certain condition of being, its ability to disclose itself.[33] Our being already *is* visible form, and we come into being already placed within this condition of being (GL1 22). He perceives it as a troublesome sign when being is no longer understood as form. The ability of being to be revealed or "seen" is crucial to von Balthasar's understanding of aesthetics. In connection with the first task of theological aesthetics to behold and perceive the beauty of form in the world, von Balthasar admits that he is using the Kantian concept of the aesthetic as something that has to do with sense perception (GL1 10).[34] Multiple remarks that he makes throughout the volumes of *Herrlichkeit* confirm that this is what his understanding of aesthetics is, although it is never fully articulated. For von Balthasar, beauty is first of all associated with the concept of form (*Gestalt*, GL1 19), but also with splendor, or the process of shining forth that reveals this form (GL1 20). However, what plays a crucial role in von Balthasar's aesthetics and places him firmly within the classic philosophical tradition of interpreting aesthetic experience as revealing—from Kant to Heidegger and Gadamer—is how this revelation takes place. The beautiful "brings with it a self-evidence that en-lightens

---

32. R. Fisichella, "Fundamentaltheologisches bei Hans Urs von Baltahsar," in *GW* 301. As in many other cases (e.g., with the Stoics [see below] or Kant), the terms *a priori* and *a posteriori* prove inadequate. The apparent a posteriori of starting with sense perception or "vision" in this case, as in the case with the Stoics, seems to rest on a hidden a priori assumption that such true perception or vision is possible: in the case of von Balthasar, on the assumption that perception matches the contents of revelation. For this reason, the use of the terms *a priori* and *a posteriori* in this study will be only occasional (where they occur in primary or secondary literature), and will not be crucial for our conceptual framework. In most such cases in Western European intellectual history, however (see the following chapters), the most convincing and persuasive element has been, it seems, either the aesthetic (from perceiving actual reality) or the quasi-aesthetic (immediate intellectual "seeing") perception of foundational principles, which might suggest, in fact, the fundamental unity of the principles of a priori and a posteriori that have been historically unnecessarily dichotomized.

33. That being is able to reveal itself, and that we are governed by this ability of being to reveal itself is, of course, also one of the main ideas in Gadamer; it creates the basis for his analogy between aesthetic and hermeneutic experience: see Chapter 1.

34. Cf. Steck, *Ethical Thought*, 7, 16, who also describes von Balthasar's understanding of aesthetics in terms of theory of perception.

without mediation" (GL1 37), that is, it reveals truth immediately, without a concept, and signals something that is self-evident and manifest.

The importance of verification through aesthetic experience in von Balthasar signals that he has a "widened" view of knowledge that goes beyond the truth of correspondence, with its established procedures that are supposed to lead us to certitude. Von Balthasar's emphasis on aesthetics reveals his anti-rational move toward finding a foundation of truth in human experience itself, e.g., in aesthetic contemplation, and toward seeking certitude or justification precisely from within this experience.[35] Von Balthasar sees the ideal of such an "aesthetic" attitude to reality in Plato and the ancient tradition:

> The idea that knowledge, and therefore also and indeed especially philosophical knowledge, be an open readiness, service and submission before 'things,' 'reality,' and should precisely be defined from that perspective, is sustained by Plato even where he deals with the highest forms of reality and thus prevents any interpretation of his thought in terms of Kantian transcendentalism. . . . Spirit is the possibility of securing something self-authenticating, self-disclosing, a genuine epiphany; it is to stand face to face with reality at every stage, right up to the highest Good. (GL4 177)[36]

This passage, filled with Heideggerian overtones (such as submission and obedience in the face of being, or the nature of reality as disclosure), stresses the importance of preserving the possibility of a certain "immediate contact" with reality that manifests itself in the self-disclosing vision, or in our ability to "see" directly. This idea of aesthetic experience as immediately revealing, by implying that a direct "seeing" or an immediate perception of reality is possible, brings von Balthasar in conflict with the transcendentalism of the group he calls "Kantians," with their denial of the possibility of a direct presentation. Thus according to Henrici (GW 243), von Balthasar rejects the transcendentalism of the Fichtean/Kantian type (for example, that of Rahner) in favor of "see-

---

35. Cf. J. Riches in AB 39–40.

36. At this point it does not matter whether von Balthasar's assessment of Plato is actually accurate or not (it probably isn't entirely so). The main point is his retrieval of the role of aesthetic experience from Plato: the issue that will be important for the next chapter. The question whether τὸ καλόν (the "highest form of reality") in the (Neo-)Platonic tradition is any more accessible than the transcendent ideas of Kant still remains to be discussed: see Chapter 5 below. At the same time, even von Balthasar himself cannot always sustain his claim that "Kantian transcendentalism" utterly lacks a grounding in "self-evident" reality: see next note.

ing" and immediate perception.[37] In other words, he rejects the model of understanding the "beyond" in terms of the transcendental conditions that are set *a priori* (the "*a priori* grounds" as in "Kantians")[38] and instead chooses the model of immediately perceiving or "seeing" the "beyond" or its presence (as, according to von Balthasar, it was in Plato), which arouses our helpless wonder at the contingency of reality.

It is precisely this understanding of aesthetic experience in terms of its revealing capacity that makes possible an analogical transition to theological topics, which can ultimately result in a theological "aesthetics." The focal point of this aesthetics is that only that which can be immediately *seen*, as in aesthetic experience, is the most convincing proof and argument (cf. GL2 100).[39] It is not enough "to 'believe' the divine content of Christ's reality, but to 'see' it in its self-evidence" (GL1 30). For von Balthasar, Christian religion is most convincing precisely because it allows us to *see* and is not based on either blind faith or reason alone. For this reason it is also the most "aesthetic" religion.[40] In fact, as he tries to show through his appeal to the tradition, many key points in Christian theology—including the idea of the unity of Christian

---

37. Von Balthasar's appellation "Kantians" is quite vague, and it appears that the charges he brings against "Kantians" (again, whether they are in general accurate needs further investigation) do not always apply to particular figures whom he tends to include among them. R. Viladesau (in private correspondence) objects to von Balthasar's categorization of Rahner and "transcendental" Thomists as "Kantians" and does not think that he had an accurate idea of what they were doing. According to Viladesau, there is less difference between their thought and von Balthasar's than the latter seems to realize. However, what is important is the set of ideas to which, having projected them on to a particular group, he objects. Kant himself, in von Balthasar's eyes, is much less guilty than the Idealist tradition that followed him. According to von Balthasar (as in GL5), Kant has the quality of being attentive to the world and to the sense of belonging to the world (which to Kant has priority), or of being "touched" by something other: cf. R. Williams in *AB* 23. Cf. Tracy, *Analogical Imagination*, 140, n. 39, who, critiquing "private taste" theories, makes the following remark: "In contrast, recall Kant's defense of the *judgment* of taste in the *Critique of Judgment*. Kant's position, in my opinion, need not have led to the 'subjectivization of aesthetic theory.'" Speaking against Gadamer (*TM* 39–73), Tracy writes that he is unpersuaded that Kant's own position, in contrast with that of neo-Kantians, "inevitably leads to those difficulties," i.e., the subject vs. object model.

38. Cf. R. Williams in *AB* 14.

39. The importance of immediate seeing, intuition, or illumination is already evident in Scheeben, who probably contributed to the prominence of this idea in von Balthasar (cf. GL1 113). The analogy between evidence and aesthetic "seeing," of course, is reminiscent of Gadamer's understanding of hermeneutics. See the discussion of the idea of immediate seeing and self-evidence at the end of the previous chapter. Again, this presentation of von Balthasar's ideas must be seen in a historical light, not necessarily in the sense that the author entirely subscribes to the theory of "seeing."

40. Cf. Kay, *Theological Aesthetics*, 61. Also cf. ibid., v: "Any theological method that fails to recognize the central role of aesthetics is doomed to be dull and unconvincing."

aesthetic vision,[41] which is the key concept of von Balthasar's *Herrlichkeit*—can be accepted only if they can be *seen* directly and immediately: they cannot be demonstrated by logical or "scientific" proofs.[42]

Understanding aesthetic experience as revealing thus provides von Balthasar with the foundation for his theological aesthetics: the analogy between beauty and revelation, or the appearance of the divine. In opposition to the Scotistic tradition, von Balthasar firmly holds on to the idea of the "analogy of being" *(analogia entis)* and rejects any univocal application of categories in Christian theology. God is nothing of being.[43] However, an analogy between God and being is possible. The idea of the analogy of beauty in von Balthasar's theology—a development of the traditional concept of the "analogy of being"—was probably inspired by the Protestant theologian Gerhard Nebel, who, according to von Balthasar, "ought to serve as an example for the Catholic inquirer" (*GL1* 67). It was Nebel who, according to von Balthasar's account, introduced the term *analogia pulchri* in parallel to the traditional *analogia entis* (*GL1* 61).[44] Noting the mediating role of beauty (*GL1* 62), Nebel goes on to state that something of God's splendor passes over into his creatures (*GL1* 64). At the same time, anything beautiful in nature has the ability to point away from itself to some other beauty. Noting the analogical relationship between *eventus pulchri et Christi*, Nebel raises the question whether "the event of the beautiful becomes a pointer to the event of Christ" (*GL1* 65). According to von Balthasar's concise formulation, the essence of the analogy of beauty is the following: if beauty is revelation or radiance from the depth of being, then the revelation of the hidden God, including the incarnation, will "itself form an analogy

41. Whether there ever was such a unity is a different matter.
42. He argues, for example, that many of Augustine's "proofs" regarding Christian theology are based precisely on their ability to be seen, rather than being derived by conceptual means or being taken on blind faith, cf.: "It can be said that Augustine's proof of the true Church is an aesthetic proof: anyone who cannot see the specific nature of this catholicity . . . cannot be moved by it" (*GL2* 102).
43. According to Henrici (*GW* 256–57), the "difference of being," or the "real distinction" between beings and Being, essence and being, common being and God, is at the center of von Balthasar's philosophy (cf. *GL5* 613–56).
44. O'Donaghue (*AB* 6) also notes that von Balthasar's "analogy of beauty" is a development of the concept of the "analogy of being"; von Balthasar embraced the concept of the "analogy of being" under the influence of, among others, Erich Przywara (*AB* 4ff.; cf. Henrici in *GW* 257). Riches (*AB* 52–54) puts the concept of the "analogy of beauty" in the context of contemporary theological debates, in particular, between von Balthasar and the Neoscholastics on the one hand, and von Balthasar and Blondel and his followers on the other.

to that worldly beauty" (GL2 11). The task of the first stage of theological aesthetics (that of "fundamental theology"), according to Henrici (GW 254), becomes "to catch sight of the radiance of divine glory in the beauty of being."

Just like beauty, divine glory—the "theological analogate" of beauty—appears. Its manifestation, just like that of beauty, is commanding, attractive, and transforming.[45] There is something about divine glory that, just like aesthetic experience that is self-evident and valued for its own sake, does not need any other justification or evidence of its worth: in this respect, the contact with divine glory is analogous to our perception of a work of art and aesthetic judgment.[46] At the same time, von Balthasar warns, the long history of iconoclasm, from Byzantium to the Reformation, must serve as a "corrective" to the aesthetic approach, which he traces back to the Patristic period: the "beauty" of revelation must not be confused with worldly beauty (GL1 41).

"The central question of so-called 'apologetics' or 'fundamental theology,'" von Balthasar writes, "is, thus, the question of perceiving form—an aesthetic problem" (GL1 173). What exactly does he understand by "form"? First of all, form means the "material" form of something: something that is "palpable," not abstract, something that can be immediately perceived or grasped by the senses. This characteristic of form (*Gestalt*) is also shared by the beautiful: "as form the beautiful can be materially grasped" (GL1 118). The form, as well as beauty, possesses a certain "splendor" and shines forth gloriously (cf. GL1 118–19). However, in order to be "beautiful," form must also possess the classic mark of aesthetic experience (von Balthasar mentions Kant and Schiller as his sources): an ability to serve as a mediator between the realms of the visible and the invisible, and to reveal something immediately about the latter. "Form would not be beautiful unless it were fundamentally a sign and appearing of a depth and a fullness that, in themselves . . . remain beyond both our reach and our vision" (GL1 118). In the "appearance of the form, as revelation of the depths," two moments are important: the "real presence of the depths" and a "pointing beyond itself to these depths," transcending itself. The two aspects are inseparable and constitute the "fundamen-

---

45. Steck, *Ethical Thought*, 7, 1. According to Steck, the analogy of beauty also gives a different "twist" to von Balthasar's ethics: from the "divine command" model in ethics typical of Protestant theology, he moves toward an approach that preserves some point of contact between the human and the divine, reason and faith, nature and grace etc. (cf. pp. 1–2).

46. Cf. Riches in *AB* 45–47.

tal configuration of Being" (*GL1* 118).⁴⁷ The form possesses another classic feature of aesthetic experience: the latter remains aesthetic (from the Greek αἴσθησις) only so long as the actual process of "seeing" or sense perception still goes on. In the same way, we are enraptured and transported by the depths to which the form points (the vertical dimension), but only so long as we never "leave the (horizontal [dimension of]) form behind us" (*GL1* 119).⁴⁸

Now it is precisely the ability of aesthetic form to appear that allows for an analogy between this form and the Spirit's appearing in history. Von Balthasar defends the possibility of an analogy between divine splendor and aesthetic radiance. "That we are at all able to speak here of 'seeing' . . . shows that, in spite of all concealment, there is nonetheless something to be seen and grasped" (*GL1* 120–21).⁴⁹ In stark contrast with the Protestant *sola fide* approach, "it shows . . . that man is not merely addressed in a total mystery, as if he were compelled to accept obediently in blind and naked faith something hidden from him, but that something is 'offered' to man by God, indeed, offered in such a way that man can see it, understand it" (*GL1* 121).⁵⁰ Certainly there are numerous proofs that revelation is somehow formed, and not completely shapeless and unbounded: certain archetypes are detectible in the history of faith, the saints possess their own "form," God's will to give form to humans in creation is evident, so that "it appears impossible to deny that there exists an analogy between God's work of formation and the shaping forces of nature and of man" (*GL1* 36). The analogical use of the concept of form broadens the concept, so as to embrace other phenomena, in addition to purely material or aesthetic form: from "forms

---

47. According to von Balthasar, different historical periods put more emphasis on one or the other of these two features: e.g., "real presence" in the form is characteristic of Antiquity, and "pointing beyond" the form is typical of the Romantic tradition. In fact, the form, according to von Balthasar, possesses even more specific features of the beautiful/aesthetic, traditionally understood: its ability to reveal goodness (as in Kant) and truth (as in Heidegger); the delight resulting from the form is based on the fact that "in it, the truth and goodness of the depth of reality itself are manifested and bestowed, and this manifestation and bestowal reveal themselves to us as being something infinitely and inexhaustibly valuable and fascinating" (*GL1* 118).

48. In fact, some theologians of the Patristic and medieval era could soar to such heights "vertically" precisely because they did not let go of the "horizontal" dimension (*GL1* 125).

49. Note the clear Heideggerian overtones in this passage.

50. Cf. Steck, *Ethical Thought*, 13: "excluding the idea of the beautiful form distorts the response of faith into a mere submission to divine power." Beauty preserves openness to revelation from above.

of existence" visible by a spiritual eye (GL1 24–25) to the "form of divine revelation in salvation-history" (GL1 29) to a certain real form instituted by Christ into which Christian saints are transformed (GL1 28, 36). At the same time, what remains constant is the quality of being "visible" or immediately perceptible, if only in an analogical sense.

Up to this point the appearance of God's "form" in the world has been discussed in the context of fundamental theology, which deals with the foundational ontological and phenomenological aspects of reality. However, in the Christian context the most important case of the extended understanding of the concept "form" is the notion of "Christ's form."[51] We must note that here fundamental or apologetic theology meets systematics.[52] Consequently, in elucidating the notion of Christ's form von Balthasar turns to interpreting Scripture, or to interpreting the textual tradition and reality as a whole in terms of Scripture. For von Balthasar, Christ's form is both the concrete form of the historical personality of Jesus as it appears through the Scriptures—with all its unique and individual traits—and the broader universal principle which is manifested through other phenomena. Christ's form is neither merely human nor merely divine (transcendent). It always mediates between the infinite and the finite by expressing the former through the latter. It can do so because of its lucidity and its "splendor"—which is also manifested to us in the world through the forms of particular things.[53] Perceiving Christ's form is analogous to our experience of the "natural" aesthetic form. This observation allows von Balthasar to approach the notion of Christ's form precisely by starting with our aesthetic experience of the world, or the "splendor" of being.[54] Perceiving the "universal form" in nature is a preliminary stage for the perception of the form of Christ in theology. What makes Christ's form aesthetic is that the process of perceiving it—like our perception of an aesthetic object—is by no means rational or conceptual: it consists in mere "seeing" or "sensing" (αἴσθησις) the form.[55]

---

51. Cf. ibid., 9: the decisive appearance of divine beauty, glory, is reserved for the Christ-form, which does not "point beyond" but is the infinite itself.

52. Of course, as the reader remembers, von Balthasar speaks of the essential unity of the two.

53. Cf. Kay, *Theological Aesthetics*, chap. 2 (The Theological A POSTERIORI. "Gathering the Evidence").

54. See above; cf. Kay, *Theological Aesthetics*, 1–35.

55. Hopkins's poetry gives a good idea of how it is actually possible to perceive the beauty

The form of Christ so perceived is, like an aesthetic object, fitted together without a concept and possesses a certain harmony and coherence, like a beautiful work of art which is, according to Kant, *like* nature. This "nature-like" quality of Christ's form is the strongest proof that such a form could only be produced naturally and could not have been created by the Gospel writers. If one were able to show that all the scattered details of Christ's life fit into one "naturally" harmonious form *(Gestalt)*[56] or *ethos* that is impossible to forge, one would obtain the strongest evidence for Christ's actual existence—but purely on aesthetic grounds. "The revelation of Biblical salvation-story," von Balthasar writes, "is a form set before mankind's eyes.... The contourlines have been drawn with such mastery that not the smallest detail can be altered. The weights have been poised in such a way that their

---

of the world and nature Christocentrically in terms of Christ's form. The poet makes the following record in his diary: "One day when the bluebells were in bloom I wrote the following, 'I do not think I have ever seen anything more beautiful than the bluebell I have been looking at. *I know the beauty of our Lord by it.* It(s inscape) is (mixed of) strength and grace like an ash (tree)'" (H. Thomas, "Gerard Manley Hopkins and John Duns Scotus," *Religious Studies* 24, no. 3 [1988]: 351). In "Hurrahing in Harvest" Hopkins first creates a fresh and spontaneous picture of the free play of natural forms in the late summer sky over the fields, an aesthetic impression that is immediately followed by the experience of Christ whose form is manifested, amidst a "worldly liturgy," as certain details of the beautiful landscape. In "As kingfishers catch fire . . . " Hopkins provides several descriptions of individual, contingent, and fleeting things expressing themselves and producing individual impressions, following the fundamental principle of expression. However, in Hopkins's experience of the world it is Christ who is at the basis of this principle and is perceived in all instances of such expression. In this particular poem his form is manifested in all individual human beings. Cf. von Balthasar's section on Hopkins in GL3 353–99. Also see Chapter 8 below for the medieval roots of this idea, and von Balthasar's discussion of Bonaventure in GL2 260ff. For an excellent analysis of Hopkins's theological aesthetics see P. A. Ballinger, *The Poem as Sacrament: The Theological Aesthetic of Gerard Manley Hopkins* (Louvain: Peeters Press, 2000).

56. The question whether there really is one coherent "form" of Christ in the Christian tradition is a separate one. In our private exchange, Frank Burch Brown rightly pointed out that if one studies various cultures, even those that have been traditionally Christian, the variety of forms in which the divine, or even the person of Jesus the Christ in particular, is envisioned, testifies that such forms obviously depend on the cultural context (see a recent survey of contextual theology in light of aesthetics: S. Bergmann, *God in Context: A Survey of Contextual Theology* [Aldershot: Ashgate, 2003]). At the same time, as Richard Viladesau noted, also in private correspondence, while acknowledging the problematic nature of von Balthasar's presentation of "Christ's form," the Thomistic (or any other medieval scholastic) view of "form" (in the singular) does not necessarily exclude a plurality of its "individualizations." One can say, with Tracy, that various contextual versions of the "Christ form" are different "performances" of the same "classic," or, with von Balthasar, that all cultural versions of the "form" are "played from the same score" but by different "artists" and "orchestras." In any case, if von Balthasar acts as an "art critic" here, why would a particular interpretation of a "classic" text disturb us any more than a particular artistic rendition of a classic piece of music?

balance extends to infinity, and they resist any displacement. God's art in the midst of history is irreproachable . . . the light of God which faith has *sees* the form as it is." It is "not at all a projection of the mythopoetic religious imagination, but rather the masterpiece of the divine fantasy which puts all human fantasy to naught." The form presents itself as the revelation of the inner depths of God, not by means of verbal claims that could have been composed by the disciples, "but by the very shape of its existence, by the impeccable mutual reflection between word and existence and therein, at a deeper level, by the irrefutable and yet indissoluble unity of the active-passive testimony" (GL1 172).[57]

Von Balthasar introduces a parallel with aesthetic experience in its traditional sense ("reflection on the aesthetic act can help us further here," GL1 178) by referring to actual sense-perception. Divine revelation is *a priori* in conformity not only with the mind but also with "the sensual in its perception of reality" (GL1 179)[58]—a fact of utmost importance. The potential believer "will dare take this leap [of faith] only when the evidential force of Jesus' credibility as the very appearance of God" (the *a posteriori* vision) "gains ground over the believer's own 'possibility'" (the *a priori*; GL1 180). Faith demands an object of contemplation in the same way that aesthetic perception does: the abstract idea of Christ does not suffice. "What convinces man about this objective nature of faith is that God appears to him externally, in history" (GL1 181). It is the "self-evidence" and "self-verification" of Christ's form[59]—the quality that makes it analogous to the aesthetic—that, according to von Balthasar, has the strongest evidential force for a Christian. It is the ability to *see* the splendor and magnificence of this unique form of historical Jesus that is essential for the Christian belief. It is the sight and attractiveness of this form that compels one to faith.[60] The primary response of the Christian is "doxological": to the glory, and not something taken on faith or understood by the intellect.[61] Just as beauty points out

---

57. The main examples of proportions that constitute the "interior rightness," or the "objective, demonstrable beauty of all proportions" of Christ's form (GL1 188) are those existing within the Trinity and those produced as a result of the Incarnation: the Son and the Father; man and the Son of God; lord and servant; exaltation and humiliation, etc. "We will come to see," von Balthasar writes in his theoretical introduction to the analysis of Christ's form, "that these relationships and meanings come together to build but one faultless and yet effortless equilibrium: they had all been harmonized into a sovereign unity" (GL1 189).

58. See our previous remark on the inadequacy of the categories *a priori* and *a posteriori*.

59. Cf. Kay, *Theological Aesthetics*, 56.   60. Cf. Steck, *Ethical Thought*, 20.

61. Ibid., 150.

the intrinsic worth and truth of reality, perceiving divine glory leads us to realize God's praiseworthiness. God's glory is "configured in Christ aesthetically, that is, visibly, ... attractively" and, like the aesthetic, draws us to itself immediately without consideration.[62] According to von Balthasar, the metaphysical wonder cannot be maintained merely on the basis of the *a priori* evidence: if one relies mostly on such evidence, one is led to monism and a loss of wonder. Maintaining wonder is necessarily dependent on the *a posteriori* evidence of Christ's objective form, that is, its being seen: "in the face of death it is impossible for anyone consistently to maintain a belief in Absolute Love, unless he sees the splendor of Christ's form."[63] At the same time, the perception of form automatically includes all of its contents: "from a Christian standpoint, there is no possibility of distinguishing between God's act of revelation and the content of this revelation, for this revelation is inseparably both the interior life of God and the form of Jesus Christ" (GL1 182). Christian faith thus becomes utterly dependent on such vision.[64]

In this situation, the task of theology is to lead others to "see" the balance, proportion, and tension within the form of Christ in order to be conquered by its splendor. "This selfless enrapturing vision of the splendor of Christ's form is the basic moment of self-verification in Christian theology."[65] The benefits must be clearly subordinated to the vision: instead of showing what Christ offers to us, theology must show us that we "cannot help but worship the splendor" of what we see.[66] To believe is to be disinterestedly fascinated by the object of belief. The form must be presented by a theologian in such a way as to show the inner necessity of all its constituents, exactly the way they are. This necessity is akin to the "purposeful" harmony and coherence of parts of an aesthetic object that come together without a concept. It must be shown to be the only form into which God could enter: the form which

---

62. Cf. ibid.
63. Kay, *Theological Aesthetics*, 41.
64. The question of the a posteriori vs. a priori evidence is thoroughly treated in Kay, *Theological Aesthetics*, Part 2. According to Williams (AB 14), von Balthasar's idea that the beauty of God cannot be determined by a theological a priori, and that nothing dictates the necessity of the form of beauty, except its inner logic, conflicts with the Rahnerian (or "Kantian") transcendentalist position that needs to establish epistemology on the basis of a *Vorgriff*, in advance. Instead of starting with the pre-apprehension of limitlessness, von Balthasar starts with the orientation of being (and therefore cognition) toward concrete form (*Gestalthaftigkeit des Wesens*; AB 20).
65. Kay, *Theological Aesthetics*, v.
66. Ibid.

is totally sufficient for the verification of belief. The task of a theologian, which consists in pointing out the qualities of Christ's form, is therefore not unlike that of an art critic.[67] Thus the objective of the major part of *Herrlichkeit* is precisely to examine the way the harmony of Christ's form—understood both as a universal principle and as the particular form of the person Jesus—is presented by various authors in the Christian tradition, including the writers of the Scriptures.[68]

To introduce a literary parallel, the verbal "portraits" of Jesus created by the Gospel writers could simply be perceived as a kind of fictional *ethopoieia*. However, the lucidity and "realism" of Jesus' personal character traits which appear from his deeds as described by the Gospel writers—with all their individual features—is such that they could not have been forged: that is, the Gospel writers could not be the inventors of this character. The textual description of Jesus bears an individual seal of his personality—the *haecceitas* or "inscape" of a particular being which must have had real existence.[69] This portrait, then, can further serve as evidence. It was in a similar way that the Byzantine iconodules

---

67. Of course, one might suggest that a theologian therefore can be as "subjective" as some art critics, but this, again, brings us back to the discussion of the nature and ethics of interpretation.

68. Cf. Kay on the task of a theologian to outline the aesthetic quality of Christ's form according to von Balthasar (*Theological Aesthetics*, 55): all discrepancies in Christ's form must be shown to be "expressions of necessary tensions, proportions and balances within the total form." A theologian must show the inner coherence of the form, as well as its unique and harmonious character: "His task is like that of the aesthetician who shows what the objective qualities of an art work are that merit for it the title of a masterpiece" and demonstrates "the unique law or aesthetic logic which determines what elements constitute the art work and what proportions exist between the elements." The "uniqueness and originality" of aesthetic form "are justified and grounded in its representation of the greatest freedom as the most necessary." The more perfect the work of art, the more it seems to be the only way it could be. This feeling of binding inner-necessity in a masterpiece von Balthasar applies to Christ by trying to show that his form is of that kind: "Because the fittingness, correctness, symmetry, proper proportion, etc., in Christ's form is totally without fault and therefore the most perfect possible, it is impossible to distinguish this fittingness from an absolute necessity." One is compelled to see the perfection of this form that makes it irresistible.

69. Cf. Kay (*Theological Aesthetics*): "if God reveals himself in Jesus in a way that is comprehensible and convincing for man, this revelation will occur in the full humanity of Jesus, in his full historicity. It was the evangelists' desire to present the fascinating humanity of Christ that led them to incorporate their accounts of his life into the kerygma.... They realized that an account of Jesus' life was necessary as a criterion and verification of the kerygma. His words alone would lack the power of conviction" (p. 52). The apostles in the Gospels "strove ... to delineate the form of Jesus the Christ in such a way that the reader will see why Jesus is the fullest possible appearance of God in history and why it is impossible to expect a greater prophet after him ... The task of theology is to help others see-understand-verify the form that the apostles present" (p. 54).

at the Seventh Ecumenical Council defended the value of the icon that captures the unique features of a historical person—much like the modern photograph—and in this way can serve as a proof of the actual existence of its prototype.[70] Using parallels with art works, von Balthasar reinforces the analogy between the activity of a theologian and art criticism, as well as the overall aesthetic interpretation of Christ's form:

> Seeing the form . . . presupposes that we can gain an overall sight of the form. Its contour, its relief, the relationship between its proportion and its weights, its colors and its sounds—all of this must be equally before the perceiving sense-organ and the spiritual faculty . . . if in a musical motif one single sound remains inaudible, a judgment about this 'sound-figure' immediately becomes impossible. . . . The more a great work of art is known and grasped, the more concretely are we dazzled by its 'ungraspable' genius. (GL1 186)

The closest parallel to contemplating the form "in the Christian realm" (that is, describing the "contours" of the personality of Jesus that emerge from his conversations and actions) is precisely "aesthetic contemplation" in either nature or art: neither psychological nor biographical descriptions can capture this form (cf. GL1 32–33). It must have been a similar observation that allowed Tillich, who also reflected on art and the form of the biblical picture of Christ, to draw and analogy between artistic representation, in his case the Expressionist style, and the biblical portrayal of Christ. According to Tillich (following J. Begbie's account), the way the biblical portrait of Christ affects us, "like the expressionist painting . . . does not hinge on its factual accuracy or reliability, but on its mediation of that power the first disciples experienced in their encounter with Jesus. No amount of historical research can falsify or validate the biblical portrait of Jesus the Christ."[71]

---

70. Cf. V. Bychkov, *2000 Years of Christian Culture* sub specie aesthetica (*2000 let khristianskoj kul'tury*), vol. 1 (Moscow, St. Petersburg: Universitetskaya kniga, 1999), 462. He discusses the words of Epiphanius in the context of the arguments of the iconodules from the Acts of the Seventh Ecumenical (Nicaea II) Council printed in J. D. Mansi, *Sacrorum Conciliorum nova et amplissima collectio*, vol. 13 (Florentiae: Expensis Antonii Zatta Veneti, 1759–98; reprinted Graz: Akademische Druck, 1960), 377B–C: "For brave deeds performed in wars are often depicted by both writers and painters, the former ornamenting them with words, the latter engraving them on tablets. And many men were aroused to bravery by both. For what speech presents in stories through hearing, painting in silence shows by imitation" (i.e., evidence can be persuasive not only in the form of words but also in the form of images).

71. J. Begbie, *Voicing Creation's Praise*, 56. One might recall the unrealistic "spiritual" features of personages captured in Eastern Orthodox icons. Cf. Ouspensky's work on icons cited below in Chapter 3.

Our analysis of von Balthasar's theological aesthetics paints the following picture. The first application of aesthetics, to the general task of "perceiving the form," is in the realm of fundamental theology, which deals with ontological and phenomenological aspects of reality. Understanding aesthetic experience as the process of sensing some revelation from the depths provides a good analogy with theology. The second application, to perceiving the "Christ form" in the Scriptures, signals that in this sense von Balthasar's "theological aesthetics" can be understood simply as a particular Gadamer-style approach to hermeneutics, or as a way of doing hermeneutics in theology. According to this approach, the meaning or "truth" of a text is derived aesthetically, as in an artwork. However, since von Balthasar pursues the first task (perceiving the form) by looking not at our actual experience, but at the textual record of such experiences in ancient, medieval, and modern texts, the hermeneutic aspect is present in the first task as well. It is therefore precisely his "aesthetic hermeneutics" that unites the two tasks and represents also the union of his apologetics and systematics; this puts him at the cutting edge of both hermeneutical thought and theological reflection of the past century.[72]

Appendix

Von Balthasar's main work on theological aesthetics is *Herrlichkeit: eine theologische Ästhetik*, 3 vols. (Einsiedeln: Johannes Verlag, 1961). The translation

---

72. Von Balthasar's attempt to ground a Christian theology on the "aesthetic" experience of revelation and wonder has a corollary which he himself, perhaps, never felt the need to articulate. A theology that starts with aesthetic experience, and not with an a priori principle or any other rational theological or idealist "system," can stand up to any contemporary hermeneutic challenges. It can effectively survive (of course, only as an ideology or a type of rhetoric; cf. Tracy's account of theology) even in a post-Nietzschean perspectival world that challenges the notions of truth and goodness and removes all grounds except aesthetic. Moreover, the aesthetic can still function even if one tries to replace the classic "metaphysics of presence" with the postmodern structure of the "trace," since the aesthetic does essentially have the nature of a trace. (E.g., R. Williams in his Afterword to *Balthasar at the End of Modernity* [BEM 178] proposes that von Balthasar takes a middle ground between the classic idea of presence/identity and the postmodern structure of difference/alienation.) Whether or not this trace signals a real presence behind it depends upon the individual beliefs and the type of theological discourse one espouses, but the initial phenomenological fact of appearance, manifesting, and presenting something is undeniable even to the most ardent proponents of the "trace" structure of experience. A radically Nietzschean stance, however, today seems less and less plausible. So if one assumes a "moderate" position, namely that aesthetic experience communicates some core truth (see Preface), then a particular aesthetic (a particular rhetorical discourse) will still communicate an aspect of it!

used in this monograph is *The Glory of the Lord: A Theological Aesthetics*, translated by E. Leiva-Merikakis et al., edited by J. Riches et al., vols. 1, 2, 3, 4, 5 (San Francisco: Ignatius Press, 1982, 1984, 1986, 1989, 1991); I refer to it as GL1–5. Key terms (such as *Darstellung, Schau/Visio, Verweis,* etc.) and passages have been checked against the German edition. Literature on von Balthasar and his aesthetics is enormous. Only select studies on his theological aesthetics, as well as some recent or important general studies can be mentioned: J. A. Kay, *Theological Aesthetics: The Role of Aesthetics in the Theological Method of Hans Urs von Balthasar*, European University Papers (Series 23, Theology) 60 (Bern/Frankfurt am Main: Herbert Lang/Peter Lang, 1975); A. Moda, *Hans Urs von Balthasar, un' esposizione critica del suo pensiero* (Bari: Ecumenica Editrice, 1976); M. Hartmann, *Ästhetik als ein Grundbegriff fundamentaler Theologie: Eine Untersuchung zu Hans Urs von Balthasar*, Dissertationen. Theologische Reihe 5 (St. Ottilien: EOS Verlag, 1985); J. Riches, ed., *The Analogy of Beauty: The Theology of Hans Urs von Balthasar* (Edinburgh: T&T Clark, 1986); L. Roberts, *The Theological Aesthetics of Hans Urs von Balthasar* (Washington, D.C.: The Catholic University of America Press, 1987); K. Lehmann and W. Kasper, eds., *Hans Urs von Balthasar: Gestalt und Werk* (Cologne: Communio, 1989); J. O'Donnell, *Hans Urs von Balthasar* (Collegeville, Minn.: Liturgical Press, 1992); B. McGregor and T. Norris, eds., *The Beauty of Christ: An Introduction to the Theology of Hans Urs von Balthasar* (Edinburgh: T&T Clark, 1994)—with an essay on theological aesthetics by B. Leahy (pp. 23–55); A. Scola, *Hans Urs von Balthasar: A Theological Style* (Grand Rapids, Mich.: William B. Eerdmans, 1995); A. Nichols, *The Word Has Been Abroad: A Guide through Balthasar's Aesthetics* (Washington, D.C.: The Catholic University of America Press, 1998); M. Saint-Pierre, *Beauté, bonté, vérité chez Hans Urs von Balthasar* (Quebec: Les Éditions du Cerf, 1998), with a good bibliography on pp. 353–70; L. Gardner, D. Moss, B. Quash, and G. Ward, eds., *Balthasar at the End of Modernity* (Edinburgh: T&T Clark, 1999), abbreviated BEM; C. W. Steck, *The Ethical Thought of Hans Urs von Balthasar* (New York: Crossroad, 2001); O. Bychkov and J. Fodor, eds., *Theological Aesthetics after von Balthasar* (Aldershot: Ashgate, 2008).

CHAPTER 3

Hans Urs von Balthasar
The Aesthete and the Hermeneute

Having established that von Balthasar's understanding of the aesthetic—as something immediately sensed that has the capacity to reveal the transcendent or the "unseen" through a direct intuition or "seeing"—is typical of the German Idealist tradition and its successors, we come to the observation that is crucial for the present study. Although his view of aesthetic experience is essentially modern, he claims (in *GL2* and *GL4*) to have retrieved his understanding of the aesthetic from several ancient and medieval texts, thus asserting, contrary to the typical restrictive position within the historical school (the "historicists"), that some key aesthetic (in the modern sense of the term) issues were already being discussed in antiquity and the Middle Ages, long before they were articulated by Baumgarten and Kant. Like some key elements of von Balthasar's theological aesthetics, the very idea of going back to the pre-Reformation tradition comes from Barth. Barth says that by referring to beauty "we reach back to the pre-Reformation tradition of the Church," in particular to such Patristic and medieval authors as Augustine, pseudo-Dionysius the Areopagite, Anselm of Canterbury, and Thomas Aquinas.[1] Noting Barth's proposal to go back to the pre-Reformation tradition (*GL1* 54), von Balthasar calls it a "decisive breakthrough" in Barth's dogmatics: "If his call to return to pre-Reformation theology inspires such trust, it is because he claims for his theology only those elements of Patristic and Scholastic thought which can be justified from

---

1. See *CD* II/1, 651, 656, 661. According to Kerr (*BEM* 8), Barth, finding no roots for the concept of beauty in Protestant theology, goes back to the Patristic and Scholastic tradition.

revelation itself" (GL1 56). It is precisely pre-Reformation theology that inspires Barth's approach of attaining an interior form—the main task of von Balthasar's theological approach as well—through "tranquil, attentive contemplation" (GL1 56). According to von Balthasar, Barth's call to return to the study of pre-Reformation texts is important not only for contemporary Protestant theology, which still has no place for beauty, but also for the attempt within the Catholic tradition to restore the lost aesthetic element in theology. Von Balthasar, of course, greatly expands Barth's project by including not only Christian but also ancient pagan texts.

Once again, by going back to the pre-modern tradition in aesthetics, von Balthasar hopes to rescue both aesthetics and theology: the former, by helping it overcome its narrowing into an autonomous and overly technical discipline, at the expense of the loss of "wonder" at reality, its original inspiration; the latter, by making it, again, more experience-based, and thus attractive and convincing, rather than a collection of "scientific" methods. Such a move can also be interpreted as an attempt to counter the nihilism of postmodernity. On the one hand, this move would be a shift from a theology based on a "system"—the main object of postmodern attacks—to a more "organic" and flexible hermeneutic model. On the other hand, it would provide a more positive view of reality by drawing attention to the revelatory nature of reality, with a mystery at its core—as opposed to an empty structure of the "trace."

In general, the value of von Balthasar's move to the pre-modern seems clear. However, in view of the variety of existing approaches to the hermeneutics of ancient and medieval texts described in our Introduction, the concrete aspects of his hermeneutic approach still must be clarified, because they can either validate or discredit his whole project. In addition, the main task of the current study—to re-examine von Balthasar's analysis of ancient and medieval aesthetic texts—automatically involves a judgment on the appropriateness of his hermeneutic strategies. Further, as we have already noted, in many ways von Balthasar's "aesthetics" is just another name for his theological hermeneutics. The way he handles pre-modern texts makes this clear, for he not only extracts from them the idea of aesthetic as revelatory, but he does this in a way that is essentially aesthetic, which is exactly the way he, as a systematic theologian, handles scriptural texts. Therefore, an assessment of his hermeneutics is at the same time an assessment of his aesthetics: one of our central tasks. So what are the main features of von Balthasar's hermeneutic approach and where is he situated in the contemporary hermeneutic debate?

Although he appears to form a tradition of his own, and his knowledge of contemporary works on hermeneutics is not apparent, some scholars notice strong similarities between von Balthasar and the hermeneutic thought of Heidegger and Gadamer. Thus Williams speaks of the "implicit communality of interest between Balthasar and the whole post-Heideggerian approach to philosophical hermeneutics, insisting . . . on the 'historicity of understanding'" (AB 28).[2] For example, von Balthasar shares the idea that knowledge is participatory and inseparable from history. This idea leads to his Theo-Dramatic, a work that shows an awareness of contemporary intellectual developments (AB 26–27).[3] With Gadamer von Balthasar shares the idea that our mental history is inseparable from the structures of language and culture. He actually quotes Gadamer discussing our sense of belonging to history and the past addressing us (AB 28). Finally, von Balthasar seems to be familiar with the major works of Ricoeur, one of the common issues between them being whether language can be a starting-point of speaking about God (AB 28–30). This awareness of contemporary issues in hermeneutics distinguishes him favorably from Rahner, who seems to remain within the world of onto-theology and a transcendentalist analysis of subjectivity, failing to follow later developments in Heidegger or engage recent hermeneutic thought (AB 30–31).[4] Viladesau also contrasts the "transcendental theology" of Rahner with the "more 'hermeneutical' type" of theology of von Balthasar;[5] this assessment of

2. Cf. observations on the similarities between von Balthasar and Heidegger regarding their understanding of the concept of truth above in Chapter 2. Also cf. J. Kay, "Hans Urs von Balthasar, a Post-critical Theologian?" *Concilium* 141 (1981): 84–89. Kay concurs with Leo O'Donovan ("God's Glory in Time," *Communio* 2 [1975]: 268) that, because of his attention to symbolism and aesthetics, von Balthasar stands much closer to hermeneutic trends in theology than many from his generation. Kay in particular states the importance of the symbolic and metaphorical side in von Balthasar's "systematic-poetic" theology. Within Ricoeur's "hermeneutical circle" between believing in order to understand and understanding in order to believe, liberals excel at the latter, von Balthasar at the former (p. 85). Since the critical stage has a tendency to explain the symbols away, Kay reminds us, von Balthasar also belongs to a postcritical stage, meriting the designation "prophetic" rather than "conservative" (p. 88).

3. Cf. von Balthasar's analysis of Nebel's Protestant theological aesthetics (GL1 58ff.); one of the main features of this aesthetics is that it regards the beautiful as an event, i.e., inseparable from history.

4. Williams's final assessment is that, although von Balthasar gives "no sustained or coherent account" of the "ontology of language," he regularly presupposes it (AB 31).

5. Viladesau, *Theological Aesthetics*, x.

von Balthasar's approach goes well with Tracy's conviction that in general "systematic theologies are principally hermeneutical in character."[6] According to Tracy, a systematic theologian assumes the "truth-bearing character of a particular religious tradition" and focuses on "reinterpretations and new applications of that tradition for the present." Truth, then, appears as "disclosure through hermeneutical retrieval" (p. 58).[7]

Two other fundamental features of von Balthasar's general understanding of the hermeneutic process bring him close to Gadamer. The first is his Gadamer-style parallel between aesthetic and hermeneutic experiences (cf. *TM* 484–86 and the discussion above), both of which are essentially viewed as certain immediate "seeing." The idea of aesthetic vision that von Balthasar claims to have retrieved from Augustine has a direct bearing on his own hermeneutic approach to texts.[8] As one may remember, such vision is also the focal point of his 'theological aesthetics,' a large part of which can be understood, as was shown above, as essentially a 'theological hermeneutics based on aesthetic principles.' According to von Balthasar, only that which can be immediately *seen*, as in aesthetic experience, provides the most convincing proof and argument (cf. *GL2* 100). He argues that many "proofs" regarding Christian theology, for instance, in Augustine, are based precisely on the ability to see, and not on conceptual constructs or blind faith alone.[9] Such quasi-aesthetic self-evidence and transparency of meaning is at the very root of von Balthasar's hermeneutic approach, which features a free and open engagement with the interpreted text where the reader has a role of his own. Unless the reader is allowed to *see* certain things for herself, she will never be convinced. For example, as the reader discovers in the

---

6. Tracy, *Analogical Imagination*, 58.

7. Cf. ibid., 104: "All contemporary systematic theology can be understood as fundamentally hermeneutical." As is well known, Tracy contrasts systematic theology with fundamental (see Chapter 4 below) in that "in terms of expressing claims to meaning and truth" fundamental theology is "concerned to show the adequacy or inadequacy of the truth-claims, usually the cognitive claims, of a particular religious tradition . . ." and usually does this through a discipline acknowledged in the academic community: philosophy or the philosophical dimension of social sciences. (Fundamental theology therefore is sometimes called "philosophical theology"; Tracy, *Analogical Imagination*, 58.) However, we have shown above that von Balthasar is probably a step ahead of Tracy in trying to eliminate this distinction as purely imaginary. As will be clear from Tracy's own thought (see below), even strictly "academic" traditions with accepted truth claims can be seen as "systematic" theologies of sorts, and thus hermeneutical in nature.

8. See Chapter 7 below on Augustine.

9. Cf.: "It can be said that Augustine's proof of the true Church is an aesthetic proof: anyone who cannot see the specific nature of this catholicity . . . cannot be moved by it" (*GL2* 102).

course of *Herrlichkeit,* von Balthasar's own idea of the unity of the Christian aesthetic vision—a centerpiece of his study—can become evident only if it can be *seen* directly and immediately in the traditional texts he presents: it cannot be demonstrated by logical or "scientific" proofs. Thus, as it is for Gadamer, hermeneutic experience for von Balthasar is akin to aesthetic: certain things become apparent through our ability to "see" directly. According to Tracy, this model of truth as disclosure, in the spirit of Heidegger, is most suitable for systematic theology, as in general for "all good interpretation."[10] Tracy further reinforces Gadamer's parallel between aesthetic and hermeneutic experiences in application to theology. Both art and religion disclose truth, and the task of a theologian must be "allowing that disclosure to 'happen'" through careful and attentive interpretation and involvement.[11]

The second Gadamer-style feature is von Balthasar's reaction against the idea of an "exact scientific method" in theology, which parallels Gadamer's attack on Romantic hermeneutics.[12] He remarks, regarding the loss of the aesthetic dimension in theology, that "exact sciences" no longer have time to spare for the word "beauty": "nor does theology, in so far as it increasingly strives to follow the method of the exact sciences" (*GL*1 18). Just like the "human sciences" in Gadamer's account, theology is pretending to develop an exact method: however, according to von Balthasar, "it is perhaps high time to break through this kind of exactness" which limits reality to a particular sector and loses track of the whole behind the particular (*GL*1 18).[13] A philological analysis, of the

---

10. "'Truth' in systematics ... ordinarily functions in some form of 'disclosure' model implied in all good interpretation" (Tracy, *Analogical Imagination,* 68).

11. Ibid., 67. Tracy also applies Gadamer's idea of the "classic" (as in "classic work of art") to theology, where a "classic art work" becomes a "religious classic": "When a work of art so captures a paradigmatic experience of that event of truth, it becomes in that moment normative.... It becomes a classic: always retrievable, always in need of appreciative appropriation and critical evaluation, always disclosive and transformative with its truth of importance, always open to new application and thereby new interpretation." He further stresses that "we need ... a rehabilitation of the notions of the normative, the authoritative—in a word, the classical—now freed from the private domain of elitist classicists" (p. 115).

12. Von Balthasar is not unique in his rejection of the understanding of theology as an exact science, as opposed to a more hermeneutic approach to it: cf. A. Louth, *Discerning the Mystery: An Essay on the Nature of Theology* (Oxford: Clarendon Press, 1983). Louth mostly sides with Gadamer's understanding of the process of interpreting the tradition (cf. chap. 2, pp. 29ff.) and is critical of the claim of historico-critical method over theology (cf. chap. 6, p. 132).

13. Von Balthasar's observation that whoever does not see the whole but tries to break it up into components "falls into the void" (*GL*1 20) sounds remarkably like Heidegger's state-

kind that is practiced in contemporary theology, tears "bits and scraps" from the totality, dissecting its object as in the study of anatomy, before the form has been contemplated. He quips that anatomy, however, can be studied only on a dead body (GL1 31). Noting that nowadays the emphasis is transferred to the "historical aspect" of theology that views theological facts as "accidental historical truths" and focuses on the study of the "sources" of revelation, von Balthasar comments that this study of sources—also practiced by the Catholic tradition, following Protestant Biblical criticism—"has become strictly historical to an almost unacceptable degree" (GL1 74), seizing the lead over dogmatics. "Historical theological research," von Balthasar writes, claims to be "scientifically exact . . . as presently understood in the 'human sciences.'" But such research can establish only the historical and literal sense, following the traditional classification of Biblical interpretation in Origen and Augustine. The "properly theological dimension" begins only with the understanding and the spiritual sense of the Scripture, "which can indeed be fostered by a comprehensive understanding of history, but which *can in no way be extracted from history by 'exact scientific method'*" (*exaktwissenschaftlich*; my emphasis). He says, for example, that the ancients had an imperfect understanding of the letter, but a "far deeper knowledge" of the spirit (GL1 75). In contrast, contemporary Biblical scholars either relegate the spiritual sense to the "unscientific" realm of "spirituality" or wait for the judgment of the "exact" science (GL1 76).[14]

Now according to von Balthasar it is high time to contain the tendency of the historical method "to usurp unlawful territory" (GL1 76). After such harsh criticism of the "historical" method,[15] he outlines

---

ment about the impossibility of acquiring the essence of an artwork (or any *thing*) by breaking it up: cf. Heidegger, "Origin of the Work of Art," in *Poetry, Language, Thought*, 46–47.

14. On this issue, von Balthasar is remarkably in agreement with Tracy, who underlines the problems that arise from absolutizing the historico-critical method and points out its limitations (*Analogical Imagination*, 105–6; see texts quoted above in the Introduction). In his introduction, M. Saint-Pierre (*Beauté, bonté, vérité*, 22) notes that von Balthasar does not like the historico-critical methodology and rarely uses it: "Balthasar a souvent renoncé au titre de 'théologian.' Cela ne devrait pas être compris comme une simple boutade ou une expression d'humilité, mais plutôt comme une prise de position en face de la théologie rationaliste qui s'inspire beaucoup de la méthodologie des sciences modernes pour développer des systèmes de pensée théologique. Une exemple étonnant de cela: on constate avec quelle liberté notre auteur a si peu utilisé les méthodes d'exégèse historico-critiques dans ses écrits. . . . L'expression littéraire et poétique de la Bible n'a pas besoin de tout un appareillage scientifique pour être accueillie et vécue."

15. In this respect von Balthasar seems to follow Gügler, who also criticizes theological "sciences" cut off from their root, cf. GL1 101–2.

what he thinks theological hermeneutics should be like. True theology begins only when an "exact historical science" passes over into the science of faith: a special kind of hermeneutics which presupposes the act of faith as its "locus of understanding." The concept of "science" can be applied to theology only analogously (GL1 75). It is only in the intuitive saving knowledge of God that "the vision of the distinctively theological 'form' and its specific beauty" is possible (GL1 76).

As W. T. Dickens has pointed out, von Balthasar's rejection of the historico-critical method is not absolute, since at times he acknowledges its value and uses it himself. He quotes von Balthasar's statement from GL7 112, n. 5: "The research into first the literary form, second the situations in which the text was produced, and third the pre-existing forms of thinking, speech and narration influenced by the contemporary world, is undoubtedly an indispensable means to acquire the correct understanding."[16] However, Dickens's "difficulty" in "squaring [von Balthasar's] polemical remarks with others in which he explicitly acknowledges the value of historico-critical inquiry" (p. 78) can be eliminated if one sees von Balthasar's critique as being directed against a narrow and excessive use of the historical method. As is clear from the same note in GL7, von Balthasar sees the possibility of a cooperation between "scientific" methods and a more hermeneutical exegesis that allows one to link different parts ("scientifically" unrelated) together. As Dickens also notices (p. 78), von Balthasar's critique seems to be directed at the older model of the historical method,[17] which since has seen much improvement through the incorporation of many contemporary trends that allow for grasping the view of the whole (cf. pp. 82–83). Perhaps the final judgment still remains to be made as to the value that von Balthasar assigned to the historico-critical method. The aspect of von Balthasar's position that still remains most relevant is his critique of absolutizing this method which imposes grave restrictions on interpretation.

What approach does von Balthasar suggest as an alternative? The model of hermeneutics that he suggests for theology is not unlike Gadam-

---

16. W. T. Dickens, *Hans Urs von Balthasar's Theological Aesthetics: A Model for Post-Critical Biblical Interpretation* (Notre Dame, Ind.: University of Notre Dame Press, 2003), here p. 78. The study espouses an odd view that von Balthasar supposedly attempts to recover the "author's intent" from scriptural texts, which seems to contradict what Dickens says earlier about his hermeneutics, but his book contains some valuable information as well.

17. Perhaps, as Dickens notes on p. 79, against extreme cases such as Bultmann, who thought that historico-critical methods were sufficient.

er's ideal of hermeneutics that is appropriate for the "human sciences," where the specific contents of the "science" dictates the approach.[18] Thus W. Treitler notes that von Balthasar's "method" is content-specific.[19] Theology becomes methodologically authentic when its form fully springs from its content expressed in this form. The content is primary: it is already self-formed and does not need any "outside" input for interpretation (GW 177). The bearers of the tradition, by virtue of having it, also possess the ability to interpret it. For this reason, there is nothing wrong with the approaches to interpretation traditionally practiced in the humanities: otherwise, if one assumes today's "scientific" stand, one must admit that "nearly all the truly great and historically influential Christian theologies have been dilettantish, fashioned as they were by 'amateurs' (lovers!) and 'enthusiasts'" (GL1 77). Indeed, most of the prominent Christian theologians—such as Augustine, pseudo-Dionysius, or Bonaventure—in addition to their scholastic writings, also practiced a "non-scientific" contemplative style, the one in which von Balthasar is particularly interested for his own work.

In other words, even a preliminary and general look at von Balthasar's understanding of the process of interpretation in theology shows that he appears to be much more in line with contemporary hermeneutic theory based on Heidegger and Gadamer than is, for example, Rahner. Does this understanding of hermeneutics transfer to von Balthasar's interpretation of ancient and medieval texts in *Herrlichkeit*? An examination of his treatment of traditional texts shows that his style of hermeneutics here shares at least several major traits with Gadamer's description of the process of interpretation.

One of the key ideas in Gadamer that goes back to Heidegger is that, despite the seeming impossibility of accessing the past, there is an unbreakable link between the past and present. The past and the present mutually influence each other in the fusion of horizons. Any attempt to engage a "contemporary" idea starts with its past layers that extend back in history; at the same time, any engagement of the past starts with

---

18. The present study is not the first to draw a parallel between von Balthasar and Gadamer: e.g., cf. D. Brown, *Continental Philosophy and Modern Theology: An Engagement* (Oxford: Blackwell, 1987), 19–22 (on von Balthasar) and pp. 22–26 (on Gadamer). Dickens (*von Balthasar's Theological Aesthetics*) also notes that von Balthasar follows some pre-modern approaches to exegesis, which are often not in conflict with postmodern approaches (cf. pp. 3, 79).

19. W. Treitler, "Wahre Grundlagen authentischer Theologie," in *GW* 176.

a present pre-conception or fore-structure.[20] As has been noted above, von Balthasar's whole project of theological aesthetics is inseparably connected with the idea of a return to the Patristic and medieval tradition. According to his account of the history of theological aesthetics in *Herrlichkeit*, Barth's call to return to the pre-Reformation tradition of the Church is strengthened by new trends in Catholic thought, exemplified by Scheeben—for whom he has great respect—that "took its bearings from the basic intuitions of the common Tradition" (GL1 104).[21] It is remarkable that the notion of "tradition" in von Balthasar's history of Christian theological aesthetics does not stop with the Christian Patristic tradition. According to Murillo, "the theological method that he assumes in *Herrlichkeit* and systematically spells out in 1965, promises 'to maintain an unhindered view of the Gospel . . . at the same time, without turning his back on the tradition of the Church and theology together with the pre-Christian ancient elements that they contain.'"[22] Extending the understanding of tradition back in history so as to engage the ancient period is based on "four foundational presuppositions"—culture as transmission of Christian belief, openness to tradition, rejection of reductionism that "short-circuits" Christianity on itself, and unity of philosophy and Christianity—and allows one to speak of a "pre-Christian theology" (GW 214). One can say, with Tracy, that for von Balthasar, as for any good systematic theologian, "tradition is an ambiguous but still enriching, not impoverishing reality."[23] Instead of a popular postmodern tendency to expose the hidden traditional elements in order to subvert or overcome them, von Balthasar clearly assumes the position of defending the value of the tradition by which we all have been formed, and is in favor of "dialoguing" rather than "overcoming."

Von Balthasar's extended commentary on ancient and medieval texts

---

20. We mean here, in the tradition of Heidegger, Gadamer, and Tracy, *Vorverständnis* or *Vorgriff* in the sense of our "starting point" in interpretation, not (to avoid a possible confusion) Rahner's *Vorgriff* ("pre-apprehension").

21. Cf. R. Fisichella in *GW* 301, who remarks that in bringing back the beautiful as "the point of departure for the understanding of revelation" von Balthasar draws on biblical-Patristic and Scholastic tradition. According to Steck, one of von Balthasar's important arguments for the revival of theological aesthetics is that a focus on beauty has been an important part of the tradition, which he suggests retrieving (cf. Steck, *Ethical Thought*, 12).

22. I. Murillo, "Im Dialog mit den Griechen: Balthasars Verständnis antiker Philosophie in 'Herrlichkeit,'" in *GW* 212–13, with a quote from *Herrlichkeit*, in the existing English version (GL4 16) worded in a slightly different way.

23. Tracy, *Analogical Imagination*, 66.

in *Herrlichkeit* shows that, in the spirit of contemporary hermeneutic thought, he has an acute sense of the historicity of modern ideas and is able to "feel" their "historical dimension." It is precisely because of this sense of historicity that a large portion of the work is devoted to an explicit attempt to retrieve from traditional texts the historical dimension of an essentially modern idea—the "revelatory" capacity of aesthetic experience to make us aware of the depths of the transcendent. Starting his interpretation with a fore-meaning—the idea of the analogy between worldly beauty and the glory of revelation—he gives this abstract idea "historical color and fullness" (GL2 13) by showing its continuity through a number of historical periods. In contrast with any "scientific" approach, von Balthasar acknowledges that the preconception of aesthetic experience with which he starts building his theological aesthetics is a vague and "unreflected" one. At the same time, he cautions against making it more precise (GL1 117); his caution becomes understandable in view of the task of searching a vast textual tradition for the roots of the idea.

One may suggest that it is precisely von Balthasar's position as a theologian that makes it easier to accommodate the idea of a preconception. Indeed, a theologian is expected to see his/her material, even if it is of a philosophical nature, from a certain perspective, in the "light" of revelation (cf. Henrici in GW 255). This perspective allows von Balthasar to approach traditional texts with a major preconception of the unity of experience in all these texts and authors. This preconception, which he openly states as one of his presuppositions, allows him to deal with diverse and seemingly discordant texts—within one author, within the whole of the Christian tradition, or even across traditions—as if they possessed certain unity and commonality of ideas. At the same time, one can also see this presupposition of unity as essentially hermeneutic, and not specifically theological, in view of the existing "scientific" approaches to doing theology that would definitely reject such a way of proceeding even for theology.[24]

Von Balthasar's treatment of Bonaventure is a perfect example of

---

24. Tracy includes the idea of pre-conception in his view of systematic theology precisely as hermeneutic (ibid., 130–31): "the theologian already possesses some preunderstanding of the fundamental questions of religion, some personal opinions and response on religion, some relationship . . . towards the religious tradition . . . whose history of effects, influences and interpretations is carried by the language employed in all theological discourse." At the same time, as will be suggested in the next chapter, almost all academic discourses, and not only theological, must work with pre-conceptions.

openly proclaiming preconceptions as part of his hermeneutics. Thus he starts with the postulate of the primacy of the beautiful in Bonaventure, which, he says, is the expression of Bonaventure's deep original experience (GL2 260–61). Next (GL2 283–84), von Balthasar lays out his general program for discussing Bonaventure's thought in the next few chapters. Given that this main idea does not appear as a conclusion of his analysis, but only at the very beginning, von Balthasar seems to be openly emphasizing and making known his fore-meaning, instead of starting by rejecting "contemporary biases" or avoiding any "initial projections" into his material, as the historical school recommends.[25]

From a historicist perspective von Balthasar's hermeneutic approach, which is based on the hermeneutic assumption of the continuity of modern ideas extending back in history, is guilty of another mortal sin: von Balthasar is not trying to avoid modern interpretations of ancient and medieval authors. He thus acknowledges that a traditional text somehow foreshadows modern developments, and that it is the role of the present-day interpreter to bring out these "latent" meanings. This understanding of a traditional text is in perfect accord with Gadamer's understanding of a "classic." In Tracy's interpretation of this notion as applied to theology, a classic is something that always remains relevant to, and compatible with, contemporary ways of thinking.[26] The task of a theologian as a hermeneute is precisely to make a traditional text relevant and challenging to a present-day reader, something that definitely happens in von Balthasar's work. First of all, von Balthasar's very concept of the aesthetic that he applies to traditional texts is very modern: "aesthetics" is something that has to do with the senses and their mediating role (cf. GL2 121). His treatment of Augustine's thought provides further examples of interpreting ancient and medieval ideas as historical roots of modern aesthetics. He does not hesitate to interpret Augustine's theory of "ascent" in terms of Kantian transcendental philosophy (cf. GL2 109 and 112). He also applies to Augustine the idea of the "finite form as the revelation of the infinite," which is at the center of eighteenth-

---

25. According to "historicist" studies of Bonaventure's theology, such a presupposition would be far from evident.

26. Cf. Tracy, *Analogical Imagination*, 130–31: "The systematic theologian is the interpreter of religious classics," and "systematic theology intends to provide an interpretation, a retrieval." Tracy mentions, as examples, the retrieval by Gadamer and others of notions of φρόνησις and truth in poetry, which have present-day relevance, from texts of Aristotle (103).

and nineteenth-century Romantic aesthetics (GL2 114): after describing the "basic experience" of self-manifestation of the infinite, he attempts to find in Augustine fascination with the finite form (cf. GL2 116–18). His use of Augustine oscillates between discussing concrete passages in terms of modern aesthetic ideas in a rather systematic way and referring to the whole body of his writings as part of the unified Christian aesthetic vision. He draws a broad parallel between the whole of Augustine's thought and the modern idea, especially prominent in Nietzsche, that the aesthetic is the major redeeming force that is self-evident and has the power of showing the unity of our otherwise fragmented experience. "It is enthusiasm," von Balthasar writes, "which has to fill the theoretical gap, and it can only do this, to put it briefly, by looking at the world in an aesthetic way" (GL2 124).[27] The unity of the multitude of fragmented visions is ensured by the total unifying aesthetic vision, as, for example, in Augustine's aesthetic justification of evil (GL2 127). Finally, von Balthasar is trying to restore an even broader historical context of Augustine's aesthetic vision. He draws broad parallels with the whole history of aesthetic thought, trying to situate Augustine in the "historical dimension" of the idea of the aesthetic. The main point of theological aesthetics is not "blind faith" but also being able to see. Augustine's proof of the "rightness" of the true religion is ultimately aesthetic, just as in Pascal, Soloviev and Newman.[28]

Another example of interpreting an ancient author as "foreshadowing" modern ideas is von Balthasar's interpretation of Plotinus in terms of Christian theological aesthetics. He contrasts Plotinus's thought with the German Idealist tradition (this subject is discussed in detail by I. Murillo [GW 210–22]). According to von Balthasar, Plotinus "wonders at the glory (*Herrlichkeit*) of the cosmos, as well as the theological dimension of beauty, which is lost in the aesthetics of the German Idealism, from Kant to Schiller to Hegel" (GW 220). Von Balthasar sees in Plotinus elements of a Christian theological aesthetics of glory and wonder; he says that Plotinus managed to ground his aesthetics in "glory" and make it into a "theological aesthetics outside the biblical [tradi-

---

27. Von Balthasar's spirit is, of course, very different from that of Nietzsche.
28. "In Augustine—as again later in Pascal, Soloviev, and Newman—the certainty of the ultimate rightness of the *vera religio* does not rest in mere intuitions of heart and conscience of faith, but resides in a seeing of rightness which in the broad sense must be called an aesthetic vision" (GL2 139).

tion]" (GW 220), which would allow his thought even today to contribute philosophically to a Christian theological aesthetics (GW 221).

Although, unlike Gadamer, von Balthasar does use the terms "method" and "methodology" (GL1 39), a detailed analysis of his hermeneutic technique proves that he practices no "method" in the scientific sense: it would be more correct to speak of an "approach."[29] Von Balthasar's own philology is very good: the text is used carefully, and his own translations from the Latin (e.g., cf. GL2 289) are excellent.[30] At the same time, references to secondary sources are sporadic and sometimes out-of-date (perhaps dating back to his student years),[31] but sometimes they are more recent,[32] and they abound and are rather complete in areas covered by his own previous research.[33]

Another feature that distinguishes von Balthasar's approach from the historical or "scientific" is his use of chronology and selection patterns in choosing his texts and authors. His criteria for selecting medieval texts for interpretation seem random and subjective, as he himself admits (GL2 20). This is deliberate: the discontinuity and absence of a system in selecting texts signals that "no continuous development can or should be shown" in such a vast subject as the analogy between beauty and the revelation of God (GL2 22).[34] At the same time, the absence of

---

29. B. McNeil, e.g., draws our attention to the fact that, when compared to the work of a scholar who uses a historico-critical method based on facts and textual criticism, von Balthasar's work might seem methodologically unclear and dilettantish, the concern he himself voices at the beginning of *Herrlichkeit* (McNeil, "The Exegete as Iconographer: Balthasar and the Gospels," in *AB* 138).

30. In the original German version of *Herrlichkeit*, von Balthasar left the Latin texts in the footnotes untranslated. In the English translation those Latin texts have been translated, with varying degrees of success; cf. GL2 passim.

31. Cf. references re. Plato, GL4 204, n. 329, or the majority of references pertaining to Bonaventure that date to the 1920s and 30s.

32. I.e., closer to the time of writing *Herrlichkeit*: cf. references to critical literature on Plotinus in GL4 302 dating to the mid 1950s.

33. In GL2 144–45, there are two pages of footnotes filled with references to secondary literature on pseudo-Dionysius, the author he studied profoundly while doing his research on John of Scythopolis. In general his treatment of pseudo-Dionysius is different from his treatment of Augustine, for example; it includes more references to secondary sources, background, and discussion of theories, and it sounds more like part of an academic dissertation, proving further the unevenness of his approach.

34. F. Kerr (*BEM* 4) agrees that at times von Balthasar selects for his discussion in *Herrlichkeit* seemingly marginal and unknown figures, but deliberately so: e.g., turning to "lay styles" in theology could be a calculated insult (*BEM* 5). Perhaps the selection of authors and texts itself contains part of his theological statement and should be viewed as an element of his hermeneutic approach. A. Scola (*A Theological Style*, 6) makes an interesting general re-

a system does not mean that no unity is achieved. As described above, one of von Balthasar's major theological and hermeneutic preconceptions is the unity of aesthetic "vision" in traditional Christian texts. This presupposition allows him to analyze many disjoint "voices" of the tradition, since ultimately they must all express the same unity of aesthetic vision and present a continuity of meaning. "All that develops," he makes an artistic analogy, "is a full orchestra, whose various instruments blend well with one another: their mutual harmony proves that they all play from the same score" (GL2 22).[35]

A similar pattern is observed regarding chronology. Although von Balthasar at times does exhibit some awareness of the chronological order of works of an author,[36] most of the time he completely ignores it. Von Balthasar's treatment of Augustine is a good example of this. A typical medievalist trained in a "historicist" methodological tradition would be struck by his arbitrariness in selecting Augustine's texts. Neither strict chronology nor any other system is followed (cf. GL2 95–97). Von Balthasar simply engages the whole corpus of Augustine's texts, letting them "play out" their meaning on their own (cf. GL2 99ff.). His approach, however, is justified because his hermeneutics is based on the assumption of the unity of vision that goes through traditional theological texts. It makes little difference where one might start chronologically, and one can engage any text at any point. As a result of such an engagement with Augustine, von Balthasar hopes to capture "Augustine's basic intuitions" that run through his major works and point to some sort of a hermeneutic "kernel" of his thought that is the unity of Augustine's aesthetic vision (GL2 97).[37]

---

mark on the absence of a "systematic arrangement" in von Balthasar's theological writings. According to Scola, he abhors the system, being conscious of the impossibility of "imprisoning the unseizable glory of God in an effort of human reflection. A theology, on the contrary, has to be open on all sides, like a fragment out of which glory itself can shine, if it so wishes." I.e., instead of a finished structure, a theologian must rather construct a medium or "conduit" of divine glory, analogous to a piece of conducting material, which can contain an electrical field even if it is fragmented or incomplete. That is, instead of creating a *system* that works only as a whole (such as a complete computer), a theologian should rather create a *style* that works in any fragment (such as a piece of copper wire).

35. Cf. GL2 29: "each original form breaks out anew from the center."

36. Cf. GL4 206, where he mentions the "middle period" in Plato; GL4 308, where he differentiates between earlier and later books of Plotinus's *Enneads*; or GL2 292, where he mentions, in a chronologically correct way, the sources of Bonaventure.

37. Cf. GL2 98 on Augustine's *De vera religione*: "circling, unsystematic, but in secret drawn magnetically to its true pole."

The style of the discussion of ancient and medieval texts in *Herrlichkeit* is equally remarkable. At times it consists of a short statement backed up by a quotation or a reference; at times a quotation from a primary source is followed by an interpretation; with few exceptions, no secondary sources are mentioned (cf. treatment of Plato in GL4 176, 191). Sometimes no prolonged interpretation is given, and the pattern of abrupt quotations is difficult to follow (Plato, GL4 183). Often the discussion simply becomes a paraphrase or a summary, with or without a commentary. Quotes can become extremely long, up to a full page, and the text can turn into an overwhelming patchwork of quotations from the primary sources, as if we are being offered a "directed reading" course.[38] Von Balthasar clearly lets the ancient or medieval text freely express its meaning, following on his promise to "let the reader see" for him or herself what the text communicates. What happens within this framework of quotation-commentary is also interesting. Sometimes von Balthasar's commentary is simply a smooth re-phrasing or re-stating of the author's ideas.[39] Texts that come from different places within one author or one text can be combined as if they were part of a continuous text (GL2 281). Certain interpretive choices seem uncritical and unexplained.[40] Frequently von Balthasar makes broad generalizations that do not seem to be well substantiated or based on the texts used.[41] The technique outlined above clearly classifies von Balthasar's style of interpretation as that of an exegete, rather than that of an academic scholar. His style creates a poetic and literary, rather than academic, impression. At times it even acquires elements of majestic grandiloquence, as in GL1 when he writes about the "tragic" Romantic figures.

What brings von Balthasar's approach even closer to Gadamer's hermeneutics is that he views his relationship with the interpreted text in terms of a dialogue, wherein the text functions as an active partner in a conversation, has a "voice," can express itself and needs to be lis-

---

38. Cf. the discussion of Nebel in GL1 61, of pseudo-Dionysius in GL2 178ff., and of Bonaventure in GL2 295, 300, 303, 329, 332.

39. Cf. his discussion of Bonaventure in GL2 286, 349.

40. Cf. Bonaventure, GL2 287, terminology and translation of *expressus*.

41. E.g., in GL2 277, referring to Bonaventure's *Breviloquium* I.1, von Balthasar makes a broad general statement—that Aquinas wants to safeguard reason, but Bonaventure makes reason to "retreat within its own proper limits"—that does not seem to have a textual basis. The statement from Bonaventure quoted on this occasion clearly refers to "philosophy" that comes to its limit, which is not the same as "reason," since for medieval scholars theology also contains elements of reason.

tened to.[42] He uses this form of a hermeneutic dialogue each time he engages the tradition of Christian texts in *Herrlichkeit*: by closely following the text, von Balthasar tries to make it speak and express its central points.[43] The dialogical approach is best illustrated by the way von Balthasar proceeds in order to substantiate his pre-conception of the unity of the Christian aesthetic vision. He engages in a free dialogue with the entire tradition that includes very diverse texts. His only guiding principle is constant attention to the text. During this process of interpretation, the reader has a role that is almost as important as that of von Balthasar himself. The text must be allowed to express itself. Instead of providing his own interpretation, von Balthasar leaves certain things to be discovered by the reader. The presupposed unity of aesthetic vision in the tradition must become evident by itself through hermeneutic experience: "That fascinating dialogues open up between one and another, one greeting another across the centuries . . . perhaps making expressible what was once intended in quite a new form . . . this and similar things the reader will see for himself" (GL2 22). Von Balthasar makes no secret of the incompleteness and openness of his dialogical hermeneutic technique. A true hermeneutic process, in contrast to the "scientific method," is expected to leave many things still unclear and open for further dialogue. One moves around the "center" in a hermeneutic circle, gradually elucidating the meaning, yet never achieving its completeness: "Even at the end of this volume it will not be possible to suppress a feeling of disappointment: for we shall have only circled round the Biblical and dogmatic meaning of the glory of the Lord and have not elucidated it from the very center" (GL2 30).

As in a regular dialogue, selecting your partner here is of utmost importance. One does not choose partners who would be unpleasant or

---

42. Again, a feature appropriate to systematic theology of a hermeneutic type, according to Tracy. Tracy views authoritarian and fundamentalist theologies as "ideologies," not systematic theologies (*Analogical Imagination*, 99). A true systematic theology as hermeneutic (in this Tracy, again, follows Gadamer) includes the idea of a conversation: listening, reflecting, "allowing the question to take over" (101). Cf. 131: "the theologian as interpreter will initiate some movement of dialogue with the subject matter"; "the theological dialogue will expand to include explicit reflection on the history of the influences, effects, and interpretations—the tradition—of this classic event, text, symbol, person."

43. Cf.: "in each case an effort has to be made to get the sought-after moments to express themselves as one traces . . . as exactly as possible the outlines of the work" (GL2 14). Henrici (GW 245) agrees that in von Balthasar's hermeneutic approach, meaning grows out of the texts in the process of an open dialogue.

unsupportive. In the same spirit, von Balthasar's "choice of his conversation partners falls on those who can accommodate his intention, especially his aesthetics" (Murillo in *GW* 215), and so he chooses texts and authors that will make a good case for his theological aesthetics. Most remarkably, once selected, his ancient and medieval conversation partners are often treated as his contemporaries, and magically the temporal difference seems to disappear. Thus Bonaventure, in von Balthasar's words (*GL2* 294, n. 157), "takes seriously" and "answers satisfactorily" the concerns of Karl Barth, appearing as a contemporary theologian in conversation with Barth. Further on (*GL2* 295), Bonaventure is compared to both Plato and Luther almost across the full spectrum of Western European intellectual tradition.

In his dialogues with traditional texts, von Balthasar uses an approach that is more appropriate for literary criticism: this comes as no surprise, given his background in German philology and literature. Against the background theme of the unity of vision, he follows particular "themes" that repeat throughout a certain text or an author. Finding a theme goes along with the idea of looking for "basic intuitions" in the whole body of writings of a particular author. He traces, for example, the theme of the "image of the crucified" through at least eight different works of Bonaventure. Another reappearing theme in Bonaventure's works that captures von Balthasar's attention is "expression-impression" or the idea that God expresses himself in the world and the world expresses God (cf. *GL2* 283).

Many peculiar features of von Balthasar's hermeneutics, such as ignoring the historical or logical order of works, assuming the "unity of vision" in a group of works or authors, or looking for "basic intuitions" of an author, point to a specific technique of presenting traditional texts. B. McNeil has pointed out (*AB* 139) that von Balthasar sees the theological exegete more as an iconographer than as a photographer. Instead of recording particular facts and data, an iconographer recreates a "portrait," or a whole, complete image that does not have to be realistic or "scientifically precise" but that captures some essential features of the prototype.[44] It is in this way that the icon is viewed by the Eastern Or-

---

44. Cf. a familiar observation that a photograph may look totally unrecognizable, although it is an image captured scientifically, and at the same time in an artistic sketch or a caricature a person can be recognized at a glance, although it may contain few of the actual details of the face.

thodox tradition,[45] and it is in this sense that Tillich spoke of the verbal portrait of Christ in the Gospels being "Expressionist." An important clue regarding his "iconographic" activity as an interpreter of the tradition comes from von Balthasar himself discussing his relation to Rahner in an interview. Von Balthasar indicates different points of departure for Rahner's transcendental approach (Kant, Fichte) and for his own approach, which "chooses Goethe." Although his thought is at times interpreted in terms of transcendentalism, von Balthasar clearly distinguishes between the apriorism of the "Kantians," which favors the intellect, and his own approach as the one that is based on direct "seeing" and favors immediate perception. According to von Balthasar, he "chose Goethe—as a Germanist" and his approach is based on capturing "the image (*Gestalt*), the indissolubly unique, organic, self-developing image . . . that image, with which Kant cannot really cope even in his aesthetics. . . . One can walk around an image and see it from all sides. One always keeps seeing something different, and at the same time always sees the same."[46] (Von Balthasar's description of a *Gestalt* sounds surprisingly close to Husserl's description of an object—a self-identical "synthesis" of countless aspects—that emerges as a result of phenomenological "seeing,"[47] which supports the characterization of his method as "phenomenology" discussed in the next paragraph.) Von Balthasar's description of his Goethe-style approach is crucial in elucidating the scholar's hermeneutic technique of creating the whole images or pictures (*Gestalten*) of authors or texts, painting portraits and capturing "visions," as it were, rather than breaking them down into components and analyzing.

All the peculiar features of von Balthasar's exegesis, which seems to defy any chronological or logical order and is expressed in a semi-poetic literary style, are aptly explained in Henrici's concise statement: "In its display of images or pictures (*Schauen der Gestalten*), von Balthasar's philosophical method can be named neither systematic—and of course not at all conceptual-analytic or -constructive—nor truly historical; it

---

45. Cf., e.g., L. Ouspensky and V. Lossky, *The Meaning of Icons*, translated by G. E. H. Palmer and E. Kadloubovsky (Crestwood, N.Y.: St. Vladimir's Seminary Press, 1999), 38–39. According to Ouspensky, the icon presents not all, but only the essential, features of a saint, which include the features that are characteristic of the "transfigured" or glorified state of his or her body, i.e., certain invisible traits that are essential for re-creating his or her portrait.

46. Quoted by Henrici in *GW* 243, after M. Albus, "Geist und Feuer: Ein Gespräch mit Hans Urs von Balthasar," *Herderkorrespondenz* 30 (1976): 75ff.

47. *Cartesian Meditations*, Second Meditation, §17–18 (39ff.).

most closely approaches, according to his own words, phenomenology—not without an admixture of a fair share of literary criticism" (GW 243). Von Balthasar himself admits that his study consists of "historical structures of world-pictures (*Weltanschauung*)" put together as individual stones to build a building that has a meaning "beyond and outside history (*ausser historisch*)."⁴⁸ He is thus positioned "between history and system, in the middle" and sees his method as "phenomenological," probably understanding this term more generally as "intellectual observation."⁴⁹ Henrici points out that this position explains the difficulties in describing von Balthasar's thought, since "it cannot be approached either historically-analytically or conceptually-reconstructively" (GW 243). All one can do is to describe the *Gestalten* that he leaves, but the approach itself used to create them escapes description. Von Balthasar's creative and poetic text cannot easily be vested in academic terms. It is best read itself, and the only way to capture it is either by re-telling it or by imitating it. Further on, Henrici notes that von Balthasar's thought moves over and against other *Gestalten* (*Gegen-Gestalten*) and can be defined only in terms of these other "pictures" (cf. GW 245).⁵⁰ In other words, in creating a particular "picture," his own text, as in a dialogue, is dependent on the commented text and can be read only in a dialogical manner and only in connection with this text.

The existence of this *Gestalt-Bildung* technique is apparent from von Balthasar's own description of his approach in *Herrlichkeit*. According to his own words, he will present a series of Christian theologies and world-pictures, each of which is "marked at its center by the glory of God's revelation" and try "to give the impact of this glory a central place in its vision" (GL2 13). However, instead of a systematic picture, the author will offer a number of "relatively closed and self-sufficient" pictures (GL2 22).⁵¹ Von Balthasar's technique can be compared to that of an art critic describing the style of a particular painter. Certain features of a particular style always remain the same: one can always recognize a Ce-

---

48. Henrici, GW 244; the original quote is taken from H. U. von Balthasar, *Apokalypse der deutschen Seele: Studien zu einer Lehre von letzten Haltungen*, vol. 1 (Freiburg: Johannes Verlag, 1998), 10, n. 2.

49. Henrici coins the term *geistesgeschichtlich-phänomenologisches Denken* to describe von Balthasar's approach (GW 243).

50. Henrici further proceeds to describe some individual *Gestalten* formed by von Balthasar for Plato, Plotinus, Hegel (GW 245ff.).

51. Henrici in GW 243 also sees von Balthasar more as an "interpreter of intellectual history" (*Geistesgeschichte*) than as a "systematic thinker."

zanne, no matter what the subject matter of the painting is. At the same time, his approach cannot avoid the main problem of art criticism: no matter how good the description is, one would still have to *see* several actual paintings in order to grasp the main features of Cezanne's style. Only when one has actually seen for him- or herself, does the art critic's description become intelligible. The same holds true for von Balthasar's technique of capturing the main features of an author's "vision" and style: one must see them in the texts, in order for the commentary to become comprehensible.

Von Balthasar's "*Gestalt*-painting" draws both on his dialogical approach and on his main hermeneutic assumption that it is direct "seeing," not logical arguments, that provides the most convincing proof. Although his "pictures" are often very general and only vaguely based on texts, they, like agreeable conversation partners, always seem to support his own aesthetic approach and, despite all their vagueness, seem to present the captured features persuasively.

The features of this "iconographic" approach emerge in his presentation of particular ancient and medieval authors. Thus his discussion of Plato is conducted with an assumption that the totality of his writings possesses a certain consistency (GL4 185), has its own individual *Gestalt*. In particular, he refers to this general picture of Platonic thought in his treatment of the *Republic* (GL4 175), as if some general picture could emerge from a variety of Platonic texts: the picture that foreshadows the *Gestalt* of Christian theology. Von Balthasar's discussion of Plotinus (e.g., cf. GL4 291 and further) creates a similarly general picture of his thought instead of analyzing particular texts.

Especially striking are his treatments of pseudo-Dionysius, for whom von Balthasar seems to have a special affection, and Bonaventure. He approaches the work of pseudo-Dionysius as if he were in dialogue with the corpus of Dionysian writings as a whole, and he allows "this astonishing work to exert its influence upon him" (GL2 147). He describes the whole body of Dionysian writings in broad terms, as it were, applying bold "brushstrokes" to the emerging picture. The holistic *Gestalt* of the Dionysian corpus emanates a certain "radiance." Just as in his discussion of Christ's image depicted by Gospel writers, whose truth and authenticity is self-evident from the particular harmony of this image, the worth and authenticity of Dionysian writings is estimated from the particular "organic" nature of their *Gestalt*: "And, then . . . such power, such radiance of holiness streams from this unity of person and work . . . that he can in no case be regarded as a 'forger'" (GL2 147). Von Balthasar continues with outlining the general "contours" of his image by noting that Dionysian theology assumes an "overall hymnic" character and sometimes "the tone of great poetry" (GL2 177), and commenting that this rhetorical or poetic way of writing about God can say more than theology that "works by definitions." Pseudo-Dionysius in general, according to von Balthasar, "gives atmosphere, a sense of the spiritual, he gives a deep peace and blessedness" (GL2 148). Again, the description focuses on the style and "spirit" of Dionysian writings as a whole, just as further down (GL2 150) von Balthasar speaks of the form of pseudo-Dionysius's letters as a whole. Finally, inspired by painting the Dionysian *Gestalt*, he arrives—to the great distress of the historicists, to be sure—at a vision of the emerging *Gestalt* of the whole of Church history "aesthetically" visible at a glance, the *Gestalt* that possesses the aesthetic characteristic of a musical composition: "All history is, as it were, aesthetically set at a distance, forming an eternal, sacred picture *(agalma)*, for the Church has no longer any proper history, or, if one prefers, its history forms a kind of heavenly concert, like the great polyphony of Josquin or Palestrina" (GL2 176).

Von Balthasar's treatment of Bonaventure proceeds in a similar manner, starting with a general outline of the main features or contours of Bonaventure's *Gestalt* (cf. GL2 264ff.). After outlining the general vision, he turns to the analysis of concrete texts, but without losing sight of the form of the initial unifying vision. This procedure is very difficult to follow if one holds on to the historico-critical mentality, since von Balthasar draws from various works of Bonaventure without an apparent pattern (cf. GL2 268ff.). Underlying this lack of organization, however, is the same unifying general vision, and the only way to read the text is by abandoning any analytic or critical attitude and simply "following along," allowing the text and the interpreter to "show" you the whole picture. In a particularly vivid example, he contrasts the *Gestalt* of Bonaventure with that of Aquinas (GL2 266). Von Balthasar quotes from the prologues to several different works of Bonaventure to capture the main "ethos" or "spirit" of his theology, as it can be contrasted with that of Aquinas. Outlining several motifs that permeate several of Bonaventure's writings—of the vastness of revelation, of being "lost" and "defeated from the start" in an attempt to approach it, of possessing no arrogance of a finished system—

von Balthasar, in bold strokes, paints a quick sketch of the whole of Bonaventure's thought:

> The ethos of the theology in Bonaventure is thereby quite different from the ethos of Thomas Aquinas, whose philosophical point of view tries to reflect the order of the world as rigorously and clearly as possible. In Bonaventure, there is something defeated from the very start; theology is an imposing upon that which is not to be imposed upon, a tireless proposing of new ordering... the 'blossoming wilderness' into bouquets. But in the face of this, the last word remains the experience of being out-trumped, of wonder, and of being transported out of oneself (*excessus*). (GL2 266)

The typical "motif" of the "Bonaventure-*Gestalt*" that appears in the last line—the overpowering movement beyond reason, the experience of going outside of self, of rapture, a transcending movement of the ascent and ecstatic excess—is also subsequently recreated by drawing on a variety of unconnected texts and relying solely on the assumption of the unity of Bonaventure's thought (cf. GL2 269).

In brief, the strong point of von Balthasar's contribution to the interpretation of ancient and medieval texts in terms of revelatory aesthetics is in his rejection of narrow historicism, which constrains all interpretation to the meaning "intended by the author" or "perceived by contemporaries." Instead, he offers a much more advanced model of hermeneutics based on a dialogue with the tradition,[52] bringing it alive for the present-day reader—which, according to Gadamer, is its very nature—and pointing out the continuity of ideas in their historical extension. At the same time, his intuitive-ingenious "literary criticism" style of interpretation, with its free use of text and frequent neglect of historical and textual connections, has its limitations. Indeed, it is reminiscent of the early practice of building Christian basilicas with fragments of pagan temples. If one's goal is to build a basilica, this works well as long as one finds pieces that fit the required shape. A different approach is needed, however, if one decides to trace "genealogically" how certain elements of a Christian building gradually developed out of elements of pagan architecture. In other words, von Balthasar's approach works well for a theological commentary based on the preconception of the "unity of Christian aesthetic vision" across the centuries. Operating with such an

---

52. There is a certain irony, of course, in calling "advanced" an approach that is allegedly based on going back to pre-modern thought—but a certain truth as well!

a priori framework, one can "skip a few steps," or make a few intuitive connections here and there: being "focused on the general vision" will ensure the correctness of the final results. At the same time, if one attempts to reconstruct a history of an idea—a history that has a broader appeal and is based on the immediate hermeneutic context rather than on an intuition of the general structure—one clearly needs a firmer foundation. In order to show the validity of von Balthasar's insights into the history of aesthetic ideas in Antiquity and the Middle Ages for a broader community of interpreters, one needs to pay more attention to the historical meaning of terms used to describe "aesthetic" experiences, as well as establish tighter historical connections between authors and traditions through careful textual research. After having done that, we will be able to see if von Balthasar's a priori intuitions actually correspond to the development of aesthetic ideas in Western intellectual history that is reconstructed on the basis of an analysis of the continuity of the textual tradition.

CHAPTER 4

Retreading von Balthasar's Path

In the previous chapters, von Balthasar's project of interpreting ancient and medieval texts in terms of aesthetics was shown in general to be hermeneutically valid. It was also shown that his exegesis of ancient and medieval texts could be improved upon. The re-examination of von Balthasar's extensive project by fine-tuning his hermeneutic approach, which is undertaken in Part Two of this study, is well justified. Von Balthasar's construction of theological aesthetics includes an attempt to show, through a careful interpretation of traditional texts, how an earlier tradition can be seen as a precursor to contemporary ideas. In his own readings of ancient and medieval texts he finds the roots, or the historical extension, of the idea of beauty as revelation. The importance of this insight to contemporary philosophical and theological thought warrants another look at some of these texts. The reaffirmation of the possibility of retrieving from the ancient and medieval tradition the idea that aesthetic experience is somehow revealing would be an important contribution to Western intellectual history.

In order to re-evaluate both the successes and weak points of von Balthasar's titanic project, the present study will assume a hermeneutic approach in the tradition of H.-G. Gadamer. At the same time, it will attempt to utilize all positive developments of the historico-critical method, without the accompanying limiting and restrictive mentality uncovered by the contemporary hermeneutic theory. At the present time, exclusive types of discourse based on convention are practiced in academia in application to the study of ancient and medieval philosophical and theological texts. Such habitual academic discourse clearly limits the horizon of discussion. For example, the rationalistic (analytic, Neoscholastic) type of academic discourse necessarily limits the study to closed "systems" of thought with truth-dominated discourse and often excludes references to mystical and aesthetic experience that are left "outside" the system. The idea of a "correct method" of extracting information from traditional texts—the heritage of the nineteenth-century historical school—often goes hand in hand with such rationalistic approaches. The limitations of the "historicist" approach, sufficiently discussed above, include the assumptions that, on the one hand, one can arrive at the true interpretation of traditional texts, but that, on the other hand, such texts can be viewed only from the perspective of their own time, which makes them appear rather irrelevant.

Another popular trend, the "postmodern" approach (the "new medievalism," for example), rightly criticizes the above-mentioned rationalistic approaches to texts by uncovering the fact that they themselves operate from within closed systems of discourse while laying claim to the universal validity of their "correct" interpretations. The postmodern approach does admit the historicity of traditional texts, whose "true" meaning remains forever hidden from us because our position in history is far removed from these texts. However, for this reason it relegates them to particular "closed" types of discourse whose "true meaning" as such cannot be discussed. Postmodern scholars concentrate on the few phenomena that, according to them, can still be studied by contemporary scholarship: methods of writing, types of discourse, systematizing and transmitting knowledge, ideologies, et cetera. What is studied is the system of medieval "episteme" rather than ideas that have any contemporary relevance.[1] In the end such analyses sound curious but "empty," devoid of any persuasiveness or sense of significance.[2]

Against this background, the hermeneutic approach can effectively restore the possibility of a constructive dialogue with the ancient and medieval intellectual tradition. On the one hand, the incomprehensibility of the historical past must be admitted. On the other hand, a possibility of engaging this past must be affirmed. There is some common ground of understanding (as the mode of being of the *Dasein*) that can be brought to light. The historicity of the phenomena (texts, ideas) is

---

[1]. Cf. P. W. Rosemann, *Understanding Scholastic Thought with Foucault* (New York: St. Martin's Press, 1999), especially his chapter on Aquinas.

[2]. Cf. Tracy's criticism of reductionism in contemporary art criticism (*Analogical Imagination*, 109), which could well be applied to the postmodern reductionist treatment of the tradition, according to which everything is reduced to some sort of power play, ideology, or type of discourse.

just one aspect of their *Dasein* that does not preclude us from engaging it. So one of the advantages of the hermeneutic approach is that, unlike historical-rationalistic approaches, it opens up possibilities for a closer engagement of an ancient or medieval text in showing its contemporary relevance. From a hermeneutic perspective one can simultaneously engage a number of thinkers from different periods—Kant and Bonaventure, for example, as von Balthasar has done. Since the historicity of texts and ideas is included within one's interpretive model, this procedure does not pose a "methodological" problem, as it would in a "historical" or analytic study of texts from the past: the latter two must limit the study to one particular chronological period, author, or "system of thought."

Using von Balthasar's reference to the different senses of Scripture, one can say that the historico-critical method in theology ensures a good knowledge of the "letter" and historical detail, but not the "spirit" of the text. But the same can be said about the history of philosophy and, generally, the history of ideas. A historico-critical approach can ensure historical accuracy and establish grammatical and semantic details. For these purposes it is essential. But do we normally read philosophical or theological texts such as Plato or Augustine to learn about some historical peculiarities of ancient thought or the intricacies of medieval grammar? Is such a text simply a historical record to us? Are we interested only in the "perspective of a contemporary reader"? Or do we read such texts in order to engage our own thought, because those classics can still speak and be relevant to us, provoking our thinking about "perennial" issues—that is, for their "spirit"? In the latter case, our engagement with the text cannot possibly be either described or accomplished by "precise scientific" methods. It is a semi-intuitive process of interpretation that cannot be scientifically taught and can only be more or less adequately described in terms of Gadamer-style hermeneutics.

The hermeneutic approach can also gain from comparison with the postmodern trend in interpretation. While postmodern writers do acknowledge that tradition is something that is almost impossible to overcome, they nevertheless tend to view it as something that ideally should be overcome and subverted. According to the hermeneutic approach (for example, that of Gadamer), by contrast, tradition, as a conversation partner, offers us something quite valuable. Von Balthasar who, through his hermeneutic reading of ancient and medieval texts, attempts to trace the main principles of theological aesthetics in different historical periods, can serve as a model for re-stating the value of the tradition. His careful attitude and attention to the tradition—that should set the standard for the present study—can be demonstrated by a passage defending the use of the ancient philosophical tradition by a Christian theologian (*GL4* 18–19):

> [W]e wish to characterize our method as one of *integration* and not of evolution. Today 'evolution' is in favor: it is by denying the old that one breaks through to the new and, in order to justify this turning aside, discredits the tradition . . . and so persuades the contemporary world that it is quite pointless to make the tradition one's own or even to come to know the tradition at all. But if Christianity is to understand itself it must be bound in a healthgiving way to its historical origin. . . . Accordingly, the Christian ought to have a sensibility for human tradition which must be integrated.

Von Balthasar, or theologians in general, are not alone in assuming such a view of the tradition. Creative retrievals of traditional—for example, ancient—concepts are well known in contemporary philosophy. The retrieval of Aristotle's notions of φρόνησις and truth in art,[3] as well as of the ancient concept of truth as disclosure (ἀ-λήθεια) by Heidegger and Gadamer can serve as examples. Gadamer continuously stresses the relevance of some traditional concepts for contemporary reflection. During his critique of methodologism in the human sciences, for example, noting the prominence of the concept of the beautiful in metaphysics in the eighteenth century, he remarks that "this ancient conception of the beautiful can also be of service to the comprehensive hermeneutics" that emerges from this critique (*TM* 477). In another reaffirmation of the tradition, Gadamer mentions that some aspects of the phenomenon of the beautiful that are important to his discussion of hermeneutics can be derived through a return to Plato (*TM* 480).

Furthermore, while being aware of the "type of discourse," a hermeneute, unlike a postmodernist, is also sensitive to the meaning that can be derived from the text, while preserving a historical perspective. (The historicity of meaning is presupposed as one of the features of the hermeneutic process.) From a hermeneutic perspective, the postmodern approach leaves out the "hermeneutic center"—the actual object of interpretation, or idea that appears from the traditional text—ignoring

---

3. See Tracy, *Analogical Imagination*, 103, cited above.

the observation (cf. *TM* 383) that ultimately genuine understanding, like a genuine conversation, is not directed by the motives or agendas (conscious or otherwise)[4] of the one who understands (or of conversation partners), but by the desire to clarify the subject matter under discussion.[5] It appears much more productive to allow oneself to be guided by the text and see what comes out as a result of such a dialogue. No matter how one arrives at a certain understanding at any point of the dialogue (by "insight," focused thinking, etc.), the final verification will probably still be guided by the text, that is, it will depend on whether the initial understanding "fits" the text or not. Of course one can, to an extent, say that there is no such thing as the more or less stable "hermeneutic center" but that any subject matter can be subverted and turned around to serve any purpose, which is (according to postmodernists) what really happens. Following von Balthasar, we reply that the answer lies in the hermeneutic process itself that will be offered to the reader on the following pages. If hermeneutic "seeing" is at all possible, the reader will "see," in a convincing way, for him- or herself.

An important insight into the nature of interpretation in the humanities in general, with wide-ranging implications for the present study, can be gained from Tracy's view of systematic theology as essentially hermeneutic, as well as from his development of the Gadamerian analogy between hermeneutic and aesthetic experiences. (The latter, in its turn, is based on Heidegger's interpretation of the essence of the work of art in terms of disclosure of truth in the "Origin of the Work of Art.") For Tracy, religion is similar to art precisely because both are capable of disclosing truth in a certain immediate way to those who

---

4. Although, of course, often it is, in addition to other things.

5. One could object that sometimes what the subject matter is—not to mention how one should interpret it—is itself determined by the conversation and various underlying biases. For example, one could say that in any conversation, while assuming a hypocritical stance of "looking for the truth," each interlocutor, in fact, is simply pushing forward his or her preconceived position, i.e., simply exercises power (which, of course, *is* the initial impetus of many conversations). One must counter, however, that despite the (sometimes subconscious) ever-present combination of hypocrisy and power push, the genuinely responsible and "ethical" thinkers—and, what is probably more important, those who desire to maintain the conversation—will be forced to modify their position under the pressure of the evidence around the projected or hypothetical subject matter (the "hermeneutic center" that needs to be uncovered). In the end, the feeling of "shame" in the face of an obvious disagreement between the agenda they put forward and the mounting evidence to the contrary would force the interlocutors closer and closer to the open "center" of the projected subject matter that is being formed dynamically, like the eye of a hurricane, under the pressure from opposing forces.

are receptive to it or, according to von Balthasar, those who can "see."[6] Viewing artworks as disclosing some sort of truth turns out to be extremely productive as far as explaining contemporary art is concerned. For example, it can account for the fact that in contemporary artistic practice a urinal exhibited in an art gallery can be a perfectly legitimate art object. Indeed, any object can disclose something about reality, if only the mere fact that something *is*. At the same time, there would still be spectators to whom it appears simply as a urinal. The situation is exactly the same with more classical examples of art: although certain people may acknowledge them as art objects more readily than in the first example, they will not "see" anything in them that would warrant the admiration and respect given to these objects. Most religious traditions, from Christianity to Hinduism, share this feature: they all claim that the one who is able (and willing) to see will see. One cannot be persuaded by any other means, and may subsequently be accused of "blindness"[7] (just as, in the case of an art object, one can be accused of a "lack of aesthetic taste" or feeling). Von Balthasar applies the same principle to interpreting texts. He treats a traditional text *as if* it discloses the idea of aesthetic experience as revealing. To the one who is *able* and receptive enough to "see" this, von Balthasar's interpretation remains relevant. Otherwise, he or she is relegated to the status of being "blind."

A short digression must be made at this point to elaborate on the notions of "seeing" and "blindness."[8] Indeed, one can object that the

---

6. This must not be taken to mean "those who can see—and, better, agree with—my point of view" but the general openness to intellectual investigation, without which no hermeneutic process will be possible: see immediately below.

7. E.g., cf. Jesus referring to those who "heard but have not perceived" or "saw but have not understood," or a frequent example in Hindu or Buddhist writings when the unenlightened do not "see" even what is right in front of them.

8. The following paragraph resulted from a private exchange with R. Viladesau, who pointed out a potential for misunderstanding the terms "seeing" and "blindness" in terms of religious or intellectual intolerance ("if you don't see it my way you are mistaken"), which certainly cannot take place in a hermeneutic dialogue. It is a much more difficult question, however, when one comes to the position "if you are not prepared, or not able, to see it you are irrelevant to us and excluded from the dialogue." The noble indignation that instinctively arises (in a modern-day liberal-democratic Western person used to the idea of universal inclusiveness) upon hearing such a formulation is quite beside the point here. First, it is impossible to deny, without distorting historical reality, that in most spiritual traditions, be it religious, mystical, or even philosophical, if one is unwilling or unable to see the point, he or she is excluded from the dialogue and no provisions are made for such inclusiveness. Second, it is difficult to imagine, hermeneutically speaking, *how one can in principle* avoid such a position if the other party is unwilling to join the dialogue which presupposes the participation of both sides!

same religious traditions that put forth the notion of "seeing" also use elaborate apologetics in order to persuade through argument, or create "knowledge." A deeper look at the two processes, "seeing" and argument, shows that these two are not really opposed; the process of "understanding through persuasion" is not fundamentally different from "seeing how things are." Most scholars who portray "knowing" as a process superior to "seeing" (even physical seeing) simply misunderstand the nature of cognitive processes. As is well known to neuroscientists—but was known "intuitively," long before there were neuroscientists, to groups as diverse as critics of impressionism and scholars of Russian icons—"physical" seeing is not a simple process but is as complex, and therefore as "trainable," as thinking. The nature of cognitive processes in either thinking or seeing is the same.[9] This is precisely the point that hermeneutes such as Gadamer are trying to make by drawing parallels between knowing and "seeing" (as in the arts). Argument and persuasion simply help to point the audience in a certain direction and "open their eyes," just as someone can be taught how to "see" a work of art or physical reality in general. (A religious apologetics in this case can be viewed as an "attempt to show."[10] One cannot help remembering, in this connection, Plato's and Augustine's accounts of learning and the role of the teacher: the accounts that, after centuries of ridicule, suddenly gain credibility. No teacher is actually capable of teaching anyone anything, but only points one in the right direction!) If the audience is not willing to go in that direction, arguments and persuasion will not work: the audience "will not see" what one is trying to show them. And if they are positively disposed then they will. Thus one must understand references to "seeing" (or "hearing" for that matter) in the sense of being open to reality and having a proper disposition toward different or "deeper" ways of knowing, as opposed to being willfully "blind," that is, lacking such a disposition.

---

9. I.e., starting with preexisting 'Gestalts' and proceeding to perceive or form new patterns.

10. Obviously, "being able to see" can also be tradition-dependent (cf. the general thrust of Tracy's and Lindbeck's positions), i.e., within a certain cultural context or tradition one can expect most people to see. Again, certain things, perhaps, can be seen across traditions, and some are strictly tradition-specific, so locating oneself within a tradition is important. This proves, as will be explained below, that even intellectual disciplines that are not usually associated with theology share some traits with the latter, and in a sense can be considered as "systematic theologies."

Given this deepened understanding of "seeing," Tracy retrieves Gadamer's notion of the "classic" to show that the systematic theologian, like the art critic, interprets and presents the classic in a way that helps one "see" certain aspects of a particular religious tradition in the text, in a way that makes the text relevant to the contemporary situation.

Reflecting on Gadamer's and Tracy's ideas, one cannot help asking: but isn't this also what happens in all other disciplines contained under the human sciences? In fact, Tracy, noting that all systematic theologies are hermeneutic and that the "systematic theologian's major task is the reinterpretation of the tradition for the present situation" does not fail to acknowledge that "all serious interpretation of the tradition for the situation is called systematic theology."[11] This observation has serious implications, namely, that not only theology or art criticism, but also any philosophical system or any interpretation of tradition whatsoever is a sort of a systematic theology and therefore hermeneutic in nature. This observation is in perfect accord with Gadamer's idea that all hermeneutic experience is not unlike perception of an art work and thus, despite all "scientific" claims, is very much like "art criticism" and results in a disclosure of truth. This means that all academic discourse within a certain discipline, which can be viewed as a "faith tradition," is also "quasi-theological," and therefore hermeneutic in nature. On this issue, there is no significant disagreement between the hermeneutic and the postmodern tradition. Thus George Lindbeck, speaking of "intratextuality" as certain internal coherence that exists within a religious tradition or theological discourse (see below), also remarks that "in an extended or improper sense, something like intratextuality is characteristic of the descriptions of not only religion but also other forms of rule-governed human behavior from carpentry and mathematics to languages and cultures," although "meaning is more fully intratextual in semiotic systems . . . than in other forms of ruled human behavior."[12] Lindbeck concludes that, just as theology can be intratextual, in the sense of not only explaining religion "from within" but also describing anything "outside" in terms of this religion, or in terms of the narrative structures of its foundational texts (p. 114), so also can other disciplines—that is, a certain discipline can approach any text, even one

---

11. Tracy, *Analogical Imagination*, 64.
12. G. A. Lindbeck, *The Nature of Doctrine: Religion and Theology in a Postliberal Age* (Philadelphia: The Westminster Press, 1984), 114.

produced outside the said discipline, in terms of its own internal parameters.

The implication for the present study is that, in the manner appropriate for a theological tradition, a certain school of thought or an academic discipline within the Western intellectual tradition—in this case, aesthetics—can be taken as a "systematic theology" within a certain "faith system" that already believes that aesthetic experience is of great value. It would be absolutely legitimate, then, for "aesthetics as a systematic theology"—that is, intrinsically hermeneutic in nature—to look at the ancient and medieval textual tradition as at a pre-history of aesthetics. Within this "systematic" tradition of aesthetics, ancient and medieval texts can still disclose the meaning of aesthetic categories to an aesthetician in a way that is both contemporary and relevant, rather than being relegated, using Tracy's expression, to "cultural curiosities" and "record of their time."[13]

While the current approach can be viewed as a type of "systematics" in the field of aesthetics—thus contributing strictly to aesthetics as a philosophical discipline—at the same time it can make an important contribution to fundamental (philosophical) theology from an aesthetic perspective, and, if one maintains the unity of fundamental and systematic theologies advocated by von Balthasar, to systematic theology as well. Kerr notes that one of the implications of von Balthasar's project, as opposed to Barth and his followers, who totally reject the "analogy of being," is the importance of fundamental theology for dogmatics (*BEM* 3). While von Balthasar understands dogmatic (= systematic) theology as the "theory of rapture" that sees "'aesthetics' as a theory about the incarnation of God's glory" (*GL1* 125), he describes fundamental theology as the "theory of vision," in this case understanding "'aesthetics' in the Kantian sense as a theory about the perception of the form of God's self-revelation" (*GL1* 125). That is, von Balthasar sees the analysis of concrete experience ("seeing"), as well as a philosophical aesthetics of a Kantian type, as important components of his theological aesthetics. At the same time, the project of fundamental theology goes well with a deep interest in providing meaningful answers that are based on the retrieval of the tradition. According to Rino Fisichella, "bringing to light" the "knowledge of the hidden treasures of the tradition of faith" is an important part of fundamental theol-

---

13. Tracy, *Analogical Imagination*, 105, quoted above.

ogy that, "as apologetics, would lead its contemporaries to a faith that is responsible, meaningful, and enriching in a human way" (GW 298).

Viladesau, who, using Tracy's division of theology into fundamental, systematic, and practical, categorizes von Balthasar's approach as systematic[14]—a characterization that is, perhaps, in disagreement with the way von Balthasar saw his own work[15]—rightly follows von Balthasar's spirit when he sees his own contribution to theological aesthetics precisely in adding the fundamental aspect to the systematic. In Viladesau's understanding, fundamental theology starts "from below" and examines explicitly the "truth claims that are implicit in both the systematic (poetic-rhetorical) and the practical (ethical-political) forms of Christian discourse" (p. 37). As a way of enhancing the fundamental ("transcendental/anthropological," in his words) element in developing von Balthasar's (mostly systematic) theological aesthetics, Viladesau suggests supplementing the former's "more ecclesially oriented" theological aesthetics with a "fundamental theology conceived on 'transcendental' lines" but neither rationalist nor foundationalist.[16] He suggests that the latter should provide von Balthasar's aesthetics with "a transcendental anthropological warrant that permits a wider conversation *ad extra*" (p. 38). At the same time, systematic theological aesthetics will add concreteness to the heuristic and indeterminate transcendental method. The present study can be seen as continuing the project of enhancing the fundamental component of theological aesthetics in its hermeneutic version, through a conversation with the tradition, but from a more academic perspective. The most important contribution would be to demonstrate in a more academic manner, and not only exegetically-rhetorically, that the modern idea of beauty and aesthetic experience as revealing has been continuously present in the ancient and medieval tradition.

Another important implication for the present study can be drawn from the tendency of Heidegger and his followers to undermine the model of truth as correspondence. While Heidegger is best known for replacing the model of correspondence by the model of truth as disclosure, the proponents of the theory of "intratextuality" (the "Yale

---

14. Ibid., 56–57; Viladesau, *Theological Aesthetics*, 37.
15. Cf. his idea of the unity of systematic and fundamental approaches discussed above.
16. According to Viladesau (*Theological Aesthetics*, 37), von Balthasar actually does not deny the possibility of anthropological verification, but he sees it as secondary and complementary to his approach.

school," for instance), who can be seen as developing ideas implicit in late Heidegger, suggest a coherence model, which is also important for formulating the current approach. Language creates a symbolic world of meaning that is internally coherent: in it, what is true is equated with what is meaningful, and meaning determines reference.[17] In the same way, texts can also be inwardly coherent and contain their truth within themselves, without references to anything external. According to Lindbeck's account of the intratextual, or cultural-linguistic approach, in contradistinction to an "objective" approach that refers to external realities, "for cultural-linguists the meaning is immanent."[18] Lindbeck uses Geertz's (and originally Ryle's) idea that culture is something within which all sorts of phenomena can be intelligibly (or thickly) described (p. 115). Such "thick description" is all-encompassing and is a creative and demanding imaginative exercise, whose test of faithfulness "is the degree to which descriptions correspond to the semiotic universe paradigmatically encoded in holy writ" (p. 116).

However, not only religious texts can be interpreted "in terms of [their] immanent meanings" (p. 116). For example, great novels or works of literature "create their own world" with their own interpretive criteria and set of references whose description (for example, literary criticism) is an intratextual task (p. 117).[19] For the people who are steeped in these worlds created by texts (cf. the world of Scripture) "no world is more real than the ones they create" (p. 117). In this case, the text absorbs the world, not the world the text (p. 118). As an example from the Chris-

---

17. A good account of this understanding of language in Heidegger after the "turn" is given in C. Lafont (*Heidegger, Language and World Disclosure*), especially in chap. 2 (pp. 85ff.). Heidegger's notion of language as world-disclosing (pp. 89ff.), which is its primary function (communication being secondary), eventually develops into the idea that meaning determines reference (pp. 93ff.). Lafont summarizes this understanding of meaning and reference in chap. 4 (pp. 179-80). Understanding has priority over knowing and functions as world-disclosing. This means that coherence and meaningfulness take precedence over correspondence to something "in reality," that is, internally coherent meaning ultimately determines reference, which is "entirely immanent in language" (pp. 179-80). One can agree with Lafont in her criticism of the extreme version of the "immanence of meaning" model, which leads to a "reification of language." Yet overall such an understanding of discourse contributes to the development of the very helpful coherence model of truth in contemporary theology.

18. Lindbeck, *The Nature of Doctrine*, 114.

19. One could think of an example of some absurdist novel about, e.g., chairs instead of people, which would make perfect sense and be quite engaging. Another example is early computer games with very specific rules and various computer symbols instead of actual creatures; the games presented no difficulty to intelligibility at all, once the brain adapted to the new "reality."

tian tradition, one could recall subversive interpretations of the pagan tradition in terms of the Christian Scriptures by the early Apologists[20] and Augustine, or the Christian interpretation of Aristotle in the thirteenth century. Thus Christian Scriptures or great novels can be viewed as intrinsically meaningful narrative structures that form the "external" world according to their own patterns. Of course, such internal coherence/meaningfulness is not reserved exclusively for religious or literary texts. Perhaps all great philosophies are such precisely because they are more persuasive and appealing in their internal coherence, and not because they are "truer" than others in terms of correspondence.[21]

The idea that something internally coherent can be by the same token meaningful without involving the concept of truth as correspondence is extremely important. It allows one to eliminate the need for constantly seeking some correspondence with an external object as a criterion of truth, legitimacy, or value, and instead switch to the criteria of internal coherence, that is, given the interpreted material, how well a certain interpretation holds together. For our present task, it means that creating an internally coherent "world" of aesthetics would allow one to interpret "external" material in terms of aesthetics also. Furthermore, if such an interpretation of a traditional text in terms of aesthetics is internally coherent, it can, merely by virtue of its coherence, be viewed as meaningful or true. The texts that are internally coherent and persuasive, as, for example, von Balthasar's interpretation of the tradition in terms of theological aesthetics, can still be meaningful, although they may not correspond to anything "in reality" ("medieval author's intention").

At the same time, the current study will make certain adjustments to a strictly "systematic-theological" approach to texts that is based on the principles of hermeneutics as practiced by von Balthasar and formulated by Gadamer. First, the interpretation should not turn into a pure exegesis of a theological kind, as, for example, that practiced by the Apologists, where the original text is fully subverted by the new ideology. Instead, the interpretation must be based on the text as its reference

20. Cf. D. Dawson, *Allegorical Readers and Cultural Revision in Ancient Alexandria* (Berkeley/Los Angeles/Oxford: University of California Press, 1992). Also cf. my review of this book in *Literary Research* 23, no. 1 (1995): 21.

21. After all, Neitzsche had suggested in *The Gay Science* that the success of philosophy lies not in the quality of its arguments but in changing the taste of its public: cf. Hammermeister, *German Aesthetic Tradition*, 148.

point, constantly revolving around its hermeneutic center and "listening" to what follows from its internal logic. Second, although one may treat traditional texts to a certain degree as contemporary "conversation partners," one must clearly situate the interpreter with respect to the historical dimension of the text. In the case of von Balthasar, his theological position is of great assistance to his hermeneutics. The idea of the unity of Christian theological vision allows him to draw on a number of traditional texts from different historical periods. Since they all must show unity of vision, a certain continuity is assured, and one can engage the tradition at any point. Thus von Balthasar can view history in terms of Scripture and the Christian tradition. At the same time, he is sharply aware of the fact that he is dealing with the pre-history or the historical extension of contemporary Christianity.

But how can von Balthasar's hermeneutic approach to the interpretation of traditional texts in terms of Christian theology be applied in the present case to the interpretation of ancient and medieval texts in terms of aesthetics, but not necessarily theologically? In line with what was said above, the current approach can be seen as a "systematic theology" of sorts that interprets traditional texts in terms of aesthetics. At the same time, one must take into consideration von Balthasar's attention to the historicity of texts, which, of course, is typical for the whole post-Heideggerian tradition and is stressed by Gadamer. Traditional texts will be examined not just in terms of aesthetics, but as a historical extension of modern aesthetic ideas, with full attention paid to the temporal distance. In this case, von Balthasar's idea of the unity of tradition can still be used, although in a slightly different sense. Instead of the unity of the Christian theological vision, one would, applying Gadamer's reflections on hermeneutics, examine the unity of a particular aesthetic concept—the idea of aesthetic experience as revelatory—in its historical extension. One would take this idea, which currently exists in the mind of a contemporary aesthetician, and examine how it extends in history, through various stages of its formation. The scholar pursuing the task of reestablishing the historical dimension of aesthetics will first become aware of the texts themselves that form the pre-history of aesthetic ideas in modern minds, despite the fact that, for the authors of those texts, it might not have been a unified area of experience. (Von Balthasar clearly shows that, when analyzing traditional texts, he speaks of the modern idea of aesthetics being only implicit in these texts. He states, for example, that works of Aquinas, Albert, Anselm, Bonaventure radiate this power of beauty "whether or not they are conscious of the aesthetic moment" [GL1 78].)[22] Further, after engaging in a dialogue with classical, medieval, and modern texts, a more complete picture will emerge of how this unified aesthetic concept is gradually formed from a disjointed chorus of traditional texts.

Further observations must situate the current study in relation to von Balthasar's approach. The difficulty of writing academically about von Balthasar because of the "artistic-poetic" nature of his work has been noted in scholarly literature. The only truly academic option appears to be to study his sources and influences.[23] The two other options would be re-phrasing or summarizing his work,[24] or—perhaps, the most productive option—becoming a disciple or a "Balthasarian" and writing in the manner of von Balthasar. The first two avenues having been explored in the past, the present approach most closely resembles the third option, as it develops its own hermeneutics of traditional texts in terms of aesthetics through incorporating some features of von Balthasar's approach. At the same time, while von Balthasar's treatment of traditional sources provides a hermeneutic model for this study, the latter in many ways will go beyond what von Balthasar has done. The most significant differences will be broadening his approach and at the same time making it more precise, so as to involve in the conversation non-theological circles, as well as employing the methods of the historical school, without fully subscribing to its hermeneutic premises.

Despite its potential for contributing to both systematic and fundamental theology, the current approach will be neither systematic-theological (understood as rhetorical-poetical, addressing the community of faith) nor strictly speaking fundamental-theological (as in theology addressed to academia), but more traditionally academic. It can be included under the academic discipline of the "history of ideas" or "intellectual history" that draws both on the positive achievements of the historical school and on the tools of philology.

---

22. The most extreme case of an analysis of the "implicit aesthetics" of Thomas Aquinas is a book by G. Pöltner (1978). From the point of view of the historical school, his analysis is almost entirely groundless: see criticism in L. Müller ("Das 'Schöne'"). At the same time, from the point of view of a "systematic-theological" hermeneutic approach Pöltner's analysis is entirely legitimate, and the book was praised by von Balthasar himself.

23. Cf. the collection edited by K. Lehmann and W. Kasper, *Gestalt und Werk*.

24. A perfect example is J. A. Kay, *Theological Aesthetics*.

The current study will preserve some of the hermeneutic features of von Balthasar's approach to conversation with the tradition, as well as his perceptive insights into the selection of texts with "revelatory-aesthetic" contents. However, the approach will become more rigorous, and the selection of texts will be narrowed by applying historico-chronological or thematic criteria. Applying a more rigorous thematic criterion means that our definition of 'aesthetic' must become more precise than just "direct seeing." For example, we can focus on something that necessarily involves the senses (i.e., actual aesthetic experience, in the Kantian sense), or at least on clear parallels and analogies with phenomena that are aesthetic in the true sense (such as earthly beauty). In the end, we hope to create a bridge between the more traditional academic approach and the exegetic-poetic-rhetorical style of von Balthasar.

So what are the essential features of the current approach, in contrast with that of von Balthasar? First of all, von Balthasar's approach—which fits very well within the pattern typical for systematic theology as a kind of rhetoric and exegesis—focuses not on analysis but on creating a *Gestalt* or "image" of a particular text or author. He takes the most critical issue at the core of the author's thought (the "spirit" of the work) and examines its relation to the notion of the 'aesthetic' broadly understood. Few particulars are given, only a general picture and a broad characteristic—for example, "liturgical-hymnic" aesthetics in the case of pseudo-Dionysius. Another typical feature of his approach, which is more in line with literary criticism, is the finding of repeating "themes" that recur in multiple texts within one author or tradition, or even across traditions, instead of examining just one text in detail. The current study will bypass the stage of re-creating the author's *Gestalt* and go directly to the text. Instead of the "author" as a whole, the whole corpus of writings, or the whole tradition of texts, the analysis will focus, at every particular stage, on one continuous text and provide a close reading of that text, letting it speak for itself and following the development of its inner logic. Thus, instead of focusing on the unity of a *Gestalt* or a theme, the study will use, as its basis, the hermeneutic unity of a continuous text.

The second difference is in the criteria for treating several texts or authors as a "tradition" bound by a certain unity. As a theologian, von Balthasar tries to derive a theological aesthetics from the inner content of revelation. Hence he goes back to the tradition with a preconception of the "unified vision" of aesthetic experience as revealing that permeates not only Christian but also pre-Christian texts—simply because, according to his aesthetic vision, reality itself possesses a certain aesthetic quality, or an ability to reveal instantly deeper truths, and this quality cannot escape notice during any period in history. The unity of aesthetic vision that comes from the same source can be "seen" directly and is sufficient for both provoking and discovering "fascinating dialogues . . . across the centuries" (GL2 22) between completely diverse texts from different traditions. While the initial section of this study, indeed, provides an overview of von Balthasar's own hermeneutics, as well as of the main concepts that he derives from the tradition, the analysis of ancient and medieval texts that follows does not take for granted his preconception of the unity of vision as the criterion for viewing a group of texts as one whole when examining particular ancient and medieval authors. Our dialogue with the tradition is not an attempt to derive a theological aesthetics—from the position of a Christian theologian—but is simply an attempt to find out what understanding of aesthetic experience transpires from the texts. Von Balthasar's apologetic or fundamental-theological task—to show the agreement of a variety of texts from many historical periods and traditions on the ground that there is something in reality that corresponds to the idea of aesthetic revelation in these texts—here becomes simply historical: to find out whether in ancient and medieval Western thought there is historically a consistent and continuous tradition of interpreting aesthetic experience as revealing.

The differences in the task and preconceptions spell a different attitude to the "historical method." While retaining the critical attitude to the narrowly understood "scientific" methodology of the historical school—typical for Gadamer, von Balthasar, and Tracy—the current study makes use of its important achievements: precision in tracing the continuity of ideas based on textual evidence, and the continuity of texts based on historical record. It is an attempt to present a tradition consisting of several texts (from Plato and the Stoics through Cicero to Augustine and Bonaventure) where unity and continuity are established on historical and philological grounds, such as the familiarity with, or the use of earlier texts by the later tradition. Thus, von Balthasar's "unity of vision" will be supplemented by the historically and philologically documented continuity of texts.

Even with all the precise instruments of the historical school and textual scholarship in its arsenal, the study will remain essentially hermeneutic in nature. One must keep in mind that establishing a historical or philological continuity of a textual tradition does not ground the initial hermeneutic preconception of the unity of the concept of the aesthetic that extends in history beyond the modern period where it first becomes "officially" a unified area. Such a hermeneutic enterprise, then, can only be enhanced by taking into consideration historical details, so far as they become available.

It is crucial for the current project to find the right "partners" with whom to dialogue. Von Balthasar's choice of conversation partners fell on those authors and texts that were suitable for his idea of theological aesthetics.[25] His example shows that, in spite of attempts to set rigid criteria (for example, what constitutes "aesthetic"), hermeneutic principles of exclusion or inclusion always remain rather subjective and intuitive and ultimately focus on the sources that would "make a good case" and contribute to the consistency of the discussion. In the present case, our attention must be centered on the texts that will support the concept of aesthetic as revealing. It is irrelevant to the project that there are many texts that do not contain this idea or show no interest in aesthetics, just as the existence of all the people who do not participate, or are not interested in a given conversation is irrelevant to its subject matter.[26]

A further clarification must be added. As a systematic theologian (according to Tracy's classification), von Balthasar is writing from *within* the Christian theological tradition, which is to say, he practices a rhetorical-poetic interpretation of "religious classics." In his case, certain things are taken for granted, and his selection of texts favors Christian texts as "main" over ancient or pagan texts viewed only as "precursors" of the Christian aesthetic vision. The present study does not start with an attitude that favors the Christian "aesthetic vision": it includes pagan or purely philosophical texts in their own right, not as precursors to, but rather together with, Christian.[27] The historical-philosophical

---

25. Cf. I. Murillo in *GW* 215.

26. Of course, from a postmodern perspective that emphasizes ideology, those who are excluded (or those who exclude something from their conversation) are just as important as those who are included. However, this data only determines the position of the given subject matter regarding certain power groups, or undermines any idealist claims to "universal truth." One can still address the movement of interpretation within a certain conversation.

27. Which is closer to the "fundamental" approach, if one is to use Tracy's classification.

emphasis of the study, combined with a hermeneutic approach, means that it is based, not on von Balthasar's theological preconception of "aesthetic vision," but on a general hermeneutic preconception of the modern idea of the aesthetic as extending back in history beyond the eighteenth century. Operating within the Western European[28] intellectual tradition and tracing the history of the idea of aesthetic experience as revealing, the present study views the tradition of pagan philosophy (e.g., from Plato to the Stoics and Cicero) as constituting a historical-intellectual continuity with the Christian tradition through the influence of texts and ideas, and not by virtue of a theological "unity of vision." The ancient tradition is viewed as a continuous extension of the medieval back in history, not because it can be seen as "pre-Christian theology," but on historical and philological grounds. For this reason, although von Balthasar's initial selection of texts and authors is taken as the basis, this selection will be further limited by the requirement of forming a consistent and continuous historical-textual tradition. Thus the inclusion of each author or text in the second part of the study will be preceded by a brief historico-philological introduction detailing the textual influence of earlier texts upon the text or author under discussion, and of the current text on the later tradition (the influence of Plato and Cicero on Augustine, and of the latter on Bonaventure, etc.).

We should add a few comments about the contents as a further limiting criterion in the selection of texts. The objection of the historical school that aesthetics is a modern notion and therefore should not be looked for in the earlier tradition has been effectively eliminated earlier in the discussion of the hermeneutic approach. The idea of the "historical extension" of a modern notion, as well as the idea of the "classic" always remaining relevant through reinterpretation by a "systematic" tradition, fully justifies looking back at ancient and medieval texts with the eye of an aesthetician. The possibility of seeing a pre-history of modern aesthetic ideas in traditional texts clearly has been at the center of many a scholar's approach; von Balthasar considers Plato to be the father of "philosophical aesthetic," a modern notion (GL4 213). He also applies the term "aesthetics" to Plotinus and draws parallels between the Intellect in his thought and the notion of the sublime in modern idealist

---

28. Just as is the case with von Balthasar, who freely admits that his area of competence limits his study to the Mediterranean tradition (GL1 11), this study will be limited to a certain geographic area, i.e., the Mediterranean and Western Europe.

philosophy (GL4 300). Commenting on von Balthasar's work, Murillo freely speaks of the possibility of deriving "transcendental aesthetics"— a modern notion—from Greek philosophy, as von Balthasar has done —aesthetics that is still of value for modern "theology of glory" (*Herrlichkeitstheologie*).[29] The objection that there was no special field of aesthetics prior to the eighteenth century was also addressed earlier in our study: namely, by pointing out that, for many great figures in philosophical aesthetics even after the eighteenth century, "aesthetics" did not necessarily mean focusing on aesthetic experience for its own sake, but was often simply a way of doing philosophy by using aesthetic analogies to solve other problems. Following these great figures, this study, instead of focusing on a fully articulated philosophical aesthetics—which, indeed, was almost non-existent at the time—will focus on ancient and medieval philosophical and theological discussions in which aesthetic analogies were used.

The question remains, however, what constitutes an "aesthetic analogy"; exactly what sorts of content are to be sought? Indeed, the historical fact that aesthetics was not an acknowledged discipline prior to the eighteenth century is in no way removed by the hermeneutic approach. That is to say, ancient and medieval texts themselves do not identify their contents as 'aesthetics.' It may be useful, first, to describe what types of phenomena the aesthetic analogy is employed to illustrate, i.e., what is metaphorically referred to as "aesthetic," or perceived as analogous to aesthetic. Von Balthasar, again, suggests a useful model. As was shown above, he understands "aesthetic" in a modern way, as something that has to do with direct "seeing" or intuiting without a concept. The idea clearly goes back to Kant, but von Balthasar is firm in distinguishing his direct aesthetic "seeing"—according to him, derived from the ancient Greek thought[30]—from the transcendentalism of the "Kantians."[31] "Aesthetic" in the ancient and medieval traditions,

---

29. I. Murillo in *GW* 217. Cf. ibid.: "For the biblical revelation a dialogue is possible only with a transcendental aesthetics" that can be traced from Homer to Plotinus to the Renaissance and the Baroque. The recent study *Neuplatonismus und Ästhetik* (2007) freely uses the concept of transcendental aesthetics as derivable from Neoplatonic thought, ancient to early modern.

30. See passage on Plato from GL4 177 quoted earlier, in Chapter 2, to support this conviction.

31. The term, however, does not necessarily include Kant himself who, according to von Balthasar, is more open to the possibility of direct seeing. See the discussion in Chapter 2 regarding the problems with the appellation "Kantians" as used by von Balthasar, as well as with what he attributes to them.

then, according to his view, includes maintaining a direct and immediate contact with reality. He sees a clear difference between defining the "beyond" in terms of its transcendental or *a priori* conditions and "seeing" the beyond or its presence immediately. While von Balthasar detects immediate perception or "seeing" in Antiquity and in the Middle Ages, he does not find it in contemporary thinkers (with the exception of some poets or writers), and he is vigorously opposed to the transcendental approach of the "Kantians" (among whom he lists Fichte and Rahner). We must note that this division of the Mediterranean and Western European intellectual tradition into the followers of the "transcendental" approach and the supporters of "direct seeing"—at times apparent in von Balthasar and his interpreters—is perhaps inaccurate and in any case too complex an issue to deal with in the present study.[32] For these reasons, we will not attempt to resolve any of these terminological or conceptual distinctions or classify an author in terms of these two "systems of thought."

Condensing the Balthasarian understanding of what sort of experience is considered to be analogous to aesthetic, we can now formulate a search program: to trace those instances in ancient and medieval texts where the idea of "direct seeing"—or the immediate manifestation or revelation of something hidden, taken as simply as that—is most clearly expressed and hermeneutically most transparent. The hermeneutic task will be to engage such texts and find out whether they really do refer to "direct seeing" into the nature of phenomena. As further analysis will show, Plato and the Stoic tradition (partly as transmitted through

---

32. Some of the more obvious problems are as follows. An attempt to interpret ancient or medieval philosophy in "transcendental" terms runs into the problem of a lack of division into the immanent and transcendent, e.g., in the materialistic Stoic thought, in which both the "earthly" and the "divine" are part of the same type of reality, or in late medieval philosophy (cf. Duns Scotus), in which all reality, including the divine, seems to be at least theoretically intelligible. At the same time, one wonders if Plato's understanding of τὸ καλόν (see Chapter 5 below), which is ultimately impossible to reach, really precludes all interpretation in terms of transcendental philosophy, as von Balthasar claims. The same can be said about the Neoplatonic notion of the One (Plotinus et al.) later associated with the Christian God as completely outside our reach (e.g., in pseudo-Dionysius and medieval mystics). The "transcendental" movement is even easier to ascribe to Augustine (see Chapter 7). At the same time, as von Balthasar rightly notices, Kant himself is clearly receptive to the idea of direct seeing that von Balthasar associates with Plato. For more on the topic of "transcendence" in relation to ancient thought see: J. Halfwassen, "Metaphysik und Transzendenz," *Jahrbuch für Religionsphilosophie* 1 (2002): 13–27; idem, "Philosophie als Transzendieren: Der Aufstieg zum höchsten Prinzip bei Platon und Plotin," *Bochumer Philosophisches Jahrbuch für Antike und Mittelalter* 3 (1998): 29–42.

Cicero) will definitely merit attention, as will the corpus of Augustine's writings. Regarding later medieval authors such as Bonaventure, one must answer the question whether the established theological system of their time still allowed for the phenomenon of direct seeing in the order of evidence. At the same time, many texts and authors will clearly be excluded: anything based purely on concept, for instance, or anything that has to do with the arts or beauty (formally within the purview of modern aesthetics) but has no reference to direct seeing as a way of providing evidence.

However, if we were to accept (as von Balthasar and others often do) that the mere reference to "direct seeing" in a text is sufficient to classify it metaphorically as "aesthetic" and therefore necessarily belonging in our study, we would be encumbered by a massive amount of material. (The application of such broad and unreflected criteria as "art" or "beauty" would have a similar result.)[33] At the same time, one would have to accept the charge that these texts really have nothing to do with the spirit of philosophical or theological aesthetics as defined above, since they do not explicitly contain any analogies with actual aesthetic experience. Indeed, the example of von Balthasar proves that many traditional texts can be interpreted in terms of references to direct seeing in a purely intellectual sense, that is, seeing the truth of a concept from the concept itself, as in the cases of the Stoics, Anselm, or Duns Scotus.[34] Some observations made by Kant show which experiences as such, without further "truly aesthetic" analogies, should be excluded from the purview of aesthetics. For Kant, there are no strictly speaking intellectual or moral beauties (cf. the idea of "spiritual beauty" or "beauty of virtues" common in Antiquity and the Middle Ages). According to Kant, these expressions are "not quite accurate, because beauty and sublimity are aesthetical modes of representation which would not be found in us at all if we were pure intelligences."[35] Thus the emphasis on sense experience is very helpful in further limiting the current selection. As many a scholar of ancient and medieval aesthetics has discovered, it is very tempting to include under aesthetics all that the earlier authors call "beautiful" or all that falls under "direct seeing," especially a whole

---

33. Cf. the general study by de Bruyne cited in the Introduction and a study of Augustine by Fontanier discussed below in Chapter 7.
34. These topics will be discussed below: see Chapters 6 and 8.
35. §29, *Gen. r.*, p. 111.

range of purely intellectual, spiritual, or moral phenomena. However, according to Kant, in order to qualify as "aesthetic" these phenomena must necessarily contain an *aisthetic* (in the Greek sense of αἴσθησις) or sensual element. At the same time, Kant indicates which types of moral, intellectual, or spiritual phenomena are susceptible to analogies with aesthetic experience. For example, the morally good should rather be called sublime (p. 112). The same holds for enthusism (p. 112) or *apatheia* (absence of affection, p. 113) which is also "noble," together with some "strenuous" affections (in contrast to "languid" affections, which are beautiful, p. 113). At the same time, Kant makes an important remark about the transcendental elements in moral law and religion, hinting at the possibility of extending aesthetics beyond the notions of beauty and sublimity, but only into the areas that deal directly with sense experience. "The object of a pure and unconditioned intellectual satisfaction," he writes, "is the moral law in that might which it exercises in us over all mental motives that precede it. This might only makes itself aesthetically known to us through sacrifices (which causing a feeling of deprivation . . . in return discloses in us an unfathomable depth of this supersensible faculty, with consequences extending beyond our ken)" (p. 111). The feeling of deprivation in the sensible experience of the sacrifice—like the "negative presentation" in the experience of the sublime—also triggers the feeling of the transcendent. In this way, Kant provides an important corrective to von Balthasar's broad preconception of the aesthetic as simply something that reveals or involves direct seeing. While allowing for an analogy between aesthetic experience and phenomena other than directly *aisthetic* (i.e., those that deal with the senses)—such as intellectual, moral, or religious—Kant maintains that to qualify as "aesthetic," either the phenomena themselves (in the present case, as described in texts) or at least analogies to these phenomena, in addition to being somehow directly revealing, should also involve actual sensible aesthetic experience. We thus arrive at our next limiting criterion as far as the contents of texts is concerned: the texts to be examined must contain, in addition to the idea of "direct seeing," an explicit analogy or parallel with aesthetic (as in *aisthetic*) experience—something perceptible by our senses, such as beauty or sublimity in natural objects or art. This corrective will comfortably limit the number of contexts, eliminating some of von Balthasar's examples that deal with purely intellectual experiences; at the same time it will eliminate the problem of overinterpretation and thinking too much into the text and will thereby satisfy even the most severe critics.

In sum, the primary selection of particular figures and texts for a dialogue will be based on von Balthasar's intuitive judgment about the "spirit" and *Gestalt* of the work[36] and further narrowed using more rigid criteria. First of all, the texts that have more explicit and extended references to actual aesthetic (= sensible) experience, or contain analogies with such experiences, will be preferred over those that just deal with "seeing" or purely "intellectual" beauty. For example, pseudo-Dionysius, who writes much about the concept of beauty, but is definitely not interested or deeply involved in the perception of sensible beauty in the way Augustine is, is likely to be excluded, as opposed to the authors that do engage direct sense experience.[37] Further, texts that are known historically to have been in dialogue with each other and present a continuous hermeneutic tradition will be preferred over those that are only broadly connected by being part of the same cultural tradition. This second criterion will more or less exclude such prominent figure as Plotinus, whose texts—despite his relevance to aesthetics in general and his importance to the Eastern and post-medieval Western tradition—were not directly known to the Western Middle Ages (e.g., to Bonaventure).

A brief overview of von Balthasar's selection using the criteria outlined above leaves us with the following list. Plato is the first major author who is both interested in the direct sensible experience of beauty and well known—both indirectly and directly—to the Western intellectual tradition, including the thirteenth century.[38] According to von Balthasar, with Plato "is born that philosophical aesthetic of the grand style, to which even Plotinus will be able to make no significant alteration" (GL4 213). Plato's views on beauty were eagerly incorporated into the Christian tradition, both Eastern and Western. "Transcendental aesthetics," writes Murillo, was "first thematized by Plato," and biblical revelation does not remove but only strengthens the "metaphysical depths" of τὸ καλόν (Murillo in GW 218).

36. In fact, if one browses through the secondary literature on ancient and medieval aesthetics, even the works that pre-date von Balthasar (see bibliography in the notes to the Introduction and to chapters on particular authors in Part Two), one would find that his selection of ancient and medieval texts, with a few exceptions, is actually rather standard, perhaps because some ancient and medieval authors are simply more interested in aesthetic matters.
37. To some extent this concerns Plotinus as well.
38. E.g., Büttner (*Antike Ästhetik*) also starts his analysis of ancient aesthetics with Plato.

Another group of texts—the Stoic tradition (in particular, Cicero's Latinized version of it), which is based directly on Plato in the area of aesthetics—fits all the present selection criteria but is definitely neglected by von Balthasar (and most other scholars), who leaves only a few brief phrases for it. By carefully reading the surviving texts and tracing their continuing influence in the Western Middle Ages, we came to the conclusion that von Balthasar missed an important link in the history of revelatory aesthetics that needs to be restored. The Stoic aesthetic tradition as transmitted by Cicero is incorporated directly by Augustine and, both directly and through Augustine, by the Middle Ages.

Despite von Balthasar's claim that Plotinus doesn't go beyond Plato (GL4 213, cf. above), this figure would certainly merit attention from the point of view of the subject matter. At the same time, there is no direct textual tradition of Plotinian texts in the Western Middle Ages (up to the thirteenth and early fourteenth century, where the second part of this study chronologically ends). In fact, even Augustine's knowledge of Plotinus is still a subject of heated scholarly debates (see Chapter 7). Even from the point of view of the subject matter, Plotinus presents a stark contrast with Plato, with the latter's attention to immediate experience of sensible beauty. Plotinus's pathos is very different: a mystical and meditative writer, he can be seen as using Platonic aesthetic themes as metaphors on the way to achieving another goal. Finally, Plotinian thought, with its long history of modern idealist interpretations, is such a complicated issue in itself that even von Balthasar seems to be seriously entangled in trying to determine its relation to "seeing" as opposed to the transcendental approach—one more reason not to select him as a major figure in this analysis.

Augustine presents a clear fit, with his attention to concrete aesthetic experience and his fundamental role as a direct textual and intellectual link between ancient thought (Plato and the Stoics) and the later medieval tradition, up to the thirteenth (e.g., Bonaventure) and fourteenth centuries. Pseudo-Dionysius, another late ancient/early medieval aesthetician on von Balthasar's list, is almost as influential as Augustine for the later medieval tradition, nourishing both the Franciscan (up to Bonaventure and Duns Scotus) and the German Dominican thought (from Albert the Great to Meister Eckhart). However, this mystic has little regard for sensible beauties and his treatment of aesthetics is almost purely intellectual and spiritual in kind.

Anselm—another important author in von Balthasar—will not be selected as a major figure, for the same reason. Although aesthetic criteria play an important role in his vision of the divine economy, the concept of beauty is for him mostly associated with the abstract intellectual notions of order and harmony, and not with concrete and sensible aesthetic experience. By contrast, Bonaventure, inheriting the elements of Augustinian, Dionysian, and Anselmian thought, is acutely aware of our direct experience of sensible beauty. In addition to that, he is the first to articulate clearly the aesthetic notion of "Christ's form" that is crucial to von Balthasar's theological aesthetics, and in general the Christocentric movement that is central to von Balthasar is also central to Bonaventure.[39] Who better, then, to complete this study intended to be a tribute to and development of von Balthasar's hermeneutic project?

39. Cf. Treitler, in *GW* 184.

Part Two

The Ancient & Medieval Horizons

CHAPTER 5

The Platonic Tradition

Our first ancient author, Plato, presents a challenge before we even start: to assess his legacy in aesthetics in one chapter is all but impossible. Therefore we will limit our study to a rather narrow task: Plato's contribution to the idea of aesthetic experience as revealing, where 'aesthetic' is understood as described in the preceding chapters. As will become clear from what follows, Plato is one of the main sources of inspiration for von Balthasar's discussion of theological aesthetics in Antiquity precisely as someone who noticed and described the revealing aspect of worldly beauty. However, with so much having been written on Plato's aesthetics, can one add anything new to the topic? In order to address this question, it will be useful to start with an overview of the topics and issues that have been brought up in recent academic discussions of Plato in the area of aesthetics. The work of C. Janaway and J. M. E. Moravcsik, both of whom wrote entries on Plato for the 1998 *Encyclopedia of Aesthetics*,[1] exemplifies what is currently being studied and discussed. (Their assessment of the actual terminology of "beauty" in Plato and the Greek thought in general, detailed in the aforesaid entries, will be discussed later in this chapter.)

Unfortunately, just as is the case with "medieval aesthetics,"[2] none of the studies of "ancient aesthetics" contains explicitly elaborated hermeneutic principles for approaching ancient texts in terms of modern concepts, nor is any based on such principles implicitly.[3] As will become

---

1. M. Kelly, ed., *Encyclopedia of Aesthetics*, 4 vols. (New York/Oxford: Oxford University Press, 1998).
2. See O. V. Bychkov, "A Propos of Medieval Aesthetics."
3. Cf., once again, Büttner's recent study (*Antike Ästhetik*) and my discussion of it in *The Classical Review* 57, no. 2 (2007): 308–9. The Introduction to the 2007 collection *Neuplatonis-*

clear later, some studies (such as those of Janaway and Moravcsik) are quite sensitive to the differences between ancient and modern terminology and at least try to avoid modern misinterpretations of individual terms. However, as far as defining the subject "aesthetics" is concerned, most such studies simply include issues and concepts related to "art" and "beauty" (the two notions that fall under "aesthetics" in modern times), whether they constitute a unified area of reflection in Antiquity or not. As this study will eventually show, many points of discussion that arise as a result of such an approach are rooted precisely in this unreflected and uncritical joining together on modern grounds of that which was never joined in pre-modern times. At the same time, the lack of breadth and hermeneutic consistency in such studies results in missing obvious commonalities between ancient and modern thought in the areas where the classic German Idealist tradition in aesthetics, including von Balthasar, has always perceived some continuity of issues: something that this study will attempt to elucidate more critically.

It is therefore no surprise that one of the themes prevalent in current scholarly literature on ancient aesthetics is Plato's critical attitude toward the arts (art being one of the "stock" notions of modern aesthetics).[4] As we have seen, however, the question of art as such is relevant to this study only insofar as the actual *aisthetic* experience of art is used in creating parallels and analogies that illustrate the ability of aesthetic experience to reveal something immediately. Since it is not immediately clear whether Plato's critique involves such revelatory aspects of art, we will leave the reexamination of Plato's attitude towards the arts in the *Republic* to the end of this chapter. However, the notion of the beautiful or beauty, which is more immediately relevant to our subject, is often discussed as well. Janaway, for example, attempts to fit Plato's notion τὸ καλόν within the modern Kantian concept of "aesthetic," which he understands as a special kind of pleasure (a typical stereotype of modern aesthetics).[5] His study still revolves within the old unreflected framework, which fails to examine how one can still speak of "aesthetics" in application to ancient thought in ways that are hermeneutically viable

---

mus und Ästhetik cited above is somewhat of an exception, but even there the discussion is minimal; see my review of this book in *The Classical Review* 59, no. 2 (2009): 436–38.

4. Cf., e.g., C. Janaway, *Images of Excellence: Plato's Critique of the Arts* (Oxford: Clarendon Press, 1998); also see the chapter on Plato in Büttner, *Antike Ästhetik*, where a similar pattern is followed.

5. See Janaway's chapter "The Fine and the Beautiful" in *Images of Excellence*, 58–79.

and do not represent a simple forcing of one conceptual framework onto another.⁶ We must also note that the study says nothing on the revealing capacity of τὸ καλόν in Plato, which is routinely noticed in the German philosophical tradition.⁷ The selection of dialogues discussed in the study is typical for modern scholars who deal with aesthetic issues in Plato: the *Symposion, Hippias Major,* and *Phaedrus.*

Moravcsik discusses Plato's theory of art and beauty in similar terms⁸ in relation to Kant's third *Critique*. The author coins the term "noetic aspiration," understood as "eros needed for insight and understanding," and Plato's thought is discussed in terms of this thesis. According to Moravcsik, inspiration (such as comes from art or the experience of beauty), in addition to serving enjoyment only, has an instrumental value: it contributes to the quest for understanding at higher (theoretical) levels. Such understanding of aesthetic experience is contrasted with Kant's autonomous realm for the aesthetic, where it has a value of its own.⁹ This essay examines such topics as the role and denunciation of artists in the *Republic*, and the status of artifacts as something "three times removed" from the ideas or forms. Moravcsik's conclusion, not surprisingly, is that there is no separate realm for art and beauty in Plato, but that all is aimed at some cognitively and ontologically higher realm.

6. The procedure goes as follows: such and so is the modern definition of "aesthetics" (i.e., one of many existing definitions, without a genealogical analysis of origin); let us see if it also works in Plato (without a preceding analysis of whether there are hermeneutic grounds in Plato's texts for this particular modern definition). In contrast, a more hermeneutically adaptive approach would be sensitive to the fact that if one starts with the issues and problems characteristic of the modern discipline of aesthetics and attempts to locate similar issues in ancient thought, one might not necessarily end up with the same concepts or terms that are discussed in modern aesthetics. It is only the continuity of problematics that will remain.

7. In Heidegger, Gadamer, et al. Although some German studies, such as Büttner's *Antike Ästhetik*, also say nothing about the revealing capacity of τὸ καλόν, other studies (several essays in *Neuplatonismus und Ästhetik* [2007], for example), do follow the German tradition of discussing this notion in Plato and Plotinus in terms of its revelatory capacity: see J. Halfwassen, "Schönheit und Bild im Neuplatonismus" (NA 43–57; cf. p. 43: "Schönheit bedeutet griechisch gedacht immer ein Sich-zeigen und Scheinen"); A. Schmitt, "Symmetrie und Schönheit: Plotins Kritik an hellenistischen Proportionslehren und ihre unterschiedliche Wirkungsgeschichte in Mittelalter und Früher Neuzeit" (NA 59–84, especially pp. 62–63); L. Bergemann, "Cudworth interpretiert Euripides: Neuplatonische Metaphysik und heteronome Ästhetik als Faktoren einer Transformation antiker Dichtung" (NA 152).

8. J. M. E. Moravcsik, "Noetic Aspiration and Artistic Inspiration," in *Plato on Beauty, Wisdom and the Arts*, edited by J. M. E. Moravcsik and P. Temko (Totowa, N.J.: Rowman and Littlefield, 1982), 29–46.

9. In fact, this thesis itself, although traditionally assumed as a commonplace, is questionable, e.g., when one asks why Kant needs the aesthetic and what purpose (both moral and cognitive) it ultimately serves in his philosophy.

In other words, the story repeats itself: as in most studies, there is no conceptual hermeneutic framework for working with an ancient text in terms of our present-day notions, and modern aesthetic theory is forced upon Plato. The essay becomes entangled in solving questions—such as whether the primary aesthetic principle in Plato is art or beauty—that hermeneutically could not have come out of Plato's texts. A positive aspect of the essay is a critical examination of the notion τὸ καλόν,[10] and the recognition of the fact that strictly speaking aesthetic or sensible beauty constitutes only part of the καλόν, which as a whole is not an entirely aesthetic category (pp. 43–44).[11] At the same time, there is almost no discussion of this aesthetic beauty in the study.[12] Also absent are any references to the revealing capacity of τὸ καλόν, since "aesthetic" is understood more narrowly as "pertaining to sense perception" (cf. p. 32). The dialogues discussed are, again, the *Symposion*, *Republic*, and *Phaedrus* (briefly mentioned).

In addition to traditional approaches to Plato within a hermeneutically unreflected conceptual framework of modern aesthetics, there are some studies that attempt to use more advanced postcritical approaches, applying the ideas of context and genealogy. Thus G. H. Blocker and J. M. Jeffers, in their introduction to the section on ancient aesthetics, which includes Plato, try to justify critically their attempt to apply modern concepts to ancient thought.[13] However, the actual study shows that they have not yet achieved a hermeneutic "dialogue" with Plato's texts: the traditional modern focus on the concept "art" and its functions (Plato's *Republic* is discussed in this respect) still weighs too heavily on the discussion, while there is nothing in the study about the

---

10. Pp. 31ff.; cf. his *Encyclopedia* article discussed below in note 48.

11. This is already an achievement, because many studies on "ancient aesthetics" simply translate it uncritically as "beauty" or "the beautiful"; see the discussion of terminology below.

12. For a discussion of physical beauty in Plato see H. Tarrant, "The Special Power of Visual Beauty in Plato and the Ancient Greek Novel," in *Greek Philosophy and the Fine Arts*, edited by K. Boudouris (Athens: International Center for Greek Philosophy and Culture, 2000), 175–84. His study starts with parallel descriptions of visual beauty in Plato and ancient Greek novels (on this topic cf. O. Bychkov, "ἡ τοῦ κάλλους ἀπορροή: A Note on Achilles Tatius 1.9.4–5, 5.13.4," *Classical Quarterly* 49, no. 1 [1999]: 339–41) and discusses, in a very straightforward way, relevant passages from the *Symposion* (visual beauty as a creative power) and *Phaedrus* (effects of visual beauty, images of visual beauty in the world, our automatic response to visual beauty, its reminding role etc.). The discussion of καλόν in *Hippias Major* is mentioned only briefly.

13. G. H. Blocker and J. M. Jeffers, *Contextualizing Aesthetics: From Plato to Lyotard* (Belmont, Calif.: Wadsworth Publishing Company, 1999).

revealing capacity of aesthetic experience or even about beauty. E. Faas, in the chapter on Plato's "transvaluation of aesthetic values," attempts to read Plato through Nietzsche's critique of the tradition in terms of the struggle between natural impulses and sublimated idealism, again, with the emphasis on Plato's critique of the arts in the *Republic*.[14] According to Faas, Plato gradually abandons his fascination with "natural" aesthetic reaction to bodies, sex, etc. (i.e., the Nietzschean "natural force" as the origin of subsequent cultural developments) and switches to the pure and empty "idea" which is "beyond reality" (p. 27), that is, to something like the Christian "beauty of God." It is worth noting that von Balthasar also claims that Plato gradually switches his attention from immediate aesthetic reaction to seeing to an abstract idea of order in his later dialogues. Unlike von Balthasar, however, Faas never mentions the "revealing" function of beauty in Plato. Among recent publications there are also studies not of Plato's aesthetics but of particular dialogues relevant to aesthetics. G. R. F. Ferrari's commentary on the *Phaedrus*, for example, discusses the relevant issues, such as beauty, as well as pleasure and love-madness caused by it.[15] Finally, the discussion of aesthetic issues in Plato—one of the most prominent being that of mimesis—occurs in more general studies of aesthetic and literary issues in Antiquity.[16]

A brief survey of critical literature thus shows that the predominant focus of recent studies has been Plato's condemnation of poetry and the arts, as well as (a related issue) his understanding of mimetic processes in art.[17] Even though some of the classic passages discussed by von Balthasar are cited in these studies, none except the 2007 col-

---

14. E. Faas, *The Genealogy of Aesthetics* (Cambridge: Cambridge University Press, 2002); pp. 15–27 referenced here.

15. G. R. F. Ferrari, *Listening to the Cicadas: A Study of Plato's Phaedrus* (Cambridge: Cambridge University Press, 1987), in particular, chap. 6 (pp. 140–203). See references to this very solid study below in the section on *Phaedrus*.

16. E.g., cf. J. T. Kirby, "Mimesis and Diegesis: Foundations of Aesthetic Theory in Plato and Aristotle," *Helios: Journal of the Classical Association of the Southwest* 18, no. 2 (1991): 113–28; S. Halliwell, *The Aesthetics of Mimesis* (Princeton: Princeton University Press, 2002). Also cf. chap. 3 ("Mimetic Doctrines: Plato and Aristotle") in D. T. Benediktson, *Literature and the Visual Arts in Ancient Greece and Rome* (Norman: University of Oklahoma Press, 2000), where Plato is discussed on pp. 41–53. His study contains some useful hermeneutic insights, such as that Plato's views differ from passage to passage, switching from ethical to aesthetic concerns (p. 41), which means that it makes more sense to discuss individual dialogues or texts of Plato, instead of simply writing about "Plato."

17. Mimesis is the almost singular focus of Büttner's (*Antike Ästhetik*) chapter on Plato.

lection *Neuplatonismus und Ästhetik* engages specifically the idea of the revealing capacity of beauty and art. The textual hermeneutics used in the aforesaid studies also needs improvement. Apart from Ferrari who maintains the continuity of the text in his commentary, the analysis of texts fluctuates from summarizing long continuous passages to "picking and choosing" statements on a particular issue from various dialogues (cf. Faas). A general hermeneutic feature of most studies, which can be seen as the trace of "authorial intent" hermeneutics, is that they mostly discuss how beauty or art can fit into Plato's general conceptual scheme[18]—for example, his discussion of imitation or the role of the arts. At the same time the value of his insight in these matters, or his "side" observations about the nature of aesthetic experience or the way it was understood by his contemporaries—something that might appear unreflected in Plato but is of importance for us now—are not taken into consideration. In other words, according to the scholars, what was not crucial to the general conceptual scheme of a particular dialogue is not worth discussing even now. Given this sort of approach, some of the issues that are of interest to our present study are necessarily left out and ignored. Finally, we can also draw up a list of Plato's dialogues usually viewed as "aesthetic" (the list is consistent with von Balthasar's selection): *Phaedrus, Symposion, Republic*, and, as far as the sheer terminology is concerned, *Hippias Major*.

Following the hermeneutically reflected approach outlined above, we must now place Plato's texts in a continuous tradition that culminates in modern and contemporary aesthetics. As Gadamer's analysis of interpretation clearly showed, a traditional text can be successfully engaged by a present-day reader only if it can still be made relevant to him or her. Therefore, the relevance of Plato's texts for modern and contemporary aesthetic theories needs to be examined first. There are clear indications that the texts of Plato exercised a real and palpable influence on modern and contemporary aesthetic thought, just as they did in other areas. It is interesting that the aspect of aesthetic experience that is not reflected in strictly academic literature on Plato's aesthetics—its revealing aspect—is precisely what has captured the attention of modern philosophers and theologians. Examining several such points of interest where modern and present-day thinkers saw Plato as still relevant

---

18. Büttner (*Antike Ästhetik*) is especially keen on this approach.

The Platonic Tradition ⇝ 135

will enable us to find common issues for the dialogue with Plato's texts.

It is only appropriate to start with Kant himself. Unlike von Balthasar or Gadamer, for instance, Kant almost never reveals the ancient or medieval sources of his aesthetics. However, as will be noted passim throughout the following chapters, there are so many undeniable similarities between Kantian aesthetics and the thought of Plato,[19] Stoics (via Cicero), and Augustine, that one starts to wonder if the sources of some of the key Kantian insights about aesthetic experience and its connection with cognition and morals were not, in fact, ancient and early medieval. In the absence of clear references, M. C. Fistioc has noted that the "similarities" with Plato's thought in Kant "are quite striking" and proposed simply to "show that these ideas find a parallel in Kant's *Critique*."[20] In other words, the best way to proceed, in the cases like that of Kant, is not by claiming an influence but by pointing out parallels. Kant's case, in fact, is paralleled in late Antiquity by that of Augustine (see Chapter Seven): e.g., although parallels between Augustine and Plotinus are undeniable and sometimes almost verbatim, he almost never directly quotes, or refers to, Plotinus, which prevents some scholars from ascribing direct influences. It will suffice to point out here that, although no "historico-critical" connection in such cases can be established, a hermeneutic dialogue can be. Although the present study will be restricted to continuous textual traditions where influences can also

---

19. For example, Schopenhauer in *The World as Will and Idea* (Bk. 3, The World as Idea, Second Aspect. [The Platonic Idea: The Object of Art]), in an example of a dialogue with the tradition reconciling two major figures in aesthetics from different epochs, openly proclaims that "it is clear, and requires no further proof that the inner meaning of both doctrines [i.e., those of Plato and Kant on ideas] is entirely the same" (§31, p. 222). Thus in both, according to him, the world is structured as an idea, presentation, or manifestation of the will, or the Kantian thing-in-itself (§31, p. 221). In this dialectic of the thing-in-itself and idea, Schopenhauer continues, "lies the ground of the great agreement between Plato and Kant, although, in strict accuracy, that of which they speak is not the same" (§32, p. 227). In other words, Schopenhauer detects a parallel or an analogy between the two thinkers, whose systems of thought are otherwise not identical. According to Schopenhauer, all are capable of transcending themselves and knowing the ideas in things somehow intuitively, i.e., all possess an aesthetic capacity (§37, p. 252). A genius retains this sort of knowledge of ideas and then relates them to others in a work of art: an idea that is reminiscent both of Plato's recollection and of Kant's concept of the genius. One can state further, upon Schopenhauer's own assertion, that this Platonic insight, which Schopenhauer combines with the Kantian, serves as the foundation of his own aesthetic view that aesthetics and art somehow reveal truth about reality. (Similarities with Plato do not end there: Schopenhauer even condemns certain sensual types of art, just as Plato did before him; cf. §40, p. 269.)

20. M. C. Fistioc, *The Beautiful Shape of the Good: Platonic and Pythagorean Themes in Kant's Critique of the Power of Judgment* (New York: Routledge, 2002), 97.

be traced "critically," such "parallels" (for instance, with Kant) will be noted.

If one were able to demonstrate convincingly an ancient or medieval influence on Kant's aesthetics, that would make a great case for the hermeneutic approach assumed in this study. Indeed, it will be proved that even greatest figures not only in theological, but also in philosophical aesthetics drew on ancient and medieval sources in constructing their theories. In this case the hermeneutic dialogue will receive support "from both sides"; that is, one will be able to demonstrate not only that some concerns of modern aesthetics are present already in Antiquity as "parallels," but that those modern ideas were actually inspired by ancient texts.

Returning to Fistioc's analysis—which, although she does not make a clear case for Plato's influence on Kant, nevertheless opens up many avenues and indicates possible ways in which such an influence could have taken place—let us ask: what issues in Kant's aesthetics, according to her, find parallels in Platonic thought? Locating these issues will further help us to focus the analysis of Plato's texts in this chapter. According to Fistioc, the main source of Kant's knowledge of Plato was certainly Brucker's *History of Philosophy*,[21] which he read before writing his third *Critique*. First of all, the whole project of transcendental *aisthetics* could have been inspired by Brucker's discussion of Plato's distinction between νοητά and αἰσθητά. The latter category is similar to Kant's "phenomena," which Kant understood in the Greek sense as something that has to do with the senses.[22] Fistioc also sees a parallel between Plato's ascent from the sensible realm to the realm of ideas "beyond this world" through the notion of τὸ καλόν in the *Symposion* and Kant's idea of reaching the Categorical Imperative, as well as the very idea of lawfulness lying at the foundation of the world (p. 92). Another possible connection is the idea that aesthetic pleasure is a mark of form or intelligible structure that is accessible immediately through the senses (p. 93), which supposedly is present in Diotima's speech in the *Symposion*. We are capable of directly recognizing structure or design in the world through our pleasurable reaction to certain things (p. 114), that is, aesthetic pleasure serves us as a guide to discovering patterns in

---

21. J. Brucker, *Historia critica philosophiae a mundi incunabulis ad nostram usque aetatem deducta*, 2nd ed. (Leipzig: Weidemann & Reich, 1767).
22. Fistioc, *Beautiful Shape of the Good*, 25–26.

nature.²³ Just like Plato, Kant distinguishes between the "lower" and "higher" types of pleasure (or eros in Plato) and maintains that only the higher kind must be used. Kant, Fistioc writes, outlines "a type of pleasure which is not a source of confusion but rather a guide"—a parallel to the "correct way of loving" from Plato's *Symposion*—which corresponds to "the human capacity, punctuated by pleasure, to understand purpose and to use it in creating a coherent view of the world and an equally coherent view of oneself" (p. 109). Finally, Kant's well-known link between the beautiful and the morally good, according to which the abstract notion of the end is somehow connected with the idea of immediate intuitive understanding, which has a direct grasp of reality, could also have come from Plato, according to Fistioc.²⁴ As we see, all these parallels are directly relevant to the modern understanding of aesthetic experience as revealing or guiding.

Another major thinker from recent times who uses Plato's aesthetic reflections is Gadamer. The retrieval of Plato's aesthetics is important because, according to Gadamer, "this ancient conception of the beautiful can also be of service to the comprehensive hermeneutics" that emerges from the critique of the methodologism of the human sciences (*TM* 477). A return to Plato's conception of beauty reintroduces the aspect of the phenomenon of the beautiful that is important for Gadamer's hermeneutic theory (*TM* 480). As gradually becomes evident, this important aspect of the beautiful that Gadamer sees in Plato's texts is precisely its self-evident nature. According to the Greek understanding, Gadamer interprets, "beautiful things are those whose value is of itself evident" (*TM* 477).²⁵ According to Gadamer (*TM* 481), Plato was aware of the difference between the intangible good and the beautiful, which is more accessible due to its immediate and evident nature. The beautiful in Plato appears as "the harmony between the thing and its attendant disclosure (ἀλήθεια)" (*TM* 481). The good can be seen as analogous to the beautiful because of its "effulgence," but it is the beautiful that,

---

23. Fistioc thinks that this idea in Kant comes from Plato and Pythagoras; however, cf. our analysis of the thought of Augustine (see Chapter 7), where this idea is much better articulated.

24. P. 109. However, cf. our observations in Chapter 6 on the parallels between Kant and the thought of the Stoics in this respect.

25. Gadamer mentions the Greek expression δι' αὐτὸ αἱρετόν ("preferable for its own sake"), which became a stock expression for the "aesthetic"—as well as ethical—aspects of reality in the Stoics: see Chapter 6.

unlike the good, can be directly grasped. The nature of the beautiful is to be "visibly manifest." The beautiful "reveals itself," "it is the mark distinguishing the good for the human soul," thus giving the soul a clear sense of direction. While the nature of virtue can be obscure, the beautiful possesses the ability to dispose us in its favor "immediately" by "its own radiance": here Gadamer refers to Plato's epithet ἐκφανέστατον from *Phaedrus* 250D7. The beautiful "of itself presents itself"; "its being is such that it makes itself immediately evident (*einleuchtend*)" (*TM* 481).

Of particular importance, of course, is the impact of Plato on von Balthasar's theological aesthetics: evaluating the accuracy of von Balthasar's assessment is part of the scope of this study. According to Murillo, von Balthasar's dialogue with Greek philosophy in general rests on the assumption "that the transcendental aesthetics of a philosophical kind even today must still play an important role in Christian theology and other areas of our culture" (*GW* 210).[26] Von Balthasar, Murillo continues, traces such aesthetics to the ancient insight that from beautiful manifestations of the sensible world one can go back to the source of beauty (*GW* 211). In this dialogue with the ancients, without doubt, "one of the main partners in conversation" is Plato, the pre-Socratics being mere "forerunners" of Plato's vision of the ascent (*GW* 215). Von Balthasar discusses Plato in the volume *The Realm of Metaphysics in Antiquity* (*GL* 4), using freely the term "Platonic aesthetic" (cf. *GL4* 206). Von Balthasar's major theoretical premise is that Plato gradually transitions from one model of the aesthetic notion καλόν—as something capable of immediately revealing reality in a passionate movement of the ascent—to another: τὸ καλόν as order (cf. *GL4* 210). Since the idea of the two models for aesthetic experience ("immediacy" versus "order") also surfaces in relation to Augustine and seems to suggest itself after a preliminary uncritical reading of either Plato or Augustine, this would be another important issue to keep in mind during our analysis of actual contexts. Does either Plato, as von Balthasar suggests, or subsequently Augustine ever abandon the "immediacy" model?

The model of aesthetic experience as immediately revealing is best described in the following passage from *GL4* 177:

26. Note how freely Murillo uses a modern term, "transcendental aesthetics," in connection with ancient thought. Such use of modern terms in describing, e.g., Plato, is also typical in von Balthasar.

The idea that knowledge, and therefore also and indeed especially philosophical knowledge, be an open readiness, service and submission before 'things,' 'reality,' and should precisely be defined from that perspective, is sustained by Plato even where he deals with the highest forms of reality and thus prevents any interpretation of his thought in terms of Kantian transcendentalism. From any such perspective his philosophizing derives straight from myth and stands firmly in the whole Hellenic tradition. Spirit is the possibility of securing something self-authenticating, self-disclosing, a genuine epiphany; it is to stand face to face with reality at every stage, right up to the highest Good.

Von Balthasar is thus fascinated with the importance of the aesthetic aspects of reality (self-disclosure, revelation, direct and immediate contact, etc.) in Plato. Again, his assessment of Plato must be prefaced with a caveat that the reality of this opposition between the "transcendental" and "immediacy" principles in application to Plato is questionable:[27] this issue will be partly clarified through the analysis of Plato's texts, but it remains outside the immediate scope of this study. In fact, von Balthasar himself is not very consistent in denying "transcendentality" in Plato in the Kantian sense.[28] What is important, however, is that the idea of aesthetic as immediately revealing is what von Balthasar *thought* was important in Plato, whether his description is totally accurate or not. His interest in this idea, of course, comes from the general context of the twentieth-century German philosophical tradition (as exemplified by Heidegger or Gadamer), in which the notion of self-disclosure or revelation permeates not only aesthetic but also cognitive and ontological spheres. For example, for von Balthasar, both being and truth also have the capacity to appear and shine through. He once again traces these observations back to Plato, to the "analogy of the sun" in the *Republic* (GL4 180) as well as to other contexts (GL4 181). Speaking of concrete texts, von Balthasar discusses the *Phaedrus* and has an extensive treatment of the *Symposion*.

Having discussed the dialogues from the middle period such as the *Phaedrus* or *Symposion*, which deal with the "passionate" and immediate nature of the good and the beautiful (up to GL4 204), von Balthasar

---

27. For example, cf. Halfwassen's discussion of Plato and Plotinus (in *NA*) cited above, where he freely speaks of the existence of transcendental systems in both Plato and Plotinus.

28. For example he speaks of "transcendental depths of his self" in relation to Socrates (GL4 192) and of "transcendence of knowledge" (GL4 197) and the "transcendental movement of knowledge as knowledge" (GL4 200) in relation to Plato.

now tries to locate Platonic texts that contain some criteria for the beautiful that would distinguish it from the good. The *Timaeus*, which is a later dialogue, provides such a criterion: the beautiful adds a relation to some "inner measure" or order.[29] It is not quite clear why von Balthasar poses the question about the distinction between the good and the beautiful at this point. Even if one follows the medieval scholastic definition (which von Balthasar inherits from his Thomistic background), the beautiful is distinguished from the good not only by its affinity with form or order but also by its luminous nature: the latter distinction appears as clearly in Plato's earlier dialogues as it does in the later. One should probably speak here of "yet another" distinction. In any case, according to von Balthasar, the main question of Plato's aesthetics at this point is this: is this "measure" the same for the world and for God? Von Balthasar thinks that in Plato it is the same for both (GL4 206).[30] From this point on, both von Balthasar's analysis and Plato, according to his interpretation, focus on the aesthetics based not on immediate revelation but on the concept of order. Thus, in the *Republic*, this cosmic order and harmony is transferred to areas such as ethics, society, politics, etc. (GL4 207ff.). The ethical import of the aesthetic—detecting aesthetic order leads to establishing moral order—is further exploited in the *Laws*, where the aesthetic is subordinated to pedagogical uses (GL4 212). At this point, beauty perceived in terms of order and harmony is interpreted as "objective" and as an "immutable canon."

Von Balthasar's general assessment of Plato's aesthetics is marked by a note of disappointment. The revelation of some transcendent "beyond" in early Plato is replaced in late Plato by the order and law that is immanent in the world and governs equally god, the world and everything in it: a sort of an "aesthetic ethic immanent in the world," in which there is a certain identity and harmony of balance between the

---

29. One wonders, in fact, how much von Balthasar's idea of these two models of aesthetic experience in Plato—"passionate immediacy" and "order"—is actually based on his "Germanist" (in his own words) background permeated by the Nietzschean idea of the opposition between the Dionysian and the Apollinean principles in Greek culture. Cf. the discussion below of the "manic" nature of beauty in the *Phaedrus*.

30. In a way, the oscillation between the scheme of order—according to which, on a certain level, all reality is based on the same principles that are intrinsically (if not actually) intelligible (cf. Anselm or late academic Scholasticism)—and the scheme of "divine transcendence"—or a mystical model where the divine reality cannot possibly be known, although one can have ecstatic glimpses of it (cf. pseudo-Dionysius, twelfth- and fourteenth-century mystics)—permeates the whole of the Middle Ages.

divine and the human (GL4 213). "The last glimmer of a revelation from above," von Balthasar sounds a tragic note, "—some features of which in the middle period were left to the (transcendent) Sun of the Good—fades, or rather passes over into the macrocosmic harmony which is accessible to philosophical inquiry. Now is born that philosophical aesthetic of the grand style, to which even Plotinus will be able to make no significant alteration" (GL4 213). At the same time, according to von Balthasar, it is precisely Plotinus, with his idea of true transcendence, who lays the foundation of the truly theological aesthetics, and not Plato, who doesn't quite make it. However, Plato's achievement in giving us a glimpse of what will later become a full-blown "revelatory aesthetics" is undeniable. His "aesthetic," von Balthasar remarks, lays down the foundations of Western humanism in Antiquity, the Middle Ages and modernity: "an aesthetic which seeks to draw out the glory of God which breaks upon the human scene in the direction of a human" (GL4 213).

The present survey shows that there is a clearly acknowledged influence of Plato on the development of the idea of aesthetic experience as revealing in modern and contemporary aesthetics. There are also numerous parallels with Platonic thought in this area that invite a modern-ancient dialogue, no matter whether their source can be textually traced to Plato or not. At the same time, academic studies of Plato clearly fail to do justice to the revelatory aspects of his aesthetics. To a certain extent, von Balthasar fills in this gap and pays most attention to the revealing nature of aesthetic experience in Plato's thought. However, his account is also far from being definitive. First, he is too involved in the hermeneutic task of presenting Plato as a precursor of his own theological aesthetics, and Plato's Gestalt is painted in a typically broad and "enthusiastic" style that sometimes obscures textual and historical details. Second, von Balthasar's account raises many questions—whether, for example, one can really view Plato's aesthetics as "transcendental," or whether one can, indeed, distinguish two periods in the development of his aesthetics. These considerations certainly justify a closer look at the Platonic tradition in order to see whether the retrieval of revelatory aesthetics from Plato is hermeneutically supported by texts. One of the hermeneutic rules that we established at the beginning is that the texts selected for this study should present a continuous textual tradition through Antiquity and the Middle Ages, and not simply be linked by parallels and similarities.[31] The hermeneutic "rebuilding" of the historical dimension of a later idea through a retrieval of the tradition by means of a "dialogue" will receive far greater credibility if textual continuity can be proved critically as well.

In the case of Plato, the direct knowledge of his texts within the ancient tradition, both among the Greeks and the Greek-reading Romans such as Cicero, hardly needs to be proven. Plato was just as familiar to later Greek pagan authors (such as Plotinus) and Greek Christian writers (such as pseudo-Dionysius), who can potentially enter a discussion on aesthetics. It remains to be established, then, how well Plato was known to the later Latin tradition that did not read Greek, from Augustine to the late Latin Middle Ages.[32] According to R. Klibansky's influential study, which is based on the edition of all surviving medieval Latin translations of Plato in the series *Plato Latinus*, the Latin Middle Ages had a very limited access to actual Platonic texts.[33] The only dialogue mentioned in modern discussions in connection with aesthetics that was directly accessible to a wide circle of learned readers from the sixth century onward is the *Timaeus* in a partial translation by Calcidius (Cicero's translation was current earlier but became almost extinct by the early Middle Ages) which was available in almost any good library.[34] However, Plato in the Middle Ages was very well known through an indirect tradition. Among the pagan authors who transmitted the ideas of Plato, Klibansky names (pp. 22–23) Aulus Gellius, Valerius Maximus, Apuleius (*De Platone et eius dogmate* and *De Deo Socratis*) and Macrobius (Commentary on the "Dream of Scipio"). Parts of Boethius's *Consolation of Philosophy* (e.g., Book 3, Meter 9) are almost a paraphrase of the *Timaeus* (p. 24). Those works of Cicero that were widely available through-

---

31. Finding parallels and themes, instead of precise textual connections, is characteristic, e.g., of *NA*. The current study thus can be seen as moving beyond this approach to the history of ancient and medieval aesthetics.

32. There is a persistent opinion that Augustine could read Greek, although not very well. I have not investigated the matter specifically, but I have never seen any compelling confirmation of this opinion. It certainly does not come through in his texts (at least not in the texts analyzed here) the way it does in the authors of whom we know for certain that they did know the language, e.g., in Cicero. Perhaps Augustine's knowledge of Greek was somewhat similar to the "knowledge" of Latin among present-day non-Latinist academics in the humanities, which amounts to being able to recognize some terms.

33. See: R. Klibansky, *The Continuity of the Platonic Tradition during the Middle Ages* (London: The Warburg Institute, 1939; reprint 1982), 21–29.

34. Ibid., 28.

out the Middle Ages contain some references to relevant dialogues and contexts (e.g., to *Phaedrus* 250D in *De off.* 1.4.15). According to Klibansky, Augustine was the chief exponent of the Platonic tradition among the Latin Christian authors (pp. 23, 27). Indeed, as will become clear later, there are some obvious similarities between Plato's *Phaedrus* and *Symposion* and the Augustinian idea of the ascent toward the divine principle, which starts with the experience of beauty. However, despite the similarity, the precise role of Plato's texts in the formation of Augustine's theory of ascent is far from clear. According to P. Courcelle, there is no evidence that Augustine knew either the *Phaedrus* or *Symposion* directly, and the only dialogue of Plato which Augustine appears to have read is the *Timaeus* (before the year 400, in Cicero's partial Latin translation),[35] which almost certainly influenced his theory of beauty as order. Augustine, however, was "abundantly informed on his [Plato's] philosophy" indirectly, from such sources as Cicero, Varro, Apuleius, Cyprian, and Ambrose.[36] Pseudo-Dionysius the Areopagite, a Greek author who was well known in the West, was almost as influential as Augustine.[37] His entire corpus was available in Latin in various translations from the ninth century onward; it is frequently commented on and copiously quoted in thirteenth-century scholastic treatises.[38] In particular, his *Divine Names*, a work that is heavily influenced by the Platonic tradition, contains a chapter on beauty in which he quotes Plato's *Symp.* 211A1–5 (the qualities of τὸ καλόν) almost verbatim. Klibansky's brief overview of the availability of Platonic texts is confirmed by our own analysis of the thirteenth-century textual tradition.[39] Thirteenth-century scholastic texts on beauty contain no direct quotations from any dialogues of Plato other than the *Timaeus* (in Calcidius's translation), which is used copiously.[40] Other references

---

35. P. Courcelle, *Late Latin Writers and Their Greek Sources* (Cambridge: Harvard University Press, 1969), 170, 169.
36. Ibid., 170–71. Therefore, his statement that he had read the "Platonic Books" (actually a Neoplatonic text, possibly a Latin translation of Plotinus), which occurred shortly before or at the time of writing his early Cassiciacum dialogues, is not decisive. On the other hand, whatever Neoplatonic writings he read constitute a more likely source of the ascent theory. Courcelle has a good discussion of the nature and authorship of the Neoplatonic works mentioned by Augustine.
37. Klibansky, *The Continuity of the Platonic Tradition*, 25.
38. See: P. Chevallier, ed., *Dionysiaca: Recueil donnant l'ensemble des traductions latines des ouvrages attribués au Denys de l'Aréopage* (Paris/Bruges: Desclée de Brouwer & Cie, 1937).
39. Done for O. V. Bychkov's 1999 study, "A Propos of Medieval Aesthetics."
40. References to the Latin text of the *Timaeus* in Calcidius's translation are given ac-

to Plato or his ideas are indirect and appear in connection with texts of Cicero[41] or passages from the Christian writers of a Neoplatonic orientation: pseudo-Dionysius, Augustine, or Boethius.

Thus the genuine Platonic influence on the Latin Middle Ages was mostly limited by the availability of his texts, although Platonic ideas were also accessible indirectly through the prism of the later tradition, pagan or Christian. Only the *Timaeus*, from among Plato's authentic texts—and, in fact, only a small portion of it dedicated to creation (29A–30B)—is used by the medieval schoolmen to illustrate the discussion about the beauty of the universe.[42] The most significant secondary source of Platonic (mixed with Neoplatonic) material in late medieval discussions of beauty is the *Divine Names* of pseudo-Dionysius the Areopagite, in particular *DN* 4.7, which contains the discussion of τὸ

---

cording to the edition *Timaeus a Calcidio translatus commentarioque instructus*, Plato Latinus 4, edited by J. H. Waszink (London/Leiden: Warburg Institute/E. J. Brill, 1975), later referred to as Wsz. E.g., Albert quotes the *Timaeus* directly in his *Summa theologica*, partly paraphrasing Calcidius and partly providing exact quotations: *Timaeus* 28A–B (Wsz 21.1–4) and 39E (Wsz 32.15–16) in *S.Th.* I, tr. 6, qu. 26, c. 1, a. 2.3 (p. 178.18–20); *Timaeus* 29E (Wsz 22.18–20) in *S.Th.* II, tract.II, qu. 62, membr. 1.4 (p. 597); *Timaeus* 30A (cf. Wsz 22.22) in *S.Th.* II, tr. 11, qu. 62, membr. 2, quaest. 1.2 (p. 599); *Timaeus* 30A (Wsz 22.23–23.3) in *S.Th.* II, tr. 11, qu. 62, membr. 2, qu. 3 (p. 603). The following editions of Albert's *Summa* were used: Albertus Magnus, *Summa theologica, pars I*, vol. 34.1 of *Opera omnia*, edited by D. Siedler (Cologne: Albertus Magnus Institut, 1978); idem, *Summa theologica, pars II, qu. 1–67*, vol. 32 of *Opera omnia*, edited by S. Borgnet (Paris: L. Vivès, 1895). Another example is the *Sapientiale* of Thomas of York edited in D. H. Pouillon, "La beauté," 263–329. *Timaeus* 29A (Wsz 21.21), 29E (Wsz 22.19–20), 30A–B (Wsz 23.3–4) in *Sapientiale* 2.2 (p. 325.32–33; 325.21; 324.5–6); *Timaeus* 29A (Wsz 21.14–15, 17–18) in *Sapientiale* 7.3 (p. 326.19–21, 26–27).

41. Cf. the only reference to the *Phaedrus* and the idea of ecstatic beauty in Thomas Aquinas, *S.Th.* II-II.145.2, ad 1, in the context of the discussion of *honestum* (τὸ καλόν). The short quotation from *Phaedrus* 250D is taken from Cicero, *De off.* 1.4.15.

42. This is not surprising. Plato's cosmology fitted quite well with the Christian world picture, and even was believed, on the authority of Augustine, *De civ. Dei* 11.21, to have been written under the direct influence of the Book of Genesis. In fact, Apuleius—who could have influenced both Augustine and later medieval authors—in his exposition of Platonic teachings (*De dogmate Platonis*) concentrated mainly on the cosmological theory borrowed from the *Timaeus*: "Therefore god the artisan selected the beautiful and perfect sphere as the prototype for the most perfect and most beautiful world, in order that it may lack nothing, but contain everything by enclosing and holding it together: beautiful and admirable, alike to itself and corresponding to itself" (*De dogm. Pl.* 1.8, *L. Apuleii opera omnia*, pars II, edited by G. F. Hildebrand [Leipzig, 1842], 189). Although Apuleius does portray Plato's supreme divinity as transcendent and without a name (*De dogm. Pl.* 1.5), there is not a word about Plato's theory of ascent either toward τὸ καλόν or from the experience of earthly beauty, and the only description of τὸ καλόν (*honestum*) in *De dogm. Pl.* 2.13 (p. 232) is done in distinctly Stoic terms: "Virtue is the primary good that is praiseworthy.... For this reason it must be called *honestum*: for we hold that only *honestum* is the good." Thus even the tradition of Middle Platonism already limits and shapes the contents of Platonic teaching in the way in which it will be known to the Middle Ages.

καλόν and an almost exact quotation from *Symp.* 211A1–5, 211B1, which deals with the inaccessible nature of the aesthetic notion τὸ καλόν in its most abstract and pure state.[43] A number of "aesthetic" themes found in Plato are prominent in the Latin Middle Ages. Plato's idea of beauty as an ecstatic experience that causes an ascent toward the divine principle is certainly prominent in Augustine, even if it was not directly borrowed from Plato. The Augustinian version was popular in the late Middle Ages. Plato's own authentic version is not directly reflected in the medieval tradition, partly because the corresponding passages were simply unavailable. One particular element of Plato's aesthetic theory of the middle period, the notion of the absolute καλόν, does, because of its similarity with the Christian idea of God, find its way into the medieval Latin tradition. Another aspect popular in the Latin West, both because of its compatibility with the Christian doctrine and because of the availability of the text, is Plato's cosmology and the theory of the beautiful world order as it appears in the *Timaeus*. This late element of Plato's teaching was popularized by Augustine and maintained its influence throughout the late Middle Ages. Finally, Plato's discussions of various aesthetic terms (in *Hippias Major*, for example), such as the "beautiful" (καλόν) and the "fitting" (τὸ πρέπον), find their way into the Latin tradition through Cicero's rendering of Stoic discussions. Like von Balthasar, the medieval tradition, in its reception of Plato, is drawn to two broad areas of aesthetic interest: the ascent to higher principles, and the concept of order. Unlike von Balthasar, the medieval tradition is very much interested in the concept of order, and therefore in Plato's late dialogue *Timaeus*.

At this point we are faced with a major hermeneutical problem. What are the exact meanings of Plato's Greek terms for aesthetic experience, and, in general, is it appropriate to interpret certain ancient Greek notions in terms of aesthetics? The problem is now posed not from a general methodological point of view (whether or not it is appropriate to discuss ancient thought in terms of modern categories), but from the point of view of the particular practical aspects of interpreting concrete Greek texts. As stated in the Introduction, one must not underestimate the significance

---

43. This version of τὸ καλόν as an absolute "transcendent" principle and the source of all goodness certainly bore a striking resemblance with the Christian idea of God, and fitted very well with the Christian theological framework. Perhaps for this reason it was borrowed almost without any change by the early Greek Fathers, and thenceforth was readily accepted by every subsequent medieval Christian tradition.

of terminological issues, not only for interpreting ancient texts—as is the case here—but also for dealing with contemporary disciplines, especially one as broad and vaguely defined as aesthetics. A lack of awareness of the precise meaning and range of terms in the history of aesthetics can lead to a confused and muddled picture of contemporary aesthetic thought, which, as was shown above, always includes its historical extension.

The problem with aesthetic terminology in general is that even presently we apply the terms that more specifically describe our aesthetic experience—"beautiful" and "ugly"—more broadly or analogically, so as to include, among other things, moral issues. (For example, we refer to human actions as "beautiful" or "ugly" instead of using the more proper appellations "noble" and "shameful.") In some languages, such as Russian (root *prekrasn-*) and German (root *schön-*), the word for "beauty" is also routinely used for evaluating realities other than aesthetic (in its meaning "excellent"). Now it is a well-known fact, confirmed by the present study, that such terms in the pre-modern period have an even broader meaning of evaluation and almost entirely conflate aesthetic, moral, and evaluative semantic fields. The exclusively "aesthetic" understanding or application of such terms as "beauty," when they start to be reserved mainly for our aesthetic experience, does not come until the appearance of the bourgeois theories of taste in modern times.[44] This means that, since in the ancient and medieval world there was no separate area of the aesthetic, there was also no conscious attempt at that time to separate or distinguish the aesthetic meaning from other connotations. The difficulties that arose during any attempt to reflect on these divisions of meaning become obvious in, for example, the discussion in Plato's *Hippas Major* and the Stoic arguments about τὸ καλόν. We should not, however, conclude that such terms of evaluation carried no aesthetic meaning, but only that that meaning was not differentiated from the moral or generally evaluative.

Regarding particular terms, the word κάλλος (with its Latin equivalent *pulchritudo*) poses less of a problem, since it refers consistently, even from a historico-critical point of view, to physical or aesthetic beauty and is applied to other areas by analogy, and so even without the precise context it can safely be assumed to have an aesthetic meaning. The story is very different with a much more important and frequently used notion τὸ καλόν. One can safely assume that the term was elevated to its crucial status by

---

44. Cf. Bürger, *Theory of the Avant-garde*.

Plato, in whose works it plays an important role in the discussion of aesthetic issues. It is precisely the term τὸ καλόν that has an extremely broad meaning and needs a thorough explanation at this point. Its Latin equivalent *honestum* and another important ancient term for aesthetic experience, τὸ πρέπον (the Latin *decorum*) will be discussed in the next chapter.

Even a cursory perusal of the texts of Plato and the subsequent Greek tradition, especially the fragments of Stoic texts, reveals major difficulties with the interpretation of this Greek term as "the beautiful" or "beauty." On the one hand, it does have an obviously aesthetic meaning in some texts (cf. the discussion in the *Symposion* below), which some scholars interpret as a license to render all instances of τὸ καλόν in Greek texts as "the beautiful."[45] On the other hand, it also has an obviously moral meaning, especially in Stoic texts, which makes many scholars swing in the opposite direction and interpret τὸ καλόν as a purely moral category, deprived of any aesthetic connotations, and meaning something like "morally right," "moral rectitude," or "morality."[46] A slightly more "aesthetic" but still quite moral rendering is "noble" or "nobility."[47] J. Moravcsik stresses the problematic nature of either purely aesthetic (beauty) or purely moral interpretations. He proposes the adjectives "outstanding" or "fine" as the closest parallels in contemporary English:

> To be sure, English translations use "beauty" as an equivalent to the Greek καλόν in many places, but this is misleading. The Greek word designates a wide genus that applies to much of what we might call "outstanding" . . . Something that is καλόν is taken to have intrinsic value, but this value need not have either strictly aesthetic or moral connotations. Since it is used in what we might call moral contexts, translators at times render καλόν as "noble"; but this is just as bad a translation as "beautiful." . . . "Fine" is probably the best equivalent for καλόν in modern English.[48]

---

45. Cf. passim in K. Boudouris, ed., *Greek Philosophy and the Fine Arts*. Büttner (*Antike Ästhetik*) is also prone to this interpretation, as well as to an even more extreme one, rendering references to τὸ καλόν as if they were to "art"!

46. For "moral rectitude," cf. passim in A. A. Long and D. N. Sedley, *The Hellenistic Philosophers*, vols. 1–2 (Cambridge: Cambridge University Press, 1987) (henceforth referred to as LS with a reference number). For "morality," cf. Cicero, *On Moral Ends*, Cambridge Texts in the History of Philosophy, translated by R. Woolf, edited by J. Annas (Cambridge: Cambridge University Press, 2001), xxxviii.

47. Cf. Aristotle, *Nicomachean Ethics*, Cambridge Texts in the History of Philosophy, edited and translated by R. Crisp (Cambridge: Cambridge University Press, 2000), pp. 207–8.

48. J. Moravcsik, "Plato: Plato and Modern Aesthetics," in vol. 3 of *Encyclopedia of Aesthetics*, edited by M. Kelly (New York/Oxford: Oxford University Press, 1998), pp. 529–30. Cf. this statement from C. Janaway's article, "Plato: Survey of Thought," in the same volume:

Von Balthasar is also aware of this problem, which is reflected even in one of his chapter titles in the section on Plato in GL4 (*The Breadth of the Kalon*). Thus in GL4 201 he remarks that, in addition to the meaning "beautiful," τὸ καλόν also includes the right, fitting, good, appropriate, integrity, health, etc.[49] In particular, in GL4 223 he mentions, although only briefly, the issue of the interrelation of the aesthetic and the ethical in τὸ καλόν.[50]

In sum, this breadth of meaning of ancient terms for evaluation results in fluctuations between their moral and aesthetic meanings within one work, and from one tradition to another. This is especially true for translations (Greek to Latin), which may have emphasized one or another aspect of the original meaning. One must simply bear in mind that an aesthetic connotation is always present in ancient terms of evaluation, and that the only way to determine whether it is the most important one in any particular context is through a careful hermeneutics of actual texts. Because the same Greek, but especially Latin terms (both on their own and as technical translations of the Greek), can acquire a different meaning over a certain time, the analysis of ancient and medieval texts also requires a certain attention to historical changes and variations of meaning in different texts and authors. Sometimes it is necessary to trace the "genealogy" of the term—not only accounting for the immediate textual context but also remaining aware of the broader historical perspective on how the term is regularly used in this particular author or tradition. However, even when one determines from the context the exact meaning of the term, further difficulties face a scholar working in English. Thus while languages such as Russian or German have almost perfect semantic matches for the ambiguous Greek term καλόν, which can mean both "visually beautiful" and "high on the evaluative scale" (that is, "excellent"), the English language has no such match. For example, "excellent" does not have aesthetic connotations, "fine" is not always "high on the evaluative scale" or isn't always aesthetic enough, "noble" describes well the moral meaning implied by καλόν but only partially the aesthetic, and so forth. For all these reasons, throughout this study the term τὸ

"The term for beautiful in Plato's Greek is καλόν. It is a wide term of approbation, sometimes translated as 'fine'" (p. 520).

49. Von Balthasar's attempt to explain the breadth of this category by presenting, in the Thomistic tradition, the beautiful as a "transcendental" (i.e., the Aristotelian "transcategorial") in GL4 202–3 must be taken with caution.

50. "... aesthetic wonderment is always channeled at once into the ethical...."

καλόν (and later τὸ πρέπον) will be left without translation if its meaning is ambiguous or the discussion of its meaning itself is at stake. If the meaning is clear and consistent, "fine," "excellent," "noble" and "beautiful" will be used variously to render it.

Turning to Plato's own texts, it would be interesting to gain from his own account an insight about the contemporary range of meanings for τὸ καλόν. The best-known terminological analysis of the aesthetic terms τὸ καλόν and τὸ πρέπον in Plato is contained in the *Hippias Major*, the fact acknowledged by von Balthasar (GL4 202–3), among other scholars.[51] Plato's authorship of this dialogue has been disputed, but many scholars now tend to accept its authenticity. *Hippias Major* was completely unknown to the Western Middle Ages. However, the discussion therein of categories related to τὸ καλόν (such as "the fitting," τὸ πρέπον) probably shaped the Stoic understanding of them, which was transmitted through the texts of Cicero (the discussion of *decorum*) and Augustine (the question of *pulchrum* and *aptum*) and influenced medieval Western terminological discussions.[52]

The problems that the interlocutors face make it clear from the start that τὸ καλόν in the dialogue is not understood narrowly as an aesthetic category, but is a much broader notion. Here we have an excellent opportunity to examine the full range of meanings of τὸ καλόν as they appeared unreflected to the Greek mind. The dialogue is of interest precisely because it documents these spontaneous reactions to the notion τὸ καλόν; Plato's own position, as is often the case, remains unclear, but the range of meanings is unfolded in the course of a heuristic discussion, especially from the concrete examples that are used to illustrate certain points.

From the very beginning (287D), Socrates introduces as a topic of discussion the concept of τὸ καλόν as an abstract idea which makes all other things beautiful or excellent (cf. also 289D). Hippias immediately

---

51. See more on *Hippias Major* and aesthetic problems in C. Kahn, "The Beautiful and the Genuine: A Discussion of Paul Woodruff, Plato, *Hippias Major*," *Oxford Studies in Ancient Philosophy* 3 (1985): 261–87; M. T. Liminta, *Il problema della bellezza in Platone: analisi e interpretazioni dell'Ippia maggiore* (Milan: Vita e pensiero, 1998). The OCT edition of Plato will be used: *Platonis Opera*, vols. 1–5, edited by I. Burnet (Oxford: Clarendon Press, 1901–2). The text of *Hippias Maj.* is in vol. 3. Many of the passages used in this study also appear in A. Sheppard and O. V. Bychkov, *Greek and Roman Aesthetics*, where all translations from Latin texts have been made by Bychkov. For the present work, all the Greek was independently translated by Bychkov.

52. See O. V. Bychkov, "Traditional Stoic Ideas," and "A Propos of Medieval Aesthetics."

becomes angry at Socrates' suggestion that they discuss the "beauty of a pot" and explains that the name "beautiful" only applies to something solemn and grand (288D), probably not unlike the Kantian "sublime":⁵³ "it is an uneducated person who thus dares to assign base names (φαῦλα ὀνόματα) in connection with a solemn matter (ἐν σεμνῷ πράγματι)." The discussion soon runs into the related notion τὸ πρέπον and switches to the relation of τὸ καλόν to τὸ πρέπον in 290C–D. The question is raised whether it is that which "is fitting" (πρέπει) that makes a thing "beautiful" (καλόν), that is, whether 'what is fitting' is that absolute idea of beauty, or τὸ καλόν. However, τὸ πρέπον is rejected as a candidate for the role of τὸ καλόν, because it expresses something relative, and not absolute (291B). As we shall see, the notion of τὸ καλόν as some absolute quality appears with great consistency throughout the whole corpus of Platonic writings. Another useful observation about the nature of τὸ πρέπον which emerges in the context of its comparison with τὸ καλόν (293Eff) is that τὸ πρέπον does not make things beautiful but makes them "appear beautiful" (294A, ποιεῖ φαίνεσθαι καλά).⁵⁴

The interlocutors then attempt to define the relationship between τὸ καλόν and the good (τὸ ἀγαθόν). An attempt to define τὸ καλόν as "useful" or "serviceable" (χρήσιμον)—to put it closer to τὸ ἀγαθόν, which was routinely defined as "useful," fails (296B–D). However, τὸ καλόν is then defined as "helpful" (ὠφέλιμον, 296E), and moreover, "helpful toward the good," that is, able to bring about the good. Thus τὸ καλόν in fact becomes the cause (αἴτιον) of the good, which means that, as the cause of the good, it ceases to be identical with it (297A–C). This conclusion, although it appears to be merely a step in the dialectical altercation between Socrates and Hippias, is actually in agreement with the typical Platonic position that τὸ καλόν is something that points toward the good, and is not itself the good. Here Plato, voicing his opinion through Socrates, seemingly contradicts the common, if unreflected, Greek assumption that τὸ καλόν is also somehow good, or actually is the good (an understanding that even surfaces in some dialogues of Plato). No wonder, then, that this conclusion does not at all please Hippias (297C9). Later the Stoics, who made the identity between τὸ καλόν and

---

53. Referring to καλόν as "solemn" confirms the possibility of interpreting καλόν as "noble." Cf. Stoic equivalents of τὸ καλόν related by Plutarch, especially σεμνόν.

54. This remark must have contributed to the awareness of the manifest and apparent nature of πρέπον or *decorum* in Stoicism and Cicero.

the good absolute, had to shift some of the former's "pointing" or revealing aspect to τὸ πρέπον (*decorum*). However, the fact that τὸ πρέπον in Stoicism *is* a variation of τὸ καλόν, simply confirms that "pointing toward the good" always has been an indispensable feature of τὸ καλόν.

Another question arises at 297Eff.: Is τὸ καλόν linked to the higher "aesthetic" senses, vision and hearing?[55] That this proposition is refuted can be interpreted as another indirect confirmation of the transcendent nature of τὸ καλόν, which is not directly dependent on concrete aesthetic experience. Τὸ καλόν as an absolute idea appears one more time in 300B. By rejecting the definition of τὸ καλόν as something in which we can participate as a group (as in "being two") but not one by one, Socrates seems to present τὸ καλόν as something altogether independent, although capable of being participated in—not as a quality of a compound body or an aggregate of parts which is present only when such an aggregate works together as a system.[56] The interlocutors finally (302E) come to the conclusion that the nature of τὸ καλόν is elusive and one cannot determine its essence by definitions, which leads Socrates to repeat a proverb: "beautiful things are difficult" (χαλεπὰ τὰ καλά) (304E). It is perhaps this realization that makes Plato recur to myths on all other occasions where he decides to speak about τὸ καλόν. Now if even the best ancient Greek minds had trouble defining τὸ καλόν in their own language, because of its extremely broad semantic field, our only hope is a careful analysis of concrete contexts and examples that could bring out its meaning on each particular occasion.

At this point we have a sufficient hermeneutical basis for approaching Plato's key texts on aesthetic experience, i.e., on the notion of beauty and the aesthetic aspects of the broader notion τὸ καλόν: the *Phaedrus*, the *Symposion*, and the *Timaeus*. While the first two are universally recognized as his main aesthetic texts, the *Timaeus* must be added because of its importance for the medieval Latin tradition. At the end of the analysis—in light of a deeper understanding of aesthetic issues in

---

55. Vision and hearing are traditionally considered the higher senses, up to the modern times (e.g., cf. Kantian aesthetics). In Antiquity similar ideas were expressed by Plato; in addition to the mention at *Hippias Maj.* 297E 6–7 and 298A 6–7, he takes up the subject in *Philebus* 51Bff., where vision and hearing (but not only these two) are listed among the pleasures that are pure and unmixed with pain. Plotinus (*Enn.* I.6.1) also expresses this idea. In the Latin West Augustine elaborates it in *De ordine* 2.11.32.

56. This position, at least on the surface, contravenes the subsequent Stoic and, later, Augustinian theory of beauty as "harmony of parts," but it supports the position of another successor of Plato, Plotinus.

Plato—it would be interesting to reexamine the puzzling problem of "banishing the arts" in the *Republic*, another dialogue frequently referred to in secondary literature on Plato's aesthetics. The generally accepted chronology of Plato's works suggests that three of these four dialogues, the *Phaedrus*, the *Symposion*, and the *Republic*, belong roughly to the same period. The *Timaeus* is one of the later dialogues; it would be interesting to see whether any of Plato's earlier ideas about aesthetic experience are carried over into the later period or, as von Balthasar and some others suggest, there is a change of models from "immediacy" to "order." Since—and especially in the case of Plato's heuristic way of dialoguing—it is not a hermeneutically sound procedure to construct some sort of a unified systematic view of Plato's aesthetic theory, the analysis will simply follow each particular text carefully as it unfolds. Aesthetic issues will appear in various lights and from various angles. It will be our final task to find any repeating patterns and attempt to recreate certain features of Plato's aesthetic.

One of the most important aesthetic texts traditionally has been the speech of Socrates in *Phaedrus* 244A–257B, where the topic is presented in a mythological form.[57] The term used in the *Phaedrus* is mostly κάλλος, and therefore it is safe to assume that Socrates has in mind what we can call aesthetic beauty; examples from the context—references to the physical shape of the body, facial features, etc.—confirm the correctness of the assumption. Socrates indicates that the subject of his speech is the experience of a manic or ecstatic type, as he claims that "as it is, the greatest of goods come to us through madness" (διὰ μανίας) (244A 6–7). Since it is obvious that souls are not always "winged"— "wings" being a metaphor for the ecstatic state ("madness")—the main task of his speech is to present the reason for the loss of the wing by the soul (246D 3–4). The wing, Socrates comments, whose natural ability is to carry things upward into the divine regions,

> has somehow more in common with the divine (τοῦ θείου) than with bodily things; the divine, however, is beauty (καλόν), wisdom, goodness, and everything that is of this kind; and it is precisely on these things that the soul's feathers, indeed, feed and grow best, but become thinner and wither away from the opposite, such as the bad and shameful or ugly. (246D7–E4)

---

57. The Greek text of the *Phaedrus* will be quoted according to the OCT edition: *Platonis Opera*, vol. 2, edited by I. Burnet (Oxford: Clarendon Press, 1901; reprint 1953).

The Platonic theory of reincarnation explains why the soul, in its earthly existence, is excited by these echoes and traces of the divine; the theory implies the stage when the souls have direct access to the divine before birth which they can later recall. While gods freely contemplate true essences (τὰ ὄντα ὄντως), the fate of the souls in their pre-existent state can be of the following three kinds (248A–B). Even the more advanced can hardly keep their heads "above the surface" in the eternal realm in order to be able to look at the essences. The less advanced merely get a glimpse of the eternal realm (ἡ τοῦ ὄντος θέα; note the idea of "aspect" or "show") now and then, and the remainder can get no access at all, but break their feathers, fall down, and live on opinions. Thus the "pasture of truth" makes the wings of the soul grow (248B5–C), but the soul that is precluded from seeing it sheds feathers and falls down upon the earth (248C5–D).

During subsequent reincarnations, the souls receive according to what they have seen of the eternal ideas (248Dff.); artists and poets are among those who have seen the ideas already, which gives them a better ability to recognize their resemblances on earth (248E).[58] What we have here is clearly a mythical presentation of what in modern thought (for instance, in Kant) is described as the *a priori* correspondence between the "natural" experience and activity of the soul on the one hand, and the "supra-natural" or "transcendent" world of ideas on the other.[59] The precondition of the possibility of this correspondence is that "every human soul by its nature has seen true reality, or it would not have come into this kind of animal" (249E). Indeed, one of the ways to explain the situation wherein we desire something that we not only do not have, but cannot possibly have or even have access to in our present state, is to conjecture the prior unity with, and the knowledge of, the object of our desire, and then the subsequent split between the two that results in the loss of the desired.[60] In Plato and some Eastern dualistic traditions, the split is a result of the natural process of incarnation in matter;

---

58. Cf. the Kantian idea (later common in both German Idealist and Romantic thought) that artistic genius has a better chance at presenting aesthetical ideas in art, or the Freudian idea that the conscious mind of an artist has an easier access to the subconscious.

59. This correspondence appears in Kant as the idea of a common supersensible ground of our experience.

60. A good analysis of this model can be found in G. Bataille, *Theory of Religion* (New York: Zone Books, 1992), 23–24, 35, 41, 45, 56; also cf. examples from all major world mythologies, including the Genesis story.

for the Christians it is a result of the original sin. The existence of this original unity, however, always implies a theoretical possibility of an ascent toward the formerly possessed reality—since the realities that were previously united must retain some degree of kinship or correspondence between them. In the present case, the feeling of kinship or correspondence that triggers an ascent is caused by the perception of beauty, goodness, wisdom, and other phenomena of the same rank, beauty being singled out as the most conspicuous of them all. "Rightly speaking," according to Socrates, "only the intellect of a philosopher becomes winged" (249C; cf. 249A1–2), for the process of recollection includes a rational component (λογισμός). Recollection, Socrates continues, is "of those things which our soul saw at a certain point, when it accompanied god (συμπορευθεῖσα θεῷ), looked down upon those things which we now say exist and lifted up its head toward true being (τὸ ὂν ὄντως)." Returning to his opening statement, Socrates describes the process of recognition of the divine through its vestiges as ecstatic: "for when such a person abandons human affairs and clings to the divine, the crowd treats him with caution as being out of his mind (ὡς παρακινῶν), and he, in his turn, being inspired (ἐνθουσιάζων) shuns the crowd" (249C–D).

At this point Socrates presents the general scheme of the ascent to the higher principles from aesthetic experience. The ascent occurs through the recollection of the realm of ideas: by looking at beautiful things the soul remembers, or becomes aware of, its origin. The role of beauty in this case is that of a "symbol" of the beyond—in the original Greek sense of σύμβολον as one of the two matching tallies: looking at one of them, its possessor remembers its counterpart in the possession of a friend. Another characteristic feature of the Platonic ascent is its ecstatic, emotional, and almost irrational nature. The influence of beauty is described when Socrates speaks about the "fourth madness" (τετάρτη; 249D4ff.). First, earthly beauty evokes the idea of beauty "when someone, seeing beauty here on earth and recalling the true beauty, becomes winged." The wings start to grow, he tries to fly, but, being unable to fly, and on the other hand not caring about earthly things, is "seized by madness." However, this passion is the best of madnesses, and "the lover touched by such madness is called the lover of beautiful things" (249E).

However, beauty is a special kind of symbol, for unlike regular symbols, which can be quite dull, it possesses an especially clear and attractive nature. This symbol first attracts and draws to itself by its intrinsic qualities, before pointing to something else. Beauty's particularly evident and luminous nature makes its position exceptional in our earthly experience, by contrast with justice, wisdom, etc. (250B):

> Indeed, here on earth the likenesses (ὁμοιώμασιν) of justice, wisdom, and all other things prized by souls completely lack all splendor (φέγγος). In fact, very few, and even those with difficulty, see the nature of what has been represented (τοῦ εἰκασθέντος) here through the blurred perception of their organs when they approach their likenesses (εἰκόνας) . . .

Beauty (κάλλος), however, even before the reincarnation, when we contemplated that "blessed sight and spectacle," was "clear (λαμπρόν) to our vision,"[61] and even now, after our incarnation in matter, still remains the most conspicuous and evident phenomenon (250D):

> As for beauty, just as we said, it shone (ἔλαμπεν) among those things beyond. Now having come here, we also discovered it—flashing brightly and clearly (στίλβον ἐναργέστατα)—through the clearest (ἐναργεστάτης) of our senses [i.e., vision, also called the "keenest of our bodily senses"].

However, even vision cannot directly perceive wisdom (φρόνησις) or other objects of love, for if they could be seen directly it would be too dangerous (250D4–6): "for if some such clear image (ἐναργὲς εἴδωλον) of it [wisdom] were offered to our vision directly it would arouse passionate love." Beauty thus is the only reality from the realm of the "beyond" that can be seen more or less directly: "but now only beauty has this fate: to be the most evident (ἐκφανέστατον) and most desired."[62]

---

61. Cf. the interpretation of τὸ καλόν and its variations as having "luminous" qualities in the Stoics and Cicero. Socrates also speaks of beauty as seen during the contemplation of ideas "in the pure light" (ἐν αὐγῇ καθαρᾷ).

62. As the reader remembers, Kant has a similar idea: it is only in aesthetic experience (in particular that of the sublime) that the transcendent ideas can be presented more or less directly (although not completely), i.e., "felt"—and thus the discipline of transcendental *aisthetics* is justified. *Phaedrus* 249–250 is, of course, one of the most celebrated passages widely discussed in scholarly literature. Von Balthasar makes note of it in *GL*4 187 in his discussion of the revealing aspect of aesthetic experience in Plato. Moravcsik ("Noetic Aspiration," 44) notices that beauty has a special role among the forms in *Phaedrus* 250A–B precisely because of beauty's sensible nature. Tarrant ("Visual Beauty in Plato," 181) mentions *Phaedrus* 250B–C as an example of our automatic response to visual beauty and its reminding role (cf. references to 255C–D, pp. 178, 180–81). Among recent studies, Ferrari's *Listening to the Cicadas* has the longest discussion of the passage. Sketching the ascent from visual beauty (pp. 141ff.) in *Phaedrus* 249–51, he also mentions the specific qualities of beauty, among other forms—its ability to shine most clearly and brightly and be perceptible to the sense of vision (pp. 141–42,

The experience of beauty thus evokes the feeling of the beyond, or opens a link to the other realm. The effect of catching a glimpse of our primordial state through beauty is twofold: it arouses dread, but also the feeling of awe and something sacred.[63] Thus "when those souls happen to see some likeness of the things beyond, they experience a shock" (250A6). Also, someone who saw the ideas before birth, "when he happens to see a godlike face, or some shape of a body which has imitated beauty so well (κάλλος εὖ μεμιμημένον), at first shudders, as if one of the awesome terrors of that time has come upon him, and then having his eyes fixed on it worships it as a god" (251A).[64] Socrates clearly describes what German Idealists would call a process of "presenting the ideas" through their similitudes, likenesses (ὁμοίωμα), or imitations (μεμιμημένον). Under the influence of this "flow of beauty," Socrates continues, the pain of budding feathers disappears, the feathers grow (251B–D), and the soul "regaining the memory of the beautiful . . . rejoices" (251D6–7). Thus what we have in the *Phaedrus*, if translated into Kantian terms, is a mythological description of the feeling of the "transcendent ground," which in human experience is brought about most efficiently through the mediation of beauty.[65] At this point Plato's particular focus is the ecstatic, emotional, and almost irrational character of

---

145)—although he does not engage any specifically aesthetic issues. He also lists (p. 142) and critiques several scholarly interpretations of what this "brightness" might mean, and finally provides his own. Ferrari's own interpretation is that beauty "is salient" and "announces itself . . . as an object of concern" (p. 145) and "points the beholder beyond the immediate pleasure he takes in the spectacle of beauty" (p. 147). However, according to Ferrari this future "concern" is care for the "person of interest" at the center of this aesthetic experience, which can be either of a sexual (regular person) or intellectual (philosopher) nature. This care for a person of interest ultimately leads one to learning who he/she truly is. The "brightness" of beauty, according to Ferrari's interpretation at this point, means that one can more immediately discover one's philosophical way of life in an encounter with beauty (pp. 148–49). Ferrari, like many others, makes no link between *Phaedrus* 250 and Heidegger's, Gadamer's, or von Balthasar's interpretations of Plato's account of aesthetic experience in revelatory terms. His close attention to the text does, indeed, provoke a similar understanding of beauty as a "mystic revelation" (p. 155). However, his interpretation of what beauty reveals to us (i.e., "who we are") does not seem to follow hermeneutically from the text of the *Phaedrus*, which rather suggests—an idea that is closer to either theological aesthetics or Kant's transcendental aesthetics—that beauty immediately reveals the "true nature of reality" or the "beyond."

63. Cf. Freud's *Totem and Taboo* on the ambivalent attitude to the sacred among tribal people.

64. Cf. 254B4–6 on the effect of beauty: "and they see the striking face of the beloved. And when the charioteer sees it, his memory is drawn back to the nature of beauty."

65. Fistioc's comparison between Kant and Plato's *Symposion* gains ground from the analysis of the *Phaedrus*, if only by adding more "parallels" between the two general schemes.

the influence of beauty. In the experience of beauty as "madness" in the *Phaedrus*, beauty is a certain ecstatic way of connecting to the beyond.

Another key text on aesthetics in Plato is the discussion of τὸ καλόν in an exchange between Socrates and Diotima in the *Symposion*,[66] where all important statements are put into the mouth of the priestess. The context of the discussion of καλόν is the nature of love (ἔρως). This passage is habitually referred to as the prime example of an ancient discourse on "beauty." However, this is precisely the point that we need to clarify first, before turning to the essence of Diotima's view. Does the context of Diotima's statements support the claim that they are about aesthetic "beauty," or are they simply about the broader notion of τὸ καλόν as "excellence" in the sense of evaluation? From the introductory statements we learn that, in addition to something good (τὰ ἀγαθά), love is, and is in need, of τὰ καλά (201E5), that is, of fine and excellent things; it is not an expression indicative of exclusively aesthetic beauty. A slight move in the direction of purely aesthetic beauty (Aphrodite, love's companion, is presented as καλή in 203C3–4) is thwarted by a statement that wisdom is among the things that are most καλά (κάλλιστα; 204B2–3). So by 204D3, when the interlocutors return to reexamine the initial statement that love is of τὰ καλά—a key point in the dialogue—there is still no clarity about the exact range of the term.

The opening statement that love is of τὰ καλά is gradually refuted. One loves τὰ καλά and wants them to happen to him. However, if τὰ καλά happen to someone, it is difficult to say what exactly it is that happened to him: questioning in this direction goes nowhere. On the other hand, if we substitute 'good things' for καλά (what happens to the person who loves and pursues good things?), we can get a very clear answer: he to whom good things happen is "happy" (εὐδαίμων; 204E6). Questioning does not need to go further in this direction because, first, we have a clear answer, and second, happiness is a goal in itself (205A). The interlocutors come to the conclusion that love is not at all of καλά but of the perpetual possession of the good, that is, of perpetual happiness (205E7–206A12).

Now the question arises as to what sort of way of pursuing the perpetual good love is, or what sort of activity exactly it involves (206B). Diotima proposes enigmatically that love is associated with "giving birth

---

66. The text of the *Symposion* is quoted according to Burnet's OCT edition, vol. 2.

in [the presence of] the καλόν"[67] (τόκος ἐν καλῷ; 206B7–8), both in the body and in the soul. Τὸ καλόν is thus brought back into play, and from this point on this is the term that is consistently used. The mysterious statement about "giving birth" is explained as follows in a metaphorical way. Humans burst with (pro)creative energy, both bodily and psycho-mental, experiencing great pain.[68] Approaching a certain point, we desire to give birth. We are not able to give birth in the presence of the shameful and ugly. However, "when that which has conceived approaches the excellent and beautiful, it becomes gracious . . . and gives birth. . . . Whence, indeed, great joy in connection with the καλόν seizes the one who has conceived and already swells up, on account of the relief from his great travail-pain" (206D3–5, 7–E1). Giving birth is necessarily associated with τὸ καλόν because giving birth and perpetuating oneself in one's progeny—either physical or "spiritual"—is the only way to imitate eternity and approximate a divine status on earth (206C6–7).[69] At the same time, the shameful (αἰσχρόν) does not befit (ἀνάρμοστον) the divine, and τὸ καλόν does (ἁρμόττον). Therefore the only phenomenon that inspires in us some sense of the divine is τὸ καλόν, and having been thus inspired we are, naturally, seized with a desire to approximate the divine, and the only way for us to achieve this is by imitating eternity through procreation, physical or intellectual (206C).[70] In sum, our love is actually of birth and reproduction in the presence of τὸ καλόν (206E5)—understood both as real birth and, for the most part, as a metaphor for creativity—which gives us relief from pain. The reason why our love is aimed in this way (206E8–207A2; cf. 207D1–3) is that propagation by birth is reminiscent of immortality, and immortality is part of what we want (that is, a perpetual possession of the good, cf. 205E7ff.); therefore our love of immortality is transformed into our love of giving birth.

---

67. "In the presence of" is an addition based on the context; the addition describes how the process actually happens. Some translations prefer to leave the enigmatic "in the beautiful."

68. Many authors focus on the idea of physiological procreation in this passage and miss the equally important idea of creativity or "psycho-mental" procreation of virtues: cf. Faas, *Genealogy of Aesthetics*, 23–24.

69. Also cf. 207D and Aristotle's *De anima* 2, c. 4. In light of this theory, the "disinterested" nature of the lover's behavior in pursuit of τὸ καλόν (in the interest of lovers, family, society etc.; cf. 208D) can, in fact, be interpreted as contributing to the "interest" of gaining eternity! This observation, once again, calls into question the modern idea of "disinterested" or "autonomous" aesthetics.

70. Cf. an interpretation of "noble" deeds as profitable in respect to gaining eternity, which makes them καλά, in 208D.

The conclusion that love is not of τὸ καλόν but of that which is *brought about* by τὸ καλόν is extremely important for the present discussion. It means that the role of τὸ καλόν in the *Symposion* is that of a mediator or catalyst (Socrates' "midwife") in giving birth and achieving relief from pain. The desire is aimed primarily at pain relief (the good), and only secondarily at τὸ καλόν as a way of achieving it.[71] Τὸ καλόν is therefore seen as a pointer or indicator that points us in the direction of the good, or, one could say, reveals and presents the true way to the good. This interpretation frees τὸ καλόν from being directly associated with utility and obvious practical goals.[72] It is he who has the good (i.e., pain relief) who is "happy," as one who has achieved his goal, but not so in the case of τὸ καλόν. In fact, one cannot even "have" it: τὸ καλόν, as it were, shines eternally as an inaccessible beacon that points in the direction of the good.

Just like Hippias in the *Hippias Major*, some present-day scholars are not particularly happy about the interpretation that τὸ καλόν is not identical with the good, which follows consistently from the discussion of "giving birth in the καλόν" in the *Symposion*.[73] However, such an understanding of τὸ καλόν in Plato is in general consistent with the interpretation of the role of aesthetic experience (beauty in particular) in the West after Plato, up to the twentieth-century tradition in aesthetics. The aesthetic is a pointer (von Balthasar's *Verweis*) that reveals and presents; it is the revelatory aspect of reality, rather than its "value" aspect (the good). Incidentally, a deviation through the modern assess-

---

71. Cf. the *Phaedrus*: upon seeing beauty, an "uplifting" capacity appears. Also cf. the Stoics: because of its manifest nature and identity with the good, τὸ καλόν is an indicator of the good.

72. It is, perhaps, this text that has influenced the Stoics: according to them, just as in Plato, we do not normally perceive any apparent utility in τὸ καλόν, and one should merely aim at it, which will automatically result in the acquisition of the good.

73. Thus even von Balthasar, who has an extensive treatment of the *Symposion* in GL4 188ff., and of this particular passage on p. 190, seems to be under the impression that one can actually reach "the beautiful" (his interpretation of τὸ καλόν; cf. GL4 204 with a reference to *Symp.* 204DE), which is tantamount to reaching the good. However, textual evidence does not support this interpretation. Instead, it points to our interpretation, that τὸ καλόν is not identical with the good, but only points to it. E.g., Fistioc (*Beautiful Shape of the Good*, 83), speaking of *Symp.* 206B, E, also recognizes that "what one really searches for ... is not just beauty, but rather birth in beauty" (again, her rendering of τὸ καλόν). Contemporary attempts to engage in the sophistry of some medieval scholastics by claiming "real identity" and "conceptual difference" for the good and the beautiful, with the beautiful acting as a "transcendental," must be deemed inappropriate for various hermeneutical and historical reasons: see some comments on this subject in Chapter 2.

ment of the pointing role of aesthetic experience might allow us to understand the exact nature of τὸ καλόν in Plato's *Symposion*. Indeed, if one assumes Gadamer's model of the historical extension of ideas, the modern understanding within the context of a continuous tradition must have roots in ancient thought. Thus what has gradually developed out of these roots cannot be entirely without any foundation in the original tradition. In modern and present-day thought, aesthetic experience is perceived as analogous to understanding, perceiving moral laws, experiencing the divine, and the process of interpretation precisely because all these phenomena share one common feature: they all include a revelatory or "pointing" aspect. The difference between the good as sheer value and the aesthetic is the presence of this revelatory or pointing aspect. Now if what is most important in the notion τὸ καλόν in the *Symposion* is its revelatory, manifest, or pointing aspect, then Plato is interested precisely in its aesthetic qualities rather than its value aspect.

Apart from pointing out the clearly revelatory nature of τὸ καλόν, what does the context of the *Symposion* tell us about the other criterion of aesthetic experience? Can τὸ καλόν be qualified as "aesthetic" on the basis of its connection to direct sensory input? Clearly, τὸ καλόν has a physical aspect (the truly aesthetic), since "beautiful bodies" have already been mentioned in 209B4–5. The analysis of the next section of Diotima's speech also confirms that at least the initial stage of one's familiarity with τὸ καλόν does include a clearly aesthetic experience of "beautiful bodies" (καλὰ σώματα; 210A6). However, the process of deepening of one's sense of τὸ καλόν also includes the καλόν perceived in souls (moral qualities), the abstract notion of the καλόν, and finally its pure idea. It is also quite clear that "birth in the καλόν" is not seen as merely physical: one can "procreate" in the soul (virtue) and in the mind (wisdom) and therefore one is also looking for the sort of καλόν (moral or intellectual) in the presence of which to give birth to good morals or ideas (209A–B). Thus, in contrast to a heterosexual couple, the two men attracted to each other's καλόν produce not children but "more beautiful and eternal children," that is, moral virtues and mental qualities.

All this creates the impression that τὸ καλόν in the *Symposion*, unlike in the *Phaedrus*, remains an undefined and general notion, and thus one cannot refer to this context as primarily aesthetic. However, the following observations will allow us to place the discussion of τὸ καλόν in the *Symposion* more precisely as regards the aesthetic. The description of the soul that is perceived as καλή includes such epithets as γενναία and εὐφυής (209B6), which are related to the notion of *nobility* ("of noble birth," "freeborn"). The fact that in the Greek mind τὸ καλόν was associated with "nobility" is confirmed historically by Cicero's translation of this root by the Latin *honestum/honestas* and the use of its close synonym *liberalitas* ("nobility," "the quality of the freeborn") in close proximity with *honestas*. Both notions are associated with some clear outward manifestations: "noble" behavior is immediately evident to all. Thus it is the "noble" aspect of moral behavior that is important if one describes it by the term καλόν. In this way, although the actual context of the *Symposion* shows that Plato's τὸ καλόν is a broad conflation of physical beauty and superior moral or intellectual qualities, it is clear that it is not the value aspect of these things that is most important. Indeed, even in the examples that do not include direct sensory (that is, aesthetic) experience, it is the revelatory or "signaling" aspect that is important. The object of revelatory experience is immediately but not rationally attractive; its value is obvious without any rational explanation. This means that even if these examples are not strictly speaking aesthetic (that is, sense-based), they are at least *analogous* to our aesthetic experience of beautiful bodies. It is precisely these qualities analogous to actual aesthetic experience that serve as an indication to us that such things have other intrinsic value (cognitive or moral).[74] However, according to the definition of aesthetics derived hermeneutically in the introductory chapters, something "analogous to the aesthetic" found in other areas is precisely the focus of many modern and contemporary aesthetic theories.

The discussion of the nature of τὸ καλόν in the *Symposion* is followed by a description of the ascent to higher principles from the aesthetic experience of physical bodies (210A–212A).[75] It is perhaps the most celebrated and most important statement in Plato's aesthetics which has influenced, directly or indirectly, the whole of the Western European intellectual tradition, from pagan Neoplatonism, to Christian Neopla-

---

74. This revelatory function in the Stoic tradition was transferred from τὸ καλόν more specifically to τὸ πρέπον.

75. Stressing that it is the ascent that is most important, Fistioc concludes (in connection with *Symp.* 211) that the feature, common to our aesthetic experience of physical things and such things as wisdom, that allows both to be called beauty is precisely that both trigger the ascent (*Beautiful Shape of the Good*, 84).

tonic elements in Augustine and later medieval authors, to nineteenth- and twentieth-century theological aesthetics. Diotima hints at the importance of this insight in 210A1–3 by referring to it as the ultimate and highest mystery, which the human mind might not necessarily be able to perceive—the rest of the discourse having been a mere preparation for it. One starts the ascent at a young age by focusing on "beautiful bodies" (210A6). After learning how to love one body, one realizes that beauty is a universal quality common to many bodies (210B). Up to this point Diotima clearly speaks of aesthetic beauty, as suggested by the term τὸ κάλλος. Once one forms an abstract notion of beauty and starts to pursue the generic καλόν, and not particular instances of it, one realizes that beauty (κάλλος) in all bodies is "one and the same" and learns how to love all beautiful bodies generically, and not one in particular. Note that at this point the terms τὸ καλόν and κάλλος are used interchangeably, thereby suggesting, also given the examples of bodies, an emphasis on the aesthetic meaning of τὸ καλόν. This is helpful when, at the next stage, the aspirant proceeds to the beauty of souls (κάλλος), which is perceived as more worthy than bodily beauty (210B6). At this point, from a present-day perspective, we are clearly dealing with an *analogy* with physical beauty. However, just as clearly, it is an analogy with *beauty*, an analogy in which the aesthetic element is the most important one. A similar beauty or aesthetic element (τὸ καλόν: probably "nobility" in this case) is found in deeds and laws (210C3–4). Already at this point bodily beauty is looked down upon. The aspirant further proceeds to the beauty (κάλλος) of sciences (210C6)—perhaps what present-day scientists would call "elegance"—and now is looking not at some particular instances of beauty but at the "immense sea ... of beauty," until one finally arrives at "one single science" of the καλόν (210D3–4).

The terms used to describe this experience here and below are all related to seeing or the revelatory aspect of the aesthetic: "behold," "contemplate" (θεωρεῖν); "see," "gaze" (θεᾶσθαι); "look," "observe," "perceive" (ὁρᾶν, καθορᾶν). Also, what follows next is clearly not a formation of a concept but a *vision* of τὸ καλόν:[76] an intellectual "eidetic-phenomenological" vision, to be sure, but analogous to an aesthetic vision. It is noteworthy that Diotima speaks of "seeing" as opposed to possessing (as one possesses the good) τὸ καλόν which, as becomes clear from what follows, is perceived

---

76. Cf. 211D2–3: θεωμένῳ αὐτὸ τὸ καλόν; 212A3: ὁρῶντι ᾧ ὁρατὸν τὸ καλόν.

as a certain absolute and inaccessible principle.⁷⁷ Thus after a prolonged contemplation, the lover "looking (θεώμενος) at the beautiful things continuously in the right manner, and already approaching the end of his amorous pursuits, will suddenly see (ἐξαίφνης κατόψεται) some beauty of an amazing nature" (210E3–5). It is precisely for the sake of this vision that he endured all the preparatory stages. In addition to its "visual" nature, this experience shares another important feature with the aesthetic: it is immediate (ἐξαίφνης), or akin to the Kantian "without a concept."⁷⁸

To be sure, the ultimate vision of τὸ καλόν is somehow associated with the possession of the end: "Indeed, when someone, ascending from those things below through the right way of manly love, starts to see (καθορᾶν) that beauty above, it is almost as if he seizes something of the end" (211B5–7). However, as before, it is quite clear from the context that τὸ καλόν itself is not the end and always remains, and should remain, something ungraspable. Indeed, the "right way of loving," or the correct way of behaving toward τὸ καλόν, the only way in which one can use it for the ascent, instead of being stalled at a particular lower level, is not to focus on the beautiful thing itself by trying to possess it, use, or take delight in it.⁷⁹ To focus on the aesthetic object itself means precisely to miss the point of the aesthetic and its anagogical and revelatory function. An aesthetic object is aesthetic precisely insofar as it always points to something else—in the case of Plato, the good. Once it becomes the end object of our desire, it ceases to be aesthetic and becomes the good itself. This would count for a "disinterested aesthetic attitude" even by eighteenth-century standards.⁸⁰

77. This is evident from the passage that immediately follows (211A1–5, B1ff.), which contains the famous dialectical description of τὸ καλόν that presents it as eternal, unchanged, and absolute (i.e., not relative to any other principle). The description itself is not particularly relevant to the present study, but it is worth mentioning that this understanding of τὸ καλόν was taken over by the Neoplatonists (because of its similarity to the unchangeable One) and became extremely popular with the Christian Patristic authors because it exhibited some features of the Christian God: e.g., this passage from the *Symposion* was quoted almost verbatim by pseudo-Dionysius in *Divine Names* 4.7, and hence it became very well known, from the Latin translations, to medieval schoolmen.

78. Von Balthasar also notices the immediacy of this vision in the *Symposion* in GL4 188ff. Commenting on the term ἐξαίφνης he paraphrases Plato's text in terms that strikingly resemble his own: these experiences, he writes, "suddenly reveal the glory of the wondrous vision of the eternal and immutable Beautiful-in-itself" (GL4 190).

79. The examples of an incorrect way of treating τὸ καλόν in 211D4–7 are looking in amazement (θεᾶσθαι, ὁρῶν ἐπέπληξαι) at such beautiful things as golden objects or clothes, or trying to be with them or even have sex with them (boys).

80. The term "disinterested" should be taken under erasure, in light of the discussion of

Diotima at this point gives a concise formulation of the principle of the ascent, which sounds surprisingly similar to Augustine's *De ordine* 2.14.39. In short, she says, "the right way to love"[81] means "to ascend (ἐπανιέναι) continually, like someone climbing a ladder (ἐπαναβαθμοῖς), starting from particular beautiful things down below in pursuit of that beauty above" (211C1–2). The main steps are now recounted briefly once again. It is remarkable that the original aesthetic (that is, sensible, physical) element always remains present throughout her discourse, even at the stage at which she discusses the vision of the immutable καλόν. Thus in 211A6, trying to separate the absolute καλόν from the process of "imagining" it as a particular instance of καλόν, Diotima again mentions beautiful "face," "hands," and "bodies" as particular examples of the general principle.

As her final observation, Diotima presents two alternative models of "aesthetic seeing"—the idea of seeing being continuously present over the whole course of the ascent. Thus seeing (ἰδεῖν) the real, divine, pure and unmixed καλόν serves as a "trigger" for producing virtue itself (211E–212A). (Note that here in *Symp.* 212A as elsewhere, τὸ καλόν itself is not identical to that virtue [or the good] which is produced as a result of looking at it. Indeed, one has a *vision* of τὸ καλόν and is able to "see" it, but what one really pursues is the production of virtue.) At the same time, if one happens upon merely an image (εἴδωλον) of τὸ καλόν, that is, those beautiful things we see on earth, only an "image" of virtue is produced, not the true virtue produced when one looks at the true καλόν (212A4–5). This scheme of the pure idea of τὸ καλόν and its image in this world (beautiful things) brings out some commonality between the ways this notion is understood in the *Symposion* and in the *Phaedrus*, where earthly beauty also serves as a clear image of the idea of καλόν from the eternal realm. Thus the idea of τὸ καλόν—either real καλόν or, as its image, earthly beauty—being somehow the very visibility of the eternal principles is not as directly stated in the *Symposion* as it is in the *Phaedrus*, but it still emerges hermeneutically from the text.

---

the aesthetic in this study (cf. the nineteenth-century idea of the aesthetic as a teaching mechanism aimed at the ethical), not to mention the postmodern critique of the term (can anything be strictly speaking disinterested?). It always turns out that there is some interest involved at a certain point, depending on how one understands 'interest.' What we mean is that Plato's τὸ καλόν is "disinterested" in the same imperfect sort of way as the modern aesthetic is, i.e., it is devoid of immediate utilitarian interests.

81. τὸ ὀρθῶς ἐπὶ τὰ ἐρωτικὰ ἰέναι (211B7–C1).

The revelatory function of the aesthetic in the *Symposion* can be briefly described as follows. The notions τὸ καλόν ("beauty/excellence") or καλά ("beautiful things") here are broad and all-encompassing, and the focus is definitely not on physical beauty but on the general concept of "beauty," taken in its true sense or analogically. However, these notions are still of interest to the study of aesthetics because at all stages they do include elements that are aesthetic in the modern sense (that is, having to do with sense perception), first in the proper sense (beautiful bodies) and then analogically. The uniting theme in Diotima's speech in the *Symposion* is that the aesthetic, or the analogue of the aesthetic, is something that is not the goal in itself but a pointer *(Verweis)* that shows the way to the goal. The main aesthetic principle, τὸ καλόν, works as a catalyst of sorts. What one strives for and finally achieves is the good (happiness resulting from a relief from pain). One also strives to approach the divine (eternal) state and comes close to it in one's reproductive and creative activity under the influence of the vision of beauty. Τὸ καλόν itself, however, is not "achieved" but facilitates reproduction and creativity; it *points the way and guides,* and so our interest is not aimed at it directly. One could say again, that, as in many modern aesthetic theories, the aesthetic is not the goal in itself here, but something that helps achieve desired results: for example, our experience of beauty can serve to improve our morals, et cetera. When beauty and aesthetic experience are used for non-aesthetic purposes it is also typical to use them as analogies to other processes.

The main "educational" or "training" mechanism in the *Symposion* is the ascent from the visual experience of physical beauty to the higher levels and degrees of "seeing" that are, from the modern perspective, only analogical to aesthetic seeing. The focus is thus not on physical beauty as such but on the analogical value of the experience that could help, by providing an easy reference to something to which all have access, at the more difficult levels of intellectual and spiritual progress ("moral" or "intellectual beauty"). An important thing to remember, though, is that despite the fact that it is the higher levels of τὸ καλόν that are of primary importance, even its "lowest" level, physical beauty, is still as valid a pointer as any higher variety of it. As for its educational value, it seems simply indispensable, since humans have no direct access to the higher levels except through the process of recollection triggered by the lowest ones. Another important point is that τὸ καλόν, perpetually maintaining its role as a "catalyst" of the ascent, even at its higher levels, still preserves, if only analogically, its aesthetic aspect, which is always closely associated with our sense experience. At the same time, to the very end the "pointer" and "beacon" of beauty remains outside the reach of the initiate: misunderstanding the task and reaching for the beacon instead of the actual goal results in the loss of one's direction.

We can now turn to the *Timaeus*.[82] This dialogue is significant for two reasons: first, because of its importance for the Western Middle Ages as one of the main sources of Platonic aesthetics, and second, because of the claim that, by the time of this dialogue, Plato switches from the model based on the "aesthetics of immediacy" or "revelation aesthetics" to the model based on the "aesthetics of order." It is quite clear that the greater part of the dialogue—beginning with 28A, where Timaeus starts his discussion of the creation of the universe—is indeed dedicated to the description of the general order of the universe. However, since the concept of order as one of the main aesthetic principles is commonplace even in Presocratic thought[83]—as it still is in present-day "biological" aesthetics—it is not credible that there was ever a time when Plato did not subscribe to it and that the theory expanded in the *Timaeus* is something new to Plato. We must therefore focus on the question whether or not Plato at this point still subscribes to his earlier view that the aesthetic element in reality stands for something that immediately reveals its hidden principles and laws.

Timaeus hints that such hidden principles are indeed the subject of his speech. In *Timaeus* 29C5–D3, and especially in D1-3 he suggests—a statement similar to the one pseudo-Dionysius makes at the end of his *Mystical Theology*—that he will try to describe some of these divine mysteries in familiar terms, but that one ought not venture anywhere beyond that, into the area that eludes description by human speech. The discourse about these "unspeakable" mysteries starts, though, precisely with the notion of physical or visible beauty. Fortunately it is clear from the context that the term καλός is used here in its aesthetic sense ("beautiful"), since Timaeus refers to the directly visible beauty of the cosmic order (the stars, planets, the arrangement of the elements, and

---

82. The text is quoted according to the OCT edition: *Platonis opera*, vol. 4, edited by I. Burnet (Oxford: Clarendon Press, 1902; reprinted 1978).

83. Cf. H. Diels, ed., *Die Fragmente der Vorsokratiker*, vol. 1 (Berlin: Weidmann, 1951), 469.36–37.

other visible signs of order). The major premise introduced at the very beginning of Timaeus's speech is that as long as the Demiurge—the creator of the universe—looks at the eternal and unchangeable exemplar (τὸ κατὰ ταὐτὰ ἔχον, τὸ ἀίδιον) during his work, he makes everything he creates beautiful, and insofar as he looks at something which has arisen (τὸ γεγονός)—not beautiful (28A5–B2). The argument then develops as follows (29A2–6):

> For if, indeed, this universe is beautiful, and the Demiurge good, it is clear (δῆλον) that the latter was looking at the eternal exemplar, but if not—which is sacrilegious even to suggest—then at the exemplar which has arisen. Surely, it is clear (σαφές) to anyone that he was looking at the eternal exemplar, for the one [i.e., the universe] is the most beautiful of all that has arisen, and the other [the Demiurge] is the best of all causes.

The minor premise (or at least an important part of it) is, then, that the universe is, indeed, the most beautiful, which leads to the conclusion that the Demiurge used the eternal exemplar in creating it. What is most important to our discussion of Plato's aesthetics here is that, according to Timaeus, the proof of the minor premise—or at least of the part about the beauty of the universe—does not rest on any rational argument: the statement in the minor is absolutely "obvious" and "clear" (σαφές), or, in modern terminology, self-evident. The conclusion that it was the eternal exemplar that was used during the process of creating the universe rests, in modern terms, on the purely *a posteriori* evidence derived from the beauty of the world, which is assumed to be evident to any observer without argument. It is thus rather difficult to claim that Plato's view of the role of aesthetic experience in the *Timaeus* undergoes a significant change. To be sure, the lengthy quasi-mythological explication of the principles of order used by the Demiurge during the creation of the universe does not seem to fit in the "revelation" scheme, but we also remember that the account in the *Phaedrus* similarly starts with a lengthy quasi-mythological explication of the pre-existent state of the human soul. The most important point in Plato's aesthetics, however, is how one becomes aware that this is the case: that there is a realm of ideas, that the soul did have contact with this realm before birth, that the universe is indeed based on some eternal orderly principles, et cetera. It is at precisely this point that the immediately revealing nature of aesthetic experience (of beauty, in this case) comes into play. We may speculate theoretically about why something is the case, but it is through our immediate experience of beauty that we become aware with certainty that it is indeed so.

It is only after presenting this initial *a posteriori* aesthetic insight into the nature of the principles underlying this world that Timaeus, indeed, moves on to portraying the principle of order as superior. (This move inadvertently elevates the position of beauty in the Middle Ages, because of the conflation of the "creation stories" of the *Timaeus* and Genesis.) The explanation for why the Demiurge did his best in producing the world (29E–30A7) runs as follows: He is good and has no envy; for this reason he tried to make all as good as possible, and order seemed to him better than disorder:

> For this god, wishing all to be good . . . thus taking all that was visible, which was not in the state of rest, but moving discordantly and disorderly, brought it from disorder to order, thinking that the latter was in all respects better than the former. For it neither was nor is appropriate for the very best to produce anything else but the most excellent or beautiful (κάλλιστον).[84] (30A2–7)

For the purpose of binding the universe in an orderly arrangement, Timaeus continues, the most beautiful kind of bond appeared to be proportion (ἀναλογία):

> For the best kind of (κάλλιστος) bond is that which would in the best way bring unity to both itself and what it binds together, and it is proportion which is naturally able to accomplish this task most beautifully (κάλλιστα).[85] (31C2–4)

These statements are followed by the well-known account of the construction of the world according to the harmonic ratios of musical intervals.

The aesthetic demonstration of the qualities of the intelligent cosmic principle from the visible order and beauty of the universe in the *Timaeus* also provides an excellent historical link to the later ancient and the medieval traditions: as a text that was both well known to them and contained ideas prominent in later ancient and medieval authors writing about beauty and aesthetic issues. For example, in the last sentence of the dialogue (92C6ff.) Timaeus gives a brief description of the beauty of the present universe (incidentally, the Greek κόσμος also means "beauty" or "ornament"), which results from its orderly arrangement.

---

84. The terms κάλλιον and κάλλιστον also appear in 30B.
85. It appears that in both of the above contexts the term καλός/κάλλιστος is not used purely aesthetically, but in its broader connotation 'fine' or 'excellent.'

This passage sounds very close to Cicero's account of Stoic teachings in *De natura deorum*: "a visible living creature containing visible things, a sensible (αἰσθητός) god—an image of the intelligible god—the greatest, the best, the most beautiful, and the most perfect it came to be" (92C6–8). There is also a distinct similarity between the *Timaeus* and the Augustinian theory of beauty as order, which is hardly surprising, given Augustine's familiarity with the dialogue in Cicero's translation.[86]

In brief, the main proof in the *Timaeus* of the eternal and unchangeable nature of the exemplar used by the creator of the universe is precisely the fact that the universe possesses striking aesthetic qualities. In line with Plato's earlier understanding of it, beauty, in this dialogue, is something immediately evident, and it points to, it reveals, other, normally hidden, principles. The idea of order as the main aesthetic principle is indeed prominent in the dialogue. However, initially this order is demonstrated or perceived *a posteriori*, through our aesthetic experience, and is not derived *a priori*. In other words, this order, according to the *Timaeus*, contains in itself the possibility of being revealed and perceived immediately without rational argument.

It appears that in Plato τὸ καλόν, which includes the area of experience described by the modern notion of aesthetic beauty, is consistently understood as the revelatory aspect of reality that points one in the direction of the good and provides a "teaching mechanism" for both ethical behavior and intellectual contemplation. Armed with the knowledge of this broad aesthetic notion, we can now re-examine the treatment of the arts in the *Republic*,[87] the text most frequently discussed in studies of Plato's "aesthetics." The reason why this text continues to puzzle present-day aestheticians is simple. If "beauty" and aesthetics in general are so important to Plato, why does he censure the "arts" and even expel "artists" from his ideal city? Indeed, much of the discussion in Book 2 about poets "telling lies," as well as the condemnation of imitative poetry and art as something "twice removed" from the ideal exemplar and thus highly imperfect in Book 10—topics that neither could nor need to be discussed here—on first reading do suggest a negative attitude toward the "fine arts." However, as with other dialogues, one must hermeneutically examine the context and see if Plato's main aesthetic principles,

---

86. Cf. P. Courcelle, *Late Latin Writers*, 169.
87. The text of the *Republic* is quoted according to I. Burnet's OCT edition, vol. 4 (see above).

that is, his attitude to τὸ καλόν, in the *Republic* are really different, and if not, try to explain his attitude to poetry or other arts in light of these principles.

A discussion from Book 3 seems to offer a key to this puzzle. The context of the discussion led by Socrates is the right type of "music" that can be used in an ideal city and whether musicians should be admitted to the city. The ancient notion "music" in this case, in addition to elements of music properly speaking, includes much of what would nowadays be treated under "poetry" or "literature," but with a focus on such purely aesthetic components of literature as meter, rhythm, style, diction, and so forth. It is not surprising therefore that in Socrates' statements in Book 3, musical and literary elements seem to be mixed together. One must keep in mind, however, that the emphasis here is precisely on the aesthetic elements in both that have a more direct and immediate "biological" or psychological impact (that is, *aisthetic*, or aesthetic even in the modern sense), rather than anything that has to do with conceptual thinking, ideas, or even metaphors and imagination.

The discussion of music proper, that is, rhythms, pitch, melodies, types of scales (or musical modes), develops within the framework of examining it in terms of imitation. It was long acknowledged by ancient Greeks (at least from the time of Pythagoras) that certain types of music, and in particular musical modes, have some affinity to psychological moods or even types of human character (Socrates refers to this phenomenon in 399A); they can "imitate" such states or even characters. Socrates makes a more immediate connection between the aesthetic impact of music/poetry and ethics. According to him, "fine language, decorum, gracefulness and eurhythmy all follow from good character" (400D–E)[88]—"good character" (εὐήθεια, which is an ambiguous term in Greek) in this case, Socrates explains, meaning precisely a "mental disposition which constitutes a truly good and fine character."[89] In fact, all human skills (painting is mentioned as a particular example), and even our bodies, Socrates continues, "contain either gracefulness or lack of grace. Now lack of grace, ineptness, and being out of rhythm are closely related to poor speech and bad character, while their opposites are closely related to, and imitate, the opposite, that is, a moderate

---

88. Εὐλογία ἄρα καὶ εὐαρμοστία καὶ εὐσχημοσύνη καὶ εὐρυθμία εὐηθείᾳ ἀκολουθεῖ. . . .
89. ἀληθῶς εὖ τε καὶ καλῶς τὸ ἦθος κατεσκευασμένη διάνοια.

and good character" (401A).⁹⁰ Now from this close association between aesthetic elements and the human character, Socrates derives a possibility of a *causal* connection or influence of one upon the other. Grace and beauty in music and other products of craftsmanship surrounding young people can have a positive influence on their morals by developing similar qualities—beauty, grace, good rhythm, decorum, et cetera—in their souls. Analogies that involve the notion of "health" make it clear that this balanced "aesthetic" state of the soul is perceived as a kind of good "mental health," which is paralleled by graceful and natural movements of one's healthy physical body. (This way of thinking seems to be a constant feature of ancient Greek thought.) According to Socrates,

> we must seek out those craftsmen who have a natural sense for tracking down the essence of the fine (καλοῦ) and graceful, so that young people, like those who live in a healthy environment, could benefit from everything: where they might happen to see or hear something, because of the presence of fine and beautiful things, which, just like the air from wholesome regions that brings health, straight from childhood would lead them imperceptibly to imitate, have a liking for, and be attuned to fine and beautiful speech and thought.⁹¹ (401C–D)

Socrates' most important statement about the role of music reads as follows:⁹²

> Isn't . . . this precisely what provides most educational benefit in music, namely, that rhythm and melody penetrate most deeply into the inner parts of the soul, and get hold of it most powerfully, bringing gracefulness (εὐσχημοσύνη), and make a person graceful, if he is rightly brought up, and the opposite if he is not? Further, the person appropriately brought up in this area would [certainly] have the keenest feeling for things that are wanting and are either not finely manufactured or naturally lacking in beauty. Now such a person, being rightly upset by such things, would praise beautiful things and, rejoicing in them and receiving them into his soul, would feed upon them and become fine (καλός) and virtuous. At the same time, he would rightly condemn and hate what is ugly and shameful, even *before he is old enough to think rationally.*

---

90. . . . ἐν πᾶσι γὰρ τούτοις ἔνεστιν εὐσχημοσύνη ἢ ἀσχημοσύνη. καὶ ἡ μὲν ἀσχημοσύνη καὶ ἀρρυθμία καὶ ἀναρμοστία κακολογίας καὶ κακοηθείας ἀδελφά, τὰ δ' ἐναντία τοῦ ἐναντίου, σώφρονός τε καὶ ἀγαθοῦ ἤθους, ἀδελφά τε καὶ μιμήματα. . . .

91. The idea that observing harmony and grace in visible objects and music leads one to consider following the same principles in morals, speech and thought is echoed, e.g., in Cicero's rendition of Stoic theories in the *De officiis*.

92. Note again that the term "music" here includes artistic skills which we normally associate with metered poetry.

When, however, rational thought comes to the person who has been brought up in this way, would he not be best positioned to embrace it, recognizing it because of its familiarity? (401D–402A; my italics)

Socrates concludes his discourse on the educational value of music and poetry by outlining the ancient Greek ideal of a person, in whom a beautifully shaped physical body is matched by a "beautiful" disposition in the soul: "So if fine (καλά) character traits present in someone's soul happen to match and harmonize with [the beauty of] his physical form, which is modeled on the same pattern, wouldn't that be the fairest of sights for those who can see it?" (402D)

It is quite obvious then that at least some types of music and poetry in the *Republic*—those that can be called καλά (fine, excellent) and εὐσχήμονα (elegant, graceful, harmoniously composed)—are highly praised and considered important from an educational point of view. A reference to kinship between such types of music and rational thought in 402A is perhaps based on the observation that rational thought shares such aesthetic qualities of music as being well organized or "elegant," as in the case of some logical or mathematical proofs.[93] Thus there does not seem to be any radical discrepancy between Plato's understanding of the positive and important role of aesthetic experience in the *Republic* and that in his other dialogues. Indeed, according to Plato, harmonious and well-organized music or poetry does contribute to developing proper morals, and Plato never departs from this idea. Moreover, Plato says, it works by making us aware, even prior to conceptualization, of the universal principles of harmony and organization that hold true both for physical bodies and for our souls. Being aware of such general principles, we "transfer" our observations from aesthetic experience to morals and try to observe the same rules in our moral behavior, thought and speech. In this case, Plato singles out music, or what is "musical" in poetry, as the most direct way of conveying aesthetic laws but the same holds true for other media as well.[94]

We see, then, that the object of condemnation in the *Republic* is

---

93. Τὸ καλόν, which reveals the foundational principles of reality, including truth, has an affinity with such principles, including rational discourse. Rational discourse, in its turn, just like τὸ καλόν, possesses aesthetic qualities (harmony, order, grace, etc.).

94. The idea of such "aesthetic education" is popular throughout Antiquity and in some medieval authors, and remains so until the modern period, e.g., in Schiller: Plato stands, therefore, at the dawn of a long, continuous tradition.

clearly not all artistic production, not even within one particular medium, but certain types or examples of such production. He rejects certain styles of music that do not contribute to good character, and so also, presumably, poetry that does not follow the laws of "gracefulness" and harmony. However, not only formal elements such as these deserve condemnation but also certain types of contents (fiction, or the "lying" aspect of poetry). We come to an observation about the fate of imitation in general in Plato: some types or styles of imitation are clearly praised (for example, imitation of courageous character in music), and only some types are rejected. Can all these diverse criteria and attitudes be consistent with a particular point of view?

There seems to be only one explanation. The modern perplexity about why Plato banishes "the arts," whereas "beauty" seems to be important for him, comes from a very crude application to his text of the modern understanding of aesthetics. It is a very modern notion of aesthetics that joins together art and beauty under one roof and always presents art, together with beauty, as aesthetic. The two do *not* always go together in pre-modern times, nor do they in the postmodern period. Moreover, the meaning of both concepts in modern studies of Plato's aesthetics is also used anachronistically. It has already been shown that Plato speaks of our aesthetic "beauty" only on some occasions, and that in the context of Plato one should really speak of the much broader notion τὸ καλόν. Present-day critical studies also apply to Plato a very modern, and thus anachronistic, interpretation of the concept of art as "high art" (his craftsmen thereby become "artists" practicing such art). In fact, as far as Plato and ancient thought in general are concerned (interpreting both the Greek τέχνη and the Latin *ars*), one must speak merely of "craft" and "craftsmen." Ancient crafts could have more or less to do with aesthetic (in the modern sense) aspects, or even with the ancient principle of καλόν, just as is the case with contemporary "arts and crafts" that are often (and have been historically) ugly, tasteless, tacky, and kitsch from the point of view of the "high" standard.

One must remember instead that what is most important to Plato's ancient mind is that aesthetic aspects are always connected to (or "channeled into," as von Balthasar well said) the ethical. That is, speaking of the main thrust of Plato's "aesthetics," one should rather speak of "pursuing τὸ καλόν in the right way," which means, in the way that uses aesthetic experience as a "step" toward something higher: the moral or even the divine. In other words, the right question to ask in evaluating an example of craft or of a craftsman would be: is this particular occupation or craft, as well as its products, conducive of τὸ καλόν? Do they contain an aesthetic element that can point to the ethical? To be sure, unlike in the Christian culture with its idea of "vain beauty," beauty in Plato and ancient Greek thought in general is always connected to the good. And nevertheless, there is always a possibility that one can stop at a lower level (that is, indulge in aesthetic pleasures for their own sake) and miss the movement of the "ascent" that is the whole point of pursuing τὸ καλόν. This means that a certain type of craft can even be "aesthetic" from the modern point of view (as far as pure aesthetic experience is concerned) and still fail to contribute to the moral drive—that is, it can be not καλόν. It is clear at this point that the real question Plato's characters ask in the *Republic* is: Does this particular craft, or its individual instance contribute to τὸ καλόν? In the case of the arts that are banished (mimetic-fictional literature for pure amusement, as well as certain "lascivious" types of music), one learns they do not, but remain at the level of purely aesthetic pleasure and entertainment.

Even in the *Republic*, then, Plato seems to be far from denying the true power of artistic activity that is capable of generating strong aesthetic response; a review of his positive account of the influence of music on good morals proves that. The criterion for banishment, however, is whether this particular type of music contributes to the ascent through τὸ καλόν, that is, provides a beneficial combination of aesthetic and moral elements. Although the aesthetic element in art, and in particular in music, is recognized as a powerful force, some art or music does contribute to τὸ καλόν and some fails to do so. And so, just as all craft that lacks the moral-aesthetic features of τὸ καλόν is rejected, so also any type of craft or any other activity that contains this revelatory element in it—that points either to the higher reality of the ideas or to the moral order—is supported.[95] In brief, an analysis of Plato's texts defi-

---

95. Plato's ambivalent attitude toward the power of aesthetic experience derived from the arts, and in particular music, is mirrored by later developments in the history of Christianity, where the attitude toward the arts and music ranged from banning them altogether to considering them an important means of connecting to the divine; see a good discussion of the Christian attitude in R. Viladesau, *Theology and the Arts: Encountering God through Music, Art and Rhetoric* (New York/Mahwah, N.J.: Paulist Press, 2000), 11–58, and some further examples and an attempt at a theoretical grounding in O. Bychkov, "Image and Meaning: Canonicity in the Eastern Orthodox Tradition," in *Image Makers and Images Breakers*, edited by

nitely allows a modern interpreter to see them as a historical extension of the idea that aesthetic experience has a revelatory aspect. This view of aesthetic experience appears consistently and clearly in a number of texts of Plato from various periods. Plato thus lays down the foundation of some aesthetic principles that endure until modern times.

J. A. Harris, 83–91 (New York, Ottawa, Toronto: Legas Press, 2003). Since this ambivalent attitude in the Western European tradition historically and culturally seems to have multiple sources, Plato in this case represents the general trend, which is not specific to his thought.

CHAPTER 6

The Stoic Tradition

A careful analysis of ancient and medieval texts shows that despite the disappearance of the Old and Middle Stoa as a continuous textual and school tradition, Stoic ideas did play an important role in ancient and medieval aesthetic thought. The surviving texts fit well within the textual tradition under consideration in this study. At the same time, as will become clear from what follows, von Balthasar fails to present this tradition adequately, perhaps for the reasons outlined immediately below. The Stoic tradition in aesthetics thus deserves a particularly close look.

The presence of what a present-day scholar would call "aesthetic ideas" in the thought of the Stoics and some authors influenced by Stoicism is not universally acknowledged. On the one hand, certain studies tend to ignore the aesthetic element in Stoic thought, and even eliminate all traces of it altogether, for example, by translating the main aesthetic term τὸ καλόν (*honestum*) as "moral rectitude," "morality," "the good" *(le bien)* or at most "nobility,"[1] or equating the term τὸ πρέπον *(decorum)* with ἁρμόττον *(aptum)* as meaning merely "suitability" *(convenance)*.[2] On the other hand, numerous studies either refer to "Stoic aesthetics" in the title or in the text of the discussion,[3] or at least mention the in-

---

1. A. A. Long and D. N. Sedley's *The Hellenistic Philosophers (LS)* is the prime example; see full citation, as well as other examples, in Chapter 5. *Honestum* is translated as *le bien* by Zagdoun (p. 37), see full ref. below.

2. Thus Desmouliez: see below.

3. For use of the term in a title, cf. C. S. Floratos, Ἡαἰσθητικὴ τῶν Στωϊκῶν (Athens: n.p., 1973). Some examples of use in text: von Balthasar uses the term "aesthetics" in application to the Stoics in GL4 226; W. Tatarkiewicz does likewise in *The History of Aesthetics, vol. 1,* edited by J. Harrell, translated by Adam and Ann Czerniawski (The Hague: Mouton, 1970), 190–97. Also cf. Büttner, *Antike Ästhetik,* 108–27.

terest of the Stoics, and authors influenced by Stoic ideas, in various aesthetic issues.⁴ It would be appropriate to start with the analysis of recent literature on the subject. What do such studies mean by "Stoic aesthetics," and what aspects of Stoic thought do they investigate? A recent collection of essays provides a good sample of the state of contemporary research in the area of Stoic aesthetics.⁵ A brief look at this and other studies (such as that of Büttner) shows that, following the general trend in the scholarship on "ancient aesthetics," such topics as the theory of "fine arts" and "philosophy of art" tend to be included uncritically under the general category "aesthetics." This very modern and broad delineation of the subject—the fact which most scholars themselves notice—is applied to Stoic thought as if all these areas already constituted a unified discipline in Antiquity, and no discussion is offered of hermeneutical issues.⁶ At the same time, many issues that are seemingly important to ancient aesthetics, such as the revelatory aspect of beauty, are left out. The fact that studies of Stoic aesthetics are sparse also suggests that scholars of Stoic thought normally do not think of it in aesthetic terms. For example, H. Karabatzaki, who carefully reviews earlier literature on "Stoic aesthetics,"⁷ concludes (p. 66) that "the study of Stoic aesthetics has been relatively neglected by specialists in Stoic philosophy and historians of aesthetics alike." Although her own study does provide such general information as the Stoic definitions of art (p. 68), she focuses on poetry (the issues of analogy and etymology) and does not discuss beauty or other important aesthetic notions.⁸ M.-A. Zagdoun also thinks that there existed a "Stoic philosophy of art" (p. 37).⁹ She admits that aesthetics is a modern term (p. 43), but, like

---

4. Cf. remarks in M. L. Colish, *The Stoic Tradition from Antiquity to the Early Middle Ages*, vol. 1, Studies in the History of Christian Thought 34 (Leiden: E. J. Brill, 1985), 45, 147; and C. Gill, "Personhood and Personality: The Four-Personae Theory in Cicero, *De officiis* I," *Oxford Studies in Ancient Philosophy* 6 (1988): 173 (Cicero's *De officiis* is discussed here as part of the Stoic tradition because it is influenced by Stoicism).

5. *Greek Philosophy and the Fine Arts*, edited by K. Boudouris, abbreviated as *GPFA*.

6. Cf. my critique of Büttner's approach in my review of his book in *The Classical Review* 57, no. 2 (2007): 308–9.

7. H. Karabatzaki, "The Stoics on Poetry" (*GPFA*, vol. 1, 65–87). She reviews the study by Floratos cited above, and an earlier study on Cicero's notion *decorum* by P. Costil, "L'esthétique stoïcienne," in *Actes du Ier congrès de la Fédération Internationale des Associations d'études classiques. Paris, 28 août–2 septembre 1950*, 360–64 (Paris: C. Klincksieck, 1951).

8. She does, however, mention that many Stoic authors were interested in art, music, and poetry: cf. p. 67, 68, 82.

9. M.-A. Zagdoun, *La philosophie stoïcienne de l'art* (Paris: CNRS, 2000).

others, she develops no hermeneutic basis for why it can be applied to Stoic thought, and instead turns to straightforward, "objective" descriptions of various topics that can be related to modern aesthetics. While touching upon most of the themes discussed in this chapter, she focuses mainly on "objective" criteria of aesthetic phenomena and mentions neither the revelatory aspect of the aesthetic nor its "guiding" function in morals and religion. Büttner (*Antike Ästhetik*) follows others in focusing on the Stoic theories of art, but adds an analysis of the role of sense perception and psychology in the arts according to the Stoics. He does touch briefly upon the subject of "the beautiful" and its connection to morality (pp. 117–18), but does not discuss its revelatory aspects. A number of more specialized studies deal either with particular concepts in Stoicism usually included under "aesthetics" in modern times, such as beauty,[10] or with particular authors relevant to the discussion of aesthetic issues in Stoicism, such as Cicero. For example, a very thorough study by A. Desmouliez uses the term "aesthetics" freely in application to Cicero and discusses many of the passages from his *De officiis* also selected for the present chapter—moreover, all in the context of aesthetics.[11] One of the more interesting, although not so recent, studies devoted to Cicero's interpretation of Stoicism that incidentally touches upon aesthetic matters simply by virtue of the textual material it uses is an early work by M. Pohlenz.[12] This study is significant not only because in it an important twentieth-century authority on Stoicism ac-

---

10. Cf. H.-J. Horn, "Stoische Symmetrie und Theorie des Schönen in der Kaiserzeit," in *Aufstieg und Niedergang der Römischen Welt. Teil II: Principat*, edited by W. Haase and H. Temporini, 1454–72 (Berlin/New York: Walter de Gruyter, 1989). Horn focuses only on the question of symmetry as a criterion of physical beauty, as well as on Plotinus's discussion of the Stoic definition of beauty as "symmetry of parts."

11. A. Desmouliez, *Cicéron et son goût: essai sur une définition d'une esthétique Romaine à la fin de la république*, Collection Latomus 50 (Brussels: Latomus, 1976), 272, 279, 281–84. The sections of this study that are relevant to the concept of aesthetics as discussed in the present chapter focus on the notion of the "fitting" (*decorum*), e.g., sect. 2 (pp. 285ff.) which is devoted to the "aesthetic application" of *decorum*. *Decorum*, the study determines, is one of the main principles that governs Cicero's taste judgments (taste being another important category in modern aesthetics). However, most of this section is devoted not to conceptual analysis but to concrete exampes of what, according to Cicero, is "fitting" in speech, i.e., to the concrete analysis of Cicero's aesthetic taste (cf. pp. 287ff.). On Cicero's aesthetics also see: P. Kuklica, "Ciceros ästhetische Ansichten," *Graecolatina et Orientalia* 11–12 (1979–80): 17–29; N. A. Fyodorov, "The Genesis of the Aesthetic Component in the Semantics of the Lexical Group decus-decorum-decere-dignitas," *Vestnik Moskovskogo Universiteta (filol. sek.)* 1 (1981): 49–61 (in Russian; the study is based on Cicero's texts).

12. M. Pohlenz, *Antikes Führertum: Cicero* De officiis *und das Lebensideal des Panaitios*, Neue Wege zur Antike 2/3 (Leipzig/Berlin: B. G. Teubner, 1934).

knowledges the existence of Stoic aesthetics: this work also comes close to noticing the revelatory aspect of aesthetic experience as presented by the Stoic thought (see passim below). A brief review of academic literature on aesthetic issues in Stoicism thus suggests, first of all, that aesthetic aspects are present in Stoic thought, and, further, that the subject is understudied. These studies also exhibit the usual lack of articulation of their hermeneutic approach, and their focus in the area of aesthetics is mostly different from the one chosen for the present study.

The influence of Stoic ideas on modern and contemporary aesthetic thought is not such a clear issue either, on the one hand because almost no early authentic Stoic writings survive, and on the other hand because their thought was incorporated by so many authors, including Christian, that it is sometimes almost impossible to determine the exact source of this or another idea that is reminiscent of Stoicism. At the same time, at least while reading pre-modern texts, one cannot avoid noticing striking similarities with Stoic thought, which are occasionally brought to light by some scholars.[13] Speaking more concretely about modern and contemporary aesthetics, one finds that little to nothing is said about the influence of Stoicism. At the same time, as this chapter will show, even if one is not able to trace direct influences, there are far more indirect parallels between Stoic ideas and, e.g., Kant's aesthetics than is usually acknowledged. Using Fistioc's approach of consulting Brucker's *History of Philosophy* (1767) for Kant's sources of ancient thought, we see that Brucker was almost definitely not the source of parallels with Stoic thought in Kant's aesthetics, although one could derive some connection between ethics and aesthetics in Stoics from his account.[14] However, as

13. Cf., e.g., M. Spanneut, *Permanence du stoïcisme: de Zénon à Malraux* (Gembloux: Duculot, 1973), and G. Verbeke, *The Presence of Stoicism in Medieval Thought* (Washington, D.C.: The Catholic University of America Press, 1983).

14. My analysis of Brucker's vol. 1 shows that he has almost nothing on Panaetius, who was, according to some studies, the main inspiration behind Cicero's aesthetic ideas in the *De officiis*. Nor does he have much relevant information on Cicero himself (cf. vol. 2, pp. 34ff.), although in vol. 1 he does use this author regularly as a source for Stoic thought. In addition, he generally does not seem to have a very high opinion of the Old Stoa which, according to him, is entangled in useless disputes (cf. p. 960). At the same time, he has a long analysis of the teachings of the Old Stoa (cf. vol. 1, pp. 896–967), including a good discussion of the so-called criterion of truth (pp. 815–17), which is relevant to aesthetics, as well as a discussion of Stoic moral philosophy (pp. 953–67), another locus of their aesthetic observations. Brucker's account of Stoic ethics lists most of the ideas that provide the context for Stoic aesthetic observations: e.g., that only *honestum* is good and must be sought for its own sake, etc. (pp. 956–58). Also, the fact that he frequently renders τὸ καλόν not as *honestum* (the standard Latin translation) but as *pulchrum* ("the beautiful") could contribute to reading Stoic ethics in aesthetic terms. Cf. his

a Latin major, Kant must have read all the main works of Cicero,[15] of which *De officiis* (by far the most popular and most widely available work in the pre-modern period) contains most of the relevant material on Stoic aesthetics. In fact, Kant's observations on the natural beauty of the starry skies and the universe in his early works are stunningly reminiscent of cosmological-aesthetic observations of Cicero *(De natura deorum)* and Seneca.[16] Since Hegel noticed formal similarities between the thought of Kant and the Stoics in his *Lectures on the History of Philosophy*, although not in the area of aesthetics, it would be an important contribution to the history of ideas if one could determine whether Hegel's insights can be supported by any similarities in their aesthetic views. Finding such similarities would further confirm the historical continuity of aesthetic ideas from the ancient period to modern times and prove the value of turning to ancient thought in contemporary theological aesthetics.

Modern and contemporary Western thought most commonly turns to aesthetic experience when the need arises for an analogy with a direct and clear intuition ("seeing," "insight," "appearance," "presentation," et cetera), whenever such intuition or "seeing" is employed to resolve key philosophical or theological questions.[17] Several thinkers, Heidegger, Gadamer, and von Balthasar among them, also thought that in order to

---

formulation of one of the main principles of Stoic ethics in par. VI (pp. 954–55) based on Stobaeus: "for the beautiful (τὸ καλόν), the good, and virtue, as well as what comes through virtue, are equivalent terms." Cf. par. XXII (p. 957) based on Diogenes Laertius, Bk. 7: "the perfect good is called the beautiful, because . . . it is in perfect proportion."

15. Fistioc mentions that Kant was a Latin major *(Beautiful Shape of the Good*, 11). Büttner, *Antike Ästhetik*, 119, comparing Cicero's analysis of the judgment of the senses in *De Oratore* 3.45.178–46.181 (useful things also look beautiful) to Kant's *Urteilskraft* (beautiful things look purposeful) makes the following observation (my italics): "One can very well imagine that *Kant, who knew works of Cicero well (ein guter Cicero-Kenner war)*, was inspired by passages like these when he was composing his *Critique of Judgment* and the definitions of artistic and natural beauty."

16. Cf. excerpts from Kant's early work *The Natural History of the Heavens* (1755) quoted here as they appear in GL5 483–84: " . . . the view of the star-filled sky on a clear night gives a kind of pleasure which only noble souls can know. In the universal stillness of Nature and of the senses, the hidden cognitive faculty of the imperishable spirit speaks an ineffable language and conveys inarticulate concepts which cannot be described but only experienced" *(ThH* III, conclusion [2, 421–22]). "The structure of the world inspires in us a state of silent wonder on account of its immeasurable grandeur and the infinite variety and beauty which radiates from it on all sides. When the idea of all this perfection touches the imagination, then the intellect is seized by another kind of ravishment as it reflects on how so much splendor, so much grandeur flows from a single universal rule in an eternal and precise order" *(ThH* II, 7 [2, 353]).

17. Again, it must be stressed that the issue is here approached historically, and the author does not try to determine the actual validity of the idea of "seeing" or revelation as a means of acquiring knowledge.

show historical continuity it was important to retrieve this key idea of a revelatory capacity of aesthetic experience from ancient thought, before it could be used in their aesthetics, epistemology, theory of interpretation, or theology. As the reader remembers, the focal point of von Balthasar's theological aesthetics is the idea that the most convincing proof is presented by that which can be immediately "seen," *as in aesthetic experience*. His view is that the idea of aesthetic analogy is as clearly present in Stoic thought as it is in Plato and many other ancient authors. In this sense the Stoic tradition does contribute to his contemporary project of retrieving theological aesthetics. However, he says very little about the Stoic tradition and claims that the Stoics "were saying nothing new" in this area (GL4 224), in the sense that they add nothing new to Plato.[18] If in the present study we can locate in the Stoic tradition significant, previously unidentified attempts to use the analogy with aesthetic experience to illustrate the possibility of relying on direct intuition as a means of solving crucial philosophical and theological questions, we shall have made a substantial contribution to von Balthasar's project.

While the connection between Stoic ideas and modern aesthetics is either weak or not yet sufficiently acknowledged, there is substantial evidence that Stoic passages, disseminated through texts with Stoic influences such as some works of Cicero, were an important source of ideas on beauty for the medieval tradition. Establishing the continuity of the textual transmission of Stoic ideas in the area of aesthetics between Antiquity and the Middle Ages is, of course, crucial to the validity of the present project. The influence of Stoic sources on medieval ideas of beauty has been studied extensively by the author,[19] and thus only a brief account of the influence of Stoic texts on aesthetic issues in the Middle Ages will be offered here. Many relevant passages from Cicero—especially from the *De officiis* or *De natura deorum*—were incorporated in influential Patristic writings, such as those of Augustine or Ambrose, the latter reworking almost the entire *De officiis* into his

---

18. There is no special section on the Stoics; the Stoics are mentioned several times in passing (GL4 220–27), but remarks are brief and general. Murillo (GW 216) notices this as well.

19. For a discussion of this influence, as well as a fuller bibliography on the influence of the Stoic texts on the medieval tradition see (cited in full in the Introduction): O. V. Bychkov, "Traditional Stoic Ideas," "A Propos of Medieval Aesthetics," and "Aesthetic Explanation of Evil." An especially detailed account of the dissemination and influence of Cicero's texts that contain Stoic ideas on beauty in the Middle Ages is found in "A Propos of Medieval Aesthetics," 118–23 (dissemination), 123–39 (influence). For a shorter account of the same, see Bychkov, "Traditional Stoic Ideas."

own work (*De officiis ministrorum*). Cicero's *De natura deorum* and *De officiis* were widely circulated in manuscript form and as part of various florilegia. Relevant passages from Cicero's texts influenced by Stoicism, especially from the *De officiis*, were widely used in thirteenth-century discussions of beauty and other related topics, by such authors as Philip the Chancellor, Alexander of Hales, Albert the Great, Thomas Aquinas, Thomas of York, and Ulrich of Strassburg.

It seems at this point that reexamining Stoic material as a "historical dimension" of both medieval and modern aesthetic theories, in particular in the area of "revelatory" aesthetics, is both appropriate and needed to fill in the existing gap. However, two hermeneutical concerns must be addressed before approaching the actual texts. First of all, the interpretation of terminology will follow the principles outlined in the previous chapter. Thus the terms κάλλος/καλός, especially when references to physical reality are clear, will be translated as "beauty"/"beautiful" and understood in terms of aesthetic beauty. All the difficulties associated with the broad range of the term τὸ καλόν—by that time already a "technical" term—will be taken into consideration: its meaning will be determined from the context and the term itself will be mostly left without translation. The situation with the Latin equivalents of Greek terms—as our sources will often come from the Latin tradition—is as follows. Whenever Greek roots are rendered by the Latin *pulchritudo/pulcher* there is little doubt that the meaning is aesthetic, in the modern sense ("beauty"/"beautiful," or "analogous to beauty"). The technical term τὸ καλόν is rendered by Cicero and the subsequent tradition as *honestum*, which poses no less difficulty than the Greek prototype: the problems with its interpretation will be addressed below where appropriate. Finally, there will be a special discussion of the term τὸ πρέπον and its Latin equivalent *decorum*.

The second issue concerns the very term "Stoic." Since no authentic early Stoic texts survive (apart from the late tradition of Roman Stoicism), one must rely on secondary sources: either polemical works against the Stoics or compilations of Stoic ideas (such as those of Cicero)[20] that come from other traditions and are often influenced by other schools or are imprecise. Therefore, in retrieving Stoic material, one must, first of all,

---

20. About Stoic influences on Cicero, in the context of his aesthetics, see Desmouliez (*Cicéron et son goût*), 87–92.

refer only to the texts that contain explicit references by ancient authors to traditionally recognized Stoics. Second, the tradition of the transmission of Stoic ideas must be clearly identified: e.g., as Cicero's version of Stoicism.[21] Another issue is that many Stoic ideas originated in earlier traditions. As will become clear from the similarity of issues and phrasing, many of their views on beauty and aesthetic experience can be traced back to Plato and Aristotle. Horn, for example, traces all Stoic definitions of beauty as symmetry back to those two authors.[22] However, to simplify matters, the present discussion will refrain from any systematic tracing of influences on the Stoic texts, apart from noting the continuity and marking any obvious parallels in passing. Thus the surviving Stoic material will be treated as part of a self-contained tradition.[23]

The analysis of Stoic thought shows that the Stoics often attempt to ground their foundational principles in certain experiences that possess a particularly clear nature—something that von Balthasar would call 'aesthetic.' For example, appeals to such clear experiences play an important role during the Stoic discussion of one of the key philosophical issues, the criterion of truth. Sextus Empiricus reports that, for the Stoics, certain sensory and intelligible data are true, and the validity of the sense data is established through the corresponding intelligible, or cognitive, impressions.[24] The theory of "cognitive impression"

21. In addition to the book by Long and Sedley (1987), I will refer to the following collections of Stoic fragments: I. von Arnim, ed., *Stoicorum veterum fragmenta*, 3 vols. (Leipzig: B. G. Teubner, 1921), henceforth, *SVF* with a volume and reference number; M. Van Straaten, ed., *Panaetii Rhodii Fragmenta* (Leiden: E. J. Brill, 1962), later, Panaetius with a reference number; L. Edelstein and I. G. Kidd, eds., *Posidonius. I. The Fragments* (Cambridge: Cambridge University Press, 1972), later, Posidonius with a reference number. Von Arnim's collection, although still extremely valuable regarding its content, is certainly out of date in respect to references to works and editions. Therefore, while keeping his reference numbers, I will, if necessary, provide more recent information in citing the works. I will quote ancient authorities on Stoicism according to the following editions: M. *Tullii Ciceronis scripta quae manserunt omnia* 1/4 (*De finibus, Tusculanae disputationes*), 2/4 (*De natura deorum, De legibus*), 3/4 (*De officiis*) (Leipzig: B. G. Teubner, 1864, 1866); Plutarchus, *De Stoicorum repugnantiis*, in vol. 6/2 of *Plutarchi Moralia*, edited by M. Pohlenz (Leipzig: B. G. Teubner, 1952); Diogenes Laertius, *Vitae Philosophorum*, edited by H. S. Long, vol. 2 (Oxford: Clarendon Press, 1964).

22. Horn, "Stoische Symmetrie," 1461, 1464. Also see occasional references to parallel passages in earlier ancient texts in this chapter.

23. Regarding problems encountered in reconstituting Stoic views, in application to their aesthetics, see Zagdoun, *Philosophie stoïcienne de l'art*, 37–38. She suggests approaching the problem by describing major concepts or themes in Stoicism, something that was done in this chapter.

24. *Adv. Math.* 8.10 (πρὸς λογικούς 2.10): "For those of the Stoa, indeed, say that some sensible and intelligible things are true; however, the sensibles are not immediately [perceived to

(καταληπτικὴ φαντασία) is a well-known element of the Stoic discussion of the criterion of truth.[25] The Stoics claimed that certain particularly clear ("cognitive") impressions are necessarily true and reveal to us the true state of things. The subsequent problem that follows from this theory, and which they tried to obviate by "aesthetic" means (by claiming that this state of affairs is immediately obvious, as is the value of an object of aesthetic experience), is created by the fact that underlying their theory was an unproved assumption that nature arranged it that way that things are knowable to us and that our senses are designed to perceive their "true" nature.[26]

Before proceeding further with the analysis of Stoic thought one must note that the idea of "direct seeing" as a type of demonstration or acquisition of truth was quite common in Antiquity throughout the period when authors of Stoic orientation were active and was employed by a variety of disciplines, from philosophy to rhetoric. This idea can be expressed by the key term ἐνάργεια ("making clear," "clearness," "illustration," "manifestation"), an object of a recent study by A. Manieri.[27] According to the ancient understanding, ἐνάργεια is a particular quality of discourse, whether scholarly or literary, as well as a general quality of our conscious experience, which, instead of engaging conceptual activity, causes some sort of a clear visualization of the matter under discussion (or of the object of our perception) which is *like physical seeing*.[28] Many ancient authors, from poets and rhetoricians to philosophers, considered such a way of presentation as providing a higher degree of

---

be such], but through a recourse, in a way, to the corresponding intelligibles." Sextus is quoted according to the edition: *Sexti Empirici opera*, edited by H. Mutschmann, vol. 2 (Leipzig: B. G. Teubner, 1914).

25. A brief outline of this discussion, as well as textual fragments, can be found in LS 40. The word κατάληψις (or καταληπτική, from κατα-λαμβάνω) can be literally rendered into English as "grasping."

26. The theory of "clear perception" is extermely interesting in itself and is, e.g., at the core of Anselm's "proofs" of the existence of God, or Duns Scotus's elaboration of a similar idea that concepts, if clear enough, include the "mark" of whether they can correspond to real things or not. One of the more recent attempts to revive this theory is Husserl's transcendental phenomenology, which uses the language that is reminiscent of that of the Stoics when they speak of "cognitive impressions." Of course, the problem inherent in Stoicism is removed in transcendental phenomenology by simply "cutting off" as "non-sense" anything that does not enter the field of phenomenological observation (and the latter is always transparent to analysis; see E. Husserl, *Cartesian Meditations* [1960], 84–86).

27. A. Manieri, *L'immagine poetica nella teoria degli antichi: phantasia ed enargeia* (Pisa: Istituti editoriali e poligrafici internazionali, 1998).

28. Ibid., 105–6.

reliability in demonstration, evidence, or proof (p. 110). Clear visualization creates a closer correspondence between a representation and its original object, signals the exclusion of doubt and error, and provides a criterion of truth and certitude (p. 109). Manieri traces the origin of the most common description of ἐνάργεια, as when something is "placed before one's eyes," to Aristotle's *Poetics* (p. 102),[29] where it appears side by side with the notion τὸ πρέπον.

The notion of "clear demonstration" is used both in philosophical discussions about the criterion of truth (pp. 113ff.)[30] and in manuals of rhetoric teaching students how to present the matter most clearly and convincingly (pp. 123ff.). While the philosophical aspect of "clear impressions" will be discussed immediately below, it is important to summarize briefly, using a survey of secondary literature,[31] the use of the principle of ἐνάργεια (or *evidentia* in Latin) in ancient rhetoric, since Cicero, one of our main sources of Stoic aesthetics, is located right in the midst of this tradition. From its origin in the Greek tradition, the term is applied to a situation in which an orator appeals to the sense of vision in the audience and, as it were, "shows" the subject matter to the audience who "sees" it, being, as it were, transformed from listeners into spectators.[32] In such cases the exposition is particularly clear, and truth is not only "spoken" but "shown" (cf. Quintilian, *Inst. Or.* 4.2.64), or made directly available to the audience's eyes.[33] In addition to creating

29. Cf. Aristotle's *Poetics* 1455a 23–27, where he says that the plot should be constructed in such a way "as to be placed right in front of one's eyes as best you can; in this way, seeing things most clearly (ἐναργέστατα), just as one who happens to be right in the midst of the action, one would find what is appropriate (τὸ πρέπον)."

30. Manieri specifically connects the notion ἐνάργεια with the problem of the criterion of truth in Stoicism (pp. 114–15; cf. pp. 45–47). In particular, using the evidence presented by Sextus, *Adv. math.* 7.200, she presents ἐνάργεια as certain "clear sense impressions" that come even before one has a "cognitive impression" that causes assent. According to Manieri (p. 116), ἐνάργεια is not a sufficient condition of truth but a *sine qua non*, i.e., if something is against ἐνάργεια, then it is clearly false. Ἐνάργεια operates at all levels, from the senses to reason (p. 117) and is sometimes equivalent to the term φαντασία (image in the imagination). In the latter case "the immediacy of evidence is a guarantee of perfect correspondence between an image in the imagination and the sensible forms that generated it." Thus φαντασίαι are always true, whereas opinions can be false, because they are not derived immediately but by the mediation of reason (cf. von Balthasar's idea of "immediate seeing"). John Duns Scotus will later adjust this view, claiming that certain clear concepts are just as true as clear sense impressions.

31. Another good study, in addition to Manieri, is D. T. Benediktson, *Literature and the Visual Arts*, in which chap. 4 deals with philosophical and rhetorical traditions and has a discussion of Cicero (pp. 94–108).

32. Manieri, *L'immagine poetica*, 123, 129.

33. Manieri provides an abundance of contexts from the Latin tradition, including Ci-

a "visual" experience for the audience, an orator may even move a step further in the direction of a truly synesthetic experience. Thus Cicero, speaking of the style of oration he calls "clear" or "transparent" (*illustris*) in *Partit. Orat.* 6.20,[34] describing it traditionally as "reconstituting the subject matter almost before our eyes" so that we could "see" it, and stating that it is most of all the sense of sight that is affected in such a presentation, adds that "other senses as well, and mostly the mind itself, can be moved" by it. Cicero also praises Caesar's "clear" style as letting one not only see but also feel, taste, et cetera, what he describes.[35]

Let us note in passing that the issue itself of "converting listeners into spectators"—in modern terms, switching between linguistic-conceptual and visual circuits in the cortex[36]—calls into question the viewing of conceptual and visual (or other sense-based) processes as entirely different types of activities. It also calls into question von Balthasar's inclusion of all phenomena related to such "clear seeing" under aesthetics. Certainly, if one assumes von Balthasar's understanding of 'aesthetic' as 'something that has to do with direct seeing,' or, as it is more often the case, with any analogy with direct seeing, the phenomenon of ἐνάργεια would fall under the 'aesthetic' (that is, sensory or quasi-sensory) mode of presentation. At the same time, as was noted above, the issue is complex and it is not clear whether one can pinpoint a radical difference between 'purely conceptual' and 'purely visual.' Thus the presence of an actual sensory input may be the only distinguishing criterion available. Another consideration that complicates the topic is as follows. Such experiences, according to ancient thought, are supposed to create particularly clear and transparent patterns. However, if one looks at the modern understanding of aesthetic experience—Kant's version of it, for example—one notices that it is precisely some lack of an entirely clear pattern, or something that cannot be grasped by reason, that characterizes aesthetic experiences as contrasted with conceptual experiences (that is, if one still maintains a clear division between the two). For all those rea-

---

cero, on pp. 138–41 (cf. p. 147), which all can be summarized as follows: ἐνάργεια is a particularly clear exposition of the subject matter that enables the audience to turn from listeners into "spectators" present at the scene, which unfolds right in front of their eyes. Cf. a comparison with the term ἔκφρασις (description) understood in the Greek tradition as creating a mental picture (pp. 150–51). Benediktson, *Literature and the Visual Arts*, also provides copious material on terminology in the area of "clear presentation" in rhetoric: cf. pp. 99–100.

34. The passage is mentioned in ibid., p. 100.
35. See references in ibid., 101, 104.
36. See the issue described in more detail in O. Bychkov, "Image and Meaning."

sons, although the theory of ἐνάργεια and "clear impressions" as a criterion of truth can serve as a background for the present study, the discussion of Stoic aesthetics as such will have to move on to the material that contains examples that are aesthetic in the proper sense.

It is important to stress, at the same time, that the function of ἐνάργεια in rhetoric, unlike its function in philosophy, is not so much to "reveal truth" as to make a speech particularly persuasive.[37] This aspect is especially interesting in view of the contemporary models of understanding "truth," some of which equate "truth" with "being coherent and convincing." The process of presenting truth in this case can be seen as an exercise in a kind of rhetoric. These observations call into question, starting already with the ancient period, what it is exactly that "clarity of presentation" accomplishes: does it "reveal truth" ("objectively") or does it simply persuade one that something is the case? And what do these early observations tell us about the nature of "evidence" as such? Although these issues are not the main focus of this study, the present discussion can contribute to answering some of these questions in the future.

Returning to the Stoic argument about "clear" cognitive impressions, we see that Sextus realizes that it involves a certain circularity, which presents a problem: "A cognitive impression is judged to be 'cognitive,' according to the Stoics, from the fact that it is derived from something really existing … but, in its turn, something really existing is considered to be 'really existing' on account of generating a cognitive impression" (*Adv. Math.* 11.183 [πρὸς ἠθικούς 183]). Sextus criticizes the Stoics for the apparent logical mistake (*petitio principii*) of trying to determine the "cognitive" character of an impression through its correspondence to a real object, and the real status of the object through its ability to generate such an impression. This circularity of thought in the argument about "cognitive impressions" was also noticed by Hegel in his *Lectures on the History of Philosophy*, where he compares the Stoic technique of argumentation with that of Kant.[38]

---

37. Manieri, *L'immagine poetica*, 144ff.
38. The following edition of the *Lectures* has been used: G. W. F. Hegel, *Werke*, edited by E. Moldenhauer and K. Markus Michel, vols. 19, 20 (Frankfurt am Main: Suhrkamp Verlag, 1971); volume and page reference provided in brackets. References to the English translation are given according to *Hegel's Lectures on the History of Philosophy*, 3 vols., translated by E. S. Haldane and F. H. Simson (London: Routledge and Kegan Paul, 1955), referred to as *H*; this translation is based on an edition of *Lectures* that is slightly different from the German ver-

How can such circularity be explained, given the fact that the Stoics were highly reputed for their command of logic? Let us examine what stands behind the Stoic affirmation of the possibility of clear cognitive impressions. For the Stoics, what reveals truth is a particular intelligible impression, which is derived from reality and owes the latter its self-evidence: there is certain luminosity in nature that indicates truth. It is precisely this aspect of the Stoic teaching that becomes a matter of dispute with other schools; the very existence of such "cognitive impressions" which possess such clarity and are immediately perceived was not taken as fact by some ancient schools of thought. Sextus, in *Adv. math.* 7.257, 259 (πρὸς λογικούς 1.257, 259; *LS* 40K), presents this theory in the following way: a cognitive impression is "clear by itself" (ἐναργής) and "compelling us towards approval"; this "cognitive impression is necessarily the criterion . . . nature providing us with a capacity for sensation (αἰσθητικὴ δύναμις)—together with a cognitive impression which happens through the latter—as with light (φέγγος) in order to assist us in our knowledge of truth." According to the Stoics, this self-certifiability of cognitive impressions rests on two premises.[39] First, nature itself helps intelligent beings make accurate judgments in order to live in accordance with nature[40]—by creating cognitive impressions (*LS* 40K). Second, the faculty of assent is naturally determined to give its approval (συνκατάθεσις) to such impressions, that is, there is a pre-existent harmony between nature and the mind (*LS* 40B, N, O).

However, there still appears to be a certain circularity of thought. The idea of "cognitive impression" is grounded on the above two premises, but the truth of these premises is, in turn, derived from the reliability of the "cognitive impressions" that were used by the Stoics to derive these premises.[41] The most probable explanation is that, although the

---

sion given above. Cf. comparisons between the Stoic and Kantian positions: in the section on the Stoics in vol. 2 of the *Lectures*, where Hegel discusses the Stoic theory of cognition and criteria of truth (19.293, cf. H 2.273); in vol. 2 of the *Lectures* in the context of Stoic ethics (19.284 and 281); in the section on Kant in vol. 3 (20.368, cf. H 3.460).

39. Cf. *LS* 40T (vol. 1.250–51) and 40 B, K, N, O (vol. 2.244, 250–52).

40. This theological principle of the Stoics is described well by Diogenes Laertius (7.88): the universe is governed by the eternal law (ὀρθὸς λόγος or Zeus); it is possible to achieve harmony (συμφωνία) between the human and the universal will; to live in such harmony is virtue (ἀρετή).

41. E.g., cf. the "aesthetic" proof of the existence of the gods described below. As in the case of von Balthasar or in the Kantian tradition, one runs into the inadequacy of classifying evi-

Stoics tried to prove these positions and present them in the form of arguments, their truth and validity ultimately rested on a direct and immediate intuition, or "seeing"—in Balthasarian terms—the way things really are (the order or "truth" of reality). This explanation clarifies why the Stoics, in order to ground the possibility of cognition of truth, persistently appeal to the apparent and clear (immediately evident) nature of the experience that results in cognitive impressions, which are particularly clear and manifest types of perception.[42] Their "demonstration" of the existence of cognitive impressions, then, is based neither on empirical evidence nor on rational arguments, but solely on what we can call an "aesthetic" proof, the nature of which will be discussed in more detail later, and which will persist well into the late medieval thought.

A further examination of the various accounts of Stoic thought reveals that similar appeals to immediately evident and clear types of experience—that is, using "aesthetic" proofs, or establishing the truth-value of things by a process analogous to aesthetic perception—are made at several other key points. What is important to this study is precisely that

---

dence into a priori and a posteriori: certain things appear evident from direct experience, but our trust in the reliability of such self-evidence rests on the assumption of some pre-existing condition of correspondence that makes this self-evidence possible. As before, we will not try to resolve this problem. In general, it appears that the a posteriori (from direct experience) verification plays a powerful, if not a decisive role in Stoic thought, as it does in von Balthasar.

42. Although Hegel (*Lectures on the History of Philosophy*, vols. 2 and 3; see n. 38) perceives similarity between the Stoics and Kant (in both cases argumentation involves a certain circularity or "apriorism" and does not seem to be based on standard logical proofs), he seems to miss the element of "immediacy" and "clear insight" or "seeing"—an element that von Balthasar by analogy would qualify as "aesthetic"—which really stands behind such "circular" proofs. The common point that Hegel perceives is the way of grounding (or justification of) morals in Kant and the way of deriving true statements in the Stoics. Since duty does not always make sense logically—its contents can contradict itself, as Hegel mentions later in the same paragraph (*Lectures*, vol. 2, 19.293)—one must offer another justification: in the case of Kant, according to Hegel, it is the assumption of some transcendental ground, on the basis of which something *ought to be* right. Hegel perceives a similar technique of argumentation in the Stoic statements concerning the criterion of truth; according to his interpretation, they argued that something is reliable simply because it is thought. Hegel, though, misinterprets their concept of "cognitive impression," first, by mistakenly translating the term κατα-ληπτική/graspable (through the translation sequence *con-ceptio—Be-griff* ["concept"]) as "what is thought"; and second, by attributing the Kantian a priori, or "transcendental" principles, to Stoic thought. In any case, it seems best to avoid using the term "transcendental" in comparing traditions of thought as distant as Stoics and Kant, since it presents a clear difficulty. The term *a priori* also has its limitations (see n. 41). It is much more advantageous to use von Balthasar's distinction between references to "direct seeing" in obtaining evidence and an absence thereof. In this sense, a clear similarity can be seen between the Stoics, Kant, and other traditions in their attempts to grasp intuitively the nature of certain phenomena, for instance, morality, and in their use of aesthetic parallels to substantiate their procedure.

at those key points the Stoics use direct analogies with experiences that even in modern terms would be considered aesthetic; most frequently they use an analogy with the experience of physical beauty.[43] In some of the cases, in fact, the Stoics go even further: the aesthetic experience of beauty not only functions as an analogy, but appears as the intuition itself of some fundamental principles. According to Cicero's account in the *De natura deorum*, one such case is the Stoics' attempt to prove the idea of the existence of the universal divine law—which is at the very core of their teaching—through the phenomenon of beauty. In this case, the discussion is certainly about aesthetic beauty, since the information used here comes from the Latin sources and the term *pulchritudo* is unambiguous; moreover, it is not used analogically, because Cicero's characters speak mostly of the physical beauty of the universe.

This way of thinking certainly predates Stoicism. In Plato's *Timaeus* 29A, Timaeus asserts that it is "obvious" (σαφές) that the exemplar that the Demiurge used in the creation of the world is the unchangeable one, the main witness being the beauty of the world. There are also more recent texts that express a sentiment that is very close to Cicero's account of Stoic "aesthetic" cosmologies, for example, pseudo-Aristotle's *De mundo (On the Cosmos)* mentioned by von Balthasar in GL4.[44] Chapter 5 of *De mundo*, a hymn to the cosmos that is eternal and stable as a whole, is unusually rich in aesthetic parallels and comparisons. Thus the universal principle itself that allows for a beautiful and stable whole to be composed of seemingly opposite and incompatible parts finds its parallel in artistic activity that follows the principles of contrast and antithesis (*De mundo* 396b 12–19):

It seems that even art, imitating nature, does this. Indeed, painting, by mixing together the natures of white and black, or of green and red colors, produces images that are concordant with their originals. In its turn, music mixes together high and low, as well as long and short sounds, producing a single melo-

---

43. For certain contemporary authors, such as von Balthasar, similarity to "seeing" and such qualities of experience as clarity or immediacy would suffice to classify an experience as "aesthetic." However, some aestheticians consider this understanding to be too broad. At the same time, hardly anyone would disagree with classifying the experience of the beautiful (as in natural beauty, or beauty of the human body) as aesthetic.

44. The Greek text is taken from the following edition: Aristotle, *On the Cosmos*, The Loeb Classical Library 400, edited by G. P. Goold (Cambridge: Harvard University Press, 1992). Relevant passages are found on pp. 378–82.

dy with diverse notes. At the same time, grammar, fusing together consonants and vowels, builds its whole art upon them.

In the same way, the world is "aptly put together" (διεκόσμησεν) as a structure with all its diverse elements held together by means of "one harmonious arrangement" (μία ... ἁρμονία; 396b23–26). The passage that immediately follows is particularly resonant with the accounts provided by Cicero and Seneca and mentions various opposing principles (light and heavy, the four elements, etc.) coming together according to the rules of harmony. As a result it becomes evident that there is one force that maintains the universe, which produces a "cosmos of utmost beauty" (397a5). This universal order is equally manifested through the regular changes of seasons, night and day, revolutions of the sky at precise intervals, and so forth (397a9–10), which are all perceived as beautiful (397a7–17): "and everything excellent or beautiful (καλόν), as well as [everything] well-arranged is named after this, being called 'well-ordered' or 'adorned' after 'universal order' or 'ornament' (κόσμος)." It is also interesting that, as in the *Phaedrus*, this beauty is the most clear and brilliant phenomenon: this world is not only the greatest, but also "in brightness most brilliant" (λαμπρότητι δὲ εὐαυγέστατος; 397a15–16). The idea itself was so powerful and convincing that it was later taken over by early Christian writers, e.g., by Minucius Felix in *Octavius* c. 17.1–11, 18.1–4, and in the West actively explored by Augustine and continued to be extremely popular in medieval scholasticism.

Like earlier ancient authors, the Stoics must have felt the evidential power and immediately convincing nature of the experience of beauty that was suited well to substantiate an otherwise rather abstract claim about the existence of the divine law that governs the universe.[45] As a result, the "cosmological proof" of the existence of the gods and divine providence from the beauty of the universe becomes one of the distinc-

---

45. There are other examples where the Stoics in general perceive some affinity between aesthetic experience and the divine. For example, Philodemus records an opinion of Cleanthes—of which he himself is critical—to the effect that "demonstrations based on poetry and music are better [or "more abiding," according to Delattre's version]. Indeed, while philosophical speech is able to give a [more] precise account of both divine and human things, it does not, in its dryness, have words that are suitable for the divine greatness. [On the contrary,] poetic meters, melodies, and rhythms approach most closely the truth of contemplating the divine" (Philodemus, *De musica* col. 28, 1–15 [= Delattre col. 142; *SVF* 1.486], quoted according to Philodemus, *De musica librorum quae exstant*, edited by J. Kemke [Leipzig: B. G. Teubner, 1884], 97–98).

tive features of Stoic thought.⁴⁶ Cicero describes Cleanthes' fourth proof of the existence of the gods in the following way:

the fourth and, surely, the greatest proof is the uniformity of motion in the revolution of the heavens, as well as the distinctive character, variety, beauty, and order of the sun, the moon, and all the stars. The very sight of these things, according to him, sufficiently indicated that they are not fortuitous.⁴⁷

Cicero records a similar opinion of Chrysippus: "if you were to consider a world so lavishly adorned, such great variety and beauty of heavenly things . . . to be your dwelling, and not that of the immortal gods, would you not clearly seem to be insane?"⁴⁸ Within the Latin tradition of transmitting Stoic ideas, Cicero is not alone in his interest in this subject. For example, Seneca expresses a similar admiration for the beauty of the universe, describing, in words that are strongly reminiscent of those of Cicero, the disinterested sense of awe that strikes the beholder at the sight of the starry sky and other natural phenomena.⁴⁹ One also

---

46. Cf. sections *De natura deorum* in *SVF* 1.528–47 and 2.1009–21. On the connection between aesthetic and religious experience in Stoicism, and in particular on Cicero's account, see Zagdoun, *Philosophie stoïcienne de l'art*, pp. 81ff., 97ff.; Karabatzaki (*GPFA*, vol. 1, p. 69). Cicero expresses a similar idea about the universal design that allows one to see the worth of things directly from their aesthetic form in *De oratore* 3.45.178–46.181.

47. *De nat. deor.* 2.5.15; *SVF* 1.528, *LS* 54C. Cf. Kant's expression of a similar sentiment in his early works quoted above.

48. *De nat. deor.* 2.6.17 (*SVF* 2.1012). Cf. also *De nat. deor.* 2.22.58 (*SVF* 1.172; "that the world is most fit for continuous existence; also, that is lacks nothing; however, mostly that it possesses extraordinary beauty and every sort of ornament"); *De nat. deor.* 2.34.87 ("all parts of the world have been put together in such a way that they could neither be more useful nor more beautiful in appearance"); and passim in *De nat. deor.* 2.4.12 (*LS* 54C); 2.7.18; 2.13.35; 2.13.37; 2.14.38; 2.14.39; 2.16.43; 2.21.56; 2.22.58 (*SVF* 1.172); 2.30.75–76 (*LS* 54J); 2.37.93 (*LS* 54M); 2.44.115. M. Colish (*Stoic Tradition*, vol. 1, 117) notices the aesthetic nature of the Stoic arguments on divine providence in *De nat. deor.* 2.29.73–61.153. In addition to the *De nat. deor.*, Cicero comments on the phenomenon of the beauty of the universe in *De oratore* 3.45.178–79 and *De divinatione* 2.72.148: "For . . . the beauty of the world and the order of celestial bodies forces one to admit that there is some superior and eternal nature that must be respected and admired by human kind." Colish (p. 122) confirms Cicero's appreciation for the Stoic "aesthetic" proof in this passage: "Insofar as there is any philosophical doctrine that promotes religious belief, says Cicero, it is the Stoic doctrine of the beauty, order, and harmony of the cosmos."

49. Cf. *De beneficiis* 4.23.2, 4 (Sénèque, *Des bienfaits*, edited by F. Préchac, vol. 1 [Paris: Les Belles Lettres, 1961], 122): "However, to put aside those [useful aspects], would not the sun by itself provide a suitable spectacle for the eyes that is worthy of reverence, even if all it were doing was to go by? And would not the moon be worthy of esteem, even if it were only passing by, an idle star? How many times through the night does the cosmos itself pour down its lights and glimmer with such a great multitude of innumerable stars, keeping everyone fixed on [the show]? And who thinks of any profit while admiring these things? . . . Those things that you think are scattered about for decoration only"; cf. *De beneficiis* 4.24.1 (p. 123): "What? You

finds striking parallels to these Stoic texts in the Christian tradition, for instance, in Augustine, according to whom perceiving the orderly arrangement and beauty of the universe also confirms the existence of a divine design.[50] However, it must be stressed that, just as in other cases of calling on immediately evident phenomena, the observation of the beauty of the universe is not strictly speaking a "proof," but rather an appeal to "see" directly the divine presence revealing itself in the beautiful and orderly structures of the universal design.[51]

The Stoic authors also turn to the analogy of beauty in their medical and psychological theories in order to provide a more vivid and clear justification for the necessity of the harmonious arrangement of psychic powers in the soul, which, according to the principle of harmony with the powers of the universe, must determine its proper functioning. The Stoics compare such arrangement in the soul to the analogous arrangement of elements in the body, which results in health and beauty. It is important that it is beauty, as something immediately evident and visible, that is the main convincing element that eliminates the necessity of any further explanation. Indeed, one clearly *sees* what such harmony does for the body.[52] Thus, according to Galen (*Plac.* 5.2.158), "Chrysip-

---

would not be taken by the sight of such a great magnitude, even if it did not protect, guard, cherish, generate, and nourish you by its spirit? For . . . these things are extremely useful, necessary and vital, but nevertheless it is their majestic appearance that fills the whole mind at once." On Seneca's aesthetic ideas see: K. Svoboda, "Les idées esthétiques de Sénèque," in *Mélanges de philologie, de littérature et d'histoire anciennes offerts à J. Marouzeau par ses collégues et élèves étrangers*, 537–46 (Paris: Les Belles Lettres, 1948).

50. Augustine's passages on this topic are reminiscent of Cicero's *De nat deor.*: cf. *De civ. Dei* 22.24 (CCSL 48, 851); *Enarr. in Ps.* 41:7 (CCSL 38, 464); *De vera relig.* 29.52 (CCSL 32, 221); *Enarr. in Ps.* 144:13 (CCSL 40, 2099.1–3); *Enarr. in Ps.* 144:15 (CCSL 40, p. 2099.18–19). See a more detailed discussion below in Chapter 7. The similarity between Cicero, *De nat deor.*, and Augustine, *De civ. Dei*—although not necessarily regarding the question of beauty—was noticed by M. Testard: cf. *Saint Augustin et Cicéron*, vol. 2 (Paris: Études augustiniennes, 1958), 69–70; also cf. idem, "Note sur le *De Civitate Dei*, XXII, 24: Exemple de réminiscences cicéroniennes de saint Augustin," in vol. 1 of *Augustinus Magister: Congrès international augustinien, Paris, 21–24 septembre 1954*, 193–200 (Paris: Études augustiniennes, 1954).

51. Von Balthasar notices that in the acient tradition "astonished wonder in the face of this dazzling splendor of the heavens . . . makes it possible for the whole cosmos to appear as a 'temple of the divine' . . . " (*GL4* 221). According to him, the vision of the starry heavens "leads directly from the frozen fixity of astonishment to the relaxed calm of understanding wonder: what is made manifest to it is glory and order together or rather . . . glory as order . . . as meaning and purposiveness" (*GL4* 223). However, he only makes a brief reference to Cicero's *De nat. deor.* 2.39–60.

52. On the Stoic views on the nature of the body and soul see section περὶ παθῶν in *SVF* 3.456–90; also cf. *LS* 61, *LS* 65R = Posidonius 163 = *SVF* 3.465ff, *SVF* 3.471–72. Cf. Zagdoun,

pus clearly wants to draw a certain analogy between that which is in the soul and that which is in the body."⁵³ Cicero, who relates a Stoic point of view in *Tusc. disp.* 4.13.30–31, explains this analogy in detail:

> Just as the balanced composition of the body, when those elements of which we consist agree with each other, is called bodily health, so, when judgments and opinions in the soul are in agreement, this is called its health . . . [31] And just as there exists some fitting shape of bodily members with some sweetness of colour, which is called beauty, so the uniformity and consistency of opinions and judgments in the soul . . . is called beauty.⁵⁴

However, it is in the Stoic moral theory that the analogy with the revealing power of beauty is used most extensively. In general the analogy between the moral and aesthetic realms comes as no surprise: the ancient Greek tradition perceived a connection between the two at least from the time of Plato. Moreover, the central notion of Stoic ethics, τὸ καλόν, is a broad term that includes both ethical and aesthetic aspects. It remains to be investigated, then, whether the aesthetic element was simply carried over into Stoic ethics traditionally, by virtue of the term they used (as von Balthasar had thought)—or whether it is genuinely important to their argument and whether they truly found some new ways of using the parallel between the ethical and the aesthetic.

Turning to the issue of "aesthetic" terminology in Stoicism: while the

---

Philosophie stoïcienne de l'art, 90ff.; Horn, "Stoische Symmetrie," 1460–61, 1465; Karabatzaki (*GPFA*, vol. 1, 73, 85).

53. Claudius Galenus, *De placitis*, vol. 5 of *Opera omnia*, edited by C. G. Kühn (Leipzig: Cnobloch, 1823), 438–39 (*SVF* 3.471, *LS* 65R, Posidonius 163).

54. Cf. *De off.* 1.27.95 and 1.28.98 (Panaetius 107). The context of Galen's statements is similar to that of Cicero's: thus, Chrysippus "defines health as proportionality of [physical] elements, and beauty (κάλλος) as proportionality of parts" (*Plac.* 5.3.161, p. 448, *SVF* 3.472). By contrast, the disproportion of members or powers results in disease or ugliness: "For this reason the harmony or disproportion which arises between hot, moist, and dry elements is health or disease . . . and the harmony or disproportion of members—beauty or ugliness" (*Plac.* 5.2.159, p. 440). Also cf. Stobaeus, II.110 (*SVF* 3.278): "just as the beauty of the body is harmony of its members . . . so the beauty of the soul is harmony of reason and its faculties" (Ioannes Stobaeus, *Eclogarum physicarum et ethicarum libri duo*, edited by A. Meineke, vol. 2 [Leipzig: B. G. Teubner, 1864], 32.25–29). The origin of this analogy certainly predates the Stoics: e.g., cf. Plato, *Rep.* 4, 444D–E, where virtue is described in terms of the health, beauty, and well-being of the soul. Plato also starts with the analogy between, on the one hand either bodily health or disease caused by, accordingly, either harmony or dissonance in the body, and on the other hand either righteousness or an unjust disposition in the soul: "For virtue, it seems, would be, in a certain sense, health and beauty (κάλλος) and good disposition of the soul, while vice would be disease and deformity (αἶσχος) or disability." The harmony between the soul and the body is described in terms of musical harmony in *Phaedo* 85Eff.

difficulties with the interpretation of the notion τὸ καλόν were addressed earlier, another terminological issue must be resolved before proceeding further. Much of the available information on the subject of Stoic aesthetics comes from the Latin sources, where Greek aesthetic terminology undergoes the process of translation. In this particular case it is the term *honestum*, the Latin equivalent of τὸ καλόν introduced by Cicero, that requires a thorough invesigation.[55] Medievalists frequently claim that, in the Latin tradition after its translation as *honestum* by Cicero, τὸ καλόν definitely loses its aesthetic connotation—starting to mean something like "morally right," or at most "honorable" or "noble"—which is later restored by Augustine for the medieval tradition.[56] As a result, one can conjecture, medieval schoolmen had a very aesthetic reading of certain Stoic passages in Cicero precisely because they were reading them through the prism of Augustine. It may well be true that Augustine's (or, for that matter, pseudo-Dionysius's) aesthetics did color some of the readings of ancient texts in the Middle Ages. Textual research clearly shows that such things do happen: for example, the aesthetic connotation of Cicero's term *decorum* in the thirteenth-century Western scholastic tradition—where it becomes a synonym of *pulchrum*—is enhanced under the influence of the Latin translations of pseudo-Dionysius, Plato's *Timaeus*, and probably even the Bible.[57] However, the opinion that the aesthetic meaning was *introduced* into Cicero's accounts of Stoic thought later in the Middle Ages (by Augustine, in the case of *honestum*), rather than simply being enhanced but already pre-existent, is certainly incorrect. Even late medieval authors had a lot better sense for the real nature of ancient discussions of aesthetic issues than they are credited with by the aforementioned medievalists. Present-day philological tools make the situation even more clear. The aesthetic range of meaning of the term *decorum* will be discussed below, but even the continuous presence of

---

55. On the Stoic background of *honestum* as "moral beauty" in Cicero see M. Pohlenz, *Antikes Führertum*, 21ff.; also see LS passim.

Benediktson (*Literature and the Visual Arts*, 107) notes that one should not underestimate the historical ramifications of Cicero's innovations in terminology. "Additions to the critical terminology . . . ," he writes, " . . . (especially from other disciplines) has been identified as one of Cicero's most significant contributions" and his terminological innovations "influenced aesthetic and poetic doctrine significantly until the eighteenth century."

56. See: de Bruyne, *Études d'esthétique médiévale*, vol. 3, 92ff.; Pouillon, "La beauté," 271; Aertsen, "Beauty in the Middle Ages," 87.

57. See a detailed discussion of this issue in O. V. Bychkov, "A Propos of Medieval Aesthetics," 67–74.

the aesthetic element in the term *honestum* already in Cicero is proved by the contexts in which he uses the term (which often happen to be related to Stoic thought). For example, discussing the "fourth kind of *honesta*" (*temperantia*), in *De fin.* 2.14.47, Cicero suggests that something similar to the "*honestas* in speech and actions" is seen "in the beautiful appearance and dignity of forms"[58]; clearly, the range of meaning of *honestum* includes aesthetic beauty.[59] In *De fin.* 2.15.49 Cicero suggests that there is an intrinsic sense in human beings to perceive *honestum*. *Honestum*, "even if humans were ignorant of it . . . nevertheless would remain praiseworthy because of its beauty (*pulchritudo*) and manifest appearance (*species*)." Other classical Latin authors express similar views; for example, according to Seneca, *honestum* possesses "beauty" and the "wonder of splendor and light."[60] Thus we are faced here with the same difficulty as existed in the case with Plato's aesthetics: the key aesthetic terms τὸ καλόν/*honestum*, and later τὸ πρέπον/*decorum* are ambiguous and have both aesthetic and moral connotations. Therefore, just as in the case with Plato, these two terms will be left without translation if their meaning is ambiguous or if it is precisely their meaning that is in question. Again, the main hermeneutic criterion for determining whether the aesthetic meaning of these Greek terms or their Latin equivalents in a particular case is the most important one will be their immediate context.

According to the Stoics, τὸ καλόν (*honestum*)—as a *moral* category probably best understood as 'excellence' or 'nobility'—is identical with the good, or virtue (ἀρετή), and is postulated as the only goal of life. Starting a discussion about the foundations of Stoic ethics in *De fin.* 3.3.10, Cicero's character Cato outlines the Stoic position in the following way: "For should you proclaim that anything, apart from that which is *honestum*, is to be sought after, or should be counted among the good things, you would certainly extinguish this very *honestum*: this, as it were, lu-

---

58. . . . *in formarum specie ac dignitate*; *species* in this case most certainly means "beautiful appearance"; the presence of *forma* excludes the interpretation of *species* as "shape," and *dignitas* suggests positive evaluation; cf. *De off.* 1.4.14.

59. The meanings of *honestus*, according to the *Thesaurus Linguae Latinae* (Leipzig: B. G. Teubner, 1910), vol. 6.3/16–17, cols. 2901–13, range from nobility and moral goodness to external beauty (*pulcher, speciosus, elegans* [*de specie externa*]). The most important meanings of *honestas* (cols. 2895–2900) lie within the moral range, but it can also signify, on occasion, external beauty (*pulchritudo, splendor* [*species externa*]).

60. *De beneficiis* 4.22.2 (vol. 1, 121). Cicero also speaks of the "beauty" and "splendor" of virtue in *Tusc. disp.* 1.28.70 and *De off.* 2.10.37.

minosity of virtue." The postulate that only *honestum* (τὸ καλόν) is the good and the goal and therefore—a development of this theme—"must be sought for its own sake" becomes a distinctive feature of Stoic moral theory;[61] it is recorded by Plutarch and repeated by Cicero on numerous occasions.[62]

The identification itself needs some discussion. As was mentioned above, even Plato's dialogues reflect the general tendency of his Greek contemporaries to think of τὸ καλόν as somehow identical with the good, which makes Socrates' position on τὸ καλόν as different from the good somewhat unsettling to a conventional thinker (Hippias, for example). Now if the Stoic identification of τὸ καλόν with the good or virtue could be interpreted simply in the sense that τὸ καλόν is always (in reality) associated with the good, that is, in the sense that pursuing it will necessarily bring one to the good, in this sense their position would be compatible with that of Plato. However, if the Stoics maintained the position (uncritically assumed by ordinary ancients, on Plato's evidence) that τὸ καλόν is simply identical with the good, then is this position conceptually consistent within the Stoic sources themselves? Is this position actually tenable in view of their own understanding of τὸ καλόν and related principles (τὸ πρέπον, for example) as something evident and clear that immediately *alerts one to the presence of* the good and allows for an aesthetic analogy with the ethical because of its similarity with purely aesthetic beauty? For if the Stoics deliberately single out the revelatory function of τὸ καλόν as something distinct, while at the same time maintaining that this function remains an integral part of τὸ καλόν, then is it not apparent that τὸ καλόν thereby always contains an element that is

---

61. The relevant texts are contained in *SVF* 3.29–37 (section "that only τὸ καλόν is good"); *LS* 60; *SVF* 3.38–48 (section "that virtue must be sought for its own sake"); *LS*61.

62. Thus Plutarch in *St. rep.* 1038D reports that "only τὸ καλόν is good," and in 1040D relates a more radical assertion that what is not τὸ καλόν is not good. Cf. Cicero: "those [i.e., philosophers, including the Stoics] who considered that all that is morally right and *honestum* should be sought for its own sake, and that either nothing at all should be counted among the good things, except what is by itself praiseworthy, or, for sure, nothing is to be considered a great good, except that which could be praised truly on its own merit" (*De leg.* 1.13.37; cf. *De Off.* 1.2.6); "the just and all *honestum* is to be sought for its own sake" (*De leg.* 1.18.48 [*SVF* 3.43]; cf. *De leg.* 1.18.49); "[Zeno] considered nothing, except *honestum*, to be good" (*De leg.* 1.20.54). The position that "all that is *honestum* must be sought for its own sake" is held in common by many philosophers, "but especially by those [the Stoics] who did not wish to count among the good things anything but *honestum*" (*De fin.*, 3.11.36 [*SVF* 3.41]; cf. *De fin.* 3.11.38–39). The idea that certain types of good, and in particular τὸ καλόν are only "for their own sake" goes back to Plato: cf. *Rep.*, Bk. 2 (357C-D). The origin of the Stoic pronouncement that "all good is καλόν" can probably be traced back to *Timaeus* 87C–88C.

clearly not identical with what it means to be "good," but is something specific to τὸ καλόν alone?[63] For example, Cicero in *De off.* 1.27.95 (where he represents a Stoic point of view; see below), while claiming a real identity between *decorum* (an integral part of *honestum*) and virtue, or the good, nevertheless does see a conceptual distinction between them. Yet, despite this conceptual difference between the two he still asserts that all good includes *decorum* and *honestum*. The most plausible answer to this puzzle is probably that the Stoics simply had a rather qualified and limiting understanding of the good: the things that were "good" (that is, useful or helpful) from the common point of view were simply not so for the Stoics, but instead fell under the category "indifferent." Only that which possessed the quasi-aesthetic characteristics of beauty, nobility, and conspicuous excellence qualified as the good in its proper sense.

Such a limiting interpretation of the good must have been difficult to justify. Indeed, it appears, from the variety of arguments and "proofs" (discussed below), that the position that τὸ καλόν is the only good and the thing to be preferred was far from being evident to their contemporaries, and that the Stoics felt the pressure to substantiate it. Diogenes Laertius (7.94), for example, describes a common contemporary understanding of the good as "profit," "benefit" (τὸ τὶ ὄφελος), "utility," or "helpfulness" (ταὐτὸν ἢ οὐχ ἕτερον ὠφελείας). At the same time, pursuing τὸ καλόν, or virtue, if one follows some of the Stoic suggestions, sometimes seemed quite far from being "helpful" and required an austere way of life or even taking one's own life. Thus Plutarch relates that "for this reason it sometimes becomes a duty for the happy ones [i.e., the Stoic sages] to take their own life" (*St. rep.* 1042D), and Cicero, relating Stoic ideas in *De fin.* 3.8.29, proves that courage is based on contempt of death, that is, on the assumption that death is not an evil (which, if one takes the common notion of the good, it would be). (In fact, according to the position assumed by the Stoics, only what is *turpe*, or "morally ugly," is evil; consequently, it is only *honestum* or the "morally beautiful" that is good.)

One of the Stoic justifications of the exclusive status of τὸ καλόν or *honestum* is based on its origin in the general order of things. In *De fin.*

---

63. That is, it is a specific aspect or variation of the good, not the whole of the good. Cf. the standard Western medieval distinction between *bonum* and *pulchrum* as the former's formal and revelatory aspect.

3.6.20 (*LS* 59D), Cicero's Cato contends that one must follow things "according to nature," or natural impulses (ὁρμαί), and reject things contrary to nature, a statement that is expected to be commonly approved. *Honestum*, or moral actions, historically come later than natural impulses; however, they *naturally* replace and overpower them, and therefore should be followed. Thus, according to *De fin.* 3.6.21, there is a certain natural "order" and "harmony" in human conduct (*ordo, concordia*, or *convenientia* rendering the Greek ὁμολογία), in which the *summum bonum* is posited. Therefore "*honestum*, which alone is considered to be among the good things, comes later in time: nevertheless, it alone must be sought on account of its own nature and dignity (*vi sua et dignitate*)," but nothing else. The natural origin of the moral principle of τὸ καλόν is sometimes proved by pointing out that even irrational creatures follow it.[64] The general sense of these texts seems to suggest that at the present moment the "rationale" behind moral drives (which could be, for example, our natural impulse toward self-preservation) may have been lost, and all that is presently remaining is our natural inexplicable feeling of τὸ καλόν. In other words, τὸ καλόν can be seen as a sort of a "sublimated" expression of the general law of being in harmony with nature (ὁμολογία). Even though it is no longer clear what exactly we are *in harmony* with in this case (one might remember Kant's "transcendent ground" of our experience), the quasi-aesthetic formal nature of this phenomenon (the "in harmony" part, something harmonious, orderly and dignified) still remains, and is conspicuously evident.[65]

It appears, however, that ultimately such a transition from natural drives to "noble" moral principles was difficult or impossible to demonstrate by argument. Hence the Stoic explanation from the natural order and harmony falls short of proving definitively the exclusive position of τὸ καλόν, and, again, sounds more like a rigid axiom, which is described by Diogenes Laertius as follows: "However, virtue, according to them, is a harmonious arrangement (διάθεσις ὁμολογουμένη); and it must be chosen for its own sake, and not because of fear, or hope, or some other thing outside of it; and happiness is posited in it, as it is nothing but the

---

64. E.g., Sextus Empiricus in *Adv. math.* 11.99 (πρὸς ἠθικοὺς 99, *SVF* 3.38) asserts that the Stoics, "thinking that only τὸ καλόν is good, believe that this is proved because the former naturally has to be chosen (αἱρετόν) even by irrational animals."

65. E.g., if a certain example of behavior is *perceived* as especially harmonious ("beautiful" or "fitting"), it *must be* an example of being "in harmony with nature" and must be followed.

soul itself disposed towards harmony (ὁμολογία) throughout its whole life" (7.89; *SVF* 3.39 LS 61A).⁶⁶

As one might expect, the Stoics also tried to apply logic—their most powerful tool of persuasion—to prove that only τὸ καλόν is the good, in the sense that being τὸ καλόν is a necessary condition of being good.⁶⁷ An efficient way of doing this would be through a syllogistic demonstration of the reverse, showing that all good is necessarily τὸ καλόν (*honestum*). Cicero (*De fin.* 3.8.27 [*SVF* 3.37; LS 60N]; cf. *Tusc. disp.* 5.15.45) relates the Stoic syllogism about τὸ καλόν most fully: "That which is good is all praiseworthy; however, that which is praiseworthy is all *honestum*; therefore that which is good is *honestum*." Perhaps perceiving that the transition from 'good' to 'praiseworthy' in the major may be unclear, the Stoics, as witnessed by Cicero, refine the argument by inserting several terminological transitions that gradually smooth out the differences between the key terms 'good' and 'praiseworthy':⁶⁸

For it is most absurd to assert that the good is something that does not have to be sought after, or that that which must be sought after is not something pleasing, or, if this, also not something loved; therefore also something approved; and thus also praiseworthy; the latter, however, is *honestum*. In this fashion it happens that what is good is also *honestum*.⁶⁹

This syllogism is related in Greek by Plutarch (*St. rep.* 1039C; *SVF* 3.29) almost word for word: "the good is that which must be chosen; however, the latter is that which necessarily pleases; the latter is praiseworthy; but what is praiseworthy is καλόν."⁷⁰ Plutarch's testimony also adds interest-

---

66. Cf. the Stoic assertion of the universal harmony reported by Laertius in 7.88, the passage discussed in n. 40.

67. That is, 'only τὸ καλόν' does not mean that, e.g., 'educational' cannot be 'good,' but that it can only be good if it is also τὸ καλόν.

68. The logical transition in the minor from 'praiseworthy' to *honestum* is less clear in the Latin (and, incidentally, in the English translation), which is Cicero's word for word rendering of the Greek where it holds better (as it would in some other languages, e.g., in Russian with *prekrasno*): ἐπαινετόν ("praiseworthy") always follows καλόν in its connotation of positive evaluation, i.e., qua "excellent." Indeed, something 'excellent' is always 'praiseworthy.'

69. Quod est bonum, omne laudabile est: quod autem laudabile est, omne est honestum. Bonum igitur quod est, honestum est . . . . Illud autem perabsurdum, bonum esse aliquid quod non expetendum sit, aut expetendum, quod non placens, aut, si id, non etiam diligendum: ergo et probandum: ita etiam laudabile: id autem honestum. Ita fit ut, quod bonum sit, id etiam honestum sit.

70. καὶ μὴν ἐν τῷ περὶ Καλοῦ πρὸς ἀπόδειξιν τοῦ μόνον τὸ καλὸν ἀγαθὸν εἶναι τοιούτοις λόγοις κέχρηται· τὸ ἀγαθὸν αἱρετόν, τὸ δ' αἱρετὸν ἀρεστόν, τὸ δ' ἀρεστὸν ἐπαινετόν, τὸ δ' ἐπαινετὸν καλόν. . . . The terminology used by Plutarch shows that the Stoic syllogism that links τὸ καλόν and the good through the "praiseworthy" (ἐπαινετόν) is probably derived from Plato.

ing details about the nature of this Stoic proof. He relates another formulation of the syllogism, this time with another set of categories: "the good"—"delightful" (χαρτόν)—"awesome" (σεμνόν)—καλόν.[71] The new terms, unlike the ones of mere positive evaluation ("praiseworthy," "worthy of approval") add some qualitative specifications to the understanding of the notion τὸ καλόν in the Greek tradition: something of a certain greatness, grand, solemn, awe-inspiring, i.e., in modern terms closer to the Kantian sublime.[72] Plutarch's refutation of this syllogism in *St. rep.* 1038–39 confirms this interpretation of τὸ καλόν. It is based on degrees of excellence: where is the threshold beyond which a human action starts to qualify as something καλόν? The argument reveals that it is only great virtues, and not minor things ("enduring a bite of a fly," "courageously extending one's finger," or "abstaining from an old hag" being traditional examples), that can merit the name of noble or beautiful.

Why did the Stoic argument need these additional qualifications that stress the "awesome" and "solemn" nature of τὸ καλόν? And what can be gained from the fact that it is precisely the threshold beyond which something can be called τὸ καλόν that happens to be the weak point in the Stoic argument? The best answer, probably, is that no simple logical sequence was able to prove definitively anything about τὸ καλόν, just as it was impossible to demonstrate by argument where exactly the "threshold" of τὸ καλόν lay. Both the use of the terms "solemn" and "awesome" and the failure to demonstrate clearly where one must start treating something as τὸ καλόν reveal that the argument, in its nature, relies not on logic but rather on an appeal to direct intuition and "seeing." It is not possible to prove logically why something "good" is "awesome" or why something "awesome" is τὸ καλόν. However, it can be clearly "seen" once one has an example of such a thing, for instance, a noble action. The same holds for establishing the "threshold": while it is not possible logically to determine when exactly something becomes τὸ καλόν, one

---

Thus in *Cratylus* 416C–D in the course of an etymological discussion, διάνοια is defined as τὸ θέμενον ὀνόματα, i.e., as τὸ καλοῦν ("that which names"). On the other hand, all that is produced by διάνοια is ἐπαινετά: therefore all ἐπαινετά are καλά by virtue of having been produced by τὸ καλοῦν.

71. Something that is καλόν is associated with σεμνόν as far back as *Hippias Major* 288D (see Chapter 5). Horn, "Stoische Symmetrie," 1467, lists another context in Albinus, who associates the good with both καλόν and σεμνόν.

72. Cf. Plato, *Hippias Major* (288D), where Hippias explains that the name καλόν applies only to something solemn and grand (σεμνόν). Of course, the fact that it is an expression of universal *harmony* also makes it somehow akin to the Kantian notion of the beautiful.

cannot fail to see the "beauty" and nobility of a particular action. In fact, even the final form of the argument, which is frequently quoted as a stable formula, shows that it ultimately, if inadvertently, rests on an appeal to a direct intuition of the nature of τὸ καλόν. This, for example, is how it is reported by Diogenes Laertius (7.101; *SVF* 3.30): "they say that only τὸ καλόν is good … hence, if something is good, therefore it is καλόν; but it *is* καλόν; therefore it is good."[73] While the major premise (whatever is good, is καλόν) is proved by argument, as has been shown above,[74] the absence of proofs of the minor in this syllogism shows that the minor was certainly expected to be self-evident in any particular case of τὸ καλόν. However, since the self-evident minor ("but it *is* καλόν") contains a reference to τὸ καλόν, it shows that what was supposed to be immediately evident to everyone is precisely the presence of τὸ καλόν: it is the connection between the "noble" and the good, or the presence of the good in this case that needed to be proved.

In sum, the analysis of the texts suggests that while purely moral categories (virtue, or the moral good) were often too abstract or contradictory to be evident to the ancient mind, τὸ καλόν, by virtue of an immediate aesthetic response that it provoked, appeared more real and filled with contents. The logical problems with the syllogisms about τὸ καλόν, which could not sustain serious criticism (in Plutarch or Sextus, for example), show clearly that their persuasive power—despite the attempts of the Stoics to put them in the form of a logical argument—was, in fact, based on pure insight and intuition: the Stoic authors could "see" clearly that τὸ καλόν alone had to be the good. Like their description of the criterion of truth, the Stoic identification of τὸ καλόν with the good can hardly be supported by anything except the immediate "aesthetic" qualities of this phenomenon: the manifest "nobility" of τὸ καλόν, which is expected to be universally and immediately perceived. In fact, it is only an appeal to this universal sense of beauty and nobility—which is most obvious in the case of sensible beauty, or aesthetic experience—that could sustain the Stoic claim that we must never choose anything but τὸ καλόν. Always preferring such noble and "beautiful" behavior cannot fail to lead one in the

---

73. Λέγουσι δὲ μόνον τὸ καλὸν ἀγαθὸν εἶναι … ἐπεὶ γάρ ἐστιν ἀγαθόν, καλόν ἐστιν· ἔστι δὲ καλόν· ἀγαθὸν ἄρα ἐστί.

74. At the same time, it has been shown also that this "argument," in its turn, is more an appeal to direct experience than an argument.

right direction. The sense for τὸ καλόν thus becomes a certain "beacon" of moral righteousness.[75]

But can this discussion be seen as "aesthetic"? Where are direct aesthetic analogies in the Stoic discussion of the moral καλόν? On the one hand, in the case of the broad moral-aesthetic notion τὸ καλόν, an additional "aesthetic analogy" is hardly necessary: the experience of the moral καλόν basically *is* quasi-aesthetic, that is, analogous to the experience of the physical καλόν. On the other hand, there is still an implicit analogy here. If the Greek audience was not quite clear about the characteristic features of the moral καλόν, they could easily supply such features at any point by turning to the more accessible and evident physical, or aesthetic (in the modern sense) καλόν. This operation (transferring characteristics back and forth between the two referents of an equivocal term), though improper from the point of view of formal logic, would nevertheless help clarify, analogically, certain characteristics in the nature of τὸ καλόν.

These frequent appeals to direct intuition by the Stoics in discerning what is moral—the moral feeling being analogous to the experience of sensible, or aesthetic beauty—may explain the interest of some Stoic authors in τὸ πρέπον (the "fitting" or "appropriate"), which appears in the Stoic tradition as the most conspicuous variation of τὸ καλόν. Again, a question may arise whether τὸ πρέπον can, indeed, be interpreted, from the modern point of view, in aesthetic terms.[76] It is easy to explain why,

---

75. As the reader remembers, this idea goes back at least as far as Plato. Especially significant is the idea, which appears in *Symposion* 206ff., that τὸ καλόν serves merely as a guiding mechanism, or a means of achieving the good, or happiness, which is the primary object of our desire. It is, perhaps, this text that influenced the Stoics most: although they fail to prove the immediate usefulness of τὸ καλόν (which is obvious in the case of something good), they still assert that one must aim at it, and that that will ultimately result in attaining the good. As was mentioned before, such an understanding of τὸ καλόν puts in question its identity with the good, one of their main postulates, which is perhaps another one of the famous inconsistencies in Stoic thought that Sextus and others tried to point out.

76. One of the most important studies of τὸ πρέπον in the Stoic tradition is M. Pohlenz, *Antikes Führertum*. Pohlenz discusses the aesthetic meaning of τὸ πρέπον in the Greek tradition (pp. 58ff.) and its relation to the aesthetic meaning of τὸ καλόν (p. 60). According to Pohlenz, the beautiful (*das Schöne*) presents a particular problem, and Panaetius tries to resolve it through the notion τὸ πρέπον, which "stems from the theory of arts" (p. 58). Zagdoun (*Philosophie stoïcienne de l'art*, 37) calls *decorum* "le beau moral" and speaks of the "aesthetization of moral beauty" (pp. 95ff.). Desmouliez (*Cicéron et son goût*, 266–70, 277, 281) discussed this notion in Stoicism and Cicero, as well as in the Greek thought predating Stoicism, speaking of the aesthetic meaning of *decorum* as "moral beauty." The Stoic discussion about the rela-

in the Greek tradition, both aesthetic and moral meanings in this notion are intertwined, just as they are in the case of τὸ καλόν. The aesthetic understanding of τὸ πρέπον as something clearly perceived or manifested naturally follows from its etymology in Greek: πρέπειν means "to be clearly seen," "to be conspicious," "to shine forth," "to appear," and therefore "to be conspicuously fit," "to be–seem."[77] However, since the main witness for the late Stoic theory of τὸ πρέπον is Cicero, who uses the Latin equivalent *decorum*, it is especially important to examine the relationship between *decorum* and "aesthetic beauty" (*pulchrum*). Could *decorum* in Cicero and the Latin tradition be applied not only to moral but also to purely aesthetic (in the modern sense) phenomena? The root *decor-* (*decor, decorus*) in the Latin tradition is often used synonymously with *pulchr-* (*pulchritudo, pulcher*), which denotes "beauty," the usage that continues in the late ancient and medieval periods.[78] One might further doubt whether the technical term *decorum* retains the aesthetic qualities embedded in its root. However, the aesthetic connotation of *decorum* in Cicero—not only as an analogue of visual beauty in morality, but also as a principle governing the arts and applicable to outward appearance—has been noticed by many scholars.[79] Thus *decorum*, according to Cicero,

---

tion between τὸ καλόν and τὸ πρέπον was probably influenced by Plato, *Hippias Major*, 290Cff. (cf. *GL*4 203; also cf. Aristotle's *Poetics* ch. 15, 1454a; *Rhetoric* 3.7, 1408a–b). On τὸ πρέπον, also see studies cited at the beginning of this chapter, e.g. by Tatarkiewicz and Floratos.

77. Cf. its derivatives εὐπρεπής ("seemly," "well-looking"), διαπρέπω ("to appear prominent or conspicuous") and διαπρεπής ("eminent," "illustrious"). Regarding the various meanings of τὸ πρέπον also see D. Guetter, "Making Sense of 'The Appropriate'" in Plato's *Timaeus* (Ph.D. thesis, University of Toronto, 1997).

78. E.g., the meanings of the terms *decorus* and *pulcher* often overlap in the Vulgate. Cf. the following contexts (all in Jerome's translation): Gen. 24:16 ("beautiful girl": *decora* and *pulcherrima*); Gen. 29:17 (Rachel has a "beautiful" [*decora*] face and a "pleasant [*venustus*] appearance"; the same is repeated about Joseph in Gen. 39:6); 1 Sam. (1 Reg.) 16:12 ("of beautiful [*pulcher*] appearance and with a beautiful [*decora*] face"); Iudith 10:4 (God increases her "beauty" [*pulchritudo*] and she appears to be "of incomparable beauty" [*decor*]); Esther 2:7 ("very beautiful [*pulchra*] and with a beautiful [*decora*] face"); Cant. 6:3 ("you are beautiful" [*pulchra* and *decora*]; the same is repeated in Cant. 7:6). Augustine, e.g., in *Enarr. in Ps.* 44:3 (ed. D. E. Dekkers and I. Fraipont, CCSL 38, 496.59–61) also uses the terms *pulcher* and *decorus* interchangeably. Such usage (reinforced by the Latin translations of pseudo-Dionysius's *Divine Names* 4.7 that used either *decorum* or *pulchrum* to render τὸ καλόν) perhaps contributed to the more aesthetic interpretation of Cicero's term *decorum* in the late Middle Ages.

79. See M. Pohlenz, *Antikes Führertum*, 60. Cf. Colish, *Stoic Tradition*, 147: Cicero "also applies the term *decorum* to the arts, both literary and musical, acknowledging the aesthetic value of moral *decorum* and vice versa, as Panaetius had done." She also notices (p. 45) aesthetic elements in *decorum* in *De off*. 1.4.14: "Finally, there is the desire for order, measure, and *decorum*, an aesthetic as well as a psychological drive, which may be ordered by reason to the virtue of temperance." Cf. also C. Gill's comments on *De off*. 1.28.98 ("Personhood and Personality," 173): "The quality of *decorum* is presented as being the outward aspect of moral

The Stoic Tradition ~ 205

concerns all things (Cicero, *De off.* 1.35.126), and, apart from moral issues, can be applied to human bodies (*De off.* 1.36.130ff) and speech (1.37.134).[80]

The best description of the theory of τὸ πρέπον is given by Cicero in *De officiis* 1.[81] Cicero starts with the four—traditionally Stoic—constituent elements of *honestum* as a moral category (*De off.* 1.4.11–14; the four principles are summarized in 1.5.15).[82] The primary source of all aspects of *honestum* lies in natural impulses, or life according to nature:

---

excellence (*honestum* and *virtus*); it is thus a kind of moral beauty which 'shines out' (*elucet*) in the life of the virtuous person."

80. Cf. Cicero, *De off.* 1.35.126: "This *decorum* shows in all that is said and done, and in addition in the motion and posture of the body; and consists of three things: beauty of shape, order, and adornment appropriate for the action (these things are difficult to enunciate, but it will be sufficient to understand what they are)." Ambrose's interpretation of Cicero preserves the similarities in meaning between *decorum* and *pulchrum*: cf Ambrose, *De officiis ministrorum* (PL 16) based on Cicero's *De officiis*. J. M. Fontanier notices that Augustine perceived *decorum* as almost identical in meaning with *pulchrum*: see J. M. Fontanier, "Sur le traité d'Augustin *De pulchro et apto*: Convenance, beauté et adaptation," *Revue des sciences philosophique et théologiques* 73 (1989): 415 (cf. his 1999 study). Finally, *decorum* is understood in the same way in the thirteenth century by Philip the Chancellor, who compares the effect of *decorum* on the soul to the effect of external light on the eye. According to him, *decorum* is a *spirituale lucidum* which "pleases and delights the soul" when it is seen: *De quatuor cardinalibus virtutibus*, pars 3 (*De temperantia*), qu. 4 (Philip the Chancellor, *Summa de bono*, 2 vols., Corpus Philosophorum Medii Aevi 2/1–2, edited by N. Wicki [Bernae: Francke, 1985], 872); cf. ibid., qu. 5 (p. 877ff.).

81. Although most scholars do not doubt the Stoic origins of the theory of *decorum* in this work—the fact is openly asserted by Cicero himself at the very beginning of Book 1 (1.2.6); cf. Pohlenz, *Antikes Führertum*, or Van Straaten (Panaetius 107), who attributes Cicero's theory of *decorum* more precisely to Panaetius—Cicero's transmission of the Stoic tradition here must be treated with caution and further qualified as *Cicero's version* of Stoicism. For this reason, in what follows the present study will refer to Cicero, instead of Panaetius or any other recognized Stoic figures. Cf. Büttner's discussion of this work in the context of Stoic aesthetics, *Antike Ästhetik*, 177.

82. The Stoic origin of this fourfold division of virtues is also confirmed by Diogenes Laertius, 7.100: "there are four kinds of τὸ καλόν: justice, manliness, orderliness, wisdom" (εἴδη εἶναι τοῦ καλοῦ τέτταρα, δίκαιον, ἀνδρεῖον, κόσμιον, ἐπιστημονικόν). *Decorum* in this case appears as κόσμιον ("order," "decency," "decorum"). Some of these subdivisions of virtue, perhaps, can be traced back to Aristotle, *Rhet.* I.9.5 (1366b). However, Aristotle mentions neither τὸ πρέπον nor κόσμιον, which suggests that these might have come from some other source, perhaps, Plato. Plato does use κόσμιον side by side with καλόν in *Rep.* 403A. In *Gorgias* 506D–E he establishes a connection between σωφροσύνη—which in the Stoic tradition transmitted by Cicero appears as "temperance," or the "fourth virtue"—and the soul that is κοσμία (in the Stoic tradition related by Cicero it is τὸ πρέπον or *decorum* that is linked to temperance). Regarding the question of the fourfold division of virtues see H. F. North, "Canons and Hierarchies of the Cardinal Virtues in Greek and Latin Literature," in *The Classical Tradition: Literary and Historical Studies of Harry Caplan*, edited by L. Wallach, 164–83 (Ithaca, N.Y.: Cornell University Press, 1966). North discusses Cicero and the Latin tradition on pp. 175–76. In particular, he makes a remark (p. 175) that Cicero in the *De off.* "transmits a view developed in the Middle Stoa concerning the relative value of the four *principales virtutes*." Pohlenz (*Antikes Führertum*) discusses Cicero's theory of the four virtues on pp. 24ff., and in particular the virtue of temperance (where *decorum* belongs) in *De off.* 1.27.93–151 on pp. 55–84.

our instinct for self-preservation, love for the offspring, et cetera. The first element, wisdom, consists "in the ability to perceive truth and in intelligence" (1.5.15), or in "seeking and investigating truth" (1.5.15) that is necessary for happiness and most appropriate for the human nature (1.4.13). The second element is justice: it consists "in preserving human society by rendering each what is his due and being faithful in keeping agreements" (1.5.15), or in a desire for the just and legitimate government (1.4.13). The third element is fortitude which lies "in the firmness and greatness of an elevated and unconquered spirit" (1.5.15) that despises trifling matters (1.4.13).

The fourth is a certain feeling for order, which consists "in the order and proper limits of all that is done or said, in which there is moderation and due balance (*modestia et temperantia*)" (1.5.15).[83] It is this feeling that is later referred to as the sense of *decorum* (τὸ πρέπον). *Decorum* is an inseparable component of *honestum*,[84] which allows for an interpretation that the latter shares in all its qualities.[85] Cicero provides a more detailed description of these qualities of *decorum* after the discussion of the first three subdivisions in the section on temperance towards the end of *De off.* 1.[86] Thus, according to him, the aspect of *honestas* "which can be called *decorum* in Latin, but is called πρέπον in Greek" includes "modesty and, as it were, some adornment (*ornatus*) of life, as well as temperance, moderation, complete calming of the soul's passions, and due limits in things" (*De off.* 1.27.93). *Decorum* (τὸ πρέπον) is clearly the most "aesthetic," in the modern sense, of Stoic moral categories. In addition to the cases where it is compared directly to the external beauty of the senses, *decorum* also possesses two typically aesthetic intrinsic qualities. One of them is its balanced and harmonious nature, which, unlike the awesome nature of τὸ καλόν, would qualify it as the beautiful (in the Kantian sense), rather than as the sublime. The other is its immediately

---

83. Cf. Diogenes Laertius (7.100; cf. 7.99) who also asserts that τὸ καλόν is a certain feeling for order (τὸ τελέως σύμμετρον).

84. *Decorum*, remarks Cicero, "cannot be separated from *honestum*" (*De off.* 1.27.93), and pertains to all aspects of *honestas* (1.27.95). According to him, it is easier to understand than to explain the difference (1.27.94); *decorum* is really identical with virtue and only conceptually distinct (1.27.95). The phrasing of some of Cicero's statements even suggests complete identity between the two terms, e.g.: "posita in decore tota, id est in honestate" (*De fin.* 2.11.35); "illud ipsum, quod honestum decorumque dicimus, quia per se nobis placet" (*De off.* 2.9.32).

85. Therefore, all aesthetic analogies valid for *decorum* apply also to *honestum*.

86. A very close parallel to Cicero's description of *decorum* in *De off.* 1.27.93–99 can also be found in *Orator* 21.70–22.74.

evident nature, which is the traditional mark of aesthetic experience, especially for the whole tradition of German Idealist aesthetics, including von Balthasar. Thus, according to Cicero, *decorum* "pertains to all *honestas* . . . in such a way that it is immediately evident *(sit in promptu)*, and not perceived by some obscure reasoning" (1.27.95). This observation is stressed several times in the same passage: thus *decorum* is "manifest with a noble appearance" *(appareat cum specie quadam liberali;* 1.27.96)[87] and "shines forth in life" *(elucet in vita,* 1.28.98). It is undoubtedly this evidential nature of *decorum*/τὸ πρέπον, an all-pervading element of τὸ καλόν, that strengthened the Stoic argument in favor of the main principle of their ethics—that τὸ καλόν must be sought for its own sake—by appealing to self-evident experience, which made any further argumentation unnecessary.[88]

The key element in Cicero's discussion of the role of *decorum* in morals is his analogy between the moral principle of *decorum* and bodily, or aesthetic, beauty. This analogy represents perhaps the closest link between aesthetic experience and morality in the Stoic tradition. Cicero introduces the aesthetic such parallel in his discussion of *decorum* in *De off.* 1:

> Just as the charm and beauty of the body cannot be distinguished from health, so this *decorum*, about which we speak, is totally blended with virtue, though at the same time being distinguishable from it conceptually by the mind . . . (1.27.95). For just as the beauty of the body moves the eye by a fitting arrangement of its members and delights by the very fact that all parts harmonize with each other with a certain gracefulness, in the same way that *decorum*, which shines forth in life, brings about the approval of those with whom we live through order, steadiness, and moderation in all words and deeds.[89] (1.28.98)

---

87. The idea that moral beauty somehow appears externally is quite common in the ancient tradition. Cf., for example, an extreme case in Plutarch's *Eroticus* 766E–F, where a virtuous soul is said to show clearly through the grace of the body, just like the natural beauty of the foot is emphasized by a well-fitting shoe.

88. There are numerous other passages in Cicero that emphasize the manifested-ness, self-evidence, and an almost visual nature of *honestum* and virtue in the Stoic tradition, presumably through its association with *decorum*: "the esteem for corporeal things is eclipsed by the splendor and greatness of virtue" (*De fin.* 3.14.45); "on account of the likeness between *honestas* and glory" (*De leg.* 1.11.32; i.e., τὸ καλόν shares with glory its conspicuousness and manifested-ness); an observation that it is the most obvious fact that *honesta* are sought for their own sake (*De fin.* 3.11.38–39); "for equity shines forth by itself" (*De off.* 1.9.30), etc.

89. Ut venustas et pulcritudo corporis secerni non potest a valetudine, sic hoc, de quo loquimur, decorum totum illud quidem est cum virtute confusum, sed mente et cogitatione distinguitur . . . (1.27.95). . . . Ut enim pulcritudo corporis apta compositione membrorum movet oculos et delectat hoc ipso, quod inter se omnes partes cum quodam lepore consentiunt, sic hoc decorum, quod elucet in vita, movet approbationem eorum, quibuscum vivitur, ordine et con-

Decorum appears as "moral beauty" that is a manifest and clearly "visible" sign of a harmonious arrangement of virtues in the soul, or an appropriate moral disposition, in parallel to physical beauty that clearly indicates a healthy disposition of the body. However, Cicero's description of our natural feeling for order in *De off.* 1.4.14 reveals that physical beauty does much more than merely to serve as an analogy or simile in order to provide a more clear understanding of *decorum*:

> Nor is this an insignificant arrangement of nature and reason, that this living being alone [i.e., human] perceives what order is, or what the appropriate thing is, *(quod deceat)* or what proper limits exist in deeds or words. In the same way, no other living being senses the beauty, charm, and harmonious arrangement of parts in those things that are perceived by sight. Now our natural capacity and reason, *drawing an analogy (similitudinem) between the visual domain and the soul*, judge that beauty, steadiness, and order must be even more carefully observed in decision-making [i.e., morality], and tries to avoid doing something in an unbecoming or effeminate way.[90]

The Stoic origin of this point of view can be further confirmed by another text of Cicero (*De fin.* 2.14.47) that deals with visual aesthetic beauty as an analogy to moral "beauty," while its Stoic roots are hardly questioned:

> After we have mentioned these three kinds of *honesta*, there follows the fourth [i.e., *decorum*]—which possesses the same beauty and arises fittingly from the above three—in which there is order and moderation, so that perceiving its likeness in the beauty and dignity of material forms, one passes over *(transitum est)* to the nobility *(honestas)* of what is said and done.[91]

In both passages quoted above, Cicero states clearly that the aesthetic experience of the beauty of material form is not merely *like* the moral

---

stantia et moderatione dictorum omnium atque factorum ... (1.28.98); cf. *Tusc. disp.* 4.13.30–31 quoted above.

90. "Nec vero illa parva vis naturae est rationisque, quod unum hoc animal sentit, quid sit ordo, quid sit quod deceat, in factis dictisque qui modus. Itaque eorum ipsorum, quae aspectu sentiuntur, nullum aliud animal pulcritudinem, venustatem, convenientiam partium sentit. Quam similitudinem natura ratioque ab oculis ad animam transferens multo etiam magis pulcritudinem, constantiam, ordinem in consiliis conservandam putat cavetque, ne quid indecore effemminateve faciat. . . ." My emphasis. The key phrase *similitudinem . . . ab oculis ad animam transferens* cannot be translated literally. Its meaning can be expanded as follows: our reason transfers its observations (i.e., the beauty and symmetry it perceives in the objects of sense) from the visual domain to the qualities of the soul, where it perceives some similarity with the former.

91. Atque his tribus generibus honestorum notatis quartum sequitur et in eadem pulchritudine et aptum ex illis tribus, in quo inest ordo et moderatio, cuius similitudine perspecta in formarum specie ac dignitate transitum est ad honestatem dictorum atque factorum.

feeling. By forming a basis for an analogy to moral phenomena within the natural order, the aesthetic experience of material things actually serves the purpose of preserving moral "beauty," order, and fittingness. Reason starts with aesthetic experience as something most immediate and evident, and then "transfers" (*transferens* or *transitum est*) its observations and conclusions—for example, that the natural order must be preserved—from visible phenomena to morals (*ab oculis ad animam*), or "draws an analogy" between the aesthetic and the ethical domains. Beauty thus serves as a guide to moral life by indicating clearly what must be preferred in morals (moral "beauty") by analogy with what is preferred among visual forms, and encouraging one to rely on one's immediate "feeling" rather than on abstract reasoning.[92]

The broader picture can be described as follows. According to the Stoics, the possibility of agreement between human actions and the universal law is established through the idea of the universal harmony and connection that applies to both human actions and the rest of reality (cf. Diogenes Laertius, 7.88 cited above). Τὸ πρέπον (*decorum*, or κόσμιον) is the most evident manifestation of this harmony: the manifestation that reveals this harmony in both physical bodies and morals (cf. Plato's καλόν). Τὸ πρέπον is a type of immediate and clear perception, naturally given to us (cf. the theory of "cognitive impressions"), which allows one to judge that something is fitting or suitable: humans clearly have this power of insight regarding bodies or speech, for example. Taking the observations a step further, when one realizes that τὸ πρέπον (and, in general, τὸ καλόν) possesses similar clarity in the area of morality—this clarity serving as a sign that its nature is identical in all its various manifestations—it becomes clear to him or her that τὸ πρέπον must also be indicative of fittingness or suitability in application to morals. It follows that one must observe τὸ πρέπον in morals for its own sake, just as one always naturally chooses aesthetic beauty, which is not dependent on any other goal.[93] In this way, the link between human actions and the eternal law, as well as the possibility of agreement between them, is made immediately evident through the analogy of beauty which, by bringing to our attention our natural disinterested af-

---

92. Cf. Schiller's idea of aesthetic education described in Chapter 1. The idea itself, of course, can be traced at least as far back as Plato, *Rep.*, Bk. 3, 401E–402A: see Chapter 5.

93. Cf. the syllogism about τὸ καλόν, which is also based on our natural ability to detect it, rather than on logic; see above.

fection for itself, also indicates which moral actions should be preferred *per se* on the basis of their "beauty" and noble appearance.⁹⁴

The attempt of the Stoics to present the aesthetic experience of the beautiful, noble, or awesome as a guide to moral life at least formally resembles the Kantian attempt to present the aesthetic as the symbol of morality. There are close textual parallels between Kant and the Stoics regarding the way the role of, on the one hand the aesthetic, and on the other hand τὸ καλόν (or τὸ πρέπον), is described. Thus according to Kant, "the beautiful prepares us to love *disinterestedly* something, even nature itself; the sublime [prepares us] to esteem something highly even *in opposition* to our own (sensible) interest" (§29, Gen. r., p. 108, W 357). The same kind of task—preparing to follow virtue *"for its own sake"* and even *against* one's well-being—is presented in the Stoic theory of τὸ καλόν as the only good. According to another Kantian statement, "taste makes possible the *transition*, without any violent leap, from the charm of sense to habitual moral interest" (§59, p. 200, W 462). And according to the Stoic theory of *decorum*/τὸ πρέπον, nature and reason "transfer" the sense for harmony and *decorum* "from the visual domain to the soul" (Cicero, *De off.* 1.4.14). Although Kant never mentions the Stoics in his third *Critique*,⁹⁵ the parallels are striking enough at least to warrant a thorough reexamination of the role of ancient aesthetics in Western European thought, in its continuity, as a historical dimension of modern aesthetic theories.

Thus the Stoics make a distinct contribution to revelatory aesthetics by articulating precisely the role that the revelatory capacity of beauty plays with respect to certain moral and theological issues. From the earlier tradition, including Plato, the Stoics inherit the fundamental insight that reality contains self-revealing elements, be it the clarity of certain true perceptions or the self-evidence of some moral principles. Against this background, the Stoic texts present an early example of an attempt to interpret, in clear terms, such self-revealing element in material bodies—the striking and manifest harmony and proportionality of aesthetic form—as analogous to the perception of morality and the divine law that governs the world. The nature of aesthetic perception is such that it operates in a manner analogous to certain experiences of the divine,

---

94. Pohlenz, *Antikes Führertum*, 56, also notices that in *De off.* 1.4.14 the sense of beauty leads to the understanding of morality.

95. Of course, it is almost certain that Kant was familiar with these texts of Cicero.

as well as to our moral feeling that manifests itself in such self-evident phenomena as τὸ καλόν or τὸ πρέπον. Aesthetic beauty can therefore serve as a witness to the universality of this self-revealing nature of reality and encourage us to follow our insight in theology and morals. Incorporating Stoic references to immediate aesthetic experience extends and enriches von Balthasar's effort to retrieve this fundamental aesthetic insight through the hermeneutics of traditional texts. In addition, the Stoic interest in the direct experience of the world as the source of insight into the nature of the moral and divine would support very well von Balthasar's stand against the post-Kantian "transcendentalist" position (as he sees it), with its emphasis on the *a priori* principles and a *Vorgriff* (pre-apprehension).[96] Thus, although the thrust of Stoic reflections on aesthetic experience is philosophical, they are still extremely important for contemporary theological aesthetics, for two reasons. First, the foundation of their theories—the acceptance of the universal divine law as the condition of correspondence between the human mind and reality, which is the foundation of the "aesthetic" transparency of reality to human perception—is clearly theological. Second, the idea of the revelatory nature of reality constitutes precisely that "pre-theological" insight that is so important for building von Balthasar's theological aesthetics.

As a final observation, this analogical interpretation of material aesthetic beauty in the intellectual tradition from Plato to von Balthasar can perhaps explain one of the well-known Stoic inconsistencies. Plutarch (*St. rep.* 1044C, D) criticizes the Stoics for holding simultaneously two contradictory views. On the one hand, they assert that nature delights in beauty and creates certain animals, such as peacocks, purely for beauty's sake. On the other hand, they blame people who cherish beautiful things and animals. Just as in the case of Plato who valued beauty but expelled the "artists," the inconsistency can be removed once beauty is interpreted as a pointer that reveals and facilitates something, and not as a goal in itself. True, one should not excessively cherish beautiful things, if one does this for the sake of pure enjoyment of the things themselves. However, it is equally true that beauty is naturally there as a sort of a self-revealing and clear experience, for the purpose of indicating the presence of the divine or the morally good.

---

96. Cf. R. Williams (*AB* 14). The similarity between this Stoic interest in direct experience and the position of Kant also confirms von Balthasar's evaluation of Kant. Von Balthasar does not ascribe to Kant himself the extreme apriorism characteristic of Kant's followers.

CHAPTER 7

The Augustinian Tradition

Augustine's Aesthetics and Its Influence

Augustine is of utmost importance, not only for von Balthasar, but for the whole history of theological aesthetics. However, the enormity of Augustine's contribution to Western culture, as well as the existence of a vast secondary literature about him, makes this author difficult to approach. As was the case with Plato, the only way to focus the discussion on a small number of contexts is by limiting the task to the question whether concrete aesthetic experience in Augustine appears as revealing. Augustine presents a unique case in another respect: as a figure that is transitional from the ancient pagan to the medieval Christian tradition. While being firmly grounded in the ancient philosophical tradition, he, unlike the ancient authors discussed so far, already has a developed apologetics, or fundamental theology, and is thus more focused on the task of finding revelatory elements in reality. For this reason it will be also interesting to see whether and how his apologetic stance contributes to his aesthetics, and what precisely the role of the aesthetic element is in his philosophical and theological discussions.

Augustine's interest in beauty and aesthetic issues is well known to historians of aesthetics and should be obvious to any perceptive reader.[1] First of all, he stands out among other ancient authors on account of dedicating whole works specifically to aesthetics topics, starting with the early lost work *De pulchro et apto*.[2] Augustine also continuously ex-

---

1. Unfortunately, as will be demonstrated in the analysis of secondary literature below, many non–aesthetically oriented studies tend to ignore the aesthetic element in his thought.
2. See Svoboda, *L'esthétique de Saint Augustin*, 10; Fontanier, "Sur le traité d'Augustin"; see full references below.

presses his great admiration for beauty in very strong terms: for example, according to him reason "felt that it was pleased by nothing else except beauty" (*De ordine* 2.15.42). Often he exclaims passionately: "Can we love anything but beautiful things?" (*De musica* 6.13.38); "Do we love anything but the beautiful?" (*Conf.* 4.13.20). It comes as no surprise then that, compared to other ancient and medieval authors, Augustine's thought generated perhaps the greatest amount of scholarly literature specifically on aesthetic topics. A fundamental pioneering study by K. Svoboda,[3] comparable in its significance to De Bruyne's three volumes on medieval aesthetics, collected almost all possible contexts in Augustine relevant to aesthetics. At the same time, like most early but also many recent studies in the history of aesthetics, he used no particular hermeneutic principle and understood "aesthetics" as anything that pertains to beauty, the fine arts, sensory perception, or literary theory. Since Svoboda, various aspects of Augustine's aesthetics have been discussed, such as the philosophical aspects of his theory of beauty and art; the beauty of God; beauty as a proof of the existence of God; various aspects of Augustine's aesthetic terminology.[4]

A review of some recent studies shows that the authors focus both on particular aesthetic works[5] and particular aesthetic themes. For example, M. J. Hayes's study focuses on the area of "sensible" beauty or aesthetic in Augustine specifically from a philosophical, not theological

---

3. K. Svoboda, *L'esthétique de Saint Augustin et ses sources* (Brno: Vydava Filosoficka Fakulta, 1933). Cf. another general study: V. V. Bychkov, *Estetika Avrelija Avgustina* (Moscow: Iskusstvo, 1984).

4. On beauty: E. Chapman, *Saint Augustine's Philosophy of Beauty* (New York/London: Sheed & Ward, 1939); C. Harrison, *Beauty and Revelation in the Thought of Saint Augustine* (Oxford: Clarendon Press, 1992); J. Loessl, "Religio, philosophia und *pulchritudo*: ihr Zusammenhang nach Augustinus, De vera religione," *Vigiliae Christianae* 47 (1993): 363–73. On art: R. J. O'Connell, *Art and the Christian Intelligence in St. Augustine* (Cambridge: Harvard University Press, 1978). O'Connell also attempts to fit Augustine into a contemporary framework in the chapter "Toward a Contemporary Augustinian Aesthetic." On the beauty of God: J. Tscholl, *Gott und das Schöne beim Hl. Augustinus* (Heverlee-Leuven: Augustijns-Historisch Instituut, 1967). On beauty as a proof of the existence of God: E. R. J. Ramirez, "Augustine's Proof for God's Existence from the Experience of Beauty: Conf. X.6," *Augustinian Studies* 19 (1988): 121–30. On Augustine's aesthetic terminology: J.-M. Fontanier, "Sur le traité d'Augustin," 413–21. An excellent general bibliography on Augustine can be found in a recent study: B. Stock, *Augustine the Reader: Meditation, Self-knowledge, and the Ethics of Interpretation* (Cambridge: Harvard University Press, 1996).

5. Cf. e.g., D. R. Maxwell, "Augustine's *De musica* 6.12.34–6.14.48: An Ontology of Music which Saves the Soul" (M.A. thesis, Concordia Seminary, 1998), which is mostly a simple summary of the *De musica* with an emphasis on ontological themes.

perspective.⁶ According to the author, the ultimate "objective" principles of sensible beauty in Augustine, for which he has great appreciation, are "unity" and "totality" (pp. 4–5; 236ff.), in accordance with the primacy of the One in Neoplatonic thought. While discussing this well-known subject and including most contexts important to aesthetics, Hayes is deliberately not concerned with other frequently mentioned⁷ elements of Augustine's aesthetics, such as the "ascent" to God through the experience of beauty, or in general with any "non-objective" topics: how one comes to realize these "objective" aesthetic principles, or how they are "revealed" to us. Some recent general studies on aesthetics, such as chapters 3 and 4 of Faas's 2002 *Genealogy of Aesthetics*, also discuss Augustine. The relevant sections of Faas's study contain a Nietzschean-style ideological critique and deconstruction of Augustine's "theocracy" (cf. p. 58) and therefore have little to do with aesthetics as understood for the purposes of the present study. However, Faas does single out some purely aesthetic topics. One of the best-known themes is Augustine's aesthetic justification of evil.⁸ Faas discusses this topic (cf. pp. 42–44, 50–51) in conjunction with Plotinus's theory of evil, which, he says, Augustine borrows in its entirety (p. 54).⁹ Another topic is the nature of beauty. In tune with his Nietzschean stand, Faas condemns Augustine for his emphasis on "spiritual" beauty as opposed to bodily (cf. pp. 47–48), and claims that, far from defending the body against Plato, Augustine simply "gives Plato's contempt for the body a new twist" (p. 56).¹⁰

By far the most exhaustive and erudite recent study of Augustine's aesthetics is J.-M. Fontanier's.¹¹ Like many other studies, his focuses exclusively on the notion of beauty (discussing the criteria of beauty, their historical roots, et cetera), precisely in order to avoid the hermeneutic difficulties and ambiguities of dealing with the notion "aesthetics" that

6. M. J. Hayes, "Beauty's Resting Place: Unity in St. Augustine's Sensible Aesthetic" (Ph.D. thesis, Marquette University, 2003).

7. E.g., in Harrison's book.

8. For a brief account of this subject see O. Bychkov, *Aesthetic Explanation of Evil*, 245–69.

9. As the present analysis of this topic will show, this opinion appears to be incorrect.

10. Another questionable opinion, given Augustine's fascination with the aesthetics of the resurrected body, and in general the role of bodily beauty in the ascent. On the discussion of the qualities of the resurrected body in Augustine see Colish, *Peter Lombard*, vol. 2, 706–10; J.-M. Fontanier, *La beauté selon saint Augustin* (Rennes: Presses Universitaires de Rennes, 1998), 120, 122; C. W. Bynum, *The Resurrection of the Body in Western Christianity, 200–1336* (New York: Columbia University Press, 1995), 99–100.

11. J.-M. Fontanier, *La beauté selon saint Augustin*. Occasional references to this study will be given throughout this chapter where relevant.

became the main concern of the present study (cf. pp. 16, 19).[12] As is the case with many other works, the study does not focus on the revelatory or anagogical functions of beauty.[13] Also, discussing the question of the "beauty of the soul," he leaves unanswered a question that is crucial to Augustine's theory of beauty: why is the term "beauty" used to mark the resemblance between the soul and the "image of God"? (Or, for that matter, why is the term "beauty" applied to God at all?)[14] One of the more fundamental themes engaged by Fontanier's study appears to be whether the main principle of beauty is proportion of multiple parts (as asserted, for example, by the Stoics) or unity and simplicity (Plotinus). According to Fontanier, Augustine manages to reconcile the two principles successfully.

In sum, scholarly literature on Augustine's aesthetics focuses on the following themes: the nature and criteria of beauty, of which proportion or unity are most common; aesthetic justification of the existence of evil (a theme that fits under one of the criteria of beauty, namely harmony and proportion); the idea of spiritual beauty and what this might be; the idea that beauty has something to do with God and his existence; the role of art on our way to God. The works most frequently mentioned are *De musica, De ordine, De vera religione,* and *Confessions.* There is also an impression that in Augustine's texts we face the same aesthetic paradox as we did in Plato:[15] sometimes he seems absolutely fascinated with both natural and artistic beauty, and sometimes he views the fine arts as somehow dangerous. It appears also that some scholars (especially Faas) are prepared to see the same tendency in Augustine that von Balthasar saw in Plato, a shift from an "early" fascination with aesthetic experience that can elevate one to God to the "late" idea of a dispassionate divine order that has little to do with passionate aesthetic ascents and promotes distrust of the arts in general. In the end of our analysis,

---

12. There is some mention of textual hermeneutics in the study in the sense of working with concrete texts. However, there is no theoretical justification for why this study is undertaken, nor any discussion of a theoretical framework for "beauty," and no raising of a hermeneutical problem of the present-day perception of ancient and medieval texts.

13. It is interesting that Fontanier reads and analyzes the same passages as discussed further in this chapter, but simply does not notice the issues that are of importance for the present study, although they seem to be hermeneutically transparent from the contexts: e.g., compare his analysis of *De musica* 6.13.38 on p. 49 (also cf. p. 52) or of *De vera rel.* 30.55 and 32.59 on p. 50 with the analysis of these passages given below in this chapter.

14. In other words, Fontanier ignores the theological question of the *analogy* of beauty that is so well discussed by von Balthasar.

15. Cf. Faas, *Genealogy of Aesthetics,* 62; also cf. Viladesau, *Theology and the Arts,* 18–20.

this paradox needs to be resolved, and the hypothesis evaluated. Finally, despite the many topics discussed, it comes as a surprise that most, especially recent, studies of Augustine's aesthetic thought, despite their often very detailed nature, fail to focus on, or even do not seem to notice the centrality of the ascent from aesthetic experience in Augustine, not to mention its revelatory nature. There is also very little effort to connect aesthetic issues in Augustine specifically to his apologetic theology, as von Balthasar attempted to do.[16]

The influence of Augustine on the later discussion of aesthetic issues is enormous. Not surprisingly, it is most prominent in the theological tradition of the Middle Ages. However, it is equally important for the present study to trace any Augustinian influence on modern and contemporary philosophical and theological trends in aesthetics. Because of the deliberate tendency in modern thought to distance itself from the medieval theological tradition, Augustine is mentioned hardly at all by modern philosophical aestheticians. It is, however, almost impossible to deny striking similarities between Augustine's direct observations on the nature of aesthetic judgment and, for example, the most foundational insights in this area in Kant's third *Critique*. Despite occasional protests against comparisons between Kant and Augustine, interpretations of Augustine's thought clearly in terms of Kantian transcendental aesthetics do appear in scholarly literature,[17] which means that the possibility of a hermeneutic dialogue between the two thinkers is openly acknowledged. In fact, it is quite likely that Kant did have direct knowledge of Augustine's work since, in addition to Latin, he majored in theology.[18] Another interesting parallel between Augustine and

---

16. Moreover, if one moves beyond the studies specifically dedicated to Augustine's aesthetics, there seems to be a general lack of awareness of the centrality of aesthetics in Augustine. A typical case is the general collection of essays by G. B. Matthews, *The Augustinian Tradition* (Berkeley: University of California Press, 1999), which contains nothing on aesthetics. Another case is the article on Augustine from the *Encyclopedia of Aesthetics* (ed. Kelly, 1998) which shows no knowledge of Augustine's aesthetics. It appears then that another evaluation of the role of aesthetic experience in this author will not be out of place.

17. Cf. "such er [Augustinus] nun zu zeigen, dass die Vernunft durch Reflexionen über die apriorischen Bedingungen des ästhetischen Urteils . . . zum Aufstieg zu Gott heranzieht" in J. Koch, "Augustinischer und dionysischer Neuplatonismus und das Mittelalter," *Kantstudien* 48.2 (1956–57): 125. Another author who points out parallels between Augustine and Kant's transcendental scheme is K. Jaspers: cf. *The Great Philosophers*, translated by R. Manheim, edited by H. Arendt (New York: Harcourt, Brace & World, 1957), 262.

18. Cf. Fistioc, *Beautiful Shape of the Good*, 11. Brucker—who, according to Fistioc, was an important source of information for Kant—could not have been the source of Kant's knowledge of Augustine's aesthetic ideas. Although Brucker does admire Augustine for his knowl-

modern aesthetics is the idea of an aesthetic justification of evil, which is presented both by Augustine and by Nietzsche. An objection that there could not possibly be any dialogue between Augustine's theological view and Nietzsche can be countered by an observation that Augustine's aesthetic "twist" to his theory of evil was never perceived as quite orthodox even by medieval theologians,[19] and, upon closer inspection, one might find that Augustine comes to such a view through considerations other than dogmatic or strictly theological.

Augustine's influence on contemporary theological aesthetics is certainly crucial, as illustrated by the example of von Balthasar, who has a long chapter on Augustine in GL2 (pp. 95–143). The most important element that von Balthasar retrieves from Augustine is what he calls "seeing," a process which describes either a physical seeing of aesthetic form or a mental seeing that is analogous to sensible seeing. The idea of direct seeing or vision as the best evidence or proof is crucial for the formation of von Balthasar's own theological aesthetics.[20] By looking at themes in Augustine that von Balthasar singles out for discussion, one can locate those elements of Augustine's aesthetics that can still be engaged in dialogue with modern and contemporary thought. First, von Balthasar is interested in the ascent of the mind from aesthetic judgment to "transcendent" principles in Augustine, which von Balthasar describes in terms of Kantian transcendental philosophy. For example, in GL2 109 he interprets Augustine's *De magistro* by openly mentioning Kant or describing Augustine's thought in Kantian terms.[21] Another theme that catches von Balthasar's attention is Augustine's general view of the beautiful as something in finite things that provides a connection to the infinite—hence Augustine's fascination with finite form. Von Balthasar phrases his description of this trait in a way definitely reminiscent of nineteenth-century Romantic aesthetic theories.[22] The

---

edge, he has no fundamental exposition of his philosophy (cf. *Historia critica philosophiae*, vol. 3, pp. 502–7). However, speaking on Plato earlier in vol. 1 (p. 696; according to Fistioc, Kant did study this part of Brucker's work), Brucker does present Plato's intellectual ascent in terms of "becoming alike to God," which Kant would have understood in theological terms and could have connected to Augustine's version of the ascent.

19. Cf. Bychkov, "Aesthetic Explanation of Evil."

20. Cf. GL2 99, 100 and 102; cf. GL2 139ff.

21. Cf. GL2 112: "this light, in that it informs the mind, is the transcendental condition of the mental structure of finite mind."

22. E.g., cf. GL2 114: "Only the one who loves finite form as the revelation of the infinite is both 'mystic' and 'aesthete.'"

key formal principle that governs the transition from the finite to the infinite in early works of Augustine, according to von Balthasar, is number that can be directly intuited in both types of reality (cf. GL2 116–18). However, seeing number in nature is only a preliminary "training exercise" on the way to seeing Christ's form or beauty as the main vehicle of revelation (GL2 123). Thus von Balthasar claims to have retrieved the most foundational idea of his own theological aesthetics from Augustine's thought. Finally, von Balthasar also notices that Augustine's positive-enthusiastic unifying aesthetic vision includes evil and discusses Augustine's "aesthetic justification" or "aesthetic theodicy" in terms that are very close to those of Nietzsche's aesthetic justification of the horror of reality (cf. GL2 123 and 127). Finally, Augustine is still a very live figure in the minds of some contemporary scholars of theological aesthetics. For example, F. B. Brown reworks Augustine's aesthetic views in an attempt to show the essential overlap between the aesthetic and the religious.[23]

After recognizing Augustine as a valid partner in a dialogue with modern and contemporary thought—the link that will be developed further in what follows—we also need to establish a historical and textual continuity between Augustine's texts on aesthetics and both the earlier ancient and the later medieval traditions. Fortunately, both connections are extremely well known (the medieval connection is particularly obvious from multiple direct quotations) and documented in secondary literature. They can be summarized as follows. One of the most-discussed ancient influences on Augustine is that of the "Platonists," from Plato himself to Plotinus and other Neoplatonic authors, from whom he borrows the general scheme of the ascent to God from worldly beauty through the concepts of number and order, as well as the idea of the beauty of a "higher rank."[24] A well-known influence is Cicero, including his definitions of material and moral beauty influenced by Stoic thought which Augustine often quotes directly.[25] Augustine's

---

23. F. Burch Brown, *Good Taste, Bad Taste, and Christian Taste: Aesthetics in Religious Life* (Oxford/New York: Oxford University Press, 2000), chap. 4, pp. 95–127.

24. Cf. Courcelle, *Late Latin Writers*; J. J. O'Donnell, "Augustine's Classical Readings," *Recherches augustiniennes* 15 (1980): 144–75.

25. On Augustine's use of Cicero see H. Hagendahl, *Augustine and the Latin Classics* (Göteborg/Stockholm: Acta Universitatis Gothoburgensis/Almqvist & Wiksell, 1967); M. Testard, *Saint Augustin et Cicéron*; Fontanier, *La beauté selon saint Augustin*, 24ff. Specifically on the history of Cicero's aesthetic quotations in Augustine, see Bychkov (1996), 149–51; idem, "A Propos of Medieval Aesthetics," 157–58. In particular, Augustine's understanding of the

dependence on the Stoic thought is less clear, because of the admixture of some Stoic elements in many texts known to Augustine, both pagan and Christian. One area of influence would be Cicero's passages on bodily and moral beauty influenced by Stoicism. Another possible influence concerns the theory that the beauty of the universe can serve as a proof of its divine origin. Although the idea itself was popular with the Christian apologists and can be traced to Plato, Augustine's formulation of it often sounds like Cicero's *De natura deorum*. Another much-discussed topic is Augustine's justification of the existence of evil, which is addressed below in more detail. Both the similarity of passages and some scholars suggest that Augustine borrowed many elements of this theory from Plotinus, who, in turn, was influenced by Stoicism.[26]

A much clearer issue is the influence of Augustine's texts on aesthetic discussions in the Western medieval tradition. Many passages on aesthetics were included in the early florilegia and collections of Sentences, starting with that of Isidore of Seville.[27] Many such passages make their way into Peter Lombard's collection. As a result, thirteenth-century Sentence commentaries, and the *Summae*, contain copious quotations, as well as lengthy discussions of Augustine's aesthetic texts.[28] Aesthetic themes from Augustine that are most commonly discussed in the thirteenth-century commentaries and *Summae* are the following.[29] A typically ancient theme discussed in a Christian context is the definition of bodily beauty as "harmony of parts with a sweetness of color." According to Augustine, this aesthetic principle will govern the process of restoration of bodies during the resurrection (*De civitate Dei* 22.19). An-

---

concept *honestas* as a kind of beauty based on Cicero is found in *De diversis quaest.* 83, q. 30. His definition of bodily beauty as "harmony of parts with the sweetness of color" borrowed from Cicero is contained in *De civ. Dei* 22.19. Regarding this particular definition of beauty cf. Hagendahl (1967), 319 and Testard, *Saint Augustin et Cicéron*, vol. 2, 89.

26. On the topic of Augustine and Stoicism see: G. Verbeke, "Augustin et le stoïcisme," *Recherches augustiniennes* 1 (1958): 67–89; G. Verbeke, *Stoicism in Medieval Thought*. On convergences between the Stoics, Plotinus, and Augustine on the subject of natural evil see B. A. G. Fuller, *The Problem of Evil in Plotinus* (Cambridge: Cambridge University Press, 1912); A. Graeser, *Plotinus and the Stoics: A Preliminary Study* (Leiden: E. J. Brill, 1972); B. Switalski, *Plotinus and the Ethics of St. Augustine*, Polish Institute Series 8 (New York: Polish Institute of Arts and Sciences in America, 1946).

27. On Augustine's aesthetic texts in medieval florilegia see a detailed discussion in Bychkov, "A Propos of Medieval Aesthetics," 140–46. On Augustine's aesthetic themes and texts in collections of Sentences see ibid., 148–52.

28. See ibid., 163ff.

29. A detailed discussion of the following themes, their sources, and parallel texts is found in ibid., 148–52.

other typically ancient theme is interpretation of the right disposition of powers in the soul as a kind of intelligible or moral beauty (*honestum* or *honestas*, cf. *De diversis quaest.* 83, q. 30).³⁰ One of the most prominent themes that has ancient roots but is easily transplanted onto Christian soil is the idea that beauty is not in separate parts but in the harmonious arrangement of the whole. From this point of view, even evil has its legitimate place in the beautiful arrangement of the universe by creating a favorable contrast with the good and allowing it to stand out. The following texts of Augustine used in the thirteenth century express this theme directly: *Enchiridion* 10–11, *De libero arbitrio* 3.9.24–27 (the example of moral evil, or sin, and punishment for sin), and *De civitate Dei* 16.8 (the example of monstrous bodies).³¹ The theme is developed in Augustine by using numerous parallels with aesthetic experience and aesthetic and artistic objects, many of which are used in the medieval *Summae*: a parallel with the technique of antithetical statements in rhetoric (*De civitate Dei* 11.18), with the use of contrasting colors in painting (*De civitate Dei* 11.23), and with the flow of speech when syllables are constantly dying yet are also constantly being born (*De natura boni* 8). Finally, a purely Christian theme is the form (*species*) and beauty of Christ, or the Son as the second person of the Trinity (cf. *De Trin.* 6.10.11).

Before looking at Augustine's texts, some remarks must be made concerning the terms he uses in discussing aesthetic topics. A reader faces very few problems with the family of terms with the meaning "beauty/beautiful" because Augustine mostly uses the root *pulchr-*. Since he also uses, after Cicero, the term *honestum* or *honestas* in the sense "moral beauty" or "beauty of the soul," we refer again to the opinion that Augustine "aestheticizes" Cicero's vocabulary.³² It was sufficiently proved in

---

30. The topic of the beauty of the body and soul in Augustine, which is clearly dependent on Cicero's transmission of Stoic ideas, will not be discussed here because, unlike in the Stoics, it is not related to his revelatory aesthetics. On this and related topics (as well as on dependence on Cicero), see, e.g., Fontanier, *La beauté selon saint Augustin*, 100–102, 106, 118ff., 120, 122.

31. On the theme of the beauty of the universe and the aesthetic justification of evil see Bychkov, "A Propos of Medieval Aesthetics," 161–63, and idem, *Aesthetic Explanation of Evil*.

32. The opinion belongs, among others, to Pouillon, "La beauté," Aertsen, "Beauty in the Middle Ages," and Fontanier, *La beauté selon saint Augustin*. For example, according to Pouillon, Augustine's definition of *honestum* as *per se expetendum* depends on Cicero. In its turn, Cicero's *honestum* is derived from the Greek term τὸ καλόν, in particular through the Stoic tradition. Since the original Greek term implies the meaning "beautiful," Augustine, reading Cicero, restores this meaning (*pulchrum*) to the term *honestum*. Pouillon says: "Une fois καλόν traduit chez Cicéron par *honestum*, saint Augustin savait assez de grec pour identifier de nouveau *pulchrum* et *honestum*, deux traductions différentes de καλόν" (271).

Chapter 6 that this opinion is incorrect, since the term *honestum* (like *decorum*) in Cicero already has strong aesthetic connotations, which Augustine simply detected, not reintroduced. At the same time, Augustine uses a number of other terms, and understanding them is crucial to interpreting his aesthetic theory correctly. For example, the key to an adequate rendering of many passages from Augustine's *De ordine* 2 into English is the meaning of the Latin *ratio* and its derivatives *rationabilis* and *rationabiliter* as used by Augustine. The meaning of *ratio* in Latin ranges from 'computation' and 'counting' to 'reason.' Accordingly, in the *De ordine* the semantic range of terms based on the stem *ratio-* includes anything that has to do with reckoning or reason: reason-like, planned, organized, law-like, rule-governed, orderly, arranged, systematic, et cetera. Especially when speaking of visual forms and musical harmony, one must keep in mind the more technical meaning of *ratio* as 'proportion' ('ratio') or 'musical interval.'[33] Since Augustine clearly saw all these meanings as connected, the real challenge for an interpreter is to find a single English stem that covers the range of meanings implied by 'reason'/'rational' on the one hand, and the more aesthetic connotation 'organized'/'proportionate' (as in visual forms or musical intervals) on the other. The term 'regular' and its derivatives in this case seem most fitting.[34] The key to understanding Augustine's *De musica* 6,[35] another important text on aesthetics, is the term *numerus*. Although the term has been translated by Jacobsson (*De musica liber VI*) as 'rhythm,' which sounds less awkward than 'number,' the term 'number' must clearly be preserved. The whole discussion stems from the Neopythagorean and Neoplatonic tradition, where *numerus* clearly means 'number' as the foundational principle of reality. The derivative adjective *numerosus*, which is crucial to Augustine's argument, also presents a problem for in-

33. This is how it is used, e.g., by Ficino in his commentary on the *Timaeus*; see *Compendium Marsilii Ficini in Timaeum*, in vol. 2 of *Opera Omnia*, 1438–66 (Turin: Bottega d'Erasmo, 1962, reprint of Basel, 1576 ed.). Ficino's use could not possibly have been an innovation.

34. As something 'rule-based,' 'regular' does imply the presence of a rational principle. At the same time, anything proportionate or patterned among visual objects or sounds can be called regular (for example, a face can be said to have 'regular features'). The same is observed in other languages, e.g., the Russian *pravilnyj* can mean either "correct" (according to a rule) or "regular" (as of physical shapes or facial features).

35. In fact, Augustine's term *musica* itself (from the Greek μουσική) needs explanation. It does not really mean 'music' in our contemporary understanding, but includes other arts and even mathematics. This explains why in the selections from *De musica* discussed below, Augustine mostly speaks of topics other than 'music,' including poetic meters, architectural proportions, and even number as a mathematical or metaphysical principle.

terpretation. While in classical Latin (for instance, Cicero) *numerosum* meant simply speech that "we can measure by equal intervals," speech that has meter or rhythm (cf. *De orat.* 3.48.185), Augustine clearly expands the meaning of this term to mean in general "something pertaining to number" or "something that has number nature."[36]

The Plotinian Moment

Finally, one cannot start a discussion of Augustine's aesthetic views without first looking at Plotinus in some detail, since it is clear that there are many similarities and even close textual parallels between the two, especially in passages relevant to aesthetics.[37] Yet Plotinus can not be included on these pages in his own right. In addition to the fact that there is no direct textual continuity between Plotinus and the Western high Middle Ages where this study ends, there is another important factor that is linked to the working definition of 'aesthetic' in this study as something that necessarily includes sensory experience. While Augustine's Christianity dictated a positive approach to the body and sensation, and he therefore focused on these aspects of human reality and saw them as valuable,[38] for Plotinus neither material bodies nor sense data have much value and he dismisses them outright as "echoes" and "traces" of intelligible reality without much discussion.[39] Plotinus thus speaks mostly of intelligible or "ontological" beauty (cf. *Enn.* 5.8.9). Although this is, of course, an analogical use of the term, Plotinus's text contains almost no observations on the original sensible, that is, truly aesthetic, experience that would serve as the basis for this analogy. The tremendous influence of Plotinus on Western thought, especially on German Idealist philosophy, is also outside the area of aesthetics and

---

36. The terms 'numeric' or 'numerical' (the best fit in English) often sound awkward, and so this term is translated below in a number of ways according to context, but in key places as 'numeric(al)' in order to indicate the presence of this technical term.

37. Scholars continue to argue about the extent to which Augustine read and used Plotinus's text. See the discussion of this issue in Courcelle, *Late Latin Writers*.

38. Of course, some scholars such as Faas try to portray Augustine simply as a "concealed Platonist" who has as much contempt for the body as Plato and Plotinus do. It must be noted that although such a reading of Augustine is hermeneutically possible, a more honest reading indicates that he never abandoned his fascination with sensible reality and he genuinely embraced the Christian attitude toward the body as part of the creation.

39. See some discussion below. Faas's observation (*Genealogy of Aesthetics*, 44) that Plotinus also says little about the arts, and that his comments on art are mostly derogatory, is not far from the truth, though Plotinus does use art and artists on occasion to exemplify some points.

concerns ontology, epistemology, the question of identity versus transcendence, dialectic, building monistic systems, and so forth.[40] In what follows, then, we will try to determine if Plotinus made any original contribution to ancient revelatory aesthetics, and at the same time establish both the extent of his dependence on Plato's aesthetic ideas and the extent of parallelism between his thought and Augustine's reflection on aesthetic topics.

It will be useful to start with von Balthasar's assessment of Plotinus, on whom he writes at length in GL4. The reader is first surprised that he spends much time not on what we would call "aesthetics" but on unraveling the question as to whether one should understand Plotinus's highest principle (the One, originally the Good of Plato) in terms of transcendence or "identity" (GL4 282).[41] All becomes clear once we take into consideration the nineteenth-century Idealist interpretation of Plotinus's system in terms of identity (particularly in Hegel). As the reader remembers from the previous discussion, according to von Balthasar, in a system based on identity which does not presuppose an essential rift between the immanent and the transcendent, one cannot have a theological aesthetics that deals precisely with the "revelation of the transcendent." Therefore, in order to justify the inclusion of Plotinus, von Balthasar must first present his thought as essentially based on transcendence.

A brief remark on "transcendence" will be appropriate at this point, since the same issue arises later regarding Augustine. As was noted in the case of Plato, and even earlier in the discussion of von Balthasar's own thought, the question whether any pre-modern thinker can be understood in terms of "transcendence" probably cannot be answered definitively.[42] Perhaps the most fruitful approach that has been assumed so

---

40. Plotinus's influence was either direct or indirect (through Proclus, Greek Patristic authors such as pseudo-Dionysius, etc.), and particularly powerful starting with the fourteenth-century German mystics, whence it continues into the Renaissance and nineteenth-century German Idealism (e.g., in Hegel); cf. von Balthasar's observations in GL4.

41. On the basic division between the interpretations of the First Principle as being or as something "beyond being" (a phrase that goes back to Plato and informs the subsequent Neoplatonic tradition), see J. A. Aertsen, "Ontology and Henology in Medieval Philosophy (Thomas Aquinas, Master Eckhart and Berthold of Moosburg)," in *On Proclus and His Influence in Medieval Philosophy*, edited by E. P. Bos and P. A. Meijer (Leiden/New York/Cologne: E. J. Brill, 1992), 120–40.

42. Naturally, there is a lack of precision on the part of ancient and medieval authors in expressing their thoughts on this matter, since they did not pose the question in the way it was posed by modern thinkers, not to mention the immense difficulty of the issue itself.

far is to consider the subject matter phenomenologically, in the fashion of Husserl, Schelling, or Kant. In other words, we will examine how certain experiences (aesthetic in this case) *appear* to our perception. In this case the only thing that matters is whether something *appears* to us, or is perceived by us, as transcending our intellectual capacities or not.

As for von Balthasar, in his usual fashion he proceeds to paint a *Gestalt* of Plotinus's thought that will explain both the connection between Plotinus and modern philosophy and the role this ancient thinker plays in the formation of von Balthasar's own theological aesthetics. According to von Balthasar, although some parallels can be drawn between Plotinus's s Intellect (seen from the point of view of the Soul) and the modern Idealist sublime (elevation above the phenomenal level), the main point in Plotinus is the difference between the Intellect and the transcendent One, which makes his thought truly theological (GL4 300; no wonder that von Balthasar puts Plotinus in the section on "religion," not "philosophy"!).[43] At this point von Balthasar sharply differentiates Plotinus from Idealist philosophy, especially the Hegelian tradition: "But it is just this lifting of the vision above the level of being that gives this radiating-outward of beauty a more than philosophical character and makes it specifically theological" (GL4 301). Although Fichte and Schelling briefly capture this moment, modern Idealist interpretations, especially that of Hegel, lose sight of it (GL4 301, cf. note 354). It is precisely this division into two spheres—rational and completely irrational—that allows for the descent of glory without the danger of gnosticism: "This 'descent' alone," von Balthasar writes in the language reminiscent of his own vision, "permitted him to follow though in a consistent way his aesthetics as an aesthetics of 'glory,' a non-biblical but theological aesthetics which cannot be captured in the categories of modern idealism" (GL4 301).[44]

Cf. von Balthasar himself struggling with the principles of immanence and transcendence in GL4 290, while attempting to classify ancient thinkers into one or the other category. Despite his attempts to distance himself from "identity-type" Idealism, his actual statements do not sound very different: e.g., he presents the immanent as something absolutely transcendent, or in terms of "self-unfolding" etc.

43. I.e., at this point von Balthasar starts to link Plotinus and his own theological aesthetics; cf. statements like "manifestation that breaks forth from the central depth of being itself" (GL4 301) similar to his account of his own theological aesthetics in GL1.

44. Von Balthasar's description of Plotinus's structure of reality, in fact, sounds closer to the language of Heidegger: he speaks of it as the dialectic or play of "concealment" and "unveiling" or revealing; cf. GL4 282, 308.

The sentiment that von Balthasar ascribes to Plotinus is very close to what he himself must have felt when writing his theological aesthetics. According to him, Plotinus throughout his life stood "speechless before the miracle of being that transcends all reason. That there *is* something, that what is is a world of such immense wonder, this is for him the clearest possible revelation of the source lying behind all things" (GL4 302). Von Balthasar even makes formal links between Plotinus and his own theory of form expanded in GL1 by examining the "structure of the beautiful" according to Plotinus (GL4 307). Although the beautiful subsists properly in the realm of the intellect, or form, this level of existence "subsists only as an epiphany of the mystery and summons back towards that mystery." The beautiful is an "outward radiation of reality," but "what shines upon it comes . . . from above." Although this "form" and "splendor" make up a sort of an "anatomy of beauty," there is no beauty without the more-than-beautiful (Plotinus speaks of "beauty above beauty" in *Enn.* 6.7.32), or what von Balthasar calls "glory": the "radiance sent forth by beauty at every level . . . signifies beauty itself, yet also signifies that there is *in* beauty something *beyond it*."

This division in the "structure" of beauty into a "horizontal" dimension, or form and beauty itself, and a "vertical" dimension, or glory as a "theological analogate" of beauty (GL1), of which beauty is a trace (or from which it "radiates") and to which it points, is extremely important. It is especially relevant to the understanding of the later medieval thought. At the same time, this scheme also shows that what interests von Balthasar in Plotinus is precisely the question of glory and the "more than beautiful"—a subject that falls outside of our more narrowly defined field of study—and not beauty or sensible aesthetics, which remains on the margin of his inquiry. In this, von Balthasar captures Plotinus's own spirit correctly. Indeed, even in the case of references to the original experience of "wonder" in Plotinus that leads to "theological aesthetics," it becomes apparent from the contexts cited by von Balthasar, for example, *Enn.* 3.8.9–10 in GL4 302, that Plotinus actually refers to intelligible reality and intellectual, not aesthetic wonder (the wonder of the intellect in the face of being)[45]—which is, again, not the focus of the present study.

While von Balthasar retrieves Plotinus's "aesthetics" starting with

---

45. Cf. von Balthasar's own statement in GL4 294: "Plotinus' aesthetic is founded on this statement: all being is beautiful because it is form, in its encounter with Intellect."

the foundations of his system (the relation between the One and the other levels of reality), for our purposes it would be important to determine what Plotinus's contribution is to aesthetics as understood in this study (aesthetic experience that involves the senses, such as sensible beauty). In other words, while von Balthasar in his treatment of Plotinus is mainly interested in "glory" that is "aesthetic" purely analogically (the "vertical" dimension), our focus is on Plotinus's treatment of the actual sensory experience that forms the basis for this analogy (the "horizontal" dimension): that is, aesthetic elements insofar as they create the feeling of something transcending our capacities.

Does Plotinus, indeed, speak of aesthetic "beauty" (as both von Balthasar and most English translators, e.g., A. H. Armstrong, assume)? After all, the term he uses in his key contexts starting with *Enn.* 1.6 is actually the ambiguous τὸ καλόν.[46] The context of *Enn.* 1.6.1 suggests that using the term τὸ καλόν Plotinus, indeed, starts by speaking of aesthetic, or sensible, beauty and only later switches to intellectual and moral, which we would call an analogical use of the term. *Enn.* 1.6 simply recounts the familiar scheme of an ascent from the beauty of material things to the realm of intelligible beauty originally described by Plato (in the *Phaedrus* and *Symposion*), who, as the reader remembers, already presents either τὸ καλόν or the good (in the *Republic*) as inaccessible ("transcendent") principles. For this reason, von Balthasar himself acknowledges that Plotinus adds nothing new to Plato as far as aesthetics is concerned.[47] Indeed, as far as the phenomenology, as well as the epistemological-cognitive and practical implications of aesthetic experience are concerned (that is, our perception of it and how it affects our cognition and moral-intellectual development), Plotinus's description of beauty and its effects seems to be very close to that of Plato. Thus, just as in *Phaedrus* 250, and in terms reminiscent of Plato's description, we become aware of beauty immediately (βολῇ; *Enn.* 1.6.2) and "suddenly" (ἐξαίφνης; *Enn.* 6.7.34; cf. GL4 305). As in Plato, the nature of beauty is striking: when ones sees it (especially the true "lovers") one experienc-

---

46. The text of Plotinus will be quoted according to the edition: Plotinus, *Opera*, 3 vols., edited by P. Henry and H.-R. Schwyzer (Paris/Brussels: Descleé de Brouwer/L'Édition Universelle/E. J. Brill, 1951, 1959, 1973).

47. Perhaps one could say that if one uses von Balthasar's perspective consistently, Plotinus should be seen as more persistent than Plato in implementing theological aesthetics, since, according to von Balthasar, Plato finally abandons the "ascent to the transcendent principle" model in favor of "universal order" which can be intereptated as "immanent."

es great wonder and shock (θάμβος, ἔκπληξις; *Enn.* 1.6.4), as those who have met a divine apparition.[48] As in Plato, the experience of beauty reminds the soul of its true nature, the intelligible realm (*Enn.* 1.6.2).[49] This is perhaps the one area where Plotinus makes the tightest connection between aesthetic experience and becoming aware of the higher levels of reality: he presents aesthetic experience as immediately revealing. In doing this, however, he does not go beyond traditionally Platonic thought.[50] Thus, according to Plotinus perceiving something in sensory data forces one to make an immediate connection with something intelligible. He uses the examples of musicians recognizing elements of intelligible harmony in actual sounds, and geometricians and people examining pictures recognizing the same in visible shapes (*Enn.* 2.9.16; cf. GL4 311).[51] Even the process of "training" one's inner seeing (*Enn.* 1.6.9) is similar to the one described in the *Symposion*. The ascent ultimately leads one to the good (ἀγαθόν) which is also καλόν, and upon seeing the highest principle the soul experiences love, longing, and shock (*Enn.* 1.6.7).

But what about the best-known feature of Plotinus's interpretation of beauty, which is not explicitly present in Plato: his insistence that beauty can be ultimately reduced to an absolutely simple principle, or unity, with harmony or proportion being only a particular case of unity? This is, of course, an ontological characteristic of beauty and, as far as it simply remains so, it does not concern us here. However, Plotinus also

---

48. Cf. *Enn.* 1.6.7: "but he who has seen it is astonished on account of this beauty, and is filled with amazement and delight, experiencing a shock which causes no harm."

49. The soul, "since it is by nature what it is, and belongs to the higher rank in the order of being, when it sees something akin to it, or a trace of something akin to it, rejoices and is thrilled, and returns to itself, recalling itself and its own qualities."

50. Several authors from the collection *Neuplatonismus und Ästhetik* (2007) present τὸ καλόν in Plotinus in its revelatory or "pointing" function: however, all portray this feature as genuinely Platonic, not specific to Plotinus: cf. J. Halfwassen (NA 45–47), A. Schmitt (NA 62–63), and L. Bergemann (NA 152).

51. Plotinus then makes a transition to the traditional "cosmological" proof of the existence of higher principles (*Enn.* 2.9.16): seeing the beauty of the universe, who would not ask a question about its source? However, in this context he also gives an example of recognizing the trace of intelligible reality in a beautiful face; his text ("and when one sees a face that has imitated beauty so well, he is drawn there" [ὁ μὲν ἰδὼν κάλλος ἐν προσώπῳ εὖ μεμιμημένον φέρεται ἐκεῖ]) is an almost verbatim quote from *Phaedrus* 251A3–4, which puts the whole passage within the original Platonic framework. The Plotinian version of the "cosmological proof" is of course not very far from that of the *Timaeus* or the Stoic versions of it. Cf. also *Enn.* 2.9.8 and von Balthasar's comment in GL4 283, to the effect that for Plotinus the vision of the starry heavens "directly reveals the certainty of the world's divinity."

observes that this unified principle often appears as a certain glow or shine that radiates even from bodies that are aesthetically pleasing. At the same time, in the absence of this shine of beauty even proportionate and symmetrical bodies may appear not beautiful. In fact, it is exactly this radiating quality of τὸ καλόν in Plotinus that von Balthasar uses to claim that Plotinus describes precisely the radiance of "glory" in the world.

Plotinus first makes this observation in *Enn.* 1.6 and provides a more extended discussion in *Enn.* 6.7.22. In order to prove that proportion of physical parts does not constitute the basis of beauty, Plotinus gives the example of dead faces, which no longer look beautiful; they lack a certain radiance (φέγγος), although they still preserve all the proportions. The same is observed in a statue that is proportionate as contrasted with one that is lifelike, in not-so-beautiful living things that are still more beautiful than beautiful statues, et cetera. Therefore, Plotinus concludes, beauty is not something complex (συμμετρία) in itself, but rather something that shines through in the manner of light (ἐπιλαμπόμενον) within something complex. Certain "radiance" or "splendor" (φέγγος) is also given off by virtuous (morally beautiful) souls, which contain something "conspicuous as light" (διαπρέπον οἷον φῶς; 1.6.4–5) that emanates from within and indicates a certain proximity to higher principles. Now if one reviews our discussion in the previous two chapters, it is easy to realize that Plotinus's terminology is strongly reminiscent of that of Plato, and the idea of beauty as something "shining through" in both bodies and souls is, in fact, common to Plato and the Stoics.

Plotinus also seems to be following the Platonic tradition in presenting beauty as a "beacon" that indicates the degree to which things partake in "true being" or "true reality" (being καλά is tantamount to being ὄντα ὄντως; *Enn.* 1.6.5). A high degree of participation in true being is indicated by a certain bright glow (ἀποστίλβει γὰρ πάντα; *Enn.* 5.8.10). Describing beauty in the intelligible world, Plotinus also uses the famous metaphor of "flowering" or "blossoming" (χρόα ἡ ἐπανθοῦσα; *Enn.* 5.8.10). In this case Plato's influence is seen clearly in the use of the term στίλβειν (cf. *Phaedrus* 250D).

Although Plotinus follows Plato's model, he clearly is not much interested in the truly aesthetic stage of the ascent, but only in the higher stages of it, which, from a modern standpoint, can be called "beautiful" only analogically. He stops discussing sensible beauty early in the chapter on the beautiful (*Enn.* 1.6.4) and starting with 1.6.7 presents the vision of the highest good, which has little to do with aesthetics as defined in this study.

It must be noted, finally, that Plotinus implements a more comprehensive analysis of beauty as form, which, as will become clear from what follows, is more like Augustine's than like Plato's. Thus instead of outlining an ascent from the lower to the higher forms of τὸ καλόν in general (as does Plato), he describes more specifically how one learns to understand the immaterial nature of form that is contained in things and that constitutes their real beauty (*Enn.* 5.8.2). Plotinus also pays closer attention to the very mechanism of judging form by comparing external form to an internal standard in order to evaluate its proximity to the intelligible realm (*Enn.* 1.6.3). In addition, Plotinus departs from Plato in *Enn.* 5.8 in his interpretation of the place of artistic activity with regard to the intelligible realm. For Plato, art is twice removed from the original intelligible ideas and imitates only material copies of ideas; for Plotinus (as later for Augustine), the artist imitates the ideas or forms directly, by observing them in his mind.[52] Thus art draws on the same principles as nature and, using our internal standard, can shape artifacts.

Beauty of the Whole

The main focus of most of Augustine's works discussed below is not aesthetics as such; rather, he uses observations about aesthetic experience to solve other philosophical and theological problems. However, as was noted above, this is precisely what characterizes even modern and contemporary aesthetic theories, not to mention Plato and the Stoics, and thus should not become an argument against the importance of aesthetics in Augustine. Moreover, Augustine in this case is a remarkable exception, having focused whole works specifically around aesthetic issues such as visible beauty or sensory perception of the arts, unlike Plotinus or pseudo-Dionysius, who discuss the broader notion τὸ καλόν.

Before moving on to the topics that one could call more specifically Augustinian, we will analyze two closely related aesthetic themes in Augustine that he clearly borrows from the tradition, sometimes almost

---

52. The idea itself does not belong to Plotinus, who inherits it from the earlier tradition, where it is common: cf. Cicero, *Orator* 2.7–3.10; Seneca, *Ep.* 65.7.

without modification. As a theologian, one of the main tasks Augustine faced was interpreting the world and reality in terms of a unified intelligent design by one benign divine principle. Certain obvious facts present challenges to such an interpretation: some elements do not seem to fit the universal order (appearing distorted, out of place or ugly); some appear to be contrary to any design with good intentions (such as evil). In order to solve this problem, in a traditional way, Augustine uses the observation, based on aesthetic experience, that an arrangement as a whole can still be beautiful, even though its individual parts are not. This is precisely what is at work in the universe: if it is seen as a whole, all its parts eventually fall into place, and its orderly arrangement becomes apparent—it is perceived, aesthetically, as beautiful. For example, in a concise statement of this idea in *De musica* 6.11.29–30 (pp. 66–68)[53] Augustine mentions the regular revolutions of the celestial bodies which he perceives, using a traditional Neoplatonic metaphor, as a perpetual song ("music of the spheres"), and then compares the total arrangement to a whole building or a whole poem. One with a restricted point of view, Augustine argues, necessarily fails to see the beauty of the whole.[54] He repeats the same idea in *De vera rel.* 40.76 (CCSL 32, p. 237),[55] where he makes an important

---

53. Pages given according to Jacobsson's edition: see full citation below.

54. "And what else can we call 'higher,' apart from those things that are the seat of the loftiest, unmoved, unchangeable, eternal equality: where there is no time, for there is no change, and where time originates as it is formed, ordered and shaped in the image of eternity, as the revolution of the sky brings the celestial bodies back to their starting point, obeying the laws of equality, unity, and order [by means of the regular intervals of] days, months, years, decades, and other periodic rotations of the stars? In this way earthly things, in their obedience to the heavenly, as it were, weave their numerous and repeated periodic revolutions into the song of the universe. [30] Now many things among these seem to us disorderly and confused, because we have been stitched into this order [only] according to our own capacity, and we do not know what sort of beautiful arrangement divine providence has for us. It is the same, for example, with a statue placed in some corner of a vast and most beautiful building: it will not be able to appreciate the beauty of the structure, of which it itself is a part! Nor can a soldier perceive the order of the whole army from his place in a rank. The same goes for verses. Surely, if individual syllables in a poem were allowed to live and perceive [only] for the time that they sounded, they could in no way appreciate that numeric texture and beauty of the work, because they could not perceive and approve it as a whole: despite the fact that it is made out of these very syllables that pass away and perish one by one."

55. "Accordingly, all functions and ends of all things are designed to ensure universal beauty, and that which horrifies us on its own, in fact, pleases us very greatly when considered as part of the whole. Indeed, we should not only consider one corner in judging a building, nor only hair in a handsome man, nor only the movement of hands in a good orator, nor the shape of the moon for only three days out of the whole cycle. For certain things acquire a lower status precisely because they possess perfection [only] as a whole, while their parts taken separately are imperfect. Now such things, whether their beauty is revealed in motion

distinction between truth judgments and aesthetic ("beautiful") judgments. (In this he foreshadows Baumgarten's notion of "thinking in a beautiful way.") Each and every thing, according to Augustine, must be judged as a whole. Now "the truth of our judgment," he continues, "does not depend on whether it is about the whole or a part. However, our judgment is beautiful [only] insofar as it covers the whole world, and we do not focus on a particular part of it while trying to determine the truth." In an unprecedented move that anticipates present-day discussions about types of truth, Augustine distinguishes between, presumably, judgments based on truth as 'correspondence' ("this color by itself, on the absolute scale from light to dark, is too dark") and 'beauty' judgments that are also somehow 'true,' but, as one would say nowadays, from the point of view of the truth of 'coherence,' which takes into consideration the whole picture: "this dark color balances out that bright color and creates a nice contrast."

Now according to Augustine, looking at the universe as a whole, one cannot fail to notice its striking beauty and order, which makes one immediately aware of its divine origin. In expanding the theory that the beauty of the universe confirms the presence of a divine design, Augustine simply follows a classic ancient tradition. Indeed, his phrasing is often reminiscent of that of Cicero in the *De natura deorum*.[56] The very description of universal beauty sounds similar to Cicero's account:

in the diverse and varied beauty of the sky, the land and the sea . . . in the sun, the moon and the stars . . . even in such a grand spectacle of the sea itself.[57]

I point out the greatness of the all-encompassing sea, I am astounded and amazed; I seek the artist; I look up at the sky and the beauty of the stars; I admire the splendor of the sun . . . the moon.[58]

---

or at rest, must be considered as a whole if one wants to pass a fair judgment. For the truth of our judgment does not depend on whether it is about the whole or a part. However, our judgment is beautiful [only] insofar as it covers the whole world, and we do not focus on a particular part of it while trying to determine the truth. Indeed, even the error of focusing on a part of the world is in itself hideous." Cf. *De vera rel.* 41.77 (CCSL 32, 237–38) where, trying to demonstrate that "all orderly arrangement is beautiful," Augustine presents the example of a worm, whose body is fitting and beautiful in its own sense. Page references to the *De vera rel.*, as well as to most other works of Augustine, are given according to the edition in *Corpus Christianorum, Series Latina*.

56. The similarity between Cicero, *ND*, and, e.g., Augustine, *De civ. Dei*—although not necessarily regarding the question of beauty—was noticed by Testard: cf. Testard, *Saint Augustin et Cicéron*, vol. 2, 69–70, and idem, "Note sur le *De Civitate Dei*, XXII, 24," 193–200.

57. *De civ. Dei* 22.24; CCSL 48, 851.

58. *Enarr. in Ps.* 41:7; CCSL 38, 464. Cf. *De vera relig.* 29.52 (CCSL 32, 221) where Augustine refers to the beauty of the sky, the moon, etc., which should lead to God.

For one should not vainly behold the beauty of the sky, the orderly arrangement of the stars, the brightness of light, the alternations of night and day, the monthly courses of the moon, the division of the year into the four seasons that corresponds to the fourfold division of the elements.[59]

to contemplate the beauty of the things.... And first of all one sees the whole earth.... [100] And how great is the beauty of the sea.... [103] And the moon... sends towards the earth that light that it receives from the sun.... [104] Then follows the great multitude of stars beyond description.[60]

Equally familiar is the idea that nothing can be more beautiful than this world:

Does this beauty not stand out in such a way that, one could say, nothing more beautiful could be devised?[61]

But surely of all things nothing is better than the world, nothing more stable, nothing more beautiful:[62] moreover, not only *is* there nothing better, but no such thing can even be thought of.[63]

There are striking similarities also in the ways both Augustine and Cicero phrase their argument that the beauty of the world proves its divine origin:

Now having considered the beauty of this world in its totality, does its beautiful shape itself not answer you, as it were, in one voice: it is not myself who made me, but God?[64]

Considering these things must not feed vain and short-lived curiosity, but become a step towards something immortal and everlasting.[65]

[Then] if you were to consider a world so lavishly adorned, such great variety and beauty of heavenly things, such great power and size of the sea and lands to be your dwelling, and not that of the immortal gods, would you not clearly seem to be insane?[66]

An important off-shoot of the idea of universal beauty and order is the solution of the problem of evil or ugliness. The unusual amount of at-

---

59. *De vera rel.* 29.52; CCSL 32, 221.
60. Cicero, *ND* 2.38.98–40.104.
61. *Enarr. in Ps.* 144:15; CCSL 40, 2099. Many other parallels can be found in the *Enarr. in Ps.*, e.g., 145:12, etc.
62. Cf. *De nat. deor.* 2.22.58: "that the world is most fit for continuous existence; also, that it lacks nothing; however, mostly that it possesses extraordinary beauty and every sort of ornament"; *De nat. deor.* 2.22.60 mentions the "most beautiful form" of the world.
63. Cicero, *ND* 2.7.18; cf. *ND* 2.34.87.   64. *Enarr. in Ps.* 144:13; CCSL 40, 2099.
65. *De vera rel.* 29.52; CCSL 32, 221.   66. Cicero, *ND* 2.6.17.

tention devoted to this problem in Augustine is not surprising. Making the defense of a non-dualist theology against the Manichaeans one of his primary tasks, he had to explain how an omnipotent benign deity which is the sole cause of the universe could allow the existence of such a thing as evil.[67] The traditional explanation originated in Antiquity to defend the monistic theology of the Stoics and was avidly taken over by early Christian authors. It goes as follows. Evil cannot be deliberately created by God with an evil intention, therefore either it is simply inevitable, as most opposites are, or it must have a certain positive function in the universe (for example, instructional or cautionary). However, although it is the ancient Stoa that is responsible for this impressive justification of the existence of evil, an analysis of contexts shows that the Stoic version does not have aesthetic overtones, which seem to be Augustine's genuine elaboration.

A passage from *Enchiridion* 10–11 (CCSL 46, 53) is one of Augustine's best-known texts on this topic and was frequently quoted in the Middle Ages. It demonstrates concisely by means of an aesthetic argument how evil can be assigned its due place in the universe: evil creates a contrast with the good, allowing the latter to stand out more clearly in the total arrangement, which is perceived as beautiful. According to Augustine, the totality of things is better and more beautiful than any individual thing. Even evil, if it is considered within the universal order of things, does not disturb the beauty of the whole, since it makes the good stand out by contrast. In this way God is capable of putting even evil things to good use.

however, all things in their totality are extremely good, for the admirable beauty of the universe consists of all things. And even that which is called evil in it, when it is well fitted and put in its place, makes the good things stand out more prominently, so that they might please more and be more praiseworthy when they are compared to evil things.

Both *De civitate Dei* and *De libero arbitrio* contain lengthy passages defending the same point of view. Thus *De civ. Dei* 16.8 (CCSL 48, 509–10) describes a particular example of corporeal ugliness. According to this passage, even monstrous and deformed human beings are part of God's design and have their place in the beauty of the universe. One fails to see

---

67. Perhaps, it was the threat of Albigensian heresies (which medieval theologians simply perceived as reincarnated "Manichaean" ideas) that renewed the interest in Augustine's theory of evil in the thirteenth century. For more information on the thirteenth-century discussions of this theory see O. Bychkov, "Aesthetic Explanation of Evil."

this only when one fails to look at the whole picture and observe that each part has its place in the universal order. Imperfection in God's universal design should not be inferred from the existence of particular deformed beings. *De libero arbitrio* 3.9.24–27 (CCSL 29, 290–91) presents the issue using moral examples. Sins are not necessary for the perfection of the universe, but once committed they are incorporated into the general order through punishment, which restores the balance of justice. Thus, the evil of crime is balanced by punishment, and the evil of punishment—since it is still evil for the beings that are punished—does not disturb the beauty of the universe because it contributes to the restoration of order. As a result, "the universe always stays beautiful, having been fitted with most appropriate parts."

The best indication that Augustine does see the issue of evil precisely in aesthetic terms, even from the modern point of view, appears in the parallels that he draws between the perception of evil and ugliness on the one hand, and the aesthetic mechanism of contrast employed by artists on the other. In *De civ. Dei* 11.23 (CCSL 48, p. 342)[68] and *De vera rel.* 40.76 (CCSL 32, p. 237)[69] Augustine uses a comparison with the use of dark contrasting shading in a painting, an example that was frequently employed in manuals of rhetoric to explain the use of contrasting statements.[70] In this case, an element that is of itself unattractive (black color) contributes to the beauty of the whole as part of the arrangement. This is precisely how sinners, who are ugly in themselves, can contribute to the beauty of the universe. Another prominent example from *De civ. Dei* 11.18 (CCSL 48, 337)[71] is the use of antithetical or opposing statements in rhetoric to enhance the effect of a speech. The technique was, of course,

---

68. "Just as a picture with appropriately placed black color, so the totality of things, if someone could see it all, is beautiful even with the sinners in it, although their deformity may make them look ugly when they are considered on their own."

69. "However, just as the black color in a painting becomes beautiful as part of the whole, in the same way the immutable providence of God arranges this public spectacle of life as a whole most fittingly."

70. Cf. Cicero, *De orat.* 3.26.101; the term *eminentia* here definitely refers to contrasting painting techniques, cf. *Acad. priora* 2.7.20.

71. "Indeed, God would not have created even any human being, not to mention an angel, foreseeing that he will become evil in the future, had he not known, at the same time, to what good use for the righteous he would put him, thus even ennobling the temporal world order, as one would the most beautiful poem, by some, as it were, antitheses.... Thus, just as these contrary statements opposed to their contraries result in the beauty of speech, so the beauty of the temporal world is formed through the workings of some eloquence—not of words, but of things—by way of opposing the contraries."

widely used in the pagan tradition,[72] but Augustine even cites St. Paul's writing as an example of *antitheta*. It is precisely such antithetical use that is intended for the sinners and evil things in the world. Using an analogy with the aesthetic perception of a beautiful speech in *De natura boni* 8 (CSEL 25.2, 858),[73] Augustine clarifies how even transient and temporal things, which constantly change and die, can contribute to the beauty of the world. Although particular sounds and syllables continuously disappear and do not last, the general impression of the beauty of speech does not suffer.

Although this issue exceeds the scope of the present study, a few words would be appropriate regarding the suggested dependence of Augustine's theory of evil on the Stoics and Plotinus.[74] The Stoic background of the passages quoted above cannot be confirmed by any direct textual tradition, but they exhibit considerable similarity with the Stoic views of evil, which, given the popularity of Stoic thought not only among pagans but even in the early Christian circles, is not surprising. The position that evil is absolutely necessary to the universal order can be traced back to the Stoics with a great deal of certainty.[75] The Stoics had to defend their idea of the universal Divine Law against their opponents, who pressed them to explain why this intelligent Law had created such an irrational thing as evil. This view is represented in Aulus Gellius, *Noctes Atticae*, 7.1.2–3 (SVF 2.1169, LS 54Q).[76] In *Noct. Att.* 7.1.7 (SVF 2.1170, LS 54Q) Gellius quotes Chrysippus (Bk. 4 of περὶ προνοίας), who

---

72. Both *De civ. Dei* 11.18 and *De natura boni* 8 (quoted below) can easily be placed within an established rhetorical tradition: *De civ. Dei* 11.18 is reminiscent of Cicero, *Orator* 50.50.166, and Quintilian, *Institutiones* 9.3.81. Regarding this particular passage from the *De civ. Dei*, as well as the previous one about painting (11.23), also see Hayes, "Beauty's Resting Place," 227ff.

73. "Indeed, out of things that come and pass there arises some temporal beauty of a certain kind, so that not even those things which die or stop being what they were deform and disturb the manner, form and order *(modus, species, ordo)* of the whole creation: just as a well-composed speech is always beautiful, although all its syllables and sounds constantly pass away, as it were, being born and dying."

74. For example, Verbeke, "Augustin et le stoïcisme," 85, 87, suggests that the theory of evil in Augustine comes from the Stoics. See more on this subject, in addition to the discusson that follows, in Bychkov, "Traditional Stoic Ideas," 152–53; A. A. Long, "The Stoic Concept of Evil," *Philosophical Quarterly* 18 (1968): 329–43.

75. Cf. the section "Why there are evil things if there is providence" in SVF 2.1168–86 and LS 65, vol. 1, 386.

76. 'When Chrysippus speaks against these arguments in περὶ προνοίας, Bk. 4, he says: "Absolutely nothing is more stupid than to think that there could be good things even if there were no evil things there concurrently. For since the good is the opposite of evil it must necessarily be the case that both exist in opposition to each other, as it were, propped up by mutual but adverse efforts; so, no opposite is without the other opposite."'

poses the question whether providence (πρόνοια) also created diseases and other evil. According to Chrysippus, this was not her primary intention; however, it is impossible for the good to emerge without evil as its counterpart. Thus immediately with the creation of bodies diseases necessarily come. As for the morals, Chrysippus contends (*Noct. Att.* 7.1.13), "as soon as virtue is born in men according to nature's plan, [at the same time] vices are born there due to the mutuality of opposites." There is clear evidence that Augustine knew and used Gellius, whom he quotes in *De civ. Dei* precisely on the subject of Stoicism.[77]

Further, there is a discrepancy in the ancient sources as to whether the authentic Stoic view was that the existence of evil was only necessary (Gellius) or that it was also useful in some way. Thus, according to Plutarch's account of the Stoic teaching, bedbugs and mice are useful,[78] and evil is part of the divine plan.[79] Augustine definitely supports the latter point of view by holding that evil serves to augment the universal beauty and order, which makes it also good in some way. Again, although his exact sources are not obvious, the second position is very similar to that of Plotinus. This study makes no attempt to solve the problem of the relationship between either Plotinus and Augustine or Plotinus and the Stoics (of whom Plotinus makes no mention, speaking on the question of evil). However, several similarities between the theories of evil in the Stoics, Plotinus, and Augustine can be pointed out.[80] A view that is very close to the Stoic theory of the necessity of evil as expressed by Gellius is found in *Enn.* 3.3.7.[81] In *Enn.* 3.2.5, Plotinus, like Chrysippus, starts by mentioning the necessity of diseases, which ultimately do not affect the state of goodness.[82] However, although this

---

77. Cf. Hagendahl, *Augustine and the Latin Classics*, no. 397 (pp. 179–84).
78. Plutarch, *St. rep.* 1044D, *SVF* 2.1163, LS 54O.
79. Ibid., 1050C–D, *SVF* 2.937, LS 54T.
80. On the influence of the Stoic theory of evil on Plotinus see B. A. G. Fuller, *Problem of Evil in Plotinus* (about the Stoic origin of the idea of the perfection of the world and the problem of evil see pp. 157–63; passim 189ff., 192ff., 207–9). On the influence of Plotinus on Augustine see: Switalski, *Plotinus and the Ethics of St. Augustine*, 81ff. (concerning the influence of the doctrine of evil see pp. 102–5; concerning the comparison between *Enn.* 3 and Augustine see pp. 91–92 and notes to pp. 102, 103, 105). A discussion of Plotinian parallels in Augustine's "aesthetics of evil" can also be found in Fontanier, *La beauté selon saint Augustin*, 160–61.
81. Schwyzer ed., vol. 1, 308.1ff.; cf. Graeser, *Plotinus and the Stoics*, 60. "But because there are better things, there are also worse things. Otherwise, how would there be something worse in a multiform thing without there being something better, or how would there be something better without there being something worse?"
82. Cf. Graeser, *Plotinus and the Stoics*, 63. Remarkably, this section is also called περὶ

statement seems to be in perfect accord with the view that the co-existence of good and evil is merely necessary, Plotinus emphasizes the point that negative qualities, in fact, do good and are necessary for the general perfection.[83] Thus Plotinus's view is more in continuity with the original Stoic tradition as presented by Plutarch.[84]

Clearly, Augustine uses the Stoic theory of evil precisely as it was transmitted by Plutarch, which is also the version supported by Plotinus. At the same time, contrary to what Faas claims, this view is not simply borrowed but considerably developed. The most obvious contribution that Augustine makes to the ancient theory of evil is precisely his aesthetic interpretation of it, emphasized by frequent parallels with the fine arts. Augustine combines a traditional justification of evil as necessary or useful with the insight drawn from the aesthetic proof of the divine origin of the universe based on its order and beauty. It is precisely that luminous and clear aspect in universal harmony that is evident to all that reveals the existence of a higher design in the world. Along the same lines, the necessity of including evil and ugliness in the universal design is aesthetically, not logically, evident and appealing. In order to justify the existence of evil, Augustine employs a "beautiful," not a "truth," judgment: just as the necessity of such elements as black color in a painting or a discordant sound in music, the necessity of evil in the world is something that is immediately evident, not logically but *aesthetically*. Perhaps, this is exactly why his aesthetic justification seemed far from being satisfactory or orthodox to some medieval theologians, such as Albert the Great, who otherwise recognized Augustine as an important authority.[85]

Augustine's attempt to justify the existence of evil is not only firmly rooted in the tradition preceding him but also makes a lasting impact on

---

προνοίας, that is, it bears the same name as the work of Chrysippus where the discussion about evil emerges.

83. "And these [i.e., evil] things are not altogether useless towards organizing and completing the whole . . . indeed, badness has contributed something useful to the whole pattern of justice through its emergence, and many useful things came out of it" (*Enn.* 3.2.5; Schwyzer, vol. 1, 275.7–9, 16 and p. 276.17–18; Graeser, *Plotinus and the Stoics*, 63, lists ll. 15–27; cf. Switalski, *Plotinus and the Ethics of St. Augustine*, p. 102, n. 469, who compares this passage with Augustinian texts).

84. Thus, according to Plutarch, *St. rep.* 1050F–1051B (*SVF* 2.1181, *LS* 61R), Chrysippus claims in the Περὶ φύσεως, Bk. 2, that "badness . . . does not arise without usefulness in respect to the totality of things; for [otherwise] the good things would not exist either."

85. Cf. O. Bychkov, "Aesthetic Explanation of Evil."

the post-Augustinian medieval tradition. During the high Middle Ages, following Peter Lombard's selections from Augustine, large sections of thirteenth-century *Commentaries on the* Sentences *of Peter Lombard*, as well as of theological *Summae*, are devoted to the discussion of Augustine's aestheticized version of the theory of evil.[86] At the same time, Augustine's choice to rely, at least partially, on a purely aesthetic, and not "truth" judgment in this matter makes his views on evil sound remarkably modern. Thus, a striking parallel to Augustine's aesthetic view of the problem of evil can be found in Nietzsche. According to Nietzsche, morality, evil, and the world in general can ultimately be justified only on aesthetic grounds.[87] Clearly, in the *Birth of Tragedy* Nietzsche is reconsidering the traditional question of what justifies the presence of evil in the world and the horror of existence in general. His answer is clear: only art, that is, the aesthetic drive. By contrast with the earlier traditions that find justification in the divine economy, or within the framework of rational or moral explanations, Nietzsche openly proclaims that the world and existence can be justified only on aesthetic grounds. Thus speaking of music and "tragic myth"—the expressions of the primordial Dionysian drive which in Nietzsche sometimes appears as the aesthetic *par excellence* ("the eternal and original artistic power")—Nietzsche writes:

both transfigure a region in whose joyous chords dissonance as well as the terrible image of the world fade away charmingly; both play with the sting of displeasure, trusting in their exceedingly powerful magic arts; and by means of this play both justify the existence of even the 'worst world.'

If we could imagine dissonance become man, . . . this dissonance, to be able to live, would need a splendid illusion that would cover dissonance with a veil of beauty. This is the true artistic aim of Apollo[88] in whose name we comprehend all those countless illusions of the beauty of mere appearance *(Schein)* that at every moment make life worth living at all.[89]

---

86. See ibid. and O. Bychkov, "A Propos of Medieval Aesthetics," chap. 3, 163–74.

87. Cf. his famous dictum from the *Birth of Tragedy*: "For it is only as an *aesthetic phenomenon* that existence and the world are eternally *justified*" (chap. 5, ed. Kaufmann, 52, W 43).

88. The Apollinean is another artistic principle akin to beauty that represents the harmonious aspects of the world.

89. *Birth of Tragedy*, chap. 25, ed. Kaufmann, 143.

Ascent through Beauty

We can now turn to an aspect of Augustine's thought[90] that relies on the revelatory nature of aesthetic experience to an even greater extent: his analysis of the (Neo)Platonic ascent from the sensible to the intelligible and beyond. Although Augustine's ascent scheme shares its main features with the ascent scheme found in the earlier Neoplatonic tradition, in Augustine's thought the scheme receives a considerable philosophical elaboration, which includes many precise and detailed observations about the nature of this process. The works that are usually discussed in this connection in scholarly literature are *De magistro, De musica, De ordine, De vera religione, De libero arbitrio, De Trinitate,* and *Confessions*.[91] *De magistro,* although it does not contain any observations on aesthetics as such, provides a concise outline of this crucial feature of Augustine's theological and philosophical system: the "transcending" movement through reason toward the transcendent divine source of all knowledge.

Although von Balthasar, among others, openly interprets Augustine's train of thought in *De magistro* and other works in terms of Kant's transcendental philosophy, we will apply the terms 'transcendent,' 'transcending,' and 'transcendental' with caution, and only in a phenomeno-

---

90. Which is also regularly mentioned in secondary literature but, as will be shown in this chapter, is almost never fully understood.

91. As above, the CCSL editions of these works will be used—CCSL 27 *(Confessiones)*; CCSL 29 *(De magistro, De ordine, De libero arbitrio)*; CCSL 32 *(De vera religione)*; CCSL 50 *(De Trinitate)*—with the exception of Bk. 6 of the *De musica* (originally edited in PL 32), for which the following edition is used: M. Jacobsson, ed. and trans., *Aurelius Augustinus: De musica liber VI: A Critical Edition with a Translation and an Introduction,* Acta Universitatis Stockholmiensis. Studia Latina Stockholmiensia (Stockholm: Almqvist & Wiksell International, 2002). The precise chronology of Augustine's works is not crucial for the present discussion. Thus the order of presenting particular works will be determined not only by their approximate chronology (as advancing from the earlier and formative period to the mature period), but also by the more or less developed form of the ascent theory. The chronology of the works in question, based on M. Schanz, *Geschichte der römischen Litteratur bis zum Gesetzgebungswerk des Kaisers Justinian,* vol. 4.2 (Munich: C. H. Beck, 1920), 406; P. de Labriolle, *Histoire de la littérature latine chrétienne,* 2nd ed. (Paris: Les belles lettres, 1924), table 8; and S. Zarb, "Chronologia operum sancti Augustini secundum ordinem Retractationum digesta," *Angelicum* 11 (1934): 89–91, is as follows: *De magistro* (Schanz 389–90, Labriolle 389, Zarb 389), *De ordine* (Schanz 386–87, Labriolle 386, Zarb 386), *De musica* (Schanz 389–90, Labriolle 387–91, Zarb 387–90), *De libero arbitrio* (Schanz 387–88, Labriolle 388–95, Zarb 388–95), *De vera religione* (Schanz 389–90, Labriolle 389–90, Zarb 391), *De Trinitate* (Schanz 400–416, Labriolle 398–416, Zarb 399–419), *Confessiones* (Schanz 400, Labriolle 397–98, Zarb 397–401).

logical sense.[92] Thus the 'transcendent' will be understood as something that is beyond, or transcends, our perceptive and intellectual capacities: whether it really does so or simply appears that way is of no concern. 'Transcending' movement refers to the perceptive or intellectual activity that somehow makes one aware of the existence of the transcendent, or gives one a "glimpse" of it: in this sense it is close to the Kantian meaning of 'transcendental' as that which has to do with the transition from the immanent (human consciousness) to the transcendent (for example, ideas, the divine principle). In this phenomenological sense there is no reason why the Platonic or Augustinian ascent cannot be viewed in terms of Kant's transcendental aesthetics, since in all these cases the ascent is based on the same experience of reflecting upon an aesthetic (more precisely, beautiful) object, which serves as the "mediator," and leads to a similar result (awareness of the "beyond," or at least something we were not aware of before). In Neoplatonic thought and in Augustine, just as in Kant, this transcending movement always implies a revealing aspect, in that one always becomes immediately aware of something. Thus "transcending" and "revelatory" almost always go side by side.

The main idea of *De magistro* is that, contrary to a common belief, nothing is actually learned through signs or words. Words cannot convey to us the actual things they signify: they either remind us of what we already know or admonish us to seek things on our own (10.33–11.36; pp. 192–94). The "teacher" therefore cannot really teach us anything;[93] if what he says sounds probable we assent to it, and if not we doubt (12.40–13.41; pp. 198–99). The crucial point in the Augustinian phenomenological reflection is the origin of this judgment concerning the things we do not yet know. Where does this judgment come from? Phenomenological necessity brings Augustine to the conclusion that the origin of our judgments about the things we do not know must transcend

---

92. The reasons for caution are outlined earlier in this chapter and in Chapter 4. This is especially true in view of the medieval-Aristotelian use of the term "transcendental," which causes confusion even among seasoned scholars.

In line with our main premise of the possibility of a dialogue between modern and medieval thought, we will use the term 'phenomenological' in application to Augustine and other medieval thinkers in the traditional sense it has in the modern phenomenological tradition, and in particular in Husserl: i.e., as something that has to do with the mental observation of the perceptive and intelligible structures of our conscious experience.

93. This is, of course, Plato's standard view as well.

our mind. We learn from the eternal truth itself, which is inside us, and then judge whether what is said agrees with it:[94]

But whoever is able to see clearly, on the inside is a disciple of truth, and on the outside—a judge of the speaker, or rather of the utterance itself. (13.41; p. 199)

[when "teachers" teach] . . . those who are called students consider on their own whether what was said is true, namely, by intuiting that inner truth according to their own capacities. Therefore it is then that they learn . . . [i.e.,] . . . when they discover inwardly that what was said is true. (14.45; p. 202)

Needless to say that for a Christian thinker the eternal truth within our minds is God, or Christ as his Word and Wisdom:

However, concerning all things that we understand we consult not the speaker who resounds from the outside, but the truth which inwardly presides over our mind itself—perhaps, being admonished with words to consult it. And the teacher who teaches us, after we consult him, is Christ—the immutable power and eternal wisdom of God—who is said to dwell in the inner man. (11.38; pp. 195–96)

However, the transcending ascent in the *De magistro* is purely intellectual and not "aesthetic": it is based on reflection, not triggered immediately by sense experience.

By contrast, two other early works of Augustine—*De ordine*, Bk. 2 and *De musica*, Bk. 6—clearly show Augustine's interest in aesthetic experience. The ascent motif is not developed as explicitly here as in the *De magistro* or some later works, but he makes several profound observations about the dynamics and structure of aesthetic judgment that become important building blocks in Augustine's fully developed aesthetics of the ascent.

The *De ordine* is not a specifically aesthetic work: it is devoted to the discussion of providence and the divine and human orders. Starting with the order observed in studies, the human mind can pass from corporeal to incorporeal reality. At the same time, because the concept of

---

94. Augustine's view of both aesthetic and rational judgment is in line with contemporary Gestalt psychology, which describes our perception and intellect as active, not passive, powers seeking positive matches in reality to pre-existing patterns in brain circuitry—as opposed to the old cognitive model of the brain passively receiving and abstracting regularities from accumulated experience. Augustine's "eternal truth" or "transcending judge" (like Kant's "ideas") thus correspond to the pre-wired patterns in the brain that, indeed, escape our conscious experience since they are the very preexisting, hard-wired cognitive structures, not the product, of our intellectual activity.

order in ancient thought since the pre-Socratics is tightly connected to that of beauty, the discussion of aesthetic matters is all but inevitable.[95] It is clear that the matter under discussion in *De ordine* 2 is aesthetic experience, even from a modern point of view. According to Augustine, the senses that are most "aesthetic"—those that produce the feeling of beauty—are vision and hearing, just as in modern aesthetics. These are the senses in which *ratio* (in this case meaning 'proportion' or 'regularity,' see above) predominantly resides.[96] For example, something can visually "appear to have order or regularity" (*rationabiliter apparere*), or a sound can "exhibit regularity" (*rationabiliter sonare*, 2.11.32). "We have then," Augustine writes, "so far as we were able to investigate, certain traces of regularity or proportion in our senses[97] and, insofar as it pertains to sight and hearing, in the pleasurable response itself" (*in ipsa voluptate*, 2.11.33, p. 125).

For Augustine the main criterion of beauty is order and proportion, and not purity and unity, as it is for Plotinus. In the case of vision the beautiful is, specifically, a "proportionate arrangement of parts" (*congruentia partium*, 2.11.33, p. 126). The "aesthetic" senses of vision and hearing are capable of perceiving this proportion directly. Now Augustine here, just as Plotinus in *Enn.* 1.6, does realize that some aesthetic visual or auditory data, such as perception of pure colors or single sounds is not "regular" or proportionate (2.11.33). The problem raised by Plotinus in *Enn.* 1.6 can be formulated as follows: how do such simple things, which we also perceive as beautiful, comply with the aesthetic criterion of proportion and harmony if they do not have parts? Both Plotinus (in *Enn.* 1.6) and Augustine (in *De vera relig.* 30.55 and 32.60) provide a solution by presenting harmony and proportion as a particular case of unity. Augustine, in particular, speaks of unity as the ultimate principle that governs all proportion. Although there is no disagreement on

---

95. On aesthetic issues in the *De ordine* see Hayes, "Beauty's Resting Place," 141ff.; Fontanier, *La beauté selon saint Augustin*, 77–78.

96. In 2.11.34 Augustine is careful to differentiate between *ratio* in the sense of 'regular pattern,' such as rhythm, detected directly by our sensation, and *ratio* as 'rational pattern,' i.e., as meaning understood by reason. As an aesthetician, it is the first variation that he is interested in.

97. Augustine's perspicuity in aesthetic matters allows him to come as close as he could at the time to discovering the Gestalt principle in human sensation, which explains in many ways, from the point of view of neuroscience, the phenomenon of "recognizing eternal and immutable laws" of beauty and proportion in physical reality. On this subject see I. Rentschler et al., *Beauty and the Brain*. However, as we said before, it is the phenomenology of aesthetic experience, not its "objective" causes, that is the focus of this study.

this matter between Plotinus and Augustine in principle, their views on what essentially constitutes beauty seem to disagree at least in spirit. Thus Augustine generally prefers to think of the aesthetic principle as inseparable from proportion and harmony, that is, involvement of multiple parts. For an explanation one may look to the Christian doctrine of the Trinity (which is the ultimate source of beauty) as a coincidence of relations, that is, something that lacks the perfect uniformity of the Neoplatonic One. J.-M. Fontanier, discussing the passage in question (*De ordine* 2.11.33), points to a passage in *De musica* 6.13.38, which provides a somewhat different solution to the problem of simple sense data that appear beautiful. This solution still presents aesthetic experience caused by simple sensations as a case of harmony: although no harmony is found in pure light or color itself, still it harmonizes with the organ of perception.[98]

Returning to *De ordine* 2, vision and hearing contain such proportion in its purest form: in these types of sense experience it is felt immediately in the perception or emotional reaction itself *(in ipsa voluptate)*. Here we notice a similarity with the Kantian understanding of aesthetic judgment as precisely the pleasurable response itself (in Kantian terms, disinterested) generated by an aesthetic object which appears to be "for its own sake."[99] In senses other than vision and hearing this propor-

---

98. Fontanier, *La beauté selon saint Augustin*, 77–78. "And what about the visible light itself, which is the origin of all colors? (We do enjoy color in corporeal forms, do we not?) Do you think we seek anything else in light and colors, apart from that which is agreeable to the eye? For we turn away from extreme glare, and at the same time lose interest in things which are too dark and unclear: just as we shrink from sounds that are too loud and find no pleasure in something too quiet, at the level of whisper. The latter quality is not in temporal intervals, but in the sound itself, whose function in respect to these [sounding] numbers is similar to that of light [in relation to visible patterns]. The contrary of this quality is silence, just as darkness is the contrary of colors. In all these things, when we seek something agreeable to our own nature and reject what is disagreeable . . . , is it not, again, some law of equality that makes us rejoice in these, when we realize that equal elements are paired up with each other in some mysterious ways? . . . To conclude, there is no other thing except equality or similitude that would please us in those sensory experiences. And where there is equality or similitude, there are numeric principles. And clearly nothing is as equal or as similar as one and one" (*De musica* 6.13.38; pp. 82–84). The idea is common in ancient theories of vision, except that here it appears in an aesthetic context: cf. Plato who in *Timaeus* 67C, speaks of color (χρόα) or light being compatible and proportioned with the eye (ὄψει σύμμετρον): color, i.e., "a flame that emanates from each body and consists of parts that are commensurate with being perceived by the eye." Plato was probably inspired by Empedocles; see J. I. Beare, *Greek Theories of Elementary Cognition* (Oxford: Clarendon Press, 1906). Seeing suitable sense objects as being "in harmony" with the sense organ is also typical of Aristotle's *De anima*. One must note, however, that this explanation ultimately has nothing to do with modern aesthetics.

99. This "disinterestedness" is questionable, not only in ancient thought but even in Kant

tion serves a different purpose and does not become part of our direct experience: it exists "not in the pleasurable emotional response itself, but for the sake of something else" (2.11.33, pp. 125–26). The example of this would be when smells, tastes, or tactile impressions mixed according to a certain proportion signal to us whether a certain object, such as food stuff or construction material, is suitable for our use, instead of simply showing that proportions and patterns themselves are pleasing, as in vision and hearing. This important observation means that vision and hearing—the aesthetic senses—are unique precisely because they possess a certain structure, or, in Kantian terms, purposiveness. At the same time, unlike in the case of the "lower" senses, the aim of this purposiveness is not immediately obvious. This observation is even more explicit in the following passage. To the two key features of aesthetic judgment—being able to detect regular patterns in sensory data and residing immediately in the aesthetic reaction itself—Augustine adds another crucial characteristic. Aesthetic judgment is experienced as something that has compelling necessity,[100] and yet lacks any compelling reason explaining it:

> And so, carefully inspecting the details in this particular building, we cannot help being displeased at the fact that we see one door placed to the side, and the other almost in the middle, but not quite there. Clearly, in manufactured things positioning parts unevenly without any compelling reason (*nulla cogente necessitate*) almost seems to offend our sight. As for the fact that the three windows inside [the building]—one in the middle, and one on each side of it—pour down sunlight[101] at equal intervals, how it delights us, after intent observation, and how it ravishes our mind! This is something evident and does not need too long an explanation. (2.11.34, p. 126)

The phrase "without any compelling reason" (the ablative absolute *nulla cogente necessitate*) can be taken either with the expression "positioning parts" or with "seems to offend."[102] The second possibility is certainly the more interesting one, since in this case Augustine definitely foreshadows Kant's understanding of aesthetic phenomena as possessing purposiveness (they seem to compel us to make a judgment, in this case, that they offend us) without a purpose (they seem to lack any rational

---

himself, since both view aesthetic experience as somehow helpful in advancing our morals and understanding our cognitive processes.
  100. This aspect will be expressed in stronger terms in his later works.
  101. I accepted the reading *solis lumen* provided by the PL.
  102. The current translation reflects this ambiguity.

explanation for why they do this). However, even if the first option is the correct one, it still refers to some "compelling reason" for arranging parts evenly with regularity that we naturally detect, and yet, as Augustine clearly notes in other contexts,[103] can hardly explain.

Naturally, as later in Kant's aporias of taste, the observation about the "unexplained cogency" of aesthetic judgment paves the way for the next step: an inquiry as to the source of its purposiveness and the direction in which it points. In a famous adaptation of the *Symposion* version of Plato's ascent, Augustine outlines how to proceed. The study of liberal arts teaches us about the regular nature of reality. In order to move on further to pure contemplation, one must leave the arts, with their physicality, behind, but use them as a "springboard" or "ladder." This step proves to be difficult, because of our strong attachment to sensible reality:

> Up to this point that part which receives the designation 'rational' or 'regular' was advanced by means of the liberal arts and disciplines (2.13.38, p. 128). From this point on, our reason wished to be ravished to the most blessed contemplation of the divine things themselves. But lest it fall from the heights, it sought [supporting] steps (*gradus*)[104] and attempted to make its own way using its own achievements and orderly nature. For it desired that sort of beauty which it could contemplate alone in its pure state, without these eyes. However, it was impeded by the senses. Therefore, for a little while it turned its gaze at them [i.e., the senses] who, proclaiming that they possessed the truth, with their discordant clamor called back [reason], which hastened to proceed to other things. (2.14.39, p. 129)

Augustine further enumerates several liberal arts and explains how to abstract from them. All liberal arts, according to him, lead to the observation that all sensible reality is governed by numbers. Numbers, understood by Augustine, together with Neoplatonists and Neopythagoreans, as fundamental principles of proportion and harmony that govern the universe, possess particular splendor and clarity; with some training, one can intuit them in reality directly. The transcending or revelatory movement of the trained mind beyond sensible reality happens precisely in the form of intuiting or seeing the true nature of number. It is at this moment of revelation that the mind becomes aware of the eternal and immutable nature of numbers:

---

103. Cf. the example of the arch in *De Trinitate* 9.6.11.
104. The metaphor of "steps" or "ladder" is common in the Platonic tradition: cf. Plato, *Symp.* 211C3 and Plotinus, *Enn.* I.6.1.

Thus at this fourth step [reason] perceived that it is numbers that reign and perfect everything in either rhythms or melodies. It carefully pondered of what kind they were. It found them to be divine and eternal, especially because it had constructed all the previous steps with their help. And now it could hardly bear the fact that their splendor and clarity was stained with the corporeal matter of sounds ... because that which the mind sees is always present and is acknowledged to be immortal (and numbers appeared to be of this kind),[105] but the sound, because it belongs to the sensible realm, flows by into the past and is impressed in the memory. (2.14.41, pp. 129–30)

Now traditionally, for example, in Plato or in Cicero's version of Stoicism, this cognitive function of the ascent from aesthetic experience and the liberal arts, which reveals to us the eternal source of all harmony, is also complemented by a moral function. Perceiving harmony clearly in the liberal arts, and subsequently learning to detect it in the physical world, we naturally strive to establish a similar harmony and order in our souls. As the reader remembers, the same function is attributed to aesthetics and the arts in modern times, for example, by Kant and Schiller. In this sense Augustine's aesthetics is no exception. Drawing a parallel between the arrangement of musical sounds and the arrangement of psychic powers in the soul brings one to a conclusion that harmony must be preserved in both:

For gradually [the soul] also comes to the idea of proper conduct and the best way of life: this time not by faith alone, but with the help of sure reasoning. [Indeed,] it will seem most disgraceful and deplorable to it, whose gaze is fixed on the nature and power of numbers, that verses should run smoothly, and the cithara should sound harmoniously (*concinere*) as a result of its own artistic skill, and that at the same time its own life and itself, i.e., the soul, should go astray, dominated by wantonness, and sound discordantly (*dissonare*) with the most disturbing clamor of vices. (2.19.50, pp. 134–35)

Although this ascent or revelation is indeed prepared by observations made from aesthetic experience, the transcending movement from the sensible in the *De ordine* is not presented as absolutely immediate. The awareness of the eternal principles does not come as a direct intuition or experience but rather as an intellectual process that requires a contemplative stage, despite being based initially on sensory data. Thus in

---

105. Augustine makes a distinction between "eternal truths," which can always be accessed and verified by the intellect, and the truths derived from sense data, which are stored by the memory and can be forgotten, distorted, etc.

the *De ordine* Augustine seems to follow the model of the *Symposion* rather than that of the *Phaedrus*, and the appellation the "ladder of the liberal arts"—instead of "aesthetic revelation"—is perhaps more appropriate for this version of the ascent:

> This is the order of the study of wisdom, through which everyone becomes capable of understanding the order of things, that is, of recognizing the two worlds and the father of the universe himself, of whom there is no knowledge in the soul, apart from knowing to what extent it ignores him. (2.18.47, p. 133)

> But when [the soul] has arranged and organized itself, and made itself harmonious and beautiful, it will then dare to look at God, the very source whence all true things emanate and the father of truth himself. (2.19.51, p. 135)

Augustine clearly wants to show that although it is sensible reality that triggers our intellectual insight, this reality is not worthy in itself. Thus, after the process of abstracting numbers (2.15.42, p. 130),[106] reason compares numbers and proportions in real things with the ones in the intellect and finds the former inferior to the latter (2.15.42, p. 130). It is important to remember that, despite the priority of reason and the value of purely intelligible numbers in this version of the ascent, the intellectual ascent cannot start without that immediate and apparent experience, which is precisely our aesthetic sense, or the natural feeling for beauty and harmony. It is equally important that at the initial stage of the ascent numbers are not conceptualized but are clearly seen in sensory phenomena, that is, they are perceived immediately or "aesthetically."

Bk. 6 of the *De musica* is another well-known text of Augustine that exhibits his keen interest in aesthetic experience and, this time, is specifically dedicated to its analysis.[107] As was mentioned above, the ancient discipline of 'music' goes both beyond what we call music (so as to include, for example, poetry and literature) and beyond what we call the "fine arts" (so as to include also geometry and mathematics), although, of course, the aesthetic dimension of all these arts is still part of it. It is

---

106. "Hence reason proceeded to the domain of the eyes and, inspecting the earth and the heavens, felt that it was pleased by nothing else except beauty, and in beauty by shapes, in shapes by proportions (*dimensiones*), in proportions by numbers."

107. The Latin text of the *De musica* is quoted according to Jacobsson's edition (Augustinus, *De Musica liber VI*), but the English translation is mine. On the *De musica*, and specifically on Bk. 6 see: Hayes, "Beauty's Resting Place," 152–86; A. Keller, *Aurelius Augustinus und die Musik: Untersuchungen zu "De musica" im Kontext seines Schrifttums* (Würzburg: Augustinus-Verlag, 1993); A. Schmitt, "Zahl und Schönheit in Augustins *De musica* VI," *Würzburger Jahrbücher für die Altertumswissenschaft* n.f. 16 (1990): 221–37.

not surprising, then, that Augustine starts his observations in *De musica* 6.2.3 with poetry. In one's actual aesthetic experience of reciting metered poetry one distinguishes, upon careful observation, between the actual sensory data (sounds) that can have variable parameters (feet or syllables can be shortened or drawn out in time, for example) and the rules—numbers or proportions—that govern the whole metric pattern and do not change (that is, the meter itself). Augustine's interlocutors (the Teacher and the Student) draw distinctions between various levels of perception, such as the sounding verse itself, its image or impression in our mental faculty or memory, the process of perception by this faculty, the process of judging the meter, and the rules used in judging this meter. They finally decide to categorize them into five (later revised to six) types of numbers:[108] 'sounding,' 'mnemonic,' 'occurring,'[109] 'progressing,'[110] and 'judging.'

The following observation about the fifth type of numbers proves that Augustine speaks about aesthetic experience in its modern sense. The "judging numbers" (*numeri judiciales*) are either delighted or discomforted in the perception of other types of numbers, and their delight or discomfort is that "innate sensory judgment" (*naturale judicium sentiendi*) which is the soul's immediate judgment about the presence of order or disorder (6.4.5; p. 16).[111] The observation is repeated later in the form that is reminiscent of the *De ordine* account. The interlocutors realize that there are, in fact, two types of "judging" numbers: lower or "sensory" (*sensuales*), which judge by feeling pleasure or pain, and "judging" proper, which pass an almost rational judgment (*De musica* 6.9.24; p. 58). The very pleasure derived from our perception of harmony by the lower kind of "judging" numbers (*judicialibus delectari*) basically amounts to passing a judgment. The higher judging numbers then "pass another, more definitive judgment . . . about that delight, which is itself, as it were, a judgment of those [lower] 'judging' numbers" (*De musica*

---

108. The Latin terms for these classes of numbers are: *sonantes, recordabiles, occursores, progressores, iudiciales* (unfortunately, all conceivable English equivalents sound awkward). On the functions of these five kinds of numbers see 6.2.3–6.

109. I.e., the impressions that correspond to actually sounding numbers, see 6.2.3–6.

110. I.e., the ones that control the procession of rhythms and meters as the brain generates them.

111. Sensation, according to Augustine, happens as a result of the soul's observation of the condition of the body: the soul itself is not affected but experiences pleasure when it observes harmony (*convenientia*) and pain when is finds disorder (6.5.10; p. 28).

6.9.23; p. 56).[112] The interlocutors conclude that "our sensory capacity for delight itself" must be "endowed with some numbers," or else "it could in no way express its approval for regular intervals and displeasure with irregular ones" (*De musica* 6.9.24, p. 58).

The interpretation of human sensation as a kind of a judging mechanism is of itself not particularly new.[113] However, both the context in which this judgment occurs here and the way it is described by Augustine bring his account much closer to modern theories of aesthetic judgment. First of all, the numbers present in our sensory apparatus react to orderly patterns, and for Augustine, as for many modern aestheticians, order and beauty imply each other as far as our sense experience is concerned, so the context of the judgment described by Augustine is definitely aesthetic. Second, this judgment is the very reaction of delight itself, just as in Kant's aesthetics: on the one hand it is clearly a judgment, that is, something close to rationality, but on the other hand it consists in delight, an immediate and purely sensible or emotional reaction. Thus aesthetic reaction in Augustine, as later in Baumgarten, appears as a sort of "lower cognition," which is based on the feeling of pleasure or displeasure. This type of judgment is conveyed to reason not in the form of rational conclusion, but precisely as pleasure triggered by beauty and harmonious arrangement.

An interesting observation concerning the "judging numbers" in *De musica* 6.7.19 (pp. 44–46) confirms that Augustine's insight into the manner of perceiving proportion by our senses here is strikingly similar to Kant's transcendental aesthetics, in particular to his discussion of the sublime (§25 and §29 of the *Critique of Judgment*). According to Augustine, the world is proportioned, and proportions in it do not depend on the magnitude (extension or duration) of things, which is relative; instead, they represent correlations between different things, which are permanent. While our senses are clearly limited in perceiving magnitudes (extensions or durations), our intellect is not and is able to think of certain correlations, such as proportion, even between extremely great magnitudes that are beyond the reach of our sensory capacity.

---

112. *de ista delectatione quae quasi sententia est judicialium istorum*; cf. "delight in the harmony" and being "offended by . . . discord" (*De musica* 6.9.24). Cf. later: reason's "own sense of delight" is "its favorable reaction to the intervals of time, as well as a sign of approbation for modifying such numbers" (6.10.26; p. 60).

113. For example, one can find it in Aristotle's *De anima*, Bk. 2.

Detecting this discrepancy, according to Kant, produces the 'transcendental' feeling of the sublime (when the realm of the transcendent ideas suddenly presents or "reveals" itself), and according to Augustine, leads to the realization of the supra-mental (divine) origin of numbers and proportions. For Augustine, our senses are 'mortal' in that they are linked to actual sense data from bodies and are thus limited; our intellect is not mortal, since it deals with eternal proportions and surpasses the limitations of bodies. Thus both thinkers use phenomenologically similar trains of thought in order to arrive at the idea of the supra-sensible or supra-mental.[114]

Augustine's phenomenological analysis of the mechanism of aesthetic judgment thus leads him to the idea of the possibility of an ascent from this judgment to the higher principles. He describes how one becomes aware of the higher reality through the most important concept pertaining to his theory of order, which is introduced in 6.13.38: "equality of number" or "numeric equality" (*aequalitas numerosa*). According to the interlocutors, one gradually realizes that all perfect proportions are reducible to equality. Even in the absence of internal equality (such as harmony) in simple things one can speak of an equality (some correspondence, or a good fit) between the thing and the perceiving sense organ.[115] In Augustine's model of sensation, as in Aristotle's, sense organs are best attuned to sense something in the moderate range, which they perceive as pleasant, and avoid the extremes, by which they are displeased.[116] For example, suitable colors are of "tempered" or even mixture, which makes them "agreeable to the eye" (6.13.38, p. 84).

As a next step, however, the mind detects that equality, which is a universal principle that applies to all reality, is never perfectly observed in bodies. As in the *De ordine*, the observation that in sensible reali-

---

114. Of course, for Augustine the existence of the universal law of proportion and harmony is not contingent but instituted by "God, whom it is certainly appropriate to believe to be the author of all harmony and concord" (*De musica* 6.8.20; p. 46). Augustine thus is on his path of "faith seeking understanding," or confirming through his phenomenological analysis what is predetermined by his belief.

115. This is precisely Augustine's solution—pointed out by Fontanier and discussed above—for the Plotinian dilemma as to whether it is simplicity or proportion that constitutes the principle of beauty.

116. According to Aristotle, the sense is a kind of 'mean' that operates best in the moderate range (*De anima*, Bk. 2, 424a 2–16) and is damaged or destroyed by extreme sensations (*De anima*, Bk. 2, 424a 30; 426a 30–b 8).

ty numbers and proportions are imperfect forces us to seek their true source, which makes them perfect and immutable (6.12.34; pp. 72–74):

[Teacher:] Now regarding this equality, which we did not find to be certain and permanent in the numbers of the sensible world, but instead obscured and passing: surely, our intellect would not seek it anywhere, unless it were known from somewhere? However, that 'somewhere' is not in the intervals of space or time, for the former change shape and the latter pass away. So where is it? See if you can find an answer to this. For you cannot think it is in the shapes of bodies, which you would never dare to call equal on close examination. Nor is it in the intervals of time, for we are similarly unaware if something is a little longer or shorter than it is supposed to be, if it escapes our senses.[117] I am asking you about a different kind of equality: the one we have before our mental gaze when we desire certain bodies or bodily motions to be even, and upon considering these bodies more carefully dare not trust them. Where do you think this sort of equality is?

In a powerful exposition of his theological aesthetics, Augustine shows how the realization of the imperfection of equality of the lower order by the mind initiates its upward movement to the higher reality of the divine order (6.14.44; pp. 92–94). Earthly numbers imitate the principle of equality, which in its perfection is present only in God. If what we desire is equality and likeness, Augustine asks, which is easier to love: reality, including aesthetic objects, which is but a vestige and shadow of equality, or God, in whom "nothing is unequal, nothing unlike itself" or affected by space or time (6.14.44; p. 92)?

Another element in Augustine's discussion of number as an eternal principle brings out more similarities between his train of thought here and the way the principle τὸ καλόν is conceptualized in Plato and the Stoics. No beauty is devoid of the principle of number and thus deserves our affection. The error, however, is in clinging to one's love of the inferior type of beauty. As with τὸ καλόν, which, of course, is present even at lower levels, the main point is to use the apparitions of beauty at the lower levels of reality to initiate the upward movement to the higher levels. What is sinful is not the act itself of loving beauty, but a misuse of it, lingering at the lower rungs of the ladder instead of moving up (6.14.46; p. 94):

---

117. The general meaning of this example with sounds, which is not an exact parallel to the one with visual shapes, is that sensation is imperfect and cannot be trusted in determining what perfect equality is.

Thus it is not numbers—which are beautiful in their own right—that are below reason, but the love of the lower sort of beauty that pollutes the soul. When the soul loves not only equality in that [lower kind of beauty] . . . but also [that lower] rank [itself, it means that] it has abandoned its own rank and has not risen above the rank of material things.

We see that that internal ascent in the *De musica* is mostly of an intellectual kind and is formally reminiscent of the movement of the mind in the *De magistro*, which has no aesthetic element in it. However, here, as in the *De ordine*, it includes an "external admonition" as its starting point, which triggers the process of internal recollection:

So, finally, is it not evident that he who inwardly moves towards God in order to understand the immutable truth when another person questions him, cannot be set on this path towards contemplating truth by any external admonition, unless this motion is retained by his memory?[118]

"External admonition" in this passage must be interpreted broadly, so as to include such "reminders" as the natural beauty of objects or aesthetic judgment, which may or may not be introduced by another person.

Thus these two early works of Augustine—*De ordine* and *De musica*—contain two features that are characteristic of his theological aesthetics in general: the idea of an ascent toward the supra-mental, and the recognition of the crucial role of aesthetic experience in this ascent. However, thus far Augustine fails to present the connection between the two as absolutely immediate and direct, such as in an experience of revelation (although he comes very close to expressing it this way). For this, we must turn to his later works.

A work that contains, in its developed form, the interpretation of aesthetic judgment as revelatory that will become a hallmark of Augustine's thought is *De vera religione*.[119] This apologetic work is charged with the task of bringing understanding to faith. It is mostly directed against the Manichaean dualism and starts with the already familiar discussion of the problem of evil and the harmony of the universe. The aesthetic element appears in the (thematically) second part of the work,

---

118. *De musica* 6.12.36; pp. 78–80. Although the Latin, properly interpreted according to the classical model, seems to say 'cannot . . . without admonition' (*non posse . . . nullo admonente*), which is the way Jacobsson translates it, the sense suggests that the phrase should be interpreted as 'imperfect,' containing an emphatic double negative ('cannot . . . by no admonition'), which is quite common for medieval Latin.

119. On this work, including some of the passages discussed below, see Hayes, "Beauty's Resting Place," 196ff.

which discusses the ascent to God. This section starts with a discussion of the divine plan of salvation, as well as of the authority of the scriptures. Augustine then (*De vera rel.* 29.52) moves on to explore how far one can advance on the way of the ascent to God from reason, moving from the visible to the invisible. This is precisely where the aesthetic element becomes prominent and remains so for the larger part of the section that deals with the ascent (until 36.67). That is, Augustine's aesthetics, much as it does in von Balthasar, appears in the context of apologetic or fundamental theology that deals with the rational exploration of faith. Another context where Augustine discusses aesthetic matters is in 39.72 where he presents an "ascent from aesthetic pleasure" while discussing soteriology and the idea of Christ winning over temptations (including pleasure).

Augustine's task, then, is to examine "how far reason can proceed in its ascent from the visible to the invisible" (29.52; p. 221). The idea of an anagogical interpretation of natural beauty appears at the very beginning. Augustine gives an excellent description of earthly beauty, in terms that are very similar to Cicero's descriptions in *De natura deorum* 2, and urges his audience not to look at it with vain curiosity but to use natural beauty as a "step towards something immortal and everlasting" (29.52; p. 221). Within the order of faculties, the argument proceeds in 29.53 (pp. 221–22), sensing things in nature is inferior to passing judgment about them, the latter being the prerogative of the human faculty of reason. As Augustine frequently states,[120] that which judges must be superior to what is judged, and reason makes judgments about everything, including the senses and even reason itself. The question now is (30.54; p. 222): can reason's judgments be grounded in reason itself or does it judge according to something which surpasses it? According to our observations, reason itself is imperfect since its judgment can be better or worse, depending, for example, on the level of training in a certain art that it possesses. The nature of this art, or artistic principles themselves, thus become the focus of further investigation. Augustine gives a concrete example of an artistic or aesthetic judgment of architectural structures: windows unequal in size create an unpleasant impression if placed side by side, but are aesthetically pleasing if placed one above the other (30.54; p. 222). There are two obvious observations here that, as Augustine's text further shows, eventually make one aware of

---

120. Cf. *De lib. arb.* and *De musica* 6.

the fact that the principles and laws of art transcend the human mind. First, one cannot explain why these laws are in effect, and yet we have an immediate positive or negative reaction to certain physical forms that comes as a compelling aesthetic judgment. Second, our mind can be more or less capable of judging physical objects, that is, our mind is subject to change, and yet the laws always remain the same. We conclude, then, that our mind judges according to these laws (cf. 30.56; p. 223) but does not judge these laws themselves, and that the laws themselves surpass our mind:

> Now this law that governs all the arts is absolutely immutable. At the same time, the human mind, which enjoys the benefit of perceiving this law, can err and undergo change. It is sufficiently clear, then, that that law, which is called truth, is above our mind. (30.56; p. 224)

Within the Augustinian framework, this unchangeable nature which is above the rational soul is God, or the "almighty artist" (31.57; p. 224): however, as the task of apologetic theology requires, the observation itself holds phenomenologically for any intelligent observer.

Augustine elaborates how one gradually "purifies" these eternal laws by separating them from the lower levels of reality in the process of a "transcending" ascent beyond the sensible in 30.55 (p. 223). In any art, we are pleased by "harmony," "equality" and "unity." However, it is easy to notice that in real things these principles are not present to their perfection. Since perfect qualities desired by the human mind cannot be found in bodies, the mind must have some ability to see them directly (30.55; cf. 32.60; pp. 226–27). Furthermore, the immutable laws of all arts cannot be located in place or time. Indeed, all spatial or temporal things are subject to change, and yet these laws can be applied to judging all that is in place or time, that is, they act in respect to mutable things as an unchanged criterion. The immutable and eternal law is also indifferent as to size and duration, which are present only in things that are spatially or temporally positioned. Now since the law by which all is judged is necessarily greater than that which is judged, the immutable law of art must surpass both physical bodies and even the very categories of space and time.

As above in the *De musica*, Augustine's way of thought here comes close to Kant's discussion of the sublime. His analysis of compelling judgments sounds no less Kantian. Augustine here follows the pattern of thought that becomes a characteristic element of his aesthetic theory: a compelling judgment of a certain "immediate" type (moral or aesthetic), when one feels that something "ought" to be this way, but cannot explain it rationally prompts the idea of a higher source; our reason senses that it judges with the help of some higher principle:

> Accordingly, whenever the soul feels that it is not self-sufficient even in making judgments about the shape and movement of bodies, it necessarily realizes both that its own nature is superior to that nature about which it judges, and that, at the same time, that nature according to which it judges and about which it absolutely cannot judge is superior to itself. Indeed, I can say *why* any particular body *ought* to be proportioned by way of placing similar parts symmetrically on each side:[121] because I am delighted by the highest degree of equality, which I perceive not by the eyes but by the mind. For which reason the more the things that I see with my eyes correspond in their nature to those that I intuit by my intellect, the better I judge them to be. However, *why* those intelligible things are the way they are, no one can say, nor would anyone in his right mind presume to say that they *ought* to be like that, as if they could be otherwise.[122] (31.57; p. 224; my italics)

The distinction between knowing the way something is (which is characteristic of reason) and passing a judgment that something *ought* to be a certain way, with no sound conceptual explanation being present (which is a sign of the influence from a "higher" source), is further reinforced:

> Thus pure minds are capable of knowing the eternal law, but they cannot judge or evaluate it. The difference is as follows. Knowledge is sufficiently constituted by perceiving whether something is or is not so. Judging, in addition to that, involves something else, namely, an indication that the things could be otherwise, as when we say "it ought to be like this," or "it ought to have been this way," or "it will have to be that way," as artists do when speaking of their own works. (31.58; pp. 225–26)

Two points are important in Augustine's discussion of compelling judgments. First, although he clearly has an opportunity to analyze moral judgments, he uses examples of aesthetic judgments, which to him must have appeared most clear and most compelling.[123] Second, becoming aware of the higher source of a judgment in the case of compelling aes-

---

121. Cf. an almost identical phrasing in *De lib. arb.* 2.12.34.
122. Cf. "As for why these things please us . . . no one would dare say: not even if he understands these things properly" (31.58; p. 225).
123. One could say that, like Kant, Augustine found no better way of solving some of his most fundamental problems than through aesthetics.

thetic judgments is an almost immediate occurrence, as contrasted with a lengthy reasoning process employed in the ascent schemes used so far. Both features point to a distinct similarity between Augustine's and modern, Kant-style understanding of the nature of aesthetic judgment as revelatory.

That Augustine does single out aesthetic experience as the best vehicle for revealing the eternal and immutable source of reality is reinforced by the fact that his further examples are drawn from artistic activity.[124] He uses a comparison with artists who judge what their products ought to be like by relying purely on their aesthetic sense. If one asks an artist why he does things a certain way, he will not be able to explain this rationally, but instead will turn to aesthetic terminology—which, curiously, seems to be designed precisely to mark our ignorance of the origin of this type of judgment—by saying that "it is beautiful" or "it is fitting":

> To many, of course, the human response of delight is the end.[125] They have no wish to turn their gaze upward to find out why these visible things are pleasing. Accordingly, if I ask an artist, after he constructs one arch, why he intends to build another one just like it on the opposite side of the building, he is likely to respond "in order that equal parts of the building might balance each other out." Further, if I persist with my questioning, asking why he prefers that very arrangement, he will say that "it is fitting," or that "it is beautiful," or that "it delights the beholder." He will not find anything more to say. (32.59; p. 226)

If one investigates the matter further, however, Augustine continues, one would be forced to admit that the source of artistic or aesthetic judgment is the pure idea of equality or unity: the idea that originates in God. We recall that Kant's analysis of the possibility of making aesthetic judgments ultimately leads one to the realization of the "common supersensible ground" of humanity, which is the modern equivalent of Augustine's divine ideas.[126]

Augustine completes his analysis of the ascent to supra-mental reality from the visible things (that is, mostly from aesthetic experience) by

---

124. For Augustine, as for modern aestheticians, there are two kinds of things that are *sensibiliter pulchra: natura edita* and *artibus elaborata* (*De vera rel.* 30.56).

125. Here Augustine describes two different aesthetic attitudes that are also common in modern aesthetics: one is that art and aesthetic appreciation exist purely for pleasure (for their own sake), and the other is that aesthetic experience leads to something beyond it (as in transcendental aesthetics).

126. Of course, from the point of view of neuroscience, these are the primary Gestalts that are 'hard-wired' into our brain.

providing a concise account that both resonates with Platonic parallels and at times sounds strikingly modern (39.72; p. 234):

What obstacle, then, remains for the soul on its way to recalling the primal beauty, which it has abandoned, when it can do so even from its own vices? For thus the wisdom of God extends mightily to all boundaries. Through it, that supreme artist constructed and ordered his works with one end in mind: beauty.[127] Accordingly, in his goodness, he bears no grudge against any beauty (which owes its very existence to him), from the highest to the lowest, to make sure that no one is excluded from partaking in truth itself, just as no one is deprived of some [sensible] image and likeness of truth.[128] Inquire what attracts you in the pleasurable experience derived from bodies: you will not find anything else except harmony. For just as discordant or incompatible things result in a painful sensation, so harmonious things give pleasure. Examine, then, what the highest degree of harmony would be. There is no need to go out: return within yourself,[129] for truth abides inside you. And if you find your own nature to be subject to change, transcend even yourself. But remember, as you transcend yourself, that it is the rational soul that you are transcending. Therefore, aim in that direction where the light of reason itself is kindled. For what else does any diligent thinker attain, except truth? However, since truth itself certainly does not attain itself by way of reasoning, but is the goal for those who reason, you must perceive that harmony there, greater than which none can exist, and strike an accord with it.[130] Admit that you are not as it is, for it does not seek itself. At the same time, you sought it and came to it not through the reaches of space, but through an affection of the mind, in order to reach an accord between your inner self and the indwelling truth through a pleasure that is not low and carnal, but lofty and spiritual.

While starting with an a priori theological assumption of the existence of higher reality, Augustine clearly confirms it a posteriori by his analysis of aesthetic experience, the main point of a theological aesthetics, according to von Balthasar.

---

127. The metaphor of the artist, as well as the idea that he "bears no grudge," has a striking similarity with Plato's account in *Timaeus* 29A, E.

128. *Effigies* definitely stands for the "aesthetic" (visible, auditory, etc.) appearance of truth (as a transcendental idea) in the real world: cf. a similar interpretation of aesthetic beauty as the worldly apparition or visible sign of goodness and truth in Plato's *Phaedrus* 250D. This idea foreshadows Kant's transcendental aesthetics, as well as the theological aesthetics of Hans Urs von Balthasar.

129. Cf. Marcus Aurelius, *Meditations*, Bk. 4.3–4, and Plotinus, *Enn.* I.6.

130. Cf. Anselm's *Proslogion* proof of the existence of God; also cf. Cicero's language in *De natura deorum*, Bk. 2. Augustine is trying to give the highest truth a status that is qualitatively different from that of the human mind, which is not unlike the "transcendent" status of τὸ καλόν in Plato's *Symposium*: one can aim at it but can never attain it.

Augustine's observations here stress something in the nature of aesthetic pleasure that is familiar to us from the earlier tradition: we enjoy things that have equality, harmony, and other aesthetic qualities despite the fact that they do not possess these qualities to perfection, since earthly things can possess only vestiges of these principles. What aesthetic pleasure marks, then, is only the state of transition to higher principles when sensible reality shows some resemblance with the latter. Thus in Augustine, as earlier in Plato and the Stoics, using this "pointing" or guiding function of aesthetic experience allows us to orient ourselves in the world without recurring to rational thinking, for, as we learn, the higher principles are accessible to us directly through aesthetic experience (30.54; p. 222): "Thus, nature itself [in this case, aesthetic judgment] is first consulted, as it were, to determine what it would approve."

De libero arbitrio, Bk. 2, is another significant text where Augustine introduces the idea of revealing some higher principles by means of a transcending movement of reason touched by aesthetic experience.[131] His account of aesthetic experience developed in *De vera rel.* by this time becomes rather standardized, but he continues to add new examples and fine-tune his phrasing. Like *De vera rel.*, *De lib. arb.*, a rather mature work,[132] is mainly directed against the Manichaean dualism. However, it is more than a merely polemical work and contains a complete account of his fundamental theology, and thus most of his philosophical views—for example, on the nature of certitude, external and internal senses, being, illumination, the soul, law, and virtues. It is thus another text that is well suited to clarify the place of aesthetics in Augustine's apologetics.

Bk. 1 of *De lib. arb.* examines the nature and origin of evil and attempts to determine God's role in this matter. Since the interlocutors come to the conclusion that it is the human will, or the ability to choose freely, that is solely responsible for moral evil, the next step is to answer why God gave humans the free choice of the will, that is, how it can be a good thing. This is the task of Bk. 2, which contains a discussion of aesthetic judgment. Bk. 2 starts by examining the assumption that it

---

131. On this text see Hayes, "Beauty's Resting Place," 186ff., including a discussion of one of the relevant passages on pp. 189–90. Hayes completely ignores both the "transcendental" features of Augustine's account and any Kantian parallels. Also see Fontanier, *La beauté selon saint Augustin*, who discusses some relevant passages on p. 133.

132. It is Augustine's last philosophical dialogue after conversion which was begun early, in 387 or 388, but finished rather late in 395.

is God who gave us the free will. Augustine poses the question in the form appropriate for fundamental theology: Do we see this clearly by reason or only take it on faith? As in any philosophical approach, the interlocutors start by doubting the main assumption and trying to work their way to certitude by rational means. The most basic question is, then, whether it is even certain that God exists and how this point becomes clear. In chapter 3 the dialogue sets out to prove God's existence, arguing rationally from the nature of truth—for Augustine, the question of God's existence is linked closely to the nature of certitude. The discussion starts, in a very modern way, with asserting the certainty of our own existence and then proceeds, to use Husserl's language, with a "phenomenological reduction" from self-awareness to complexes (or "syntheses") of sensations and relations between them. (At any given step, the discussion shows, reason remains aware of the situation with the senses and stays above it.) Chapters 4 and 5 gradually make a transition to the judgment of the senses, which manifests itself as pleasure and pain, whence the way is cleared for the aesthetic judgment in the true sense. One can see that the issue of aesthetic judgment does not appear randomly but has a key place in Augustine's fundamental theology, namely as part of the proof of God's existence. From chapters 6–16, which are relevant to aesthetics, it appears that it is precisely the compelling nature and the certitude of aesthetic judgments that is at stake. Thus, in chapter 6 the interlocutors agree that if they find, *with certainty*, anything that is higher than reason, that would be God. Finding something like this, however, requires an analysis of a "transcending" judgment—the best example of which appears to be the aesthetic judgment—which is performed in chapters 8–13 by establishing, in a familiar pattern, that numbers are eternal, as is truth, and that numbers transcend our minds. Since our judgment happens according to truth contained in numbers, truth must also be higher than the mind. In chapter 15, finally, the interlocutors are able to assert with certitude that God does exist, and chapter 16 contains a summary of the transcending movement of the mind that starts with the senses.

Let us retrace Augustine's train of thought in more detail. Following the familiar principle that that which judges is superior to that which is judged, our reflection determines that reason is the most powerful of our capacities. Now, according to Augustine, if we find something that is still higher than our reason, that must certainly be God (*De lib. arb.*

2.6.14). In a passage echoing the *De ordine* the thinker repeats that reason contains something that is common to all and does not change, that is, numbers (2.8.20), which, in their turn, contain the "incorruptible truth" (2.8.21). There is something "immobile," "firm," and "incorruptible" about numbers (2.8.23). Further, "interior light" helps us realize that numbers transcend our minds: "But when we start, as it were, our journey upwards, we find that they transcend even our minds (*etiam nostras mentes transcendere*) and immutably abide in truth itself" (2.11.31; p. 259). Here Augustine uses the verb *transcendere* in a clearly cognitive sense: to describe the cognitive movement of reflective reason beyond itself.[133]

The next step is to prove definitively that the truth that the mind feels is above itself is, in fact, higher than our intellects (2.12.34). The proof goes as follows: if it were not, we would then judge about it, and not according to it; therefore it must surpass our intellects:

> Surely, if it [i.e., truth] were lower, we would judge about it, and not according to it, just as we judge about bodies because they are below us, and often not only indicate that they *are* or are not this way, but also insist that they *ought* or ought not to be this way (*sed ita vel non ita esse debere*). The same goes for our souls.[134] Not only do we know that the [disposition of the] soul *is* such and such, but often also that it *ought to be.* . . . Now we make these judgments *according* to those inner rules of truth that we all discern. However, in no way does one judge *about* these rules themselves. (2.12.34; p. 260; my italics) . . . For this reason, if truth is neither lower than nor level with our minds, it must be higher and more excellent. (2.12.34; p. 261)

Thus the very necessity, the compelling nature of our judgment about harmony and proportion, implies that it has a source that surpasses our intellect, which is unable to explain its imperative nature. Augustine's description of compelling judgment here is almost identical to *De vera rel.* 31.57, and, once again, we cannot fail to notice a striking parallel with the Kantian way of thought.[135]

This time Augustine, like Kant, refers to two kinds of such compel-

---

133. A Kantian parallel suggests itself here not on the basis of the similarity of terms but because of the identity of phenomenological observations upon which the movement of both Augustine's and Kant's thought is based: the origin of certain laws seems to go beyond, or transcend, our mind.

134. That is, our morals that are certain dispositions of our souls.

135. Cf. Kant, *Of the Dynamically Sublime*, §29 (*Critique of Judgment*, 106): "In this modality of aesthetical judgments, viz. in the necessity claimed for them, lies an important moment in the critique of judgment. For it enables us to recognize in them an *a priori* principle, and raises them out of empirical psychology."

ling judgments: aesthetic (in the true sense of the Greek *aisthesis*) and moral. These two types of judgments are similar in the sense that in both, after perceiving something, one can immediately tell how it *ought* to be, or correct it, as it were, against some internal but rationally inexplicable model. Of course in Kant this parallelism between compelling judgments in aesthetic perception and compelling judgments in morals makes one aware of some connection between the two that eludes our immediate intuitive capacity, that is, makes one aware of the common transcendental ground of both. It is obvious that, phenomenologically at least, Augustine makes the same connection (and, as becomes clear from *De ordine* 2.19.50 discussed above, draws very similar conclusions):

> An example of judging in this manner about bodies is when we say 'it is not as white as it ought to have been,' or 'not as square,' and many other like statements. An example about someone's character [would be when we say] 'it is not as accommodating as it ought to be,' or 'not as meek,' or 'not as forceful,' according to what our moral standards might be. (2.12.34; p. 260)

Augustine goes on to stress the newly discovered superior status of the "inner rules of truth." Whereas things that belong to the sensible and moral realms are imperfect and therefore allow for corrective judgments of a compelling type according to the "inner rules," those rules themselves cannot be judged. Indeed, as commonly proved by experience, one cannot judge these rules themselves by prescribing that they ought to be a certain way:

> However, in no way does one judge *about* these rules themselves. For while someone may say that "eternal things *are* more powerful than temporal," or that "seven and three equals ten," no one says that it *ought to* have been so. Indeed, learning no more than *that it is* so, one makes no attempt to correct as an examiner, and merely rejoices as a discoverer. (2.12.34; p. 260, my italics)

It is remarkable that although these "inner rules" are present to our reason more or less directly in their pure form, that is, they are transparent to it, our intellect itself is clearly not these rules, because its ability to see these rules more or less clearly varies depending on the person, passage of time, conditions, et cetera. This variability allows one to judge even intellectual activity itself against certain ideal standards:

> Do you not see that we even judge about our own minds according to it, while there is no way for us to judge about truth itself? For we say "he understands less than he ought to," or "he understands as much as he ought to." But the de-

gree of understanding for a given mind depends precisely on the degree of its proximity to immutable truth and its ability to cling to it. (2.12.34; pp. 260–61)

A familiar pattern (one could call it a "typology" of aesthetic experience) thus emerges in Augustine's works. As in Plato, the Stoics, and subsequently even Kant, aesthetic reaction is viewed as one of the most important ways of making one aware of the transcendent principles. The transcending movement of reason often starts with an aesthetic reaction. When we judge and approve, that is, take pleasure in, exterior forms we realize that, since no conceptual explanation is possible, we could not judge in this way unless our judgment were governed by some laws of beauty which transcend our mind. As in the case of the *De vera. rel.*, of course, one realizes that for Augustine here the mechanism of aesthetic perception is theologically conditioned. The harmony we perceive in exterior forms by means of aesthetic judgments that use the rules of "eternal truth" is a vestige of God, that is, from Augustine's standpoint the correspondence between the earthly and divine harmony is theologically predetermined a priori. At the same time, the movement itself is accessible to anyone, either theologically or philosophically minded, and is open to phenomenological analysis (that is, as is appropriate for any apologetics, it can become *a posteriori* demonstrable):

> For wherever you turn, wisdom speaks to you through some vestiges with which it has stamped its creation, and when you slip toward external reality, it calls you back inside through the very forms of external things. For it enables you to *see* that whatever delights you in bodies and lures you through corporeal senses is proportioned *(numerosum)*, and to *inquire* where this quality comes from, and return into yourself. And then you understand that *you could not approve or reject* that which comes into contact with your bodily senses, *unless you had some laws of beauty within you*, with which you could compare any beautiful things that you sense externally. (2.16.41, p. 265; my italics)

The marked difference between the quoted passages from *De lib. arb.* and Augustine's early works is that the experience of the transcendent in *De lib. arb.* comes immediately following our perception of harmony in the sensible, or a particular aesthetic reaction, and not as a result of a gradual intellectual ascent through the study of the liberal arts, reflection upon the nature of numbers, or learning, as in the early works.[136] The immediacy of this transition is expressed textually by placing the

---

136. The reader may remember that the *De vera rel.* already moves in this direction.

whole description of the process within one sentence or a short paragraph, instead of writing a lengthy discourse. The immediacy of the occurrence makes it appear more like revelation than like reasoning. One also notices that Augustine presents the process of becoming aware of the transcendent in terms of *seeing*, which confirms that he understands aesthetic experience precisely as revelatory.

Again, as in the *De vera rel.*, Augustine uses the example of the aesthetic judgment of artists, which proves that when he describes the mechanism of our becoming aware of the transcendent principles he definitely has in mind aesthetic reaction, precisely in its modern understanding. In the following passage, artists compare their work with their internal sense for harmony and correct it accordingly:

> Look at artists skilled in the production of all corporeal forms: even their art consists of numbers, in accordance with which they fashion their works. For they move their hands and instruments in the process of production up to the point when the product that is being shaped externally is sufficiently adjusted[137] to [the standard set by] that light of numbers which is inside: that is, until it releases[138] them and pleases—through the mediation of the senses—the inward judge whose gaze is fixed on celestial numbers. (2.16.42; p. 266)

Once again using "transcendental" terminology to describe the principles according to which artists work, Augustine presents the moment of immediate revelation that follows these observations: "Therefore transcend *(transcende)* also the mind of the artist, in order to see eternal number: and at this moment wisdom will flash out at you from its inner abode and from the very sanctuary of truth" (2.16.42; p. 266). He obviously stresses the revealing aspects of artistic activity in this passage. The number that is beyond time and space is nevertheless *seen* directly and immediately in any beautiful artwork. In the form of art where artworks are not present—artistic dance—the "number" moves the very limbs of the artist and thus presents itself through the external form of the body: "Now ask what delights in dance, and number will answer

---

137. The meaning of this phrase is clear, but a verbatim translation would sound awkward in English, for which reason it has been slightly adjusted, e.g., by rendering *relatum* (probably "compared" in this context) as "adjusted," etc.

138. Augustine's use of the term *absolutio* is almost certainly a deliberate allusion to the judicial process: cf. "judge" mentioned immediately afterward. Augustine uses *absolutio* almost exclusively in the judicial and religious senses, which confirms the choice of translation. The metaphor also adequately captures the artist's experience of finally being 'released' from his 'obligation' to his artistic creation after it starts to satisfy his inner artistic sense.

you: 'Behold, it's me'" (2.16.42; p. 266). Each artwork also somehow presents or reveals its maker (God in the case of earthly beauty):

> For the artist somehow beckons the beholder of his work away from the very beauty of the work, lest he become totally fixed on it. [Rather he wants him] to glance over the beautiful appearance of the artist's creation in such a way that he may return with affection to him who has made it. (2.16.43; p. 266)

De lib. arb., then, repeats the familiar idea of the ascent from aesthetic experience. The beauty of earthly forms is not the goal in itself but an excellent medium that directs the human mind toward the source of reality that transcends both sensible reality and the mind. However, in addition to this Augustine emphasizes the immediate and revelatory nature of aesthetic experience: one becomes aware of the divine almost immediately after an encounter with an aesthetic object.

The same picture repeats in two later works of Augustine, *De Trinitate*, Bk. 9 and *Confessions*, Bk. 7, which also contain brief accounts of the impact of beauty and aesthetic reaction. To be sure, in these mature works the theme of the revelatory ascent through aesthetic experience no longer holds a central place and is simply mentioned in passing as an Augustinian *locus communis*. Unlike in his earlier works of an apologetic nature, Augustine shifts his attention to systematic or practical tasks. Nevertheless, these passages are important since they clearly show that Augustine even later in life retains his scheme of the transcending movement of reason immediately triggered by aesthetic experience. The discussion of aesthetic judgment in the *De Trinitate* appears in the context of Augustine's well-known psychological model of the Trinity that examines relations within the Trinity based on relations between various faculties in the human soul, for example, between the mind (or wisdom, memory), knowledge, and love.[139] This is how the discussion comes to the analysis of knowledge and cognition. As is clear from the discussion of the *De magistro* above, Augustine's epistemology is based on a Platonic, rather than Aristotelian, model: one derives all general truths, including our general notions about the human soul, by intu-

---

139. Augustine's Trinitarian aesthetics proper will be discussed in the next chapter. On aesthetic themes in the *De Trinitate*, including some of the passages discussed below, see Hayes, "Beauty's Resting Place," 218ff., especially p. 222. Also see multiple references in Fontanier, *La beauté selon saint Augustin*, although he mostly discusses Trinitarian aesthetics, not the ascent: pp. 57, 136–37, 144, 148. Neither author engages the topic of the compelling nature of aesthetic judgment in Augustine.

iting them in the "immutable truth," not by abstracting them from a plurality of things.¹⁴⁰ As a result, one can judge not only what is the case, but also what ought to be the case. The same model is assumed in the *De Trinitate* (cf. 9.6.9; p. 301). Discussing the way one judges sensible images by applying to them "eternal" rules above one's mind (9.6.10; p. 302), Augustine provides a well-known example of an immediate reaction to a compelling aesthetic judgment which is, in his opinion, analogous to our judgments in moral matters. According to Augustine, who starts with a moral example, in virtue we love some ideal of virtue, and not a particular person who may prove to be unworthy (9.6.11; pp. 302–3). So it happens also in our aesthetic response, since we not only enjoy the sight of some harmonious object, but also can correct the shape of an imperfect object according to our judgment:

> Likewise, when I revolve in my mind, let us say, a beautifully and evenly curved arch that I have seen in Carthage, the mind becomes aware of a certain physical object through the eyes, which is then transferred to the memory and produces a picture in the imagination. But my mind also sees something else: [namely, some criterion] according to which this piece of work pleases me, and which would allow me to correct it if I did not like it. Therefore we judge about these material things according to that form of truth.¹⁴¹ Now this form of truth we perceive by the eye of our rational mind. (9.6.11; p. 303)

The fact that the mind is able to pass a judgment about how a sensible object should be, without however being able to explain the judgment rationally, reveals to us the existence of some intelligible criteria that transcend our mind. Note that the experience is expressed in revelatory terms: one "sees" both the sensible object and the criteria by the "eye" of the mind. The experience is also unmediated by much reasoning and it follows immediately upon our observation of the sensible object.

Finally, it is not surprising to find a brief description of the scheme of the ascent from aesthetic judgment, which was so foundational to the formation of Augustine's apologetics, in *Confessions*, Bk. 7:¹⁴²

---

140. This counter-Aristotelian position is, of course, much closer to some contemporary models of knowledge: e.g., in phenomenology or in Gestalt psychology.

141. "Form of truth" as the referent of *illam* is supplied *ad sensum* from the previous paragraph.

142. On aesthetic themes in the *Confessions* see Hayes, "Beauty's Resting Place," 208ff., especially p. 272; Fontanier, *La beauté selon saint Augustin*, 130. Both authors mention the passage quoted below, but neither points out any revelatory or "transcending" aspects of it.

For I tried to find the source of my feeling of approval for the beauty of bodies, whether heavenly or earthly, and what that presence was that guided me in judging soundly about things that are mutable when I said: 'This ought to be so, and that not so.' And looking for the source of my judgments of this sort I found the immutable and eternal truth residing above my mutable mind. (7.17.23; p. 107)

From this point on, Augustine continues, his mind ascends "step by step," starting from bodies and proceeding to the level of the soul, then to its inner capacity, then to reason which judges about sensible things and abstracts from the phantasms, "all in order to find that light that pervaded it" (7.17.23; p. 107) and to arrive, finally, at the divine source of its illumination.

The case of Augustine is markedly different from the material that has been analyzed so far precisely because here we have a Christian author who attempts to philosophize about theology and show rational approaches to faith with a clear agenda of apologetic or fundamental theology that frames his analysis of the "transcending" nature of aesthetic judgment, the ascent from sensible experience, and its epistemological implications. Unlike the pagan ancient authors discussed above, Augustine fits within the same tradition as von Balthasar in that he does theology in its proper sense, as opposed to ancient authors occupied with "theology improper" (or with the "precursor" of theology properly speaking, using von Balthasar's assessment). At the same time, what sets Augustine apart favorably from modern authors is precisely the fact that he does not operate from within the framework of a developed aesthetic theory. Thus he is not biased, as is von Balthasar, in the sense of having a hermeneutic task of presenting aesthetic experience as revealing, or even as important, but is only attempting to find support for his project of apologetic or fundamental theology. It is quite remarkable, then, that even with no modern "disciplinary" bias toward the field of aesthetics, and with an agenda very different from that of ancient philosophers, Augustine is still drawn to the same sorts of observations on aesthetic experience and to the same type of material as attract both ancient and modern authors. This can mean only one thing: that aesthetic experience genuinely makes a "good case" for him too, presumably because of its power, appeal and apparent nature.[143]

---

143. Whereas Augustine follows the Christian Apologists, such as Minucius Felix, in engaging the cosmological proof of God's existence from the beauty of the universe, the devel-

Further, it seems that either some ancient aesthetic themes were seamlessly transplanted on to the Christian ground and inspired some of the apologetic topics, or that despite the new Christian agenda of apologetics some of these traditional ancient philosophical themes were retained mostly unaltered by virtue of their own attractiveness. Augustine's ambiguous attitude toward the arts—as on the one hand somehow valuable, by virtue of providing a link to the divine, and on the other hand dangerous due to distracting and corrupting the mind by their sensuousness—can be classified as one of the things he inherits from the Platonic tradition. One could say that for Augustine, as it was for Plato, whatever contributes to the ascent is positive and valuable, and whatever distracts from this ascent and allows one to dwell on the experience itself is dangerous.[144]

Out of all ancient authors, Augustine's observations on the phenomenology of aesthetic experience are most advanced. While Plato, Stoics, and even Plotinus hardly venture beyond noticing the exceptional clarity and luminosity that marks the appearance of beauty (including its intellectual and moral analogues), Augustine is more specifically concerned with the question of "transcendental" aesthetic judgment, and his analysis of it is much more advanced and detailed. In fact, medieval scholastics mostly ignore this part of Augustine's legacy, and the depth of his analysis of aesthetic judgment was not matched again in European thought until Kant. Thus in this area Augustine appears almost as a modern thinker who foreshadows many Kantian developments in the field. Even if the similarity of Augustine's and Kant's aesthetic views cannot prove definitively a continuity of ideas between the former and the latter, it must be seen at least as a remarkable case of "convergence" in the history of thought.

---

opment of the ancient discussion of aesthetic judgment has no earlier parallels in Christian authors.

144. One can refer to the two contexts that state this idea clearly, both quoted in full above: *De musica* 6.14.46 (p. 94) about the "love of the lower sort of beauty that pollutes the soul" and *De vera rel.* 29.52 (p. 221) that urges one not to "feed vain and short-lived curiosity" while considering beautiful things, but instead use them as a "step towards something immortal and everlasting."

CHAPTER 8

Bonaventure and the Late Medieval Tradition

The Place of Bonaventure's Aesthetics

Despite Augustine's tremendous contribution to theological aesthetics, he remains, with respect to aesthetics, an "ancient" author. Augustine uses aesthetics almost exclusively for apologetic purposes, with the simple aim of revealing the existence of the divine principle to the general observer: the transcendent divine principle, to be sure, but by no means a specifically Christian one. Augustine, of course, does develop a specifically Christian, Trinitarian, systematic theology, but as the contexts show, aesthetics remains in the purview of his fundamental theology.[1] It is interesting that aesthetics shares a similar fate in the hands of even later medieval authors, such as Anselm. By the time of the high Middle Ages, however, aesthetic thought takes a different turn. No longer focused on "aesthetic proofs" of the existence of God accessible to any observer, the schoolmen shift their interest to what aesthetic parallels or analogies can reveal to them about the topics of a specifically Christian systematic theology, about, for example, the nature of the Trinity and Christ as the Son, or the second person of the Trinity. Authentic Christian aesthetics must have in view the Trinity and Christ. For the medieval Christian community of interpreters, it makes sense to speak of beauty or other aesthetic topics only when they can be understood in terms of the Trinitarian doctrine or Christology. The aesthetic here, as the reader will see, does not need to lose its revelatory function, except that in this system of inter-

---

1. 'Aesthetics' here is taken in the general sense assumed for the purposes of this study: i.e., not in the sense of a purely analogical aesthetics (e.g., God as τὸ καλόν) but as something that contains references to concrete "earthly" aesthetic experience.

pretation, instead of revealing a vague "beyond," it is called upon to reveal certain qualities of the Trinity of persons, and specifically of the Son.² From this point of view such late Patristic or earlier medieval authors as pseudo-Dionysius or Anselm—included fully by von Balthasar in his discussion—are not yet building this specifically Christian aesthetics, being limited either to the discussion of God as abstract "beauty" (τὸ καλόν) or to certain aesthetic arguments explaining the economy of salvation. To be sure, the echoes of the Augustinian and Anselmian "apologetic" aesthetics are still felt strongly in late medieval thought (such as that of Bonaventure), but they merely lay down the foundation for new developments.

In this connection we recall R. Viladesau's observation that aesthetic experience as such does not lead one to the *Christian* God.³ It is only conversion—which affects all aspects of the human person, including emotional and perceptive—that "directs" one to see the specifically Christian beauty. The belief in the Trinitarian and Christological principles thus comes first, before one can "see" them aesthetically presented. This observation explains the initial disappointment that a purely academic aesthetician experiences reading either Bonaventure himself or von Balthasar's account of Bonaventure's aesthetics. Trying to read such texts as if one were reading traditional aesthetics, one cannot avoid a feeling of always being "led astray" into matters incomprehensible or irrelevant to a lay aesthetician. The discourse seems to lose its ordinary logical connections, subsequent statements do not seem to follow from what has been stated earlier, and the linkage becomes elusive, as if the text follows some "invisible" pattern that one cannot grasp. Yet for one approaching the same texts from inside the community of Christian interpreters, all these observations appear as internally necessary, relevant, and following from one another.⁴

Von Balthasar himself is aware of this difference between the specifically Christian aesthetics (which is developed during the Patristic and medieval periods) and any other (e.g., ancient) theological aesthetics.⁵

---

2. While Augustine has a detailed discussion of the Trinity, aesthetic observations either are not present or play no essential role there.

3. In the section "Christian 'Conversion' and the Aesthetic" in R. Viladesau, *Theological Aesthetics*, 204–8.

4. For example, von Balthasar's foundational idea that Christ is the "form of God," the analogy to which can ultimately be seen in the rest of reality, certainly does not follow from one's aesthetic experience but is a judgment of faith.

5. See the section *The Theological Apriori of the Philosophy of Beauty* in GL4.

First of all, "as the modern period approaches, the distinction between ancient beauty and Christian glory is more and more keenly felt and experienced" (GL4 319). In Christian hermeneutics the ancient idea of beauty is gradually "purified," so as to be seen as a manifestation of glory, and appropriated for Christianity (GL4 320). The idea of divine glory, which presses the interpreter to focus on the aesthetic systems that feature a boundary between the world and the transcendent, through which glory can be manifested, can be acquired only by faith. It is the same way with the Trinitarian principle: the Trinitarian structure of reality, as it appears in Augustine and later in Bonaventure, can be grasped only "in the light of the 'resemblance' effected by faith," or through the "insight of faith" (GL2 301). Furthermore, in his own attempt to turn aesthetic categories specifically to shed light on the mystery of Christ (cf. O'Donnell, GW 262–63), von Balthasar seems to follow in the footsteps of medieval theologians such as Bonaventure. The idea of linking aesthetics and Christology, obviously, can appear only within the framework of faith.

This does not mean, however, that such an aesthetics can only be studied within a faith-based system of interpretation by a theologian (such as von Balthasar). The task of the "insider" interpreter is, indeed, to show convincingly how certain presuppositions of a given faith tradition follow from the interpreted material. The task of an "outsider" critic or a historian could be simply to examine how well and how consistently the interpretation is carried through and whether indeed there is any hermeneutic basis for these interpretations in the texts.

It can be inferred from the picture of "Christian aesthetics" just drawn that one can speak only of analogical aesthetics here. However, while the use of aesthetic terms in application to the divine is, indeed, strictly analogical, this does not mean that one cannot find here aesthetics in the true sense,[6] at least as described for the purposes of this study. Consequently, while the main focus of Christian aesthetics remains what an aesthetic view can reveal to us about certain articles of belief, our task will be further narrowed as follows: we will focus only on the contexts that involve true (that is, non-analogical) aesthetic experiences, or analogies with actual sense experience of the aesthetic type. This means that the cases in which 'beauty' or other aesthetic categories are used simply analogically, with no reference to actual aesthetic

---

6. Some theologian-aestheticians, such as F. B. Brown, would contest the reduction of aesthetics to cases that deal with sense perception.

experience, will remain outside of this study. Although this criterion of selection somewhat impoverishes medieval aesthetic thought, it will dramatically reduce the number of authors and contexts in this study.

As it stands, a focus on the specifically Christian, that is, Trinitarian and Christological, aesthetics, together with the exclusion of the strictly analogical use of aesthetic terms, leaves us with only one main name from von Balthasar's selection: Bonaventure—the author who is crucial to von Balthasar's project. Other Franciscan (Alexander of Hales, for example) and Dominican authors (such as Albert the Great) who do discuss beauty and also comment on pseudo-Dionysius's *Divine Names* and other "aesthetic" passages from the Neoplatonic tradition,[7] must remain outside the current project. These authors either limit their discussion of aesthetics to the abstract Neoplatonic idea of God as "beauty" in the sense of the general principle of "excellence" (τὸ καλόν),[8] or, in engaging specifically Christian topics (such as the beauty of Christ or the Trinity), do not use any parallels with actual aesthetic experience. At the same time, in a surprising turn, we must augment von Balthasar's list with another medieval Franciscan, John Duns Scotus. Although Duns Scotus has few explicit pronouncements on beauty or other aesthetic issues, both his fundamental theology and, to a certain extent, his practical theology appear to be grounded on aesthetic principles. Moreover, he uses explicit analogies with actual aesthetic experience at some key points in his theological system, so Scotus definitely deserves some attention.[9]

Apart from von Balthasar's monumental chapter on Bonaventure's aesthetics in *GL2*, there is surprisingly little recent literature on the

---

7. A detailed list of all passages in these and other medieval authors related to aesthetics, analogical or not, can be found in O. Bychkov, "A Propos of Medieval Aesthetics."

8. Both Alexander and Albert have extended aesthetic discussions of the classic ancient or apologetic topics such as "beauty of the universe as a proof of the divine design" and "aesthetic justification of evil": see O. Bychkov, "A Propos of Medieval Aesthetics." However, these are non-original topics that are based almost entirely on Augustine and partly on pseudo-Dionysius (in addition to being not specifically Christian). Another popular, but, again, non-original, topic is "moral beauty" inspired by Cicero's discussion of *honestum* (subsequently elaborated by Ambrose and Augustine); this one is also popular with Thomas Aquinas: see O. Bychkov, "A Propos of Medieval Aesthetics."

9. The degree of Scotus's involvement with aesthetics will be explained in what follows, including all pertinent references to texts and secondary literature. Not all of Scotus's texts were easily available to von Balthasar at the time, and this fact probably explains his silence about Scotus. Moreover, aesthetic aspects of Scotus's theology are only now coming to light (see bibliography below), so no definitive picture of his aesthetics will result from the current study either; the subject requires a separate fundamental study.

topic. The lack can be explained, perhaps, on the one hand by the inaccessibility of the texts that have not been translated from the Latin, and on the other hand by the specific nature of his Christian aesthetics, which puzzles and hence discourages most academic aestheticians. The existing studies of Bonaventure's aesthetics, as is the case with general studies on medieval aesthetics, draw on the works of de Bruyne and Tatarkiewicz and share the same lack of hermeneutic coherence in selecting and interpreting material on "aesthetics."[10] One of the more extensive, although older, studies is by E. J. M. Spargo,[11] who, like de Bruyne, has no clear definition of "aesthetic" (cf. p. ix),[12] but acknowledges the central role of Bonaventure's theological Christocentric view of reality in his aesthetics (p. x). Spargo focuses on the concepts of image, likeness, and expression central to both Bonaventure's Christology and aesthetics. Christ, she shows, is presented as a perfect, or "express" likeness of the Father, while the created world is presented as muted likenesses or vestiges of God as the exemplar. The works of Bonaventure that she analyzes are predominantly his main academic or "scholastic" theological work, *Commentary on the Sentences of Peter Lombard*, as well as a work that is more spiritual or "monastic" in nature, the *Itinerarium* (*The Journey of the Mind towards God*). She also mentions *Disputed Questions on the Knowledge of Christ* and a few other titles. The obvious shortcoming of Spargo's work, from the point of view of the present study, is that although she connects Bonaventure's aesthetics to his theology, Spargo still speaks of "aesthetics" in terms of an academic theory of beauty and art, not of revelatory theological aesthetics as understood by von Balthasar. As a result, no consistent picture emerges and it is often not clear why certain aesthetic notions are found together with theological issues. One cannot help remembering von Balthasar's suggestion that, in analyzing the work of a theologian, one must start not with traditionally accepted aesthetic notions but with the theological system itself, in order to see whether, and what kind of, aesthetics naturally emerges from it.[13]

---

10. E.g., cf. chap. 5, "The Middle Ages," in Faas (*Genealogy of Aesthetics*, 66, 67ff.), which is entirely based on Tatarkiewicz's work.

11. E. J. M. Spargo, *The Category of the Aesthetic in the Philosophy of Saint Bonaventure* (St. Bonaventure, N.Y.: Franciscan Institute, 1953).

12. She compiles a catalogue of contexts of "aesthetic" terms and topics in all works of Bonaventure, which at times have no conceptual connection with one another.

13. Another older work on Bonaventure's aesthetics is K. Peter, *Die Lehre von der Schön-*

By far the greatest contribution to the study of Bonaventurian aesthetics is by von Balthasar himself. His analysis of Bonaventure's thought, which results in appropriation of some key ideas for his own theological aesthetics, is an example of the continuing relevance of Bonaventure's aesthetics in the modern tradition. Speaking of the Middle Ages in general, von Balthasar stresses the significance of the Franciscan school in establishing the "theological *a priori*" crucial for a theological aesthetics based on the idea of the "form." "Human existence, ascending from the beauty of worldly forms ... is confirmed *a posteriori* by the beauty of the world." However, a leap from such sensible beauty to the affirmation that being as such is beautiful cannot be attempted from below: for this, one needs a theological *a priori*, that is, the possibility of seeing the form and the subsequent ascent must be preconditioned "from above." According to von Balthasar, establishing such an *a priori* was attempted "for the first time" in metaphysics by the Franciscans, and specifically by Bonaventure, who reformulated a certain experience of being that Francis had (GL4 378).[14] In fact, a careful study of von Balthasar's work on aesthetics, together with his assessment of Bonaventure, shows how important this material was for developing his own notion of "Christ's form."[15]

Speaking about Bonaventure in particular, von Balthasar makes

---

heit nach Bonaventura (Werl: Dietrich-Coelde-Verlag, 1964). His argument does not differ essentially from the previous literature such as de Bruyne or Spargo, but only becomes more detailed. A more recent work on Bonaventure's aesthetics is L. A. Smit, "'He's all Delight': Aesthetic Knowing in the Thought of Bonaventure" (Ph.D. thesis, Boston University, 1998). The author analyzes "aesthetic knowing" in Bonaventure, which she understands as a "humble approach to beauty as an end to be enjoyed, not means to be used," or as a kind of surrender as opposed to rational approaches understood as "prying into." The analysis proceeds mostly by paraphrasing and commenting on a variety of Bonaventure's texts, including the *Itinerarium* and his Commentary on the *Sentences*. The hermeneutic framework is traditional in nature, i.e., attempting to "look through the eyes of a medieval" (cf. p. 20).

14. Although his general description of the "Franciscan impulse" is impressive, the rest of his analysis of the late medieval tradition in GL4 is not convincing and is based on older secondary literature, e.g., works of Pouillon and Grabmann. Even the section on Bonaventure in GL2, although fascinating in itself, is certainly out of date as far as the sources he uses, even for the time he was writing it: most of them date to 1920s and 30s (Bissen, Gilson, etc.), with some later familiar titles, such as de Bruyne (1946), Spargo (1953), and Peter (1964).

15. The strong impact of the Trinitarian and Christological thought of Bonaventure on von Balthasar has been long noticed in scholarly literature, e.g., cf. O'Donnell, "Alles Sein ist Liebe: Eine Skizze der Theologie Hans Urs von Balthasars," in *GW* 268–70. Specifically he notes that von Balthasar "turns to Bonaventure's theology" in thinking of the essence of the Trinity in terms of love, rather than the intelligence and will (GW 269). Like Bonaventure, von Balthasar views the world through a Trinitarian perspective, and the study of the Trinity is "the foundation of von Balthasar's theological hermeneutics" (GW 270).

several strong statements, both about the importance of aesthetics for Bonaventure and about his unique position in late medieval thought as regards the use of aesthetics in theology. Aesthetics in Bonaventure is tightly linked to the foundational experience of reality that is at the core of his thought.[16] Central to Bonaventure's theology is the Augustinian idea of the "Trinitarian" image of God in humans. Von Balthasar stresses that this image of God in humans, Trinitarian in nature, is more than a trace or pointer (in the manner of the abstract τὸ καλόν); the distinction of faculties in the human image resembles the interrelations that belong to the divine nature, that is, there is a specific structural-relational likeness between the two (GL2 302). The specifically *aesthetic* moment here is, in the tradition of von Balthasar's usual understanding of "aesthetic," the ability to *see* the image of God in oneself. One must remember, however, that, just as we indicated above, one can see this Trinitarian nature of both the human image and of God only in the light of faith.[17] This is, according to von Balthasar, precisely the "central point of Bonaventure's spirituality and of his aesthetic alike" (GL2 302).

Applying his usual hermeneutic approach of *Gestalt*-building, von Balthasar captures, in a few bold brushstrokes, the general "ethos" of Bonaventure's theological aesthetics, which, perhaps not surprisingly, bears a striking resemblance to his own. The fundamental feature of Bonaventure's approach is that it is based on seeing and wonder at the sight of the vastness of reality, or God's revelation. From von Balthasar's point of view, that makes it essentially aesthetic. Bonaventure's experience of approaching this vastness is fundamentally humbling. It is an experience of "being lost," "overpowered," or "defeated from the start," which precludes any possibility of creating a finished systematic description. This position is contrasted with the arrogance of all-knowing "finished" systems (von Balthasar refers to the thought of Thomas Aquinas) which by the very reason of their finished-ness fail to capture the

---

16. Cf.: "Of all the great scholastics, Bonaventure is the one who offers the widest scope to the beautiful in his theology: not merely because he speaks of it most frequently, but because he clearly thereby gives expression to his innermost experience and does this in new concepts that are his own" (GL2 260–61); "one sees the statements about beauty occupying so important a place in Bonaventure's theology that one begins to be afraid that there is no unity to give shape to their multiplicity" (GL2 333); "perhaps no one in the Middle Ages evaluated sense-perception so positively as Bonaventure" (GL2 334).

17. "it is only in faith that he [the spirit of man] understands himself as the expression of the triune life, and it is only in the explicit turning . . . to the trinitarian image that is above him that the image of the eternal God in him . . . is truly illuminated" (GL2 302).

vastness of experience.[18] The "pyramids of concepts," according to von Balthasar, "do not satisfy the need for fullness" (GL2 266), which warrants precisely a non-conceptual aesthetic approach of wonder that is capable of embracing even incomprehensibility.[19]

The aesthetic element in Bonaventure, according to von Balthasar, is anything that has to do with direct seeing or visibility. Thus he draws on Bonaventure's *Hexaemeron* to present his understanding of faith as involving "acts of seeing," both bodily and intellectual, which alone "give to revelation the certainty of faith" (GL2 280–81).[20] This aesthetic visibility is understood in two senses: in the traditional sense of something hidden being immediately revealed through seeing, as well as in the sense of something becoming visible through an actual, even physical, transformation or "impression."[21] (One can see that such an understanding of 'aesthetic'—including not only sensible vision but also sensible transformation—is too broad for the parameters of this study.)

Von Balthasar starts his analysis of Bonaventure's aesthetics with the theological *a priori*, or the "downward" movement, as presented in

18. "The ethos of the theology in Bonaventure is thereby quite different from the ethos of Thomas Aquinas, whose philosophical point of view tries to reflect the order of the world as rigorously and clearly as possible. In Bonaventure, there is something defeated from the very start; theology is an imposing upon that which is not to be imposed upon, a tireless proposing of new ordering . . . the 'blossoming wilderness' into bouquets. But in the face of this, the last word remains the experience of being out-trumped, of wonder, and of being transported out of oneself" (GL2 266). One can, perhaps, argue academically or textually against von Balthasar's general assessment of the thought of Thomas Aquinas, but "aesthetically" we feel that he captures well the general "spirit" of the difference between the two approaches.

19. In GL2 267 von Balthasar quotes an excellent passage from Bonaventure's *De scientia Christi* q. 6 (vol. 5, 35a): "nothing satisfies the soul except what exceeds its power to grasp." The works of Bonaventure will be quoted according to the "great" Quaracchi edition (also called *Editio Parmensis*): *S. Bonaventurae opera omnia*, vols. 1–10, edited by Collegium S. Bonaventurae (Quaracchi: Collegium S. Bonaventurae, 1882–1902).

20. Von Balthasar's assessment is based on *Hexaemeron* 8, 3 (vol. 5, 369b); 9, 10–11 (vol. 5, 374a); 9, 12–14 (vol. 5, 374b).

21. "The glory is the appearing of the Lord, and through the Spirit of the Lord . . . the open seeing of faith and . . . the configuration to the image in a process that stamps an impression are made possible in the unity between expression and impression that was found between the seraph and Francis. This apparent *theologia gloriae* . . . remains . . . for Bonaventure—precisely in its blinding brilliance—a theology of *excessus* as the believer is confronted by the ever greater fullness of God: the superabundance of what may be revealed is the hiddenness that is the true characteristic of the Christian God" (GL2 282). For the same reason, von Balthasar also calls 2 Cor. 3:18, because it contains the idea of transformation into the image of God, an "aesthetic text" (GL2 281). One could liken von Balthasar's description of the Franciscan experience of being "impressed" by the seraph to the Eastern Orthodox tradition where a saint was supposed to be physically transformed into the image of Christ, or become an expression of a resurrected body; this idea is captured well in iconic images of saints.

Bonaventure's thought. In Bonaventure, according to von Balthasar, the divine serves as the exemplar upon which everything in the created world is modeled. Bonaventure's thought is driven by the idea that the human being and the world are intelligible only on the basis of the being of God. The key category in this way of thinking is "expression": God expresses himself in the world and in Christ (who is the perfect expression or image of God), and the world expresses God (GL2 283). Thus all things, as imperfect copies or expressions, are related to the perfect expression and image. Von Balthasar, again, stresses the Christocentric and Trinitarian nature of Bonaventure's theory of expression (GL2 283).

In a summary description in GL2 Bonaventure's system appears as a typical Neoplatonic "procession-return" scheme in the tradition of the Greek Fathers (such as pseudo-Dionysius), as well as of some of their Latin imitators (such as Eriugena): God's "expression" or unraveling of himself is concluded by man's "impression" and return, where both movements are seen in aesthetic terms. Thus the realization of the Trinitarian nature of God through the process of return is for Bonaventure "the fundamental act of thinking and being that is worthy of man" (GL2 304). It is precisely the centrality of these two movements that explains why the categories of image, likeness, form—ultimately linked to the aesthetic concept of beauty—play such an important role in Bonaventure's theology which can ultimately be seen as aesthetic.

The theological *a priori* is thus set: the image "points beyond itself" and allows for the process of the "reduction, the theological transcendental reduction, the theological demonstration of the conditions of the possibility of all knowledge and striving" (GL2 307).[22] Finally, von Balthasar presents the *a posteriori* position: the analogy of the divine in the world that allows for the process of return or "reduction" to God "from below."[23] However, the section on the *a posteriori* appears much less substantial and interesting than the one on the *a priori*. In fact, von Balthasar himself realizes the limited nature of this part of his study, which is restricted to "a few" aspects about the world and Christ that are significant to his aesthetics.

After we have located Bonaventure's thought in the modern discus-

---

22. Note the echoes of both Platonic and Kantian thought in this passage.
23. "Now we must show the same phenomenon from the standpoint of the world, *a posteriori*, and then demonstrate the synthesis of descending and ascending expression in the God-man" (GL2 309).

sion on theological aesthetics,[24] it is equally important to establish a continuity between Bonaventure's aesthetics and the earlier medieval and ancient sources. As it happens, the majority of Bonaventure's statements on aesthetics—apart from the specifically Bonaventurian elaboration of the Trinitarian and Christological elements in aesthetics—can be traced with certainty to the ancient and early medieval traditions described in the previous chapters and therefore constitute part of a continuous tradition. Unlike in the case of Augustine, access to the earlier tradition in the late Middle Ages was limited by the availability of ancient and early medieval texts, and this is precisely why the issue of transmission of these texts in the later period received so much attention in the previous chapters. Summarizing the results of these analyses, the link to the Platonic tradition in aesthetics was provided through Augustine, pseudo-Dionysius, and twelfth-century authors such as the Victorines. The only Platonic dialogue that was both directly available and relevant to aesthetics was the *Timaeus*. This tradition was the main source of the view of beauty as a "pointer" that reveals the divine, and of aesthetic experience as anagogical. Many aesthetic themes filtered from the Stoic tradition through the texts of Cicero and, with significant transformations, through the works of Augustine: for example, such topics as the cosmological proof of the divine existence from the beauty of the universe, an aesthetic justification of evil,[25] and the notion of "moral beauty" (*honestum* and *decorum*).[26] Although most of the aforementioned Stoic material in Bonaventure and other thirteenth- and fourteenth-century schoolmen is related to aesthetics (as understood for the purposes of this study),[27] it is not original in nature and is not connected with the specifically Christian theological

---

24. In contrast with Plato or Augustine, it is difficult to find any direct influence of Bonaventure on modern secular aesthetics, precisely because of the specifically theological nature of his thought. However, speaking of the influence of Bonaventure's thought on modern aesthetics, apart from von Balthasar one could mention the Romantics and Hopkins. Tracy (*Analogical Imagination*, 134–35) links Bonaventure and Franciscan spirituality with the poetry of the Romantics. P. A. Ballinger (*Poem as Sacrament*), 100, argues convincingly that some of the aesthetic trends in Hopkins can be linked more successfully not to the Ignatian exercises, but to the Franciscan tradition, and not to Scotus, which is the traditional claim, but specifically to Bonaventure.

25. On these two themes in the late Middle Ages see O. Bychkov, "A Propos of Medieval Aesthetics," chap. 3, 163–74.

26. On the Stoic aesthetic themes in the late Middle Ages see Chapter 6, as well as O. Bychkov ("Traditional Stoic Ideas," "A Propos of Medieval Aesthetics," and "Aesthetic Explanation of Evil").

27. E.g., it presents the connection between the aesthetic and the divine, or between aesthetic and moral issues.

aesthetics, which is the most original contribution of this period and the focus of this chapter. At the same time, Stoic material from Cicero historically played an important role in forming connections between various aesthetic notions in the late Middle Ages, for example, in interpreting *decorum* and *honestum* in terms of beauty (*pulchritudo*), which allowed medieval authors to read aesthetic meaning into a variety of texts from very different backgrounds (for example, into pseudo-Dionysius).[28] Augustine is by far the most obvious source for the thirteenth and fourteenth centuries, but especially for the Franciscan tradition and in particular for Bonaventure and Duns Scotus, who revere this author to the point of denying that any of his statements could possibly be wrong. In fact, some sections of Bonaventure's key texts on aesthetics, such as the *Itinerarium*, are almost a paraphrase of Augustine's aesthetic works analyzed above in Chapter 7. Our review of the sources of late medieval schoolmen, then, confirms the initial decision to present such earlier authors as Plato, Cicero, and Augustine as part of a unified, continuous tradition in aesthetics, while leaving out such otherwise important authors as Plotinus, who was not directly available.

The Dionysian and Anselmian Moments

One cannot, however, start a discussion of Bonaventure without saying a few words about his other two key sources from the Patristic and earlier medieval periods: pseudo-Dionysius and Anselm. With respect to Bonaventure's aesthetics, these two sources are secondary in importance only to Augustine. Although Bonaventure inherits reverence for Anselm from other intermediary authors (such as Hugh of St. Victor), the Franciscan certainly uses the actual text of Anselm. The same holds true for pseudo-Dionysius, whose texts in various translations had become widespread by the thirteenth century.[29] Another reason for taking a look at these two authors is that both are credited with developing their own aesthetic-theological views and both are discussed by von Balthasar.[30]

---

28. On this issue see O. Bychkov, "A Propos of Medieval Aesthetics," chap. 2, 67–74.

29. Thus many schoolmen, such as Albert and Aquinas, write extended commentaries on his works, including the passage from the *Divine Names* 4.7 on τὸ καλόν, and quotes from this author are extensively used in Commentaries on the *Sentences* and Sums of theology. For more details on the transmission of the texts of this author see O. Bychkov, "A Propos of Medieval Aesthetics."

30. They do not receive full treatment in this study because their aesthetics is either pure-

Pseudo-Dionysius the Areopagite features in medieval and modern discussions of aesthetics because, writing in the Neoplatonic tradition of Proclus (but also being familiar with earlier sources, including the original texts of Plato, which he sometimes includes almost verbatim), he accepts τὸ καλόν as one of the "divine names," as discussed in his treatise *On the Divine Names* 4.7. However, as was traditional in Greek thought, τὸ καλόν here is a broad category which means "general excellence" and includes beauty as only one of its aspects. In application to God this is, again, an analogical usage. For the present study we chose to discuss only the cases where such an analogical usage is illustrated by parallels from concrete sense experience, which is precisely what does not happen in pseudo-Dionysius. In fact, even von Balthasar is forced to limit his discussion of this author only to abstract matters and to assume a very broad understanding of "aesthetic": anything that has to do with expression, manifestation, symbolism, etc.

This author is, nevertheless, important for von Balthasar for one particular reason. He serves as a figure that is transitional from the aesthetic thought of Plato and Plotinus (whom von Balthasar credits with creating a truly theological aesthetics for the first time) to the Christian Fathers. Following his hermeneutic-theological approach, von Balthasar regards Christian Patristic authors as part of a continuous tradition of aesthetic thought that smoothly transitions from the ancients.[31] In this line of succession, von Balthasar regards pseudo-Dionysius as the "most aesthetic of all Christian theologians" for showing how the "aesthetic transcendence that we know in this world (from the sensible as manifestation to the spiritual as what is manifest) provides the formal schema for understanding theological or mystical transcendence (from the world to God)" (GL2 168). Von Balthasar correctly assesses the influence of this author in the pre-Aristotelian Middle Ages as "scarcely less than that of Augustine" (GL2 148). He even credits him with creating the "clear, realized synthesis of truth and beauty, of theology and aesthetics, which was never wholly lost even in the driest realms of the

---

ly analogical, without reference to actual aesthetic experience, or not specifically Trinitarian or Christological, the focus of this chapter.

31. "Greek thought from Plato to Plotinus has an essentially aesthetic, religious structure—for the cosmos is experienced as the representation and manifestation of the hidden transcendent beauty of God . . ."; there is no wonder, then, that " . . . Christian theology takes over this aesthetic and metaphysical schema" (GL2 154).

scholasticism of the schools" (GL2 148).³² The theological-aesthetic element that von Balthasar finds in pseudo-Dionysius is, again, an emphasis on "seeing."³³ Von Balthasar describes the general scheme of the Dionysian theological system in terms that are reminiscent both of his sketches of other Neoplatonic authors and of some basic features of modern Romantic or Idealist tradition. Thus he speaks of the procession and return, which is portrayed in terms of the "aesthetic" manifestation or expression of the hidden, as well as of becoming aware of this hidden (GL2 164–65). The proportion that is perceived outwardly as "beautiful" must be suitable for manifesting what is hidden: otherwise it would not be perceived as beautiful.³⁴ It is interesting that many passages that von Balthasar himself chooses from pseudo-Dionysius sound close to the original Platonic texts, but their interpretation is worded rather in the tradition of Heidegger.³⁵

We must now look at von Balthasar's assessment of another important source for Bonaventure, Anselm of Canterbury. It soon becomes clear that the reason why von Balthasar considers Anselm's thought "aesthetic" is the same as why he thinks that way of the thought of pseudo-Dionysius and many other authors: because he supposedly puts great emphasis on "seeing" (a sort of "intellectual seeing" in this case) rather than on "reasoning." As became clear in Chapter 6 during the discussion of Stoic thought, distinguishing between 'immediate intellectual seeing' and 'thinking' is difficult. One quickly realizes that in his discussion of Anselm, von Balthasar's interpretation of all instances of "seeing" in Anselm as "aesthetic" is probably stretched too far (cf. GL2 220, 223–24, etc.). As is well known to almost any speaker of an Indo-European language (at least those used in Europe, including Germanic languages, one of which was spoken by Anselm), the verb "to see" is rou-

---

32. "The categories of the aesthetic and of art will play a decisive role" in pseudo-Dionysius's theology, von Balthasar continues, "and there has hardly been a theology so deeply informed by aesthetic categories as the liturgical theology of the Areopagite" (GL2 153–54).

33. Cf.: "No explanations can help him who does not see the beauty; . . . who cannot see *what* is manifest in the world; no apologetic can be any use to him for whom the truth that radiates from the center of theology is not evident" (GL2 166).

34. "This proportion (between spirit and what is perceptible to sense), which is the real center of the aesthetic, is, without being simply ruptured, infinitely transcended and, as it were, stretched out, when it is a matter of the relation between God and the world" (GL2 165).

35. Cf. like Plato: "the blessed beauty of the archetype shimmers through clearly (ἀποστίλβω ἐμφανῶς)" (*Eccl. h.* III.3.2 [PG 3, 428C] quoted in GL2 169); like Heidegger: "the more it reveals the more it conceals" (GL2 169).

tinely used as a metaphor for purely intellectual activities that include conceptual clarity (cf. "I don't see why" or "I see!" etc.). Whether the instances of intuiting clearly some conceptual correspondence fall in the purview of aesthetics is doubtful, especially if the metaphor of seeing is not reinforced by direct appeals to actual aesthetic experience, and that is not the case for Anselm.

It is of interest, however, to examine two main contexts in which Anselm, according to von Balthasar or other observers, comes close to connecting theology and aesthetics. The first is his famous *Proslogion* proof of the existence of God. This proof, according to von Balthasar, is ultimately not an argument but a vision (GL2 233), which is rooted in Anselm's direct "aesthetic" intuition whose evidential power is based on something shining forth and being immediately clear.[36] Such immediacy and clarity of insight or "seeing" in the case of some concepts cannot be resisted and leads one to the feeling of absolute necessity and certainty, as opposed to the "unclear" concepts of dialectical sophisms (GL2 222).[37] According to von Balthasar,

For Anselm the process of thought moves unmistakably towards the point where the subject studied appears with such clarity that one can speak of an immediate in-sight, towards the making present of the subject matter, whereby the attempt to achieve such a making-present proves whether the subject matter can be achieved and therefore true or not. (GL2 225)

It is noteworthy that von Balthasar's contemporary hermeneutics of Anselm's thought is consistent with the medieval interpretation of Anselm's *Proslogion* proof in aesthetic terms, for example, by Duns Scotus. Despite some attempts in scholarly literature to reconstruct Scotus's "aesthetics,"[38] this author is clearly not interested in aesthetics as such, and

36. The scholar calls his thought "aesthetic" and "intuitive" (GL2 232). Re. the nature of Anselm's argumentation cf.: "Reason is for Anselm the spirit's capacity for sight.... To think means to make something visible spiritually" (GL2 220). Thus in his appeals to reason or concepts Anselm in fact emphasizes "vision," seeing, clarity, transparency, evident nature, opening up of the truth, openness, revealedness, etc. (GL2 222). The conceptual and phenomenological validity of the idea of "seeing clearly" was discussed in detail above in Chapters 4 (in general) and 6 (in the context of ancient theories).

37. Cf.: such openness "compels agreement"; "the radiant obviousness of truth is something that convinces so persuasively that finally it must be described by using the keyword, as 'necessity,' that which must be so" (GL2 222); "from such apprehensibility there arises certainty" (GL2 223).

38. Cf. chapter on Duns Scotus in de Bruyne, *Études d'esthétique médiévale*; also cf. F. J. Kovach, "Divine and Human Beauty in Duns Scotus's Philosophy and Theology," in *Scholastic*

simply repeats some basic ideas already developed by Bonaventure.[39] At the same time, although Scotus does not often engage aesthetic topics explicitly, his epistemology and theory of cognition are ultimately based on aesthetic analogies with actual aesthetic experience.[40] This becomes strikingly apparent in the text where Scotus supports Anselm's "aesthetic" (in von Balthasar's assessment) argument for God's existence.

In Book I, Distinction 2 of his Commentary on the *Sentences* of Peter Lombard, in both Oxonian and Parisian versions of it, Scotus reexamines the validity of Anselm's *Proslogion* proof of the existence of God (which he supports), that is, that the existence of God is evident simply from the concept that we have of God.[41] One of the steps in proving

---

Challenges to Some Medieval and Modern Ideas, 93–110 (Stillwater, Okla.: Western Publications, 1987). De Bruyne's treatment is simply too broad and includes, e.g., Scotus's analysis of the principle of individuation on the basis that it deals with formal entities. Kovach's study is based on several versions of only one short passage in Scotus that is indeed relevant to aesthetics but is not even original enough to justify a "Scotist aesthetics." Cf. a more recent study of Scotus's concept of beauty: G. Sondag, "The Conditional Definition of Beauty by Scotus," *Medioevo* 30 (2005): 191–206.

39. Although, as is well known, Scotus's thought did happen to influence at least one great modern aesthete. Thus G. M. Hopkins wrote in his letter to R. Bridges that he "cares" for Duns Scotus "more even than Aristotle and more ... than a dozen Hegels" (Ballinger, *Poem as Sacrament*, 105).

40. Mary Beth Ingham in a recent study also detected the important role of aesthetic imagery, such as parallels with perceiving musical harmony, in Scotus's ethical thought. According to Scotus, an action becomes meritorious only due to God's acceptance of it, or, as Ingham puts it, his delight in it. Now although a meritorious action is due both to the movement of the free will and to the habit of charity, what makes it acceptable or pleasing to God is precisely making one's choice through the habit of charity. Scotus argues through a comparison with a sounding body of a musical instrument: although technically the sound is produced by the movement of the sounding body, in order to be acceptable or pleasing to the ear it is more important in which order this body is struck. Thus the most efficient action of the sounding body does not always produce the best sound, and sometimes the worst, because first of all it must be harmonic, or ordered in a certain way, to be pleasing. In ethics, it is the habit of charity, not the brute force of the will, that imposes this sort of order on the movement of the will, and it is this organizing skill or "art" of charity that is pleasing to God. Cf. M. B. Ingham, "Divine Delight: *Acceptatio* and the Economy of Salvation in Duns Scotus," in *Theological Aesthetics after von Balthasar*, edited by O. Bychkov and J. Fodor (Aldershot: Ashgate, 2008), 59–66. The discussion is on p. 65, where she also refers to her other works, such as "Duns Scotus: Moral Reasoning and the Artistic Paradigm," in *Via Scoti: Methodologica ad Mentem J. Duns Scoti* (Rome: Antonianum, 1995), 825–37, and *The Harmony of Goodness: Mutuality and Moral Living According to John Duns Scotus* (Quincy, Ill.: Franciscan Press, 1996), 117–35. The texts she refers to are *Ordinatio* I, Dist. 17, p. 1, q. 1–2, n. 152 (editio Vaticana, vol. 5, 212), with a parallel passage in the *Lectura*.

41. The texts quoted below are from *Reportatio* I-A, Dist. 2, part 1, q. 1–3, n. 71–73. A similar account is found in the *Ordinatio*. The key parallel text is in *Ordinatio* I, Dist. 2, p. 1, q. 1–2, n. 136 (vol. 2, 208), translated in A. Wolter, *John Duns Scotus: Philosophical Writings* (Indianapolis/Cambridge: Hackett Publishing Company, 1987), 72–73. The work of Scotus

The Late Medieval Tradition ~ 283

that God exists is simply to prove that some infinite being necessarily exists (in Anselm's words, "something greater than which nothing can be conceived"). In both versions of his Commentary, Scotus's strategy is to prove that the concept of 'infinite' is not incompatible with that of 'being': our intellect clearly perceives that there can be "infinite being." Moreover, our intellect always strives beyond any finite being, which means that it is clear to our intellect that there is something more to reality than finite being, since it certainly would not strive after something it does not think can exist.[42] Suddenly Scotus realizes, as the Stoics did before him, that he also needs to prove why we should trust our intellect in the first place, when it thinks that something is "clearly" the case. What if it is continuously deceived? Amazingly, in the *Reportatio* I-A (which contains an account similar to that of the *Ordinatio*) the Subtle Doctor comes up with the following way of rooting the certainty of our intellectual cognition (*Rep.* I-A, n. 72):

The sense faculties, which are less perfect cognitive powers than the intellect, immediately perceive any lack of harmony in their object, as is clear from the case of auditory perception of dissonance. Therefore, if 'infinite' were repugnant to 'being,' the intellect would immediately perceive this repugnance and lack of harmony and then, because of the repugnance, it could not grasp 'infinite being' as its object—just as it could not have something contradictory, like 'man is irrational,' as its object. But everyone experiences the opposite, since the intellect never rests with finite being.[43]

---

that will be principally used for this chapter is the latest version of Book 1 of his *Commentary on the* Sentences *of Peter Lombard* based on a student's report of his Parisian Lectures. The text and translation of the Parisian Lectures is taken from the following edition-translation: A. Wolter and O. V. Bychkov, *John Duns Scotus: The Examined Report of the Paris Lecture (Reportatio I-A). Latin Text and English Translation*, 2 vols. (St. Bonaventure, N.Y.: The Franciscan Institute, 2004, 2008). The choice is based on two considerations. First, the *Paris Report*, unlike Scotus's principal work, *Ordinatio*, is already available in English. Second, there is a strong opinion that Book 1 of this work represents the latest and most mature stage in the development of Scotus's thought before his death: an opinion expressed by Allan Wolter in private conversations with me, by Richard Cross in his recent book on Scotus (see below), and by other scholars. See a summary of arguments in defense of the use of Bk. 1 of the Parisian Lectures over that of the *Ordinatio* in O. V. Bychkov, "Introduction. The Nature of Theology in Duns Scotus and His Franciscan Predecessors," *Franciscan Studies* 66 (2008): 5–62.

42. *Rep.* I-A, n. 71. The proof that the context of this discussion can be interpreted, from the modern point of view, as "transcendental aesthetics," is supplied by a very close parallel in Kant's third *Critique*: "But because there is in our imagination a striving toward infinite progress and in our reason a claim for absolute totality, regarded as a real idea, therefore this very inadequateness for that idea in our faculty for estimating the magnitude of things of sense excites in us the feeling of a supersensible faculty" (§25, p. 88, W 336).

43. . . . potentiae sensitivae quae sunt minus cognitivae quam intellectus statim percipi-

The *Ordinatio* version sounds similar:

Now, if tonal discord so readily displeases the ear, it would be strange if some intellect did not clearly perceive the contradiction between [infinite and] its first object [viz. being, if such existed]. For if the disagreeable becomes offensive as soon as it is perceived, why is it that no intellect naturally shrinks from the infinitely intelligible as it would from something out of harmony with, and even destructive of, its first object?[44]

Thus the proof of certainty of our intellectual cognition rests on a purely aesthetic argument. In our perception of art (in this case music, but it could easily have been visual arts) our senses pinpoint the presence or absence of proportion or harmony with never-failing accuracy. In our day-to-day experience the judgment of our aesthetic sense, for example, the sense for musical harmony, does not need verification and can be absolutely trusted. At the same time, we know that it can be independently verified, for example, with the help of measuring instruments. Why, then, not trust our intellect, which is a faculty that is clearly not inferior to our senses?

The main objection to Anselm's argument is resolved in a similar way (cf. *Rep.* I-A, n. 73–74). Indeed, one can object that we can easily think of something that definitely cannot exist, for example, of absurd things such as chimaeras. Scotus answers that we do not actually have a clear and certain idea of such things. That is, it is already in our intellect that these things lack reality and certainty. On the other hand, if our intellect does see or perceive something clearly, as it happens in aesthetic perception, it is necessarily the case. In other words, like von Balthasar, Scotus understands a lack of clarity in a concept as a sign of non-truth, or of a complexity that needs to be reduced further. As early as at the conceptual level, it is possible to distinguish between the certain and the dubious.[45] One can be absolutely certain about some concepts

---

unt disconvenientiam in suo obiecto; patet de auditu respectu soni discovenientis. Ergo si infinitum repugnat enti statim intellectus istam discovenientiam et repugnantiam percipiet; et tunc non posset apprehendere ens infinitum pro obiecto—sicut nec repugnantia, ut hominem esse irrationalem, potest habere pro obiecto, quia obiectum includit repugnantiam—cuius oppositum quilibet experitur, quia numquam quietatur in ente finito.

44. A. Wolter's translation, loc.cit. The Latin reads: Mirum est autem si nulli intellectui talis contradictio patens fiat circa primum eius obiectum, cum discordia in sono ita faciliter offendat auditum: si enim disconveniens statim ut percipitur offendit, cur nullus intellectus ab intelligibili infinito naturaliter refugit sicut a non conveniente, suum ita primum obiectum destruente?

45. The pattern of thinking in Duns Scotus that we can clearly and quasi-aesthetically

that are "simply simple."⁴⁶ Therefore, if one can make a reduction to such "simple" concepts that are immediately clear and need no proof, one can be absolutely certain about some truth, which in this case, one could say with von Balthasar, is immediately "seen." Returning to the main objection to Anselm's proof in *Rep.* I-A, n. 73, Duns Scotus first proves that Anselm's concept of "the highest thing one can think of" does indeed belong to the class of such "immediately clear" or true concepts.⁴⁷ However, it is much harder to make a transition from a "clear concept" to real existence. Since, as the objection points out, one can also think of what does not exist, how can having a concept of something prove its existence? According to Scotus, the actual existence of a thing conceived does not add anything to its concept (does not make it more "intensive"). Therefore, the distinction must lie within the concept itself: that is, it should be possible to tell, from a particular clarity and consistency of a concept, whether the thing it represents is able to exist, or even whether it exists or not.⁴⁸ In the case of Anselm, the particular clarity of the concept in question indicates that it does have a real referent.⁴⁹

---

perceive certain things about divine reality is confirmed, for example, by the way in which he proves one of his well-known views that the concept of being is univocally known of both God and creatures. In *Reportatio* I-A, Dist. 3, q. 1, n. 28 (transl. taken from Wolter/Bychkov [2004]), which closely follows the *Ordinatio* account, this view is formulated concisely in the following way: "Every intellect that is certain about one concept and dubious about another, has the concept about which it is certain as other than that about which it is dubious: the subject includes this predicate; were it otherwise, one would be certain and uncertain about the same thing. But the intellect of the pilgrim is certain that God is a being, doubting whether it be a created being or uncreated, and the being is saved univocally in both; therefore the concept of being is other than both and is preserved in both; therefore it is a univocal concept." Cf. *Ord.* I, Dist. 3, q. 1 in A. Wolter (1987), 20. It is clear that the way Scotus proves the univocity of being is similar to the way he proves Anselm's argument for the existence of God. In both cases the process is analogous to our judgment of aesthetic forms: the intellect clearly sees whether this is the case or not, without any discursive deduction.

46. Cf. from the same discussion of univocity in *Ord.* I, Dist. 3, q. 1 (A. Wolter, 1987, 21): "these two concepts [of being] are irreducibly simple. Unless, therefore, they are known distinctly and wholly, they cannot be known at all. Consequently, if these concepts are not perceived as two concepts now, they will not be perceived as two later on."

47. "But contradictories do not form anything one, neither simple nor composite. Therefore, they will not form one conceivable concept. I return then to my original proposal and argue that the highest thing one can think of exists, because the highest thing one can think of is conceivable without contradiction, but it is possible for such to exist in actuality, therefore it can be thought to exist in actuality." Further argument shows that such a thing must also exist of itself and necessarily, as well as be infinite.

48. Cf. the Stoic theory of "cognitive impressions" discussed above in Chapter 6.

49. *Rep.* I-A, Dist. 2, p. 1, q. 3, n. 74: "But against this it is objected that contradictories as well as absurdities, like a chimaera or a golden mountain, can be thought of, and yet cannot come to be or actually exist. I reply: if the same conceivable thing were in the mind and in the

Examining this medieval debate, one cannot help noticing close parallels ranging chronologically from the Stoic discussion of "cognitive impressions" as a criterion of truth to modern phenomenology. However, the perennial debate of whether truth about reality can be immediately revealed must remain outside our discussion of aesthetics unless some interest in actual aesthetic perception is present. And, unlike Duns Scotus, Anselm here does not recur to any direct aesthetic parallels.

The second context is Anselm's economy of salvation. Incidentally, von Balthasar applies the same typology to Anselm that he applies to Plato and that some other critics apply to Augustine:[50] he claims that Anselm, as he matures, shifts his focus from "aesthetic reason of his early works (*Monologion* and *Proslogion*) with their, as it were, immediate apprehension of theological necessities" to other topics, such as "Christian freedom" (GL2 258–59). Although any of these broad assessments is debatable, what is true is that by and large Anselm, despite his extensive use of Augustine, ultimately does not assume the Neoplatonic "immediate ascent" model for his theology,[51] but limits himself to the model that, after von Balthasar and others, one could dub "aesthetic order" (which is Augustinian, and ultimately Platonic, in origin). One must admit, however, that there are some elements of "revelatory aesthetics" even in the model based on aesthetic order, because this order in Plato, the Stoics, and Augustine is presented as directly discernible, not rationalized. Despite the fact that this model does not rely on immediacy to a great extent, still it derives some of its transparency and convincing power from aesthetics. Thus arguments "from order" can also be seen as aesthetic to a degree.

Anselm's later work *Cur deus homo* is a good illustration of this trend. The discussion of order appears in the course of a dialogue be-

---

world of actual existence, it would not on that account be conceivable with any more intensity, although it would be conceivable [extensively] in several ways [viz. abstractly and intuitively]. And this applies to things we can think of like a golden mountain . . . [which will not be distinguished from others through a reference to actual existence, but already conceptually, as contradictory and incompatible with existence]." Scotus returns to the idea that one can know whether something could be really existing or not from its essential concept on other occasions as well. For example, answering the arguments of Henry of Ghent in *Rep.* I-A, Dist. 36, p. 2, q. 2, n. 157–58, he indicates that if something is not capable of existing then there would also be no quidditative concept of a "valid" kind for such a thing.

50. The issue was discussed above in the corresponding chapters.

51. Although, with von Balthasar, one could possibly interpret the *Proslogion* argument as such an "ascent" or "revelation."

tween Anselm and Boso, who debate the necessity of the Incarnation. The first passage is from *Cur deus homo* I.12:

Anselm: Let us go back and see whether it befits God to remit sins out of mere mercy, without any restitution for the honor which has been taken from him. Boso: I don't see why it wouldn't befit him. Ans.: To remit a sin in this way simply means not to punish. Now since to restore order rightly when no satisfaction is received for a sin simply means to punish, if [a sin] is not punished it is remitted un-ordered. Boso: What you say makes sense. Ans.: However, it does not befit *(non decet)* God to leave something un-ordered in his kingdom. Boso: If I contradict, I would be a sinner. Ans.: Therefore it does not befit God to remit a sin in this manner unpunished. Boso: It sounds logical. Ans.: There is also another logical consequence if a sin is remitted thus unpunished, for God will treat both a sinner and a non-sinner in a similar fashion, which is not appropriate *(non convenit)* for God.[52]

Anselm's choice of terms, especially those that mean "fitting" or "appropriate" *(decet, convenit)* which also occur several times before and after this passage, gives the whole discussion an aesthetic direction. Relying on what is "fitting" means that the proof here is ultimately aesthetic, and not based on "what makes sense." Anselm's use of aesthetic language is further supplemented by a direct allusion to the phenomenon of beauty: in this case, the beauty of the universal arrangement of things in the world.[53] By preserving God's honor, creatures contribute

---

52. My translation is based on the following edition of the Latin text: *S. Anselmi Cantuariensis Archiepiscopi Opera Omnia*, vol. 2, edited by F. S. Schmitt (Edinburgh: T. Nelson & Sons, 1946), 69.

53. *Cur d. h.* I.14–15, ed. Schmitt, 1946, 72–73. "Boso: . . . But I would like to hear from you whether the punishment of a sinner is an honor for him, or whether it is an honor of any sort. For if the punishment of a sinner is not an honor for him—when a sinner does not restitute what he has taken away, but is punished—then God loses his honor without recovery . . . . [15]

Anselm: Nothing, insofar as God is concerned, can be either added or taken away from his honor. For his honor remains the same: incorruptible, and in no way changeable. However, when some creature preserves, either naturally or acting from reason, its orderly condition (as it were, enjoined to it), it is said to obey God and honor him, and mostly this refers to the rational nature, which possesses the understanding of what ought to be. Now when this creature wills what ought to be, it honors God: not because it bestows something on him, but because it willingly submits to his will and decree, and preserves, in the totality of things, its own orderly position and the beauty of that totality, insofar as it is in it. However, when it does not will what ought to be, it dishonors God, insofar as the creature itself is concerned, for it does not willingly submit to his decree and disturbs the order and beauty of the totality, insofar as it [i.e., the creature itself] is concerned. . . . " However, God, Anselm continues, " . . . with his highest wisdom converts even that which it [the creature] wills or does perversely into the order and beauty of the aforesaid totality. For both the voluntary satisfaction for perversity and exacting punishment from the one who does not [wish to] satisfy, not to men-to the beauty of the universal arrangement. However, even if they fail to preserve God's honor, this can happen only so far as they themselves are concerned, because as far as God himself is concerned, he converts any disorder (sin or evil) into order, thus preserving his own honor. Despite the strong influence of Augustine here,[54] Anselm's thought incorporates only certain aspects of the Augustinian theory of order and beauty. For Augustine, aesthetic order ultimately contributes to the scheme of the ascent from the order and beauty of the universe to the divine principle: the revelatory and "transcendental" nature of this ascent subsequently becomes crucial for the development of modern theological aesthetics. Anselm, in his turn, replaces the more *aisthetic* and immediate ascent scheme with the more legalistic scheme of reconciliation between humans and God—which, nevertheless, still retains some aesthetic elements. The terminology of reconciliation is most frequent in *Cur d.h.*, II.16, where Anselm presents a view of the Incarnation as reconciliation. First, Anselm says, "it is clear that that man [Jesus] is God and the reconciler of sinners," and further he compares God to a king in relation to his subjects. The conflict between the two parties must be reconciled by a middleman (Christ) who wants to "reconcile (*reconciliare*) all by means of some service which will very much please that king," etc. As has been demonstrated, side by side with the terminology of reconciliation Anselm uses aesthetic terminology, which proves that he sees the process of reconciliation in aesthetic terms. This is clearly indicated first of all by the term 'beauty' (*pulchritudo*) which he equates with 'order,' and also by the terms with double meaning—moral and aesthetic—such as 'it is fitting,' 'it is appropriate,' 'honor,' etc.[55] Thus Anselm's discussion of beauty appears in the context of his theological attempt to describe the movement from the divine to the human, as well as their harmonious relationship mediated by Christ, as something aesthetically pleasing. The aesthetic state of the world—its harmony, balance, or nobility (*honestas*)—is theologically interpreted as conscious obedience to God and the divine law (cf. *Cur d. h.* I.15). The Anselmian idea of reconciliation is in fact reminiscent of a certain theme in modern aesthetics which

---

tion the fact that God [otherwise] makes good things out of evil things in many ways, preserve their place in that totality and the beauty of order."

54. One can clearly observe Augustinian trends in this passage, not only as regards the theory of order, but also as regards the understanding of the role of evil as contributing to the beauty and goodness of the universe.

55. Cf. our discussion of these terms above in Chapter 6.

can be described as the "reconciliation" of the two realms after a split between them.[56] In its modern version, aesthetic emotion appears as "taming" the sensible and irrational: when we experience it we are "reconciled" with the world, for we realize that the two have something in common, and our expectations are appeased. In the case of Anselm, of course, the situation is interpreted theologically as the consequence of the divine economy and put into strict legal terms. Thus our secluded and limited state is perceived as a result of debt (the original sin) which requires a reconciliation—not a psychological or intellectual one, which would occur spontaneously, but a quasi-legal and consciously performed one—that repays the debt (cf. *Cur d. h.* II c.16). At the same time, the recuperation of the former union and harmony—either salvation, which comes as a result of the Incarnation, or punishment for sins—is perceived as beautiful, as is the experience of bridging the two realms in modern aesthetic theories. It becomes more clear at this point, however, that Anselm still does not present a specifically Christian aesthetics. Both proofs—of the existence of the divine by clear seeing and of the contention that God must preserve his honor "because it is fitting"—would make perfect sense even to a pagan ancient mind, despite the fact that they are used here in the context of Christian theology.

The Beauty of the Trinity

It is now time to examine Bonaventure who, as it appears from the secondary literature, is often viewed as the father of a truly Christian aesthetics in the later Middle Ages. As has been the rule in this study, Bonaventure will be discussed as part of a continuous tradition that can be traced back—both textually-historically and conceptually—to earlier Franciscan authors such as Alexander of Hales, and even as far back as Augustine.[57] For the discussion of aesthetic issues in medieval systematic theology we will also use Duns Scotus. As was mentioned above, although Scotus rarely speaks on aesthetic issues explicitly, the aesthetic

---

56. E.g., the moral and the rational, the immanent and the transcendent, etc., in Kant, Schiller, Nietzsche, et al.; see above in Chapter 1.

57. As regards aesthetic topics, early Franciscan authors such as Alexander of Hales rely heavily on Augustine, and Bonaventure relies on both Alexander and Augustine. Many of the textual parallels in aesthetics between Bonaventure and Alexander, as well as the tradition of using Augustine's text by both authors, are presented in O. Bychkov, "A Propos of Medieval Aesthetics"; see examples below in this chapter.

analogy is at the core of his epistemology and theory of cognition. This fact places his thought firmly within the Augustinian-Bonaventurian tradition, of which he is strongly supportive. What is equally important is that the Subtle Doctor presents perhaps the most developed and profound analysis of issues in medieval systematic theology. Although Scotus does not add anything radically new to Bonaventure's treatment of aesthetic issues in systematics, his work can be seen as an elaboration of Bonaventure's statements: the latter appear much more clearly through the prism of Scotus's thought.[58]

The works of Bonaventure most frequently mentioned in studies of his aesthetics are his main scholastic work, *Commentary on the Sentences of Peter Lombard*, as well as his best-known work of a spiritual-meditative orientation, the *Itinerarium*. The present study will focus on these two works, using some other material where necessary. Following von Balthasar's approach in retrieving Bonaventure's theological aesthetics, the analysis will start not with aesthetic or artistic examples used for theological purposes, but with an examination of his systematic theology proper, in order to show if, and how, certain aesthetic issues naturally come out of solving certain theological problems. We ought to remind the reader that in this sort of approach, as von Balthasar demonstrated, the use of the terms 'beauty' or 'aesthetic' is often purely analogical: that is, aesthetic examples properly speaking merely provide analogies to certain phenomena in the divine.

Our analysis of the secondary literature already yielded several themes in Bonaventure's theology that can serve as starting points: the Trinity, the figure of Christ as the second person of the Trinity, and the notions of expression/impression, image and likeness. Notably, von Balthasar often speaks of Bonaventure's "Trinitarian" or "Christological" aesthetics. But what does the Trinity or Christ have to do with aesthetics or beauty? And what exactly is the meaning of the word 'beauty' when medieval theologians refer to the "beauty" of the Trinity or its specific persons? One of the more common uses of the term 'beauty' is when it is applied to the Trinity as a whole, that is, as something one, as one God, or as one essence. As was shown above, both Plotinus and Augustine provide solutions to the

---

58. The text and translation of Scotus's *Parisian Lectures* in what follows is quoted according to Wolter/Bychkov (2008). Some of the material on Duns Scotus's Trinitarian aesthetics appears also in my article "What Does Beauty Have to Do with the Trinity? From Augustine to Duns Scotus," *Franciscan Studies* 66 (2008): 197–212.

problem of how something one and simple can be called beautiful: while beauty in ancient and medieval times is generally understood as something that involves a degree of complexity, unity is either the simplest case of harmony of parts, or a case of harmony with a perceiving organ. The reader also remembers that the divine principle, especially in the Platonic and Neoplatonic traditions, can be viewed aesthetically in the sense of τὸ καλόν, that is, as something of a high degree of excellence, with additional connotations 'awesome' or 'magnificent.' In this sense the divine principle can also be called τὸ καλόν, or "beautiful," insofar as it is one and simple. It is clear, however, that in neither case does this usage concern the Trinity as trinity, and overall this is not even a specifically Christian problem.

The proper way of addressing the issue of the beauty of the Trinity is by speaking of the Trinity as something relational, or of Trinitarian relations. It is precisely here that Duns Scotus's meticulous analysis of Trinitarian relations is of great value in understanding Bonaventure's statements, which lack the degree of elaboration typical of Scotus and therefore are less transparent to a modern reader.[59] The first type of Trinitarian relations examined by Scotus is common relations, such as identity, equality, or likeness, which are common to all three persons insofar as they share the same essence. For example, all three persons are equal or alike in their power, wisdom, and other "pure perfections" that they have by virtue of having the essence.[60] The second type of relations are personal relations, which are specific to each person and are, in fact, the only thing that makes the persons distinct, or, according to Scotus's vocabulary, "constitutes" the persons. In other words, these are the relations of difference. For example, "active generation" is specific to the Father regarding the Son, but not to the Son, who is related to the Father through "passive generation," and so on.

If one looks at the standard understanding of beauty in Antiquity and

---

59. The discussion of relations resulted in such a tremendous effort on the part of Scotus that he is extremely concerned lest the issue at any time be deemed unimportant, which would annul his great work: because in this case, he writes, "all Catholic theologians, who take great pains to lay out the information about relations in common first, and about particular relations afterwards, would have labored in vain, filling their treatises with numerous questions" (*Rep.* I-A, Dist. 25, n. 26).

60. Cf. R. Cross, *Duns Scotus on God* (Aldershot: Ashgate, 2005), 247–48: "Scotus simply maintains that the divine persons are equal in all respects. This equality is explained by the divine essence, which is equally perfect in all divine persons." Cross lists various sorts of such equality, e.g., in greatness, eternity, or power.

the Middle Ages, the most logical locus for Trinitarian beauty seems to be precisely common relations of equality. The association between beauty and the proportion of equality or symmetry is standard in the ancient world and, what is more important for the Christian tradition, in Augustine. He repeats numerous times that equality is the main principle of beauty. Ultimately all other aesthetic principles—not only harmony but also unity, since it is the simplest case of equality—are reducible to equality.[61] God as the Trinity perfectly fits the main criterion of beauty thus understood, because, according to Augustine, "nothing in him is unequal, nothing unlike another."[62] The designation "beauty" in application to the Trinity would, of course, be strictly analogical: it is beautiful *just as* symmetrical or proportionate material objects are beautiful.

Both Bonaventure and Scotus follow Augustine closely in asserting that all persons of the Trinity are equal or alike insofar as they are founded in the one divine essence, that is, by virtue of the common relations of equality and likeness among them. Thus according to Bonaventure,[63] who echoes Augustine's *De vera religione* 30.55, beauty arises both from equality and from inequality. In God, where there is supreme perfection, beauty is found "on account of most perfect equality and likeness between equal things . . . because in each of the equal persons there is the highest perfection of all sorts." It is only in created hierarchies, which possess lower degrees of perfection, that beauty is formed "from some proportional gradation of unequal things." In *Sent.* I, Dist. 31[64] he states that the relations of equality and likeness are certainly relations (that is, something relative), but that it is precisely the identity and unity of the divine essence in all persons (that is, something essential) that founds these relations.

Duns Scotus is in perfect agreement with Bonaventure on this point. Discussing the common relations of identity, equality, and likeness in *Rep.* I-A, Dist. 31, q. 1 n. 1,[65] he presents Augustine's position on what makes the Son equal to the Father:[66] "*He is not equal* as regards being

---

61. See Chapter 7 in general, and specifically cf. *De musica* 6.12.34 or 6.13.18 discussed in that chapter.

62. *De musica* 6.14.44 (ed. Jacobsson, 2002, 92). Fontanier, *La beauté selon saint Augustin*, who uses the term "Trinitarian aesthetics" in application to Augustine (cf. pp. 136ff.), also has no other explanation as to what the beauty of the Trinity consists in except for the idea of equality.

63. *Sent.* II, Dist. 9, a. un., q. 8 resp. (ad 4).

64. *Sent.* I, Dist. 31, p. 1, a. un. q. 2.

65. My italics in quoting medieval texts in this chapter in my translation.

66. *De Trin.* 5, c. 6, n. 7 (CCSL 50, 212).

defined as the Son in relation to the Father [i.e., as regards something relative]; it remains therefore that he is equal as regards something that is defined in relation to itself." "Therefore," Scotus infers, "he is equal as regards the substance." In his reply, Scotus echoes Bonaventure in stating that, on the one hand equality is indeed something relational (n. 17), but on the other hand it is the essence that founds equality in all persons (n. 18). "For the essence," he writes, "as absolutely one in the Father, the Son and the Holy Spirit, is the foundation of equality of any particular person vis-à-vis another one, and therefore any [person] is called equal to another according to substance." Thus, while confirming that the Son *is not equal* to the Father as far as the relation of origin (that is, filiation) is concerned, Scotus stresses that he is equal if one considers the commonality of the essence in the persons.[67]

Scotus brings further precision into the matter by discussing the issue of mutuality of relations. For Scotus, real relations must be mutual, that is, if A is really related to B then B should be also really related to A. Now such mutual relations are either opposing or not. For example, relations of production are mutual but opposing: the relation of active generation in the Father is matched by the opposing relation of passive generation in the Son. In the case of the relation of equality,[68] however, a relation of equality in the Father to the Son is matched by an equal relation in the Son to the Father, that is, the persons are perfectly equal insofar as they are related by a relation of equality.

At this point, however, some problems become noticeable. For example, both Augustine and Scotus, echoing Augustine, mention that the Son "is not equal" to the Father insofar as the personal relations of origin or production are concerned: that is, the relations of difference that constitute individual persons. If the standard medieval criterion of beauty is that of perfect equality, can one speak of the beauty of the Trinity when one considers personal relations, or the relations of difference, where such equality seems to be absent?

According to R. Cross who examines "anti-subordinationist strate-

---

67. He sums up his position in n. 21: "it is clear that the Son *is not equal* to the Father from the point of view of his position in respect to the Father, that is, on account of that relation of origin [i.e., filiation] by which he is related to the Father. . . . However, the Son is equal to the Father on account of [the relation of] equality according to the first mode, [i.e., quantitatively] as well as equal to him under the aspect of substance according to the second mode, because the substance or essence is the foundation of equality in them."

68. *Rep.* I-A, Dist. 31, q. 3, n. 13.

gies" in Scotus,[69] Scotus, like Gregory of Nazianzus before him, thinks that although persons are not equal in terms of quasi-causal[70] relationships of procession, the divinity of each person is equal, and this is sufficient against any accusation of subordinationism (p. 245). Indeed, Scotus routinely holds that the divine persons have all their so-called "pure perfections," such as wisdom or infinity, by virtue of having the essence. Since they all share the same essence, they are equal as regards pure perfections. That in which they are not equal does not constitute a pure perfection and thus a particular person is not in any way deficient by not having a personal property of another person.

So the common medieval position is that essential equality of the persons is sufficient. In other words, the Trinity is already beautiful by virtue of having the essence and being divided into generic persons who are all equal by virtue of sharing the essence. But does this mean that it is not beautiful as far as personal relations are concerned, that is, purely relationally? And what about the beauty of particular individual persons? In fact, can one really speak of true "equality" if in respect to the very characteristics that constitute the persons they are not equal? In any case it seems that if "perfect equality" is required for beauty, any inequality between the persons, even relational, may fail to satisfy this criterion.

Again, Duns Scotus's meticulous analysis of Trinitarian relations is a good indicator of potential "tension points" in the question of equality of the divine persons as far as personal relations of difference are concerned. As, according to Scotus, "besides the [divine] nature nothing more is required for the makeup of the persons except [their] incommunicability," the role of relations of origin is merely to provide this incommunicability.[71] Thus the divine persons are equal in all, up to having the property of incommunicability itself, except for *the way* they are incommunicable.[72] However, why certain relations, for example, paternity, are incommunicable, and some similar ones, for example, spiration, are

---

69. Cross, *Duns Scotus on God*, chap. 18, 245–48.

70. Cross thinks that it is inevitable to think of relations of origin as in some sense causal. In our experience, this can be confirmed by Scotus's discussion of the nature of production, e.g., in *Rep.* I-A, Dist. 26, q. 3, n. 101, where some dependence in the case of generation seems unavoidable (although the official position is that no person is dependent on another): "Indeed, the product does not exist of itself, but it has its existence in an unqualified sense from another."

71. *Rep.* I-A, Dist. 26, q. 1, n. 30.

72. Cf. ibid., q. 2, n. 70.

communicable, has no logical explanation. Scotus simply affirms that this is the nature of these individual properties, or the haecceity of these relations.[73] That is to say, if any inequality or subordination is implied by the difference of relations of origin it would be "just so" by virtue of their individual nature.

The most challenging logical, or even, one could say, phenomenological problem here is how to think what is called the "priority of origin" in the divine persons. The official position that Scotus holds in common with many other contemporaries is that the Father is "prior to the Son by origin and still . . . simultaneous with him by nature."[74] Scotus further clarifies (n. 143) that simultaneity here is precisely one of nature, but not "in attaining some perfection," which can mean no other thing except that the Father is prior to the Son in attaining perfection, or even prior in perfection,[75] despite being equal in nature. Another problem appears when Scotus tries to explain why neither the Son nor the Holy Spirit can produce, as the Father does, after the productive principle has been communicated to them. Apparently, this principle, while remaining productive in the Father, ceases to be productive once it is communicated.[76]

One of the more explicit statements about the inequality of the persons comes when Scotus discusses the question whether the divine essence is of itself determined to subsist first of all in the first person.[77] Depending on the type of primacy, Scotus clarifies, the essence may or may not be determined of itself to subsist first of all in the first person.[78] In the case of the "primacy of immediateness, however" (Dist. 28, q. 3, n. 98), the essence "is [of itself] determined to assume first of all its subsistence in the first person, and not in the second or third." As before, it is the priority of origin of the first person that causes this proclivity in the essence toward the first person, although this proclivity does not

---

73. Cf. ibid., q. 1, n. 30, n. 43; also cf. ibid., q. 3, n. 100.
74. Dist. 26, q. 4, n. 141.
75. Cf. n. 145, where Scotus refers to Aristotle's idea that it is impossible for two species to be equal in perfection: "Therefore, one correlative can very well be prior to the other in perfection and at the same time simultaneous [with it] in nature."
76. Dist. 27, p. II, q. 1, n. 141.
77. Dist. 28, q. 3.
78. E.g., speaking of "the primacy of adequateness of the intensive type" (Dist. 28, q. 3, n. 96) the essence is "primarily" determined to relate to any person, not just the first (i.e., they are all equally primary and any person is adequate for the essence to subsist in, so there is equality in this regard). Also, by the primacy of adequateness of the extensive type the essence is in all three, not only in the first (n. 97).

come from the essence itself. The lack of "symmetry" between persons becomes so apparent that Scotus is forced twice to make a direct statement about the inequality of persons as regards the order of their appearance in the essence. Arguing against Henry of Ghent he states the following (n. 99): "Nor do I understand it, as some do, in the sense *that the three relations primarily rise up* or 'sprout out' *from the essence all equally* and at once."[79] And immediately afterwards he restates the same point differently (n. 100): "From this, it is evident that *they do not have a sound opinion, who say that those three modes,*[80] as it were, *in an equal manner perfect the essence* in its second act, just as the three angles in an equal manner perfect a triangle."[81]

As if the statements about the inequality of the persons resulting from the relations of origin were not enough of a problem, Scotus also consistently introduces the terminology of subordination while conceptualizing the statement that the Father works *through* the Son. He uses two related terms in application to the persons of the Trinity other than the Father—*subauctoritas* and *subauthentice*—which are difficult to interpret except in terms of subordinate authority.[82] Occasionally the term *minoritas* is also used, after Hilary and Peter Lombard, meaning the same thing, that is, some sort of a diminished authority.[83] For example, the issue of the authority of the Father and the "subauthor-

79. Scotus continues immediately after: "In fact, [I understand it in the sense] that, as has been said, [the essence] is of itself determined to subsist [most] immediately in the first relative person through the first property, to which it is determined [to lend subsistence] first: the 'first property' that makes this person 'first.' Now the essence, primarily determined [to lend subsistence] to this [first property], exists and subsists as truly as [it would have] if it were an absolute person. Further, insofar as it [i.e., the essence] has being in the first instant of origin in the first subsistence, it is communicated to the second subsistence in the second instant of origin—and insofar as it has being in both, it is communicated to the third subsistence in the third instant of origin; and this is the order among the persons in respect to having the essence."

80. I.e., relational modes, or ways of having the essence.

81. Scotus continues: "Indeed, it is true that the properties of the three persons are equally in the essence in the sense that none precedes another by nature, for all are simultaneous by nature. However, one [property] does precede another by origin, for the first one produces the second, and the first and the second [together produce] the third, and the producer *qua* producer is prior in origin than the product." Cf. the same idea restated in n. 111.

82. Richard Cross, in a private conversation, suggested the translation "derived authority," but ultimately I do not see how this makes things better: if one is not the direct source of authority, it still suggests a status below (sub-) the true source of authority.

83. Cf. *Rep.* I-A, Dist. 19, p. II, q. 2, n. 95. Scotus explains that the terms *maioritas* and *minoritas* employed by Hilary and quoted by Peter Lombard (*Sent.* I, Dist. 19, c. 4) in application to God mean the same thing as "authority" and "subordinate authority."

ity" or subordinate authority of the Son comes up during the discussion of creation and of "sending" or spirating the Holy Spirit.[84] "It must be said," Scotus sums up, "that although the works of the Trinity may be undivided, they do not, however, operate in the same way regarding authority and subordination (*subauctoritas*)." According to Scotus, it does not follow that "the Father does something that the Son does not do" but it does follow "that the Father does or creates in some way through the Son."[85] The same idea appears in Scotus's discussion of Trinitarian relations in *Rep.* I-A, Dist. 32. Although Scotus presents a hypothetical case, it is clear that he tries to work out the situation with relations of production within the Trinity using an analogy with divine creation, wherein the relation of the Father to the Son is presented as that of authority to subordinate authority.[86]

To sum up, if one looks at the relations that distinguish the persons in the Trinity, the Father appears to be prior to the other persons in origin and in perfection (or at least in attaining perfection) and has superior authority compared to them. Can this really be compatible with the proportion of perfect equality required for beauty? There has been a recent claim that one can speak of the "beauty" of the Trinity precisely because of the "peaceful interplay" of the "relations of difference," that is, something that resembles the Kantian notion of the beautiful as a

84. Cf. *Rep.* I-A, Dist. 14–15, q. 1–2, n. 12: "In this way, therefore, it would be said that 'to be sent,' by virtue of its wording, connotes the effect in the creature, but subordinately (*subauthentice*); and 'to send' connotes the effect with authority or the fecundity of sending, that is, authoritatively (*authentice*). In a similar way it is evident from an analogy: The Father is said to create through the Son, that is, to be creative authoritatively, that is, to bestow action on him; and the Son is said to create subordinately through the Father." Re. spiration see also ibid., Dist. 12, n. 37, 48. The same idea about the subordinate authority of the Son reappears in Dist. 34, q. 3, n. 20.
85. *Rep.* I-A, Dist. 14–15, q. 1–2, n. 13.
86. One could explain the meaning of "subordinate authority" in this case as follows: when the Son acts, this is an action of the Father 'in a remote way,' in the sense that the Son receives everything from the Father and therefore acts 'subordinately.' E.g. when the car brakes it is actually the brake pads that stop the wheel, but it is the driver who acts through the brake pads, so we usually say that the driver brakes. Cf. Dist. 32, q. 2, n. 35: "Whence if 'to elucidate' were formally some sort of acting, in the statement 'the Father speaks by means of the Word' that ablative would function as a reference to someone elucidating actively[, but] subordinately, exactly as [it functions] in the statement 'The Father creates by the agency of the Word' (meaning that the Father and Son are one and the same principle of creating), where 'the Word' [in the ablative] stands for the principle that acts[, except] subordinately. (Now [I stress] this would have been the case with 'speaking' *if* it were acting—but it isn't.)" In his reply to q. 1 (Dist. 32, n. 38) Scotus also mentions "subordinate authority" as regards the position of the Holy Spirit toward the Father and Son as "spirators."

free and harmonious interplay of faculties.[87] However, a careful analysis of the medieval theology of Trinitarian relations shows that in the actual history of the Christian doctrine, this understanding must be qualified at best. Thus the only type of relation that features some sort of even mutuality is a common relation, such as the relations of equality, likeness, or identity that pertain equally to all persons. However, these are not "relations of difference." At the same time, the proper relations of difference, that is, personal relations, hardly introduce any equality that would be sufficient for the appellation "beauty."

The Beauty of Christ

The examination of Bonaventure's and Scotus's Trinitarian doctrines called into question the appellation 'beauty' in respect to the Trinity beyond its common relations. However, it is well known that the appellation 'beauty' in the history of Western Christianity does go beyond common relations in the Trinity, or beyond the Trinity qua one common divine essence. It is sometimes, notably in Bonaventure, used in application to the second person of the Trinity, the Son. In what sense can the Son be viewed as "beauty"? The investigation of this issue will lead us to examine the second claim put forward in the critical literature on Bonaventure's aesthetics, namely, that it is "Christological" in nature. At the same time it will allow us, by examining aesthetic interpretations of one of the persons of the Trinity, to make an even tighter connection between aesthetics and the internal structure of the Trinity than the one allowed by a common relation of equality.

The Western medieval tradition of viewing the Son as beauty goes back to Augustine, who in *De Trinitate* 6.10.11[88] interprets a brief and unclear passage from Hilary. The passage from Hilary, *De Trinitate* 2.1,[89] reads as follows: "in the Father, the Son, and the Holy Spirit there is infinity in the eternal, beautiful form *(species)* in the image, and use in the gift." Augustine explains that the expression "beautiful form *(species)*[90] in the image" refers to the second person of the Trinity. He continues:

---

87. Cf. the section on the Trinity in D. B. Hart, *The Beauty of the Infinite: The Aesthetics of Christian Truth* (Grand Rapids, Mich./Cambridge: W. B. Eerdmans, 2003).
88. CCSL 50, 241.
89. CCSL 62, 38.
90. The *Oxford Latin Dictionary* gives the following definitions of the term *species* crucial to the present discussion: (1) something presented to view, spectacle, sight; (2) look, glance;

For an image (*imago*), if it expresses perfectly that of which it is an image, is itself equated to [its prototype], not [the prototype] to its image. Now in that [statement about] the Image he used the name *species*, I believe, on account of beauty (*propter pulchritudinem*), [for in this Image, i.e., in Christ as the Image] there is already great harmony, and equality of the first rank, and likeness of the first degree, disagreeing in no respect, and in no manner unequal, and in no part dissimilar, but continually corresponding to him of whom it is the Image.

It is clear that Augustine does not speak of the beauty of the relation of equality as common to all three persons and based on the commonality of the essence. Beauty acts here as a personal property of the Son that is specific to the Son as a person. It is also clear why Augustine associates the Son with beauty. The Son is a perfectly adequate image of the Father that is absolutely equal to him, and, as we remember, equality, proportionality, and symmetry are standard criteria of beauty for Augustine. What is different, then, is the origin of equality in this case. While equality as a common relation is based on the commonality of essence in all three persons, equality in the Son as something specific to this person is based on his ability to reflect, image, represent or express the Father adequately. The association between, on the one hand the Son as image, and on the other hand beauty, is also furthered by the general proximity between the concepts 'beauty' and 'shape' or 'form,' although this point does not receive proper elaboration in Augustine.[91]

Before turning to Bonaventure's own interpretation of Christ as beauty, it would be appropriate to present a brief history of the development of this Augustinian notion in the literature immediately preceding or surrounding Bonaventure. The incentive for the thirteenth- and fourteenth-century authors to discuss this passage from Augustine's *De*

---

(3) visual appearance, aspect; [pregn.] good appearance, beauty, attractiveness; (4) splendor, pomp, show.

91. Fontanier (*La beauté selon saint Augustin*) in his brief analysis of beauty in relation to the Trinitarian "God structure" in Augustine (cf. p. 136ff., where he also mentions *De Trin.* 6.10.11) makes a number of comments that confirm both the importance of the notion of equality in the specifically Christian Trinitarian aesthetics and the observation we made in Chapter 7 about why proportion in general is so important for Augustine as a criterion of beauty (as contrasted with Plotinus). According to Fontanier, for Augustine, God is not "beyond" beauty as he is for Plotinus and some Platonizing Eastern Fathers such as pseudo-Dionysius, but *is* beauty (cf. p. 144). For Augustine, beauty is not a metaphysical trope, but what God is, his very life. It is perhaps for this reason that Augustine is reluctant to abandon proportion, in particular that of equality, as the fundamental criterion of beauty. God is not an indefinite transcendent principle: like beauty, the proportion of equality is at the center of God's life. Thus God is beautiful precisely as something relational, as a trinity.

Trinitate is provided by Peter Lombard, who uses it in his collection of *Sentences*.[92] The schoolmen in this connection speak of the "appropriation" of certain qualities for specific divine persons, and appropriating the quality of 'beauty' or 'beautiful form' *(species)* for the Son becomes commonplace. The issue of Christ's *species*, synonymous with 'beauty' *(pulchritudo)*, appears already in the early thirteenth-century *Summa aurea* of William of Auxerre.[93] According to him, certain qualities that pertain to Christ, such as splendor and brightness, equally pertain to beauty or *species*; hence one can speak of appropriating the latter quality for Christ. In the Dominican tradition the passage is discussed, in the context of speaking of beauty, by Albert the Great and his two students Ulrich of Strassburg and Thomas Aquinas.[94] Albert refers to Augustine's *De Trin.* 6.10.11 while discussing beauty in his Commentary on pseudo-Dionysius's *Divine Names* 4.7.[95] He takes the synonymity between beauty and *species* for granted and says that according to Augustine the Son possesses the "highest degree of beauty." A more detailed discussion of the issue of *species*-beauty as a property of the Son is contained in his *Commentary on the Sentences*.[96] First, Albert raises objections against identifying *species* with beauty, but in his response to the objections he ultimately agrees with Augustine's opinion that *species* qua property of the Son must be understood to mean "beauty," for the reason that he receives the form of the Father most adequately or fittingly.

Thomas Aquinas uses Augustine's *De Trin.* 6.10.11 in his *Summa theologiae* I, qu. 39, a. 8 in the context of attributing the property 'beauty' specifically to the Son, and makes the following comment, quoted by almost all who wrote on "medieval aesthetics":

---

92. *Sent.* I, Dist. 31.2 (SB 4, 225–26). The following edition was used: Petrus Lombardus, *Sententiae in IV libris distinctae*, 2 vols., Spicilegium Bonaventurianum 4–5 (Grottaferrata/Rome: Collegium S. Bonaventurae, 1971, 1981).

93. *Summa aurea* I, tr. 8, c. 8, qu. 4 (SB 16, 175). The following edition was used: Guillelmus Altissiodorensis, *Summa aurea, libri 1–4*, Spicilegium Bonaventurianum 16–19, edited by J. Ribaillier (Paris/Rome: Centre National de la Recherche Scientifique/Collegium S. Bonaventurae, 1980, 1982, 1985, 1986).

94. Ulrich quotes Augustine, *De Trin.* 6.10.11 in his chapter *De pulchro: De Summo Bono* II, tr. 3, c. 4.1 and 4.5, Corpus Philosophorum Teutonicorum Medii Aevi 1/2, edited by A. de Libera (Hamburg: Felix Meiner, 1987), 55, 57.

95. *Super Dionysium De Divinis Nominibus*, vol. 37/1 of *Opera omnia*, edited by P. Simon, 183 (Münster: Aschendorff, 1972).

96. *Sent.* I, Dist. 31, a. 6. The following edition will be used: Albertus Magnus, *Commentarii in I Sententiarum (Dist. XXVI–XLVIII)*, vol. 26 of *Opera omnia*, edited by S. Borgnet (Paris: L. Vivès, 1893).

However, *species* or 'beauty' is alike to the [personal] properties of the Son. Indeed, three things are required for beauty: first, integrity or perfection . . . ; then, proper proportion or harmony; and also clarity. . . . As for the first, it is alike to the properties of the Son insofar as the Son has in himself truly and perfectly his Father's nature. . . . As for the second, it coincides with the properties of the Son insofar as he is the express image of the Father. . . . Finally, as for the third, it coincides with the properties of the Son insofar as he is the Word, "which is the light and splendor of the intellect."

Aquinas makes an almost identical statement on the issue earlier, in his *Commentary on the Sentences*, Bk. I, Dist. 31, which proves that the text in the *Summa* develops out of the initial discussion of Peter Lombard's *Sentences*.[97] Just as his teacher Albert did, Aquinas expressly states in his *Commentary on the Sentences* that in this case he understands *species* as identical with beauty (p. 251B), and he also agrees with Augustine's attribution of beauty to the Son. The reasons for such attribution described in *S.Th.* I, qu. 39, a. 8 quoted above—which are identical to the reasons stated in Aquinas's *Commentary on the Sentences*—can be summarized as follows. The Son is the "image and likeness" of the Father. His attribute *species*, which is synonymous with beauty, reflects adequately all aspects of the Father-Son relationship, and therefore beauty is a suitable analogy for the latter. Aquinas lists three such aspects of the Father-Son relationship that are most adequately illustrated with the help of the analogy of beauty, whose three characteristic qualities, according to Aquinas, are perfection, proportion, and luminosity or conspicuousness. Just exactly how the properties of the Father-Son relationship correspond to these three characteristics of beauty is explained in the following way. First, the Son possesses the Father's nature perfectly; moreover, the Son is an adequate or proportionate image of the Father; finally, the Son is the Word, which implies clarity.

However, in general the Dominicans are not as interested in the idea of Christ-beauty as the Franciscans, for example, Alexander of Hales and the Franciscan *Summa* ascribed to him (the so-called *Summa Halensis*, henceforth S.H.).[98] Alexander discusses Augustine's *De Trin.* 6.10.11 and

---

97. *Sent.* I, Dist. 31, qu. 2, a. 1 (p. 251B); the following edition will be used: Thomas Aquinas, *Commentum in quatuor libros Sententiarum, libri 1–2*, vol. 6 of *Opera omnia* (Parma: P. Fiaccadori, 1856). See the full text of this passage in O. Bychkov, "A Propos of Medieval Aesthetics," 82.

98. More on these two works and the relationship between them see in O. Bychkov, "A Propos of Medieval Aesthetics," chap. 1. The following editions were used: Alexander de Hales, *Summa theologica, libri I–III*, 4 vols. (Quaracchi: Collegium S. Bonaventurae, 1924, 1928, 1930,

identifies *species* in this context with beauty as early as in *Sent*. I, Dist. 31.[99] The more recent *Summa Halensis* also refers, on several occasions, to the identity between *species* and beauty in the context of the appropriation of this quality to the Son.[100] This work is also important because it served as a source of discussions of aesthetic topics for both the Franciscan and the Dominican traditions. Notably, a key passage in Bonaventure's *Commentary on the Sentences* that is discussed below was definitely influenced by a parallel passage from the *Summa Halensis*.[101]

However, in the Franciscan tradition the Augustinian association between the Son and the notion 'beautiful form' or *species* is best developed by Bonaventure.[102] In *Sent*. I, Dist. 27 Bonaventure lists several properties—appropriate for the Son as the Word—that are crucial to his discussion of the Son as beauty. The concept of "cognition" that is included in the concept of the 'word' is closely followed by "conception of likeness" and "expression" or "manifestation of something," which can be summed up by one notion of "express likeness."[103] Hence the concept of "knowledge" is tightly linked to the notions of intuiting and generating an image or likeness, which is also expressly manifested.[104] Bonaventure clearly presents equality and likeness in the Son—which make the appropriation of beauty possible—as personal, and not common or mutual qualities. Thus in Dist. 31 he distinguishes between the two senses of "equal" and "like" in the Trinity:[105] first, "insofar as they imply agreement in quantity or quality," and second, "insofar as they imply, over and above agreement, perfect imitation or expression and manifestation." In the first sense, just as with Scotus's common relations, 'likeness' and 'equality' are paired relations, so there are always two equal relations, that is, of A to B and of B to A. In this sense, equality and likeness belong to all persons. "In the second sense," Bonaventure continues, "'like'

1948); idem, *Glossa in quatuor libros Sententiarum, libri 1–4*, Bibliotheca Franciscana scholastica Medii Aevi 12–15 (Quaracchi/Florence: Collegium S. Bonaventurae, 1951, 1952, 1954, 1957).

99. *Glossa in quatuor libros Sententiarum*, vol. 12, 306.

100. Cf. *S.H.* II, pars II, inq. 1, tr. 2, qu. 3, c. 4 (vol. 3, 53); *S.H.* I, pars II, inq. 2, tr. 2, sect. 2, qu. 1 (vol. 1, 641). Both passages are quoted in O. Bychkov, "A Propos of Medieval Aesthetics," chap. 2.

101. The parallel passages are Bonaventure, *Sent*. I, Dist. 31, pars 2, a. 1, qu. 3 (vol. 1, 432–33) and *S.H.* I, pars II, inq. 2, tr. 2, sect. 2, qu. 1 (vol. 1, 641), both quoted in O. Bychkov, "A Propos of Medieval Aesthetics," 85.

102. The following edition will be used: Bonaventura, *Libri IV Sententiarum*, vols. 1–4 of *Opera theologica selecta* (Quaracchi/Florence: Collegium S. Bonaventurae, 1934, 1938, 1941, 1949).

103. *Sent*. I, Dist. 27, p. II, a. un., q. 3, resp.   104. Ibid.

105. *Sent*. I, Dist. 31, p. I, a. un. q. 3, resp.

and 'equal' add to this the [personal] notion of origin: whence 'equal' is used in the sense of 'equated' or 'made adequate' and 'like' in the sense of 'likened.' In this sense it is only appropriate to someone who is 'from another,'" or to the Son. In this second sense, the Father is not a likeness of the Son through imitation, nor is he equated to the Son through procession from someone else, but he equates the Son to himself.[106]

Duns Scotus adds nothing radically different to Bonaventure's view of beauty as a personal property of the Son, but it is significant that this meticulous mind maintains the same view without finding it problematic. Thus he attributes beauty to the Son already in *Rep.* I-A, Dist. 3, q. 3, speaking of the vestiges of the Trinity in creatures.[107] His main discussion of Hilary's and Augustine's attribution of "beautiful form" to the Son is in *Rep.* I-A, Dist. 34, q. 3. First of all, he states that in order for certain properties such as 'beauty' to be ascribed to specific persons, there should be some "specific agreement between [such] essential [properties] and the proper characteristic of some person" (n. 16). This means that Scotus, just as Bonaventure does, speaks of beauty as the Son's personal property: there must be some kinship between beauty and his personal traits.[108] Scotus further (n. 17) comments specifically on Hilary's attribution of beauty:

106. Further in Dist. 31, p. II, a. 1, q. 1, resp., discussing Hilary's scheme of appropriation, Bonaventure again affirms that "as far as God is concerned 'image' is predicated on account of expression or manifestation according to the identity of nature," and therefore 'image' qua uncreated is used in a personal or relational sense, i.e., is not grounded on the commonality of essence in the persons, for "it signifies procession" and procession due to the unity of nature is "only of a person." "So," Bonaventure concludes, "preserving the proper way of speaking, 'image' is predicated according to personal relation." 'Image' in Bonaventure has a range of meanings similar to that of 'equality' and 'likeness': is consists "in representing something not only in its substance, but also in its formal aspect (*distinctione*) and the arrangement of its elements" (*Sent.* I, Dist. 31, pars 2, a. 1, q. 1, arg. 4), and is "that which expresses and imitates the other" (ibid., resp.). In addition, the image is an "express (*expressa*) likeness, and in respect to divine things—most expressed likeness" (ibid., q. 2, arg. c), *expressa* here meaning also "visible" and "manifest."

107. Scotus reacts to Augustine's passage from *De Trinitate* 6.10.12, where Augustine says that "every created thing has number, form, and order, which are the primary origins of beauty" (n. 74). Scotus replies (n. 80) regarding this attribution of "number, beauty/shapeliness (*species*), and order": "The first two represent as a likeness, and the third as a correspondence. Number and unity can be attributed to the Father, beauty to the Son, because beauty and shapeliness come from a combination of many things that agree with one another, as is evident in bodies, and it cannot be as conveniently attributed to the Father as to the Son, who is primarily the beauty of the Father."

108. Scotus later (n. 18) discusses another property ascribed to the Son by Augustine in *De doctr. Christ.*, namely, equality, and views it this time not as a common property but as a personal property "by appropriation"—again, in agreement with Bonaventure.

Beautiful form, on the other hand, is ascribed to the Word or the Son, because it is beauty that requires integrity, due proportion, and some manifestation or disclosure of some power (and this third property harmonizes with the proper characteristic 'word'). Now the Father does not have the essence in such a way that it is measured by someone. The Son, in his turn, receives the divine essence from the Father as a whole, or integrally. Similarly, in order to be equal to the Father, he receives the essence according to some adequate and due proportion. Finally, because he is the Son and Word of the Father, he is [something] disclosing, and is like some light and disclosure. And it is in this way that Augustine in Bk. VI of *The Trinity*, chapter 9 accepts [these ascribed properties] from Hilary.

It is remarkable that Scotus's three criteria of beauty (integrity, proportion, manifestation) are identical to those of Aquinas (see above), which means that he is essentially in agreement with the Dominican here, and that the theory of the Son as beauty simply represents a widely accepted point of view. It appears, then, that the beauty of "equality" that belongs to the Son—for example, as the image of the Father—has nothing to do with equality as a common relation that is responsible for the beauty of the Trinity as a whole. This is a separate, third sense in which one can speak of beauty within the Trinity as specifically belonging to the Son.

The passage that is perhaps most important for understanding the medieval identification of the Son with beauty is in Bonaventure's *Commentary on the Sentences*, Bk. I, Dist. 31, p. II, a. 1, q. 3, where he discusses at length Hilary's attribution of the notion 'form-beauty' to the Son.[109] One of the obvious objections to this attribution[110] is that the term *species* in its meaning 'form' cannot be specifically attributed to anything, and as 'beauty' it is more appropriate for the Father who is the source and prototype of all beauty.[111] Bonaventure, however, defends the view that Hilary attributes 'beauty' to the Son as his personal property.

Answering Objection 5, he states that there are two reasons for ascribing "perfect beauty" to the Son. First, the Son is beauty "because

---

109. Von Balthasar quotes this text in *GL2* 298–99 and discusses the notion *species* and its meanings, including cognitive. This is of course not the only context where Bonaventure speaks of the appropriation of beauty to the Son, which he inherits from the tradition described above. E.g., in *GL2* 296–98 von Balthasar lists a number of other contexts: not only *Sent.* I, Dist. 31 discussed below, but also passages from the *Hexaemeron* and *De triplici via*.

110. Bonaventure's Objection 2.

111. One could say that the Father is 'beauty' in the sense of τὸ καλόν, rather than the formal type of beauty which consists in proportion, equality, etc.

he is a perfect [that is, precise and excellent] and express likeness" and "therefore he is beautiful in relation to him whom he expresses," that is, the Father. Bonaventure must be taking 'beauty' here in the sense of evaluation, as 'excellence': this is a typical pre-modern understanding implicit in both the Greek καλόν and the Latin *pulcher*, but not always in the English 'beautiful.' This observation is confirmed when he answers Objections 2–4 by providing an example of a picture that is called "beautiful" when it presents a good likeness. According to Bonaventure's medieval understanding of 'beauty,' the image is beautiful only when it perfectly expresses the prototype, and not necessarily a beautiful one. (Of course, beauty here can also be implied from the fact that a perfect image is adequate or *equal* to the prototype: another standard criterion of beauty in the Middle Ages.) Thus whatever presents the most perfect expression—one that is most adequate, or equal—possesses the highest beauty.[112] In this case equality (in the sense of presenting an adequate or perfect likeness) can be seen as a personal property of the Son who " . . . in relation to the Father . . . possesses the beauty of equality, because he expresses him perfectly, as a 'beautiful' [that is, excellent] image . . . " (ad 5).

The Son is also "perfect beauty" insofar as he is the exemplar and principle of all, or is the *cause of beauty* in all. One must stress that the Son is beauty not as the 'cause of all,' which would rather be the Father or the Trinity as a whole, but precisely as the principle of imaging and shaping, and therefore form and beauty, in all created things. In other words, he "has beauty in relation to all beauty modeled on the exemplar" (ad 5). Hilary's appropriation highlights the fundamental differences between the persons that come to light if one considers their relation to procession. Thus it is only the Son whose procession has a formal aspect that can be expressed by the terms *species* and likeness (cf. q. 2, resp.; cf. q. 3, ad 5).[113] The initial objection that the principle

---

112. "One can find a twofold principle of beauty there. . . . This is clear because an image is called beautiful when it is well proportioned [a common understanding—O. B.], and it is also called beautiful when it represents well him of whom it is the image [the pre-modern understanding—O. B.]. As for considering the latter a separate principle of beauty, this is clear because it can exist without the other one: it is in this sense that an image of the Devil is called beautiful [i.e., excellent—O. B.] when it represents well the repulsiveness of the Devil, in which case it is [actually formally] repulsive."

113. The Father does not proceed, and therefore his personal attribute (Hilary's "eternity") is the absence of beginning (*Sent.* I, Dist. 31, p. II, a. 1, q. 3, resp.) and the Holy Spirit proceeds by way of will and love (q. 3, ad 1). Bonaventure explains how the Son's procession acquires

'form' as such is not limited to the Son is thus addressed: the Son is form and beauty quintessentially, as its first instance and exemplar. Von Balthasar provides a similar assessment using the notion "expression" instead (which in Bonaventure is closely linked to the notions form, image, and likeness). He says that the Son is the quintessential principle of expression, "God as he is in being expressed" (GL2 289), "God as expression," or "*the* expression universally" (GL2 290).[114]

Just how the Son can be viewed as such a formal exemplar for all things must be further clarified. According to Bonaventure, insofar as the Son is the *species*, or the principle of form, likeness, and expression in things, he is also the principle of cognition, since cognition essentially happens through distinguishing and recognizing (copying or expressing) the form of things, be it their physical shape or concept: "by virtue of having the principle of perfect likeness he possesses the principle of cognition."[115] This idea further reinforces the connection between the Son and creatures; in relation to them he serves as the principle of knowledge (by providing something structural, or formal, which can be conceptualized, that is, identified as a pattern or form) as well as of their form (ontologically speaking, as a result of creation). The two aspects of *species* or beauty—that of "manifest likeness" and that of "cognition"—are interrelated. Since the Son "has in himself the principle of express or manifest likeness, therefore he also has the one of cognition, for express likeness is the principle of knowing."[116] Thus according to Bonaventure the Son-*species* is, on the one hand, the quintessential exemplar or principle of form and beauty for everything,[117] and

---

characteristics of form in the following way: as contrasted with the Holy Spirit, who proceeds through will and love, the Son proceeds "by way of nature" and therefore "by way of perfect and express likeness ... for nature produces something like and equal to itself" (q. 3, ad 5).

114. According to von Balthasar, God himself has expressive nature which underlies the ability of the world (God's creation) to express God: expression as the foundation of the Trinity "is the root for every outward self-expression of God" and any expression in the world (GL2 284). Since any possible copies are imperfect expressions, except for Christ who is a perfect image and likeness, the expressive nature of God can only be manifested through Christ, and all should be brought into relation with him as the principle of expression and the expressive aspect in the Trinity (GL2 283). Von Balthasar generalizes (GL2 290): "the Son, by being the expression of the Father, is at the same time *the* expression universally, i.e., the expression of everything.... The Son is therefore not only the archetype, of which images are made in the world: he is God as expression."

115. *Sent.* I, Dist. 31, p. II, a. 1, q. 3, ad 5.

116. Ibid.

117. "And since he contains in himself the principle and exemplar of all things in accor-

on the other hand, "he contains the principle of knowing" all by virtue of possessing the "blueprints" and schemata (formal layout) of things.[118]

Question Two in Bonaventure's *Disputed Questions on the Knowledge of Christ*[119] further clarifies the connection between cognition and likeness in the context of the discussion of divine knowledge.[120] According to Bonaventure, God knows things through "likenesses," which are understood as eternal ideas-exemplars, or "exemplary" likenesses (*exemplativa*). "Eternal reasons" or exemplary likenesses are capable of representing and expressing things most perfectly and are essentially the same as God himself (pp. 8–9). Following pseudo-Dionysius and Augustine, Bonaventure asserts that these eternal reasons are not the true essences of things, because the essence of God is different from the essences of things. Therefore, they must be "exemplary forms" and therefore "representative likenesses of things." Indeed, "they are the principles of cognition, because cognition, by the very fact of being cognition, implies likening or assimilation between the knower and the known, as well as [the principle of] representation (*expressio*)" (p. 8). There is also another type of likeness, the likeness of a copy (*imitativa*). This latter likeness causes the knowledge of things in us (p. 9).

In *Sent.* I, Dist. 35, a. un., q. 1, ad 3, Bonaventure makes an interesting remark about the divine idea as an archetypal exemplar or ideal likeness which, paradoxically, expresses the thing better than the thing itself:

There is another type of likeness, which is the expressive truth itself of an object of cognition, and it is likeness precisely by virtue of being truth. Now this likeness expresses the thing better than the thing itself could express itself, because this very thing receives its principle of expression precisely from that [original likeness]. Now cognition according to this [likeness] is more perfect, and it is by this [sort of likeness] that God knows.

---

dance with perfect likeness and proportion (*ratio*), therefore he also contains the principle of perfect beauty (*pulchritudo*)" (ibid.).

118. The Son "in relation to the [created] things ... possesses all their 'reasons'" (ibid.).

119. *Quaestiones disputatae de scientia Christi*, quoted according to the Quaracchi edition (1882–), vol. 5.

120. Bonaventure is not the only one to associate the notion *species* with both cognition and Christ—for example, cf. Albert the Great, *De bono*, tr. I, q. 2, a. 3: "If ... *species* pertains to cognition, then it seems to pertain rather to the Son than to the Father" (Albertus Magnus, *De bono*, vol. 28 of *Opera omnia*, edited by H. Kühle, 27.76–78 [Münster: Aschendorff, 1951]); "However, insofar as it exhibits *species*, by means of which a thing is known, it refers to the Son" (p. 27.88–90).

At this point Bonaventure speaks of divine ideas, not of *species Christi*. However, the passage from the *Disputed Questions* quoted above shows that the discussion of the divine ideas in Dist. 35 and the discussion of *species* as related to cognition in Dist. 31 can be taken as part of the same context: both issues are part of Bonaventure's discussion of the question of divine cognition or knowledge. The passage from Dist. 35, then, gives a clearer idea of how the Son can serve as the "perfect form and beauty" for the created things, precisely in this "better-than-the-thing-itself" status. The passage also explains the sense in which the Son can be seen as the perfect principle of cognition of things.

Von Balthasar notices the passage from Dist. 35 in GL2 294 and characterizes it as a sign of a "very strong downwards-tending analogy" in Bonaventure.[121] W. Treitler, drawing on A. Gerken's 1963 dissertation on Bonaventure, dubs this "downward-tending analogy" noticed by von Balthasar in Bonaventure "catalogy" (*Katalogie*),[122] an extremely apt term that describes the downward movement extending from God qua the exemplary form to creatures as its copies. The Son, then, is a perfect image and likeness of the Father properly speaking, and he is a perfect image as regards the rest of the reality in the sense of catalogy. Speaking of von Balthasar's theological method employed in his theological aesthetics, catalogy would adequately describe what he elsewhere calls the "theological *a priori*" (see above): the fact that our ability to perceive the form (or the "analogy" of form) is determined "catalogically" by the existence of the quintessential or exemplary form in God (cf. Treitler, GW 177–78). In other words, once again, an analogical movement from the worldly beauty will not result in a specifically Christian aesthetics unless it is informed by this catalogy from Christ-beauty.

The second person of the Trinity, then, Bonaventure summarizes, is unique in being connected to the Father through the principle of perfect likeness, and to the created world through the principle of imaging, form, and expression. This double connection,[123] which is specific

---

121. "In contrast to the scarcely considered upwards-tending *analogia entis*, there is a very strong downwards-tending analogy: the eternal Word of expression knows better and says better what each thing wants to say than the thing itself knows. And the creature receives its power to speak, to set it on its path, namely the *species*, which it emits from itself so that it may be grasped and understood in the sense-perception or intellect of another."

122. W. Treitler, "Wahre Grundlagen authentischer Theologie," GW 176–77.

123. Von Balthasar in GL2 298 notices this double connection: "he gives expression to the Father who is the archetype, and himself becomes an expressive archetype in relation to the world." Playing on the double meaning of *species* in Bonaventure (form qua conceptualization-

to this person, Bonaventure contends, is most adequately expressed by the term 'beauty,' which encompasses all the above meanings:

> [the Son] (1) in relation to the Father has the beauty of equality, because he expresses him in a perfect way, as a perfect image, and (2) in relation to things contains all their principles ... it is therefore clear that the principle of all beauty (*pulchritudo*) is rightly found to be contained in the Son. Thus insofar as the Son proceeds naturally, he possesses the principle of perfect and manifest likeness; and insofar as he possesses the principle of perfect likeness, he possesses the principle of cognition; and [finally] by virtue of both [likeness and cognition] he possesses the principle of beauty. For because the term *species* implies (1) likeness and implies (2) the principle of knowing, it also implies beauty.[124]

Another concise passage that describes the Son's double role as the principle of likeness is contained in *Sent.* I, Dist. 27, p. II, a. un., q. 2, resp., which adds an interesting detail:

> and it is only then that the word is uttered or generated when a likeness or image of some object of knowledge is conceived in the mind; and the word refers to the same thing as this conceived likeness.... Now because in God the power of conception conceives a likeness that embraces all in one act of intuition or seeing, he conceives or generates a unique Word, which is a likeness of the Father in the sense of imitation, and a likeness of the created things in the sense of serving as an exemplar for them, as well as providing operational power, and so *it has the position of an intermediary*.... Thus it is clear that the divine Word implies (1) a relation to the Father, from whom it is generated, who speaks it forth as most alike to himself in every way. It also implies (2) a relation to creatures by way of providing a formational exemplar as well as the power to put it into operation. (my italics)

The Son as the universal principle of form, likeness, and imaging thus plays the role of an "intermediary." This aspect of the second person of the Trinity makes it typologically akin to the modern notion of the aesthetic. (As the reader remembers, the revelatory role of the aesthetic in modern thought gives it a mediating role between the realms of the immanent and the transcendent.) Beauty-form (and therefore, one can imply, Christ precisely as beauty-form), is perfectly positioned to fulfill such a mediating role: in addition to its revelatory capacity, according to Bonaventure it has

---

knowledge and form qua beauty) in *GL2* 291, he states that the position of the Son is not only "the place of truth but also the place of beauty."

124. *Sent.* I, Dist. 31, p. II, a. 1, q. 3, ad 5.

the capacity of preserving its formal characteristics virtually intact during its transition between the prototype and the image.[125]

Despite the intensity of Bonaventure's discussion of the difficult notion *species Christi* in his *Commentary on the Sentences*, the inclusion of this discussion in thirteenth-century scholastic writings is necessitated simply by Peter Lombard's initial selection. We will now turn to a different type of writing practiced by the Franciscan, which can be broadly described as "monastic" or "contemplative"; we turn in particular to his work *Itinerarium mentis in Deum*, with occasional references to other works.[126] These writings were not directly dependent on the discussions of the Schools and can provide a more genuine evidence of the importance of this notion for Bonaventure.

The *Itinerarium* goes back to the "monastic" tradition of writing characteristic of the Victorines in the twelfth century, but is directly influenced by Augustine[127] and pseudo-Dionysius. This is apparent from direct quotations, the general similarity of the argument and examples, a certain type of phrasing and the (Neo)Platonic idea of the ascent toward the divine principle. (Despite these numerous influences, Bonaventure still maintains the specifically Christian nature of his aesthetics.) Although Bonaventure's general description of the ascent through the things of this world to God is rather traditional, the way it is phrased shows a deeper interest in sensible and aesthetic experience. Things are not merely symbols or signs of the divine—a traditional statement in Christian theology—but also some sensible presentations of the unpresentable God comparable to aesthetic objects in modern philosophy:

> all the created things of this sensible world lead the spirit of a contemplative and wise person towards eternal God, for the reason that they are the shad-

---

125. Cf. *Sent*. I, Dist. 31, pars 2, a. 1, q. 3, ad 2–4 (a passage that clearly echoes the iconoclastic disputes of the Eastern Church, in particular the words of St. Basil used to defend the icons): "Therefore, to the objection that the beauty of the image refers back to [the beauty of] its prototype one must reply that this is true. However, honor and beauty refer back in different ways. Indeed, the honor given to the image or representation refers back to its prototype in such a way that this honor does not of itself belong to that very [image]. A clear example of this is when one venerates an icon of St. Nicholas. However, beauty refers back to its prototype in such a way that beauty is no less in the image, and not only in that of which it is the image."

126. My translations from Bonaventure's *Itinerarium mentis in Deum* are based on the Quaracchi edition (1882–), vol. 5. References to individual chapters will be given in brackets.

127. Especially significant is the role of the main argument of Augustine's *De lib. arb.* 2, chaps. 3–6 which describes the movement from the senses to aesthetic judgment, but also *De musica* 6 and *De vera rel.*

ows, echoes, and pictures . . . of this first principle . . . ; they are vestiges, representations and displays offered to us for the purpose of perceiving God, as well as signs given from above; these things, I would say, are exemplars, or rather copies of exemplars, offered to the minds—until this point ignorant and submerged in the sensible—*in order that they, through the sensible which they see, might be transferred to the intelligible,* which they see not, in the same way as one is transferred to the signified through signs or signifiers. (*Itinerarium* 2.11; my italics)

Bonaventure starts by outlining the six steps of the ascent (the symbolism taken from the six wings of the seraph in Francis's vision) that correspond to the six powers of the soul: senses, imagination, reason, intellect, intelligence, and mental apex, or the spark of conscience (1.6).[128] The formal aspects of created reality that Augustine dubs "manner, form (*species*), and order"—the standard locus of beauty in the Middle Ages—belong to the sensible stage of this journey of ascent (1.11). A particularly important statement is that beauty is among the phenomena (together with order) that provide the clearest evidence of the divine power, wisdom and goodness in the world:

Indeed, the beauty of things clearly (*evidenter*) proclaims these three [divine qualities] through the variety of lights, shapes, and colors in simple, mixed, and compound bodies, e.g., in celestial bodies and minerals, as well as in stones and metals, plants and animals (1.14) [to such an extent that] he who is not illumined (*illustratur*) by such powerful splendors of created things is blind. (1.15)

On must note that, in the tradition of ancient thought that is later retrieved by modern aesthetics and subsequently by von Balthasar, 'beauty' for Bonaventure describes the capacity of reality to manifest and reveal the beyond, which one is expected to see immediately.

Of key importance is chapter 2 of the *Itinerarium*[129] where Bonaventure, detailing the process of our ascent, draws an analogy between the mechanism of sense perception and the operation of Christ (called "our ladder" in 1.3) as the second person of the Trinity through the principles of "form-beauty" (*species*) and "likeness." The sensible world enters the

---

128. Regarding Bonaventure's understanding of the term "spark of conscience" (*synderesis scintilla*) see *Sent.* II, Dist. 39, a. 2, q. 1 (vol. 2, 909–11).
129. Von Balthasar calls this chapter "Bonaventure's principal aesthetic text" (GL2 340). He says, "Bonaventure's chief concern" here is "to make this whole texture of the aesthetic sense-perceptions transparent to the theological and trinitarian" (GL2 341).

human soul "through perception," and first of all exterior sensible qualities enter through the five senses. Bonaventure provides a detailed description of sense objects entering our senses:

> They enter, I should say, not substantially, but through their likenesses, first generated in the medium, and after the medium in the organ, and after the exterior organ in the interior organ, from which they proceed into the apprehending faculty; and thus the generation of shape (*species*) in the medium, and after the medium in the organ, and the change in the apprehending faculty under its influence result in an apprehension or perception of all exterior things by the soul.[130] (2.4)

What is being transmitted here across the boundary between the object and the sense faculty is a certain formal aspect of a thing, or its *species*. (The reader already knows from the discussion of Bonaventure's *Commentary on the Sentences* that "form-beauty" is transmitted between entities almost intact.) One cannot help projecting, given what we have learned from Bonaventure's *Sent.* I, Dist. 31, that Christ as the quintessence and exemplar of the principle of *species* is bound to hold a central position in this scheme.

The next stage in the process of the apprehension of the world is pleasure (*oblectatio*) which follows the perception of compatibility between the soul and the perceived *species* (2.5). If this apprehension is of a "compatible" thing, pleasure immediately follows, for "all pleasure is due to being proportioned [in respect to something]."[131] The type of pleasure that arises in the sense faculty after it takes in an object grasped "through an abstracted likeness" is directly dependent on the various qualities of the sense object, that is, on the type of sensation. In the case of vision it is beauty (*speciositas*), but closely related is the "sweetness" (*suavitas*) of pleasant sounds and scents—the whole palette of what we now describe as aesthetic experience. Finally, a certain type of pleasure (that of "wholesomeness") can also be caused by the "base" senses—taste and touch. 'Likeness' and 'form-beauty' (*species*) are general principles

---

130. Although certain Aristotelian principles are retained here (cf. *De anima* 2, c. 12; 424a 17–b 4), the whole picture is rather reminiscent of the transmission of εἴδωλα or "shapes" in various systems of ancient Greek philosophy—except in this case they are definitely not material. For details see: O. Bychkov, "ἡ τοῦ κάλλους ἀπορροή: A Note on Achilles Tatius 1.9.4–5, 5.13.4," *Classical Quarterly* 49, no. 1 (1999): 339–41.

131. This is a traditional Aristotelian theory; cf. the idea that sensation operates best in the medium range in *De anima* 2, c. 11 (424a 1–16), and that sensation is a type of harmony in *De anima* 3, c. 2 (426a 28–b 8).

of sense perception that apply to all three areas.[132] Depending on the area of sensation, there can be three types of "proportionality" (which is the cause of pleasure) in likenesses. If one considers the purest type of likeness, "shape" (*species*) or "form," which is manifested in the sense of vision, the corresponding effect of being proportionate or in harmony is called "shapeliness" or "beauty." The perception of likeness in the case of the baser senses produces the harmonious states of "sweetness" and "wholesomeness." This, according to Bonaventure, is the triple way by which the exterior sensible qualities enter the soul through "likenesses."

After sense perception and pleasure comes judgment (*diiudicatio*; 2.6). Bonaventure's judgment is separate from the immediate reaction of pleasure and is more rational than Kant's *Urteilskraft*.[133] It determines the reason for taking pleasure in a thing, or the "cause of the beautiful, sweet and wholesome," which it finds to be the "proportion of equality."[134] Judgment, Bonaventure concludes,

> is a process which allows the sensible shape (*species*), which has been received by the senses in a sensible way, to enter the thinking faculty through purification and abstraction. And it is in this manner that all this visible world has access to the human soul through the gates of the senses.

The important fact here is that 'form-beauty' or 'likeness' acts as a sort of an intermediary between the sensory and intellectual cognition: the latter can be further "purified" from the sensible components of the former without the loss of the formal composition of the object. It is noteworthy that beauty in this scheme always remains merely one of the three elements (beauty, sweetness and wholeness), and aesthetic experience is not clearly separated from the rest of the sensory experience, for example, smell, taste, or touch. Bonaventure thus speaks of the whole area of the *aisthetic* within which 'form-beauty' and 'likeness' are the main governing principles.

---

132. Bonaventure in this case includes a broader area of sensation. Recall that Augustine (as earlier Plato) tried to separate vision and hearing into a special category that has to do with form, as contrasted with the "baser" senses.

133. This can be seen as a reflection of Augustine's separation of the judgment of the senses into the lower and higher, almost rational, types of judgment in *De musica* 6.9.24. Since Bonaventure quotes *De musica* 6 precisely in this context he was obviously well aware of the Augustinian division.

134. This "proportion" remains one and the same and does not depend on the size of the compared things, i.e., it is something absolute in relative things. Cf. the similar Augustinian idea about "immutable truth" in *De musica* and *De vera religione*.

Having outlined the process of sense perception through *species*, Bonaventure comes to the key point of the *Itinerarium*: the analogy between this process and the nature and workings of Christ (2.7). It is the first stage of "perception" (*apprehensio*; cf. 2.4) that provides the closest parallel with Christ. It is important that the second person of the Trinity does not serve as the analog of the subsequent "upper" stages of the process of perception, which Bonaventure instead compares to the influence of the "divine light," or God in general. This detail only reinforces the unique role of Christ as *species*, in that in this capacity he is analogical precisely with the sensible.[135] *Itinerarium* 2.7 reads:

> For all these things are vestiges in which we can see our God. Indeed, *the apprehended shape* (species) *is a likeness* which has been *generated in the medium and subsequently impressed upon the organ, and* through that impression *it leads back* to its origin, namely *the object of cognition.* This clearly shows, therefore, that *the eternal light* [i.e., God] *generates out of itself* a co-equal, consubstantial, and co-eternal *likeness or splendor* [i.e., the Son]. Now *just as the object of perception generates its likeness* throughout the whole medium, and *just as this shape* (species) *is united to the corporeal organ*, in the same way he who is the 'image of the invisible God,' and the 'splendor of his glory,' and the 'form of his substance' (Col. 1:15; Hebr. 1:3), he who is everywhere from the first moment of his generation, *is united* through the grace of union *to the individual of rational nature* [i.e., the human soul], in order that through that union he might lead us back to the Father, as to our original source and final object. Therefore if all knowable things have the ability to generate their own shape (*species*), they openly proclaim that the eternal generation of the Word, the Image, and the Son eternally proceeding from God the Father can be observed in them as in mirrors. (my italics)

The quoted text is important for two reasons. First, it contains an analogy between the function of 'form-beauty' or 'likeness' in sense perception, including aesthetic experience, and the generation of Christ as the 'image,' 'likeness' and *species*. Bonaventure finds distinct similarities between the functioning of these two mechanisms of mediation and presentation: on the one hand, sense perception, and on the other hand, mediation through Christ of a more spiritual kind. In both cases, at a

---

135. Thus, while the first stage of the mystical-contemplative 'perception' of God—by analogy with the sensible *species*—arouses the idea of the "primary beauty, highest proportionality and equality" (as we already know, exemplified by the Son), the second stage of 'delight' leads to the idea of the "true delight" (*Itinerarium* 2.8), and the third stage of 'judgment' (*Itin.* 2.9) makes one think of Augustine's "immutable laws" above us, which we discover by analyzing our own ability to judge.

certain point the human soul is led back by means of a *species* to the primary source of this *species* (the object of perception or the divine principle respectively), which in both cases is somehow manifested or presented. This parallel between *species Christi* and the operation of the sensible *species*—the closest analog to the aesthetic in modern terms—means that Christ's form-beauty works at least in the way that is analogous to the modern aesthetic. The analogy is strengthened by the use of identical phrasing: "through *species* as an intermediary," "through likeness as an intermediary," "through Christ as an intermediary" (*mediante specie; mediante similitudine; mediante Christo*).[136] Despite the fact that 'Christ's form-beauty' is only an analogical aesthetic, it can be legitimately included in the current analysis, just as moral and intelligible beauties, also purely analogical, were included in the previous chapters, provided that comparisons with aesthetic phenomena in the true sense (that is, involving sense perception) were present. Bonaventure, as is clear from the context, does include such comparisons.

Second, the text suggests that the mechanism of sense perception (including the aesthetic range of it), which is analogous to the workings of Christ, can trigger in us a sudden insight into the nature of Christ. Just as in modern thought analogies with aesthetic experience provide deeper insights into the nature of other phenomena, including the divine in general, in the case of Bonaventure such an analogy provides a specifically Christian insight into the nature of the Trinity and the specific qualities of the Son. One could say, once again, using the terminology of modern theological aesthetics, that sense perception in Bonaventure, including the perception of the beauty of shape and sound, can be revelatory, albeit of specifically Christian principles.

---

136. Discussing the analogy between aesthetic experience and Christ's form on the basis of the principles of 'image' and 'likeness,' von Balthasar makes important connections between the operation of the aforesaid principles in Bonaventure and key notions in modern aesthetics, including his own theological aesthetics. Thus each of the Augustinian three stages (i.e., vestige, image, and likeness) under faith can be interpreted in two ways: "as a 'reference' (*Verweis*) to the archetype, and as a 'presentation' [*Darstellung*; translated as 'representation' in GL2] (and to this extent a vessel) of the archetype" (GL2 301). The *Itinerarium*, von Balthasar remarks, is divided into several stages: "trace, image and resemblance each as a pointer (*Verweis*) and as presentation ['representation' in GL2] . . . . The pointer is in each case prior: . . . and in this way one achieves a proper understanding of the pointer as a presentation ['representation' in GL2]," i.e., creaturely being as the sign of its origin. "The sequence is determinative of this theological aesthetic: the immanent beauty of the things of the world is visible in itself only when the transient pointer to the archetypal beauty is understood and ratified. But in this, the pointer itself must of necessity be named beauty" (GL2 301–2).

It comes as no surprise, then, that among the things this aesthetic analogy reveals is the fact that Christ as *species* is himself revelatory in nature. The nature of Christ's form itself is to be manifest and apparent, and not only in a mystical sense. Just as in the case of such phenomena as τὸ καλόν or τὸ πρέπον in the Greek tradition, it is often the appearance of Christ's form that is desired, and not only its concept or dogmatic explication, as Bonaventure makes clear in some of his works.[137] Thus the soul "desires his [Christ's] presence and appearance";[138] "this devout soul seeks the manifest appearance of the Son of God, for it does not merely seek him to be present in the mind,"[139] "and it is for this reason that he necessarily had to be beclouded with flesh, that men might see and imitate him."[140] Christ thus takes over the role of a "transcendental idea" which on the one hand stands beyond presentation, but on the other hand can be presented. The Son, of course, is simply the principle of presentation par excellence.

This need for the actual sense experience of Christ's form is hardly surprising in Bonaventure. His thought, one could safely assume, reflects some features of Francis's own experience, or at least Bonaventure's own view of it. As Bonaventure remarks in his *Life* of St. Francis, the actual aesthetic experience of the beauty of the universe was vividly felt by Francis as Christ's form permeating all Creation:

Rejoicing in all the works of the Lord's hands aroused him on all occasions to love God, and all the delightful displays [of reality] lifted him up to [the awareness of] the vivifying reason and cause [of all]. In beautiful things he saw the most beautiful one, and everywhere through the traces impressed in physical reality he traced the beloved, building a ladder for himself out of all things . . . and he, as it were, perceived a heavenly harmony in the consonance of virtues and actions.[141]

These observations, again, confirm the possibility of including the discussion of 'Christ's form' in Bonaventure in a study of aesthetics. In ad-

137. Von Balthasar also notices that the second person of the Trinity becomes the locus of sensible experience of God, cf. GL2 320: "It is firstly characteristic that the chief texts identify the eternal Word as the object of this experience of God through the senses," even if these are only "spiritual" senses, i.e., senses analogically speaking.

138. *Sermo in Vigilia Nativitatis* (vol. 9, 88a).   139. Ibid.

140. Ibid., p. 90b.

141. *Legenda Major* 9.1 (vol. 8, 530a). Cf. von Balthasar's comments on this passage: "This ability to interpret nature, the flowers and birds, the powers of the elements, the whole of being as it makes its appearance, has its root in God; the eternal Son is radiating light (*splendor pulcherrimus*) as God illuminated and expressed" (GL2 347; cf. GL2 339ff.).

dition to describing actual aesthetic experiences as part of the analogy with *species Christi*, Christ's form itself in Bonaventure is sometimes experienced directly or *aisthetically*, that is, the notion of Christ's form-beauty as a "theological aesthetic" reflects actual experience, and is not merely a product of intellectual reflection. There is another reason why we can say that Christ's form incorporates, in a more than analogous way, some functions (revelatory and mediating) reserved for aesthetic experience in modern thought. As is clear from Bonaventure's *Commentary on the Sentences*, the Son as *species* is the source and highest manifestation of the principles of 'likeness' and 'image,' which also lie at the foundation of aesthetic perception. Thus he can actually be seen *as* the aesthetic (in the modern sense), except quintessentially, in an exemplary manner, thus forming the foundation of a specifically Christian aesthetics.[142]

Despite very close analogies between Christ's form and the modern aesthetic in Bonaventure, as well as all the contexts that point to the concrete aesthetic perception of this form, a modern aesthetician would probably still feel that *species Christi* remains something very alien to mainstream academic aesthetics, and that it can be called 'aesthetic' only analogously. Indeed, according to Bonaventure's *Itinerarium*, Christ is joined directly to the soul by and large through grace, and not through

---

142. The parallel between sense perception and the operation of the Son as "likeness-image-form" is not unique to the *Itinerarium*. For example, it is clearly stated in the *De reductione artium ad theologiam*, where Bonaventure examines the illumination by "sense cognition" in order to see how it can lead to theology: "Should we decide to consider the medium of cognition, we will see there the Word that is eternally generated and incarnated in time. Indeed, no object of sense moves the cognitive faculty except through a likeness acting as an intermediary *(mediante similitudine)*, which emanates from the object as an offspring from a parent.... However, this likeness does not bring the act of sensing to its completion unless it is united with the organ and faculty. When it is so united, a new perception is formed, and through this perception one is led back to the object [of sense] through this likeness acting as an intermediary.... In the same way, you must understand, a likeness, image and offspring has emanated eternally from the highest Mind, which is knowable to the interior senses of our mind. Now afterwards, *when the fullness of the time has come*, he [i.e., this likeness] was united with the mind and flesh and took on the human form, something he was never before. Through him, all our minds, which perceive this likeness of the Father through faith at their core, are led back to God." The same mechanism is observed in artistic production ("the effect of artistry emanates from the artist through likeness—which exists in the mind—as its intermediary"; *De red. art.*, chap. 12) and speech ("But if we consider speech from the point of view of its end, from this angle it is for the purpose of expressing, informing and moving; however it never expresses anything except through likeness as its intermediary"; *De red. art.*, chap. 18), i.e., it has a universal nature. I translated from the following Latin edition of *De red. art.*: *Tria opuscula S. Bonaventurae*, edited by Collegium S. Bonaventurae (Quaracchi: Collegium S. Bonaventurae, 1938), 374, 376, 379.

some *aisthetic* experience (although *analogously* to sense experience), which suggests that Christ does not function 'aesthetically,' in the modern understanding, but serves as 'form-beauty' for the special spiritual or intelligible medium and way of communication, just as the sensible 'form-beauty' functions in the physical medium (for example, air). Bonaventure speaks of Christ's mediating and revelatory role mainly in the context of spiritual and mystical, rather than sensory, experience. (According to Bonaventure, Christ arouses the "spiritual senses"; *Itin.* 4.3.) The role of Christ becomes crucial only at the point of "entering into oneself" in order to achieve a union with God, and not earlier at the stage of sense perception—although already at this stage one becomes *aware* of the fact that Christ's form acts in the manner analogous to beauty:

> Therefore, no matter how much someone may be illumined by the light of nature and acquired knowledge, he is [still] not able to enter into himself, in order *to take delight in the Lord* [Ps. 36:4] while being within himself, without the mediation of Christ [*mediante Christo*; cf. 1 Tim. 2:5] who says: *I am the door* . . . [John 10:9]. (*Itin.* 4.2)

The sensory way is clearly not sufficient, and a parallel spiritual (mystical, contemplative) way is required where Christ is the mediating 'form' leading to God.[143] Bonaventure sums up the three ways in which "one can contemplate God not only outside of us and inside us, but also above us" (*Itin.* 5.1): this can be done through focusing on sensible experience ("outside through a vestige"), on the internal constitution of one's faculties ("inside through the image"), and on the "light that is above our mind" (the Augustinian "light of immutable truth"). By means of these speculative exercises the soul "transcends" the sensible world and even itself "in the course of which passage Christ is the *way* and the *door*," as well as the "*ladder* and, as it were, the vehicle of reconciliation" (*Itin.* 7.1). The aforesaid contexts signal that the problem with the interpretation of Christ's form in an aesthetic sense, or as "beauty," still remains.

A solution to this impasse can be found in von Balthasar's distinction between 'beauty' and 'glory.' In *GL4* von Balthasar uses Plotinus to outline his general scheme or "anatomy" of theological aesthetics, which he appropriates for himself in *GL1*. The level of earthly existence, at which level the beauty of form proper is found, "subsists only as an

---

143. Cf. Viladesau's observation, mentioned at the beginning of this chapter, that aesthetics ultimately does not lead one to the *Christian* God.

epiphany of the mystery" (GL4 307), that is, of the level of existence "above being." This epiphany is revealing and anagogical in nature in that it points to that reality above being. Thus while one can speak of the beauty of form at the "horizontal" level of regular being, when one considers the "vertical" dimension of this scheme of epiphany or revelation, one speaks of "glory" instead, a certain "radiance sent forth by beauty at every level," which "signifies beauty itself, yet also signifies that there is *in* beauty something *beyond* it" (GL4 307). The scheme of the two dimensions of beauty—form and glory—perfectly fits Bonaventure's understanding of the Son as "beauty" and explains the seeming discontinuity between the earthly beauty of form and Christ as *species* (form-beauty) that puzzles any modern professional aesthetician. In fact, this is precisely the crux of Bonaventure's theological aesthetics: *species Christi* is not aesthetic beauty and does not quite work like this type of beauty. Despite the analogy between the two that allows one to understand the mechanism of Christ's form, one would have to qualify the latter, in Balthasarian terms, rather as 'glory': something that points and leads one in the vertical dimension to the level of the "beyond." Despite several known attempts to write a history of "medieval aesthetics," extensive textual research shows that in proportion to other topics, aesthetic reflection is at best of marginal interest to the schoolmen.[144] Perhaps this can be explained precisely by the fact that their time has already experienced a shift from aesthetic 'beauty' to 'glory,' and from aesthetics to theological aesthetics.

So what are the similarities and differences between Bonaventure's understanding of the notion 'Christ's form' and von Balthasar's appropriation of it for his theological aesthetics? Both emphasize the evident and manifest nature of Christ's form and its intrinsic aesthetic qualities: harmony and balance. For both thinkers Christ's form is related to cognitive functions: it can be "seen" and recognized directly in what Duns Scotus would call an act of "intuitive cognition." However, von Balthasar focuses on the historical aspects of the form: for him, it is the form of Jesus as a concrete historical figure who appears, acts, and speaks in the Scriptures (cf. GL7). For Bonaventure, Christ's form is a metaphysical-ontological characteristic of the Son, the second person of the Trinity. In Bonaventure Christ-beauty appears as a certain universal

---

144. Cf. O. Bychkov, "A Propos of Medieval Aesthetics," where most of the thirteenth-century "aesthetic" texts are listed.

principle, analogous to the modern aesthetic, which is manifested to the senses, albeit "spiritual" senses. The two stages of perceiving the form mediate between the divine and the human through sensible or quasi-sensible experience. The first stage is the anagogical movement from the experience of this world and its beauty to the recognition of the divine principle. The second stage is the continuation of this movement with the help of Christ's form, which acts as a guide in the inaccessible realm of the divine, being a sensible or quasi-sensible manifestation of the latter. The binary ancient Platonic-Augustinian scheme 'world's beauty—God' is thereby transformed, in Bonaventure's theology, into a threefold Christian scheme: 'world's beauty—Christ (or Christ's form)—God.'

But what about the broader issue of the relationship between aesthetic and Trinitarian principles? Within the developed Christian systematic theology exemplified by the Franciscan tradition of Bonaventure and Duns Scotus, beauty in application to the Trinity is simply understood equivocally. At least three senses can be distinguished in which the Trinity can be spoken of in terms of 'beauty,' all of them strictly analogous, and each sense must be analyzed separately. The first sense refers to the Trinity as a whole, qua 'one God' or 'one essence,' and denotes general excellence, like the Greek τὸ καλόν. In the second sense the Trinity is "beautiful" due to the proportion of equality and symmetry—perceived as the essence of beauty in ancient and medieval thought—between its three persons. In the third sense, it is specifically the Son, the second person of the Trinity, that contains the essence of beauty, understood as the formal principle of likeness and imaging.

It appears, then, that the High Middle Ages, compared to the thought of Augustine, by and large retain only one rather traditional aspect of his aesthetics: the idea of beauty as equality, proportion, and harmony. Bonaventure also takes over the general Platonic-Augustinian idea of the ascent from aesthetic experience. However, his scheme of the ascent is much more mechanistic: it is reminiscent rather of the version described in the *De ordine* and lacks the immediacy that is characteristic of the ascent as it appears in later works of Augustine. Moreover, Bonaventure makes it very clear that aesthetic experience as such is part of the broader area of sensibility that includes taste and touch as well. One must stress, once again, that even the "stripped down" version of the ascent still preserves the revelatory aspects of aesthetic experience that are present in the Platonic tradition, in the sense that it leads and guides one to the beyond (von Balthasar's *Verweis*). Moreover, even the principles of proportion and harmony as the essence of beauty can be seen as revelatory[145]: such harmony and proportion are immediately seen in reality, not rationalized, and they make one aware of its origin (von Balthasar's *Darstellung*). However, what is definitely lost is the immediacy of the instantaneous "transcendental movement" of revelation through aesthetic experience that was grasped so clearly by Augustine. Although with Bonaventure the thirteenth century does see the development of a properly Christian theological aesthetics, the depth of Augustine's "transcendental analysis" is lost until its recovery by Kant in the eighteenth century. It becomes clear at this point that despite the birth of an authentic Christian theological aesthetics in the Middle Ages, historically it could not achieve its highest point until after the rise of modern aesthetics, which made available profound reflections on the topic by the German Idealist tradition.

145. As the reader remembers, Christ as the Word, or something revealing, shares in this quality of beauty.

Conclusion

Our hermeneutic dialogue with ancient and medieval thought proves that von Balthasar's analysis was essentially correct: both ancient and medieval authors do notice and explore for their theological and philosophical needs the revelatory aspect of what we now call aesthetic experience. Moreover, if one understands 'aesthetics' as theology, philosophy, or hermeneutics that uses aesthetic experience (in its modern understanding) or analogies with aesthetic phenomena in order to make philosophical or theological points, then aesthetics is certainly present in both Antiquity and the Middle Ages. Perhaps it is even correct to assume that the revelatory function of aesthetic experience in modern theological aesthetics is a revival or retrieval of ancient and medieval thought, rather than an offshoot of eighteenth- and nineteenth-century aesthetic theories, since the latter, in their turn, also used the fundamental insights of ancient and medieval thought. There is no gap, then, but an essential continuity between ancient and modern revelatory or "transcendental" aesthetics: its essential components exist as early as in Plato, the Stoics, and Augustine. Consequently, referring to the transition from ancient and medieval to modern revelatory aesthetics, one should rather speak of transformations and changes in terms of terminology, precision, and the understanding of such foundational categories as "transcendental"—not of some radical shift. Revelatory aesthetics can therefore be considered a fundamental feature of Western European thought.

Our dialogue, further, shows that other common trends in contemporary theological (and some philosophical) aesthetics can be seen as retrievals of ancient and medieval thought as well. For example, an important trend that emerged in twentieth-century theological aesthetics and still continues today is not to view aesthetics, as many modern academic aestheticians do, as an "autonomous" field that deals with "disinterested" experience "for its own sake." Instead, aesthetic experience is viewed as always involved in some other area, contributing to our awareness of the divine, for example, or improving our morals: that is, as *transformative* and *participatory*. Ancient and medieval thought, of course, always viewed aesthetic experience strictly in these terms and never separated it from cognitive, moral, or theological issues. Ancient and medieval thinkers consistently link aesthetic experience with something that is meaningful and reject or ignore experiences of art objects or nature sought for pure enjoyment or "useless" pleasure. In fact, even the idea of "disinterested" (in reference to aesthetic experience), as far as it can be derived from ancient and medieval traditions, must be interpreted in the sense of the modern "transcendental": that is, not disinterested in an absolute sense, or having no goal at all except itself, but disinterested simply in the sense of having no immediately explainable goal here, in the immanent realm, but leading to a goal or interest that is imperceptible to us, or that "transcends" us. (Kant, for instance, despite declaring aesthetic experience "disinterested" and autonomous, presumably in the sense of having no immediate practical interest, still assigns to it an important role of "linking up" all areas of human experience by providing a "transcendental" insight into the nature of reality.) The aforesaid trend in contemporary theological aesthetics to view aesthetic experience as "engaged" rather than as autonomous and "disinterested" can be also traced back to ancient and medieval thought.

Engaging ancient and medieval Western thought also helps us to formulate a clearer and more robust concept of aesthetics for our present-day needs, which would account for some new features and trends in present-day aesthetics and even reconcile some conflicting tendencies in aesthetics, from Plato to the present. For example, let us use the working definition of the field of aesthetics—which both fits modern thought and can be derived from the ancient and medieval traditions—as "transcendental sensibility": something that involves the senses or analogies with the senses, but at the same time has an "elevating" or "advancing" function of going beyond the senses or even human cognitive powers. Aesthetic experience thus understood is (1) sensing, or making us aware of, some hidden principles of reality and therefore (2) orienting us toward higher spiritual, intellectual, or moral goals. Sensing of such quality and with such consequences is necessarily signaled overtly by a certain type of pleasurable (beauty) or unusual (awe, sublimity, transcendence) reaction. It is clear that the understanding of aesthetics that we derive from ancient and medieval thought can accommodate not only classic types of aesthetic experience and classic forms of art, but also contemporary art and aesthetic sensibilities, as well as attempts to censor art, which date back at least as far as Plato. For example, the experience of even great contemporary art, which may not be "beautiful" in a classic way, is still accompanied by a certain feeling of awe and an impression that the viewer gains access to some deeper principles of reality. At the same time, many types of art that are created purely for sensory pleasure were often criticized, not only by Plato but even by great modern and contemporary artists, for their lack of "spirituality" (they lacked some values that are higher than purely sensory). This critique meant that these types of art lacked the elevating function, or did not reveal any deep principles of reality, and therefore failed to qualify as "aesthetic" in the true sense of the term. Thus not only classic art forms that merely serve the pure joy of the senses (the arts that are pretty or enticing), but also contemporary artifacts that are conceptual, clever, parodic, ironic, and so forth, but lack the ability to cause the "transcending" or anagogical movement, will fail to qualify as truly aesthetic. This understanding of the field of aesthetics also automatically problematizes the definitions—common in modern literature on aesthetics and known to cause conceptual problems—that reduce "aesthetic" to "everything that involves art" or to a "certain type of pleasure."

Finally, reflections on ancient and medieval thought can help us reshape and refocus the broad, loose, and almost unmanageable field that is currently described by the term 'aesthetics.' The study of ancient and medieval reflections on aesthetics calls into question the way this field is delimited in modern and contemporary thought. In our analysis, let us once again assume the "compromise" or "one fits all" definition of aesthetics—derived from our study of the tradition—as "transcendental sensibility." Since this definition, as explained above, necessarily contains the revelatory component, that is, the idea of leading or pointing to the beyond, the experience that serves the pure joy of the senses—which would be included under academic aesthetics in modern times—will necessarily remain outside the field. But since this definition also contains a reference to actual sensory experience, the field thus defined will exclude certain areas that were part of the broader aesthetic in ancient times, e.g., purely intellectual beauty, or something that does not involve the senses. For example, the revealing aspect itself, which is crucial to the definition of aesthetics as retrieved from ancient and medieval thought, does not necessarily have to do with the senses, but applies also to purely moral and cognitive experiences. Nor is sensory experience required to produce certain phenomena that exhibit "beauty" or "harmony," and so forth. All this speaks to the inadequacy of the conceptual framework for what is understood under "aesthetics," at least if we include here revelatory or transcendental aesthetics. That is, not all sensory (*aisthetic*) experiences are revelatory and not all revelatory experiences are sensory (*aisthetic*). The fact that in this study we attempted to enforce the aforesaid definition that requires both the revelatory (transcendental) and the sensory components is not an argument to the contrary. Although we did succeed in limiting the field of study and avoiding many conceptual inconsistencies, this approach also uncovered such latent problems as the fact that ancient and medieval thought did not limit the range of the 'aesthetic' (the experience of beauty, for example, or "transcendental" awe) to sensory experience. Thus although there are clearly observations and phenomena that do fit both criteria, the field itself, even in ancient and medieval thought, extends beyond the current definition in both directions. So, how best to delimit the new field?

One way is to eliminate the criterion of sense experience (the *aisthesis* itself) as necessary for the field of aesthetics. In this case, one can construct the area usually described as aesthetics as a broader discipline that applies to all human experiences, not only sensory, since they all, in some way, include certain "aesthetic" principles, such as regular patterning, clarification, et cetera. In this case some other name, rather than 'aesthetics,' might be more appropriate for the broader discipline: perhaps, 'revelatorics.' Is the time ripe, then, for writing a new foundational study "*Revelatorica*: The Revelatory Nature of Human Experience"?

Another possibility, of course, is to proceed in the opposite direction, as F. B. Brown has done, by eliminating the revelatory criterion as necessary and focusing precisely on the "aesthetica" as the focal point of the new discipline, which should rather be styled *aisthetics* (or neo-aesthetics, in Brown's terminology). But is sensory experience a viable principal criterion? According to Brown, "part of the realm of the aesthetic . . . is the sheerly delightful within perception . . . ," that is, not meaningful or revelatory of any truth: the standard criteria in the hermeneutic model in aesthetics.[1] "Neo-aesthetics" in his opinion must take into consideration the full range of the "aesthetica," not only the sensory phenomena that are revelatory of truth. Thus the phenomena covered by the new discipline will range from purely sensory-based to mixed to more conceptually based (p. 12).

First of all, rejecting the necessity of the revelatory or "pointing" criterion for the new discipline and replacing it with the *aisthetic* criterion as the only one required creates a problem for the classification of phenomena that fall under the new discipline, or for delimiting the new field for what used to be aesthetics. For example, what do we do with "purely intellectual or moral beauties," which Kant excluded from aesthetics in its proper sense but which ancient and medieval thought, as well as some contemporary philosophers and theologian-aestheticians who retrieve this thought, consistently treat as analogical or parallel to sensory? There will be a conceptual problem whether they are excluded (the field of aesthetics will be diminished) or included (the criterion of *aisthesis* will not be followed). Revelatorics, on the other hand, does provide a more universal criterion, as well as allows one to include not only intellectual and moral phenomena but also most of the truly *aisthetic*; indeed, even aesthetic experiences that are the least "truth-revealing" still provide some sort of a connection or sense of unity with the universe or with our own nature and are thus "transcendental" or revelatory.

"Neo-aesthetics" also creates a problem for theological aesthetics proper, that is, for the "religion" component in aesthetic experience, or at least for the analogy between the aesthetic and the religious. Brown stresses the importance of sheer delight and joy in aesthetic experience. Perhaps for the Protestant or evangelical traditions in Christianity this would be very germane, as it would be for some pagan traditions that practice a type of Dionysian frenzy or immersion. However, it is not a generally accepted truth that "sheer delight and joy" is universally characteristic of the nature of religious experience. For example in the Eastern Christian tradition, religious experience has always been associated with what is called *dukhovnost'* in Russian. This term cannot be adequately rendered by the English "spirituality," since that notion has been tainted with too many extraneous connotations. What the

---

1. F. Burch Brown, *Religious Aesthetics*, 11.

Russian word really means is loftiness, elevatedness, sublimity, creating some intense feeling of higher reality. In the Roman Catholic tradition, in particular in von Balthasar, the equivalent, although not an exact one, would be the experience of awe. What *dukhovnost'* implies is definitely not "pure joy and delight," nor does it mean pure hiddenness of meaning, which is implied in the term "mystery." *Dukhovnost'* is, indeed, a kind of positive experience, but one that necessarily has to do with intellectual or cognitive faculties—with the "spirit" rather than with the "soul." The sort of cognitive reality implied (lofty, sublime) exceeds normal human powers, that is, has to do with experiences that indicate something that is beyond our reach ("purposive without a purpose"?), but not entirely hidden from view as in mystery. But this is precisely what is covered by the modern field of "transcendental aesthetics," or by the terms "transcendental" or "revelatory," since revelatory necessarily implies revelatory of something that is beyond our present reach. Moreover, many Eastern artists, Russian in particular, from icon-painters such as Rublev to abstract avant-garde artists such as Kandinsky, referred to their art as possessing *dukhovnost'*—again, meaning that this art was "lofty," "elevated," having to do with higher rungs of reality. Curiously, these same artists condemned the type of art dedicated purely to sensory pleasure (nineteenth-century Victorian art, or the decadent "art for art's sake" of the 1900s) as *bezdukhovnoe*, or absolutely lacking *dukhovnost'*. The term *dukhovnost'* thus provides a viable link between art and religion: art and religion intersect not at the point of being "enjoyable" or "aesthetic" but at the point of being "lofty" or having *dukhovnost'* or a transcendental nature. We must add that if one looks at other Eastern religious traditions such as Buddhist or Hindu, as well as at the use of art in them, the claim that they focus on purely sensory joy, to the exclusion of the "pointing" or "guiding" criterion, will be questionable at best.

Another argument against making the sensory into the main criterion for the new discipline can be made from a purely historical perspective, based on the analysis done in this study. Indeed, this analysis of the "prehistory of aesthetics" consistently shows that all of the Western-Mediterranean tradition, from Antiquity through the Middle Ages (with some of these trends carrying over into modern and contemporary thought) has always preferred viewing aesthetic experience as linked (be it in some hidden ways) to cognitive and moral in some sort of a higher "synesthesia" of all human faculties. Our historical analysis is also elucidating in respect to the criterion of sensory "joy" or pleasure. Both ancient and medieval thought, later reincarnated in Kant, consistently tend to interpret sensory and intellectual pleasures, as well as the "mixed" cases of enjoying regular patterns ("aesthetic," from the modern point of view), as a kind of judgment about the nature of things. (In the case of the "higher" senses, this sort of judgment can be called pattern recognition.) If perceived objects are judged to be perfect in their own form, they become suitable as models for morals and as pointers that lead us to the transcendent or divine (or the "essence of the universe," et cetera). Pleasures that did not contribute to this "guiding" function were often deemed illicit (as in Plato, Augustine, and some other Christian theologians). Let us consider what would happen to the field of aesthetics if we decided to include in it the component of "sheer delight," the non-patterned experience of "joy" that lacks any anagogical or cognitive features.[2] What would prevent one, then, from including *any* sensual pleasure that has no immediate practical function, such as sensual experiences that people seek "just for thrills"? Could one speak, then, of the aesthetics of bungee-jumping? It is clear that such a move would extend the area infinitely. (On the other hand, both the position of rejecting some arts on the basis of their perceived lack of the anagogical function, and also Brown's position that there are some *aesthetica* that have nothing to do with the revelatory function, ultimately may be misrepresentations of the reality of aesthetic objects. Even when aesthetic mechanisms are used for the "wrong" purposes, still their essence remains revelatory of some principles [harmony, for instance] if such objects are patterned or articulated; at the very least, aesthetic experiences still lead to some unity with the transcendent, for example, in some ecstatic sense of unity with the divine, the universe, et cetera—movement that can always be interpreted as "revealing" the transcendent.)

Ultimately, perhaps the only solution is to separate the current field of 'aesthetics' into 'aisthetics' (or neo-aesthetics, to adopt Brown's term) and 'revelatorics': two overlapping but not identical fields. Since the former already has been adequately described,[3] let us conclude by outlining the grounds for, and approaches to, the latter.

2. Or at least quasi-cognitive, as in being "purposive without a purpose," the expression that stands for the presence of some sort of a pattern.
3. Brown, *Religious Aesthetics*.

What bridge can we establish between aesthetics and revelatorics? A quick look at the new field suggests that revelatorics should include the phenomenology of purely intellectual, non-sensory processes; von Balthasar refers to them as intellectual "seeing," and pre-modern authors refer to them as perceiving "intellectual beauty." So why should the new discipline, which can be portrayed as a sort of epistemology or cognitive theory, need aesthetics in its classical sense? Is aesthetics in its proper sense essential to the future discipline of revelatorics? Some sort of a unifying framework is provided already by our analysis of ancient and medieval traditions, subsequently retrieved by von Balthasar, which often use *analogies* with the aesthetic (the fine arts and aesthetic experience) in making important observations about cognitive mechanisms, morals, and theological matters. The very fact that they use *analogies* means two things: first, that we are dealing with areas that are broader than the sensory aesthetic; second, that the sensory aesthetic often plays a crucial role in providing insights into other philosophical and theological matters, or in initiating the revelatory movement. Ancient and medieval thought thus signals that somehow the arts and aesthetics have a special place in revelatorics, the area that is in itself broader than *aisthetics*.

Looking at the history of the modern discussion of aesthetic matters, we also notice, just as we have in ancient and medieval thought, that some distinctive features about art and aesthetic experience keep them at the center of attention of Western European thinkers who investigate the ways we gain insight into cognitive, moral, and theological matters (all issues that pertain to revelatorics). As the German Idealist and subsequently the phenomenological tradition suggest, aesthetic experience and the arts possess some traits that are unique in their ability to offer an adequate insight into the revelatory capacity of reality. Specifically, those traditions focus on our ability to create art objects using our aesthetic feeling. The process of creating art objects results in something that clearly has been created by us—yet that something has already become non-created or "natural." An art object provides a unique opportunity for intuiting the essence of what is "natural" or what is not-ego, by the very fact that it is the result of the ego's activity. The ego thus receives an opportunity to transcend the immanent, which is immediately transparent to it, and to gain a unique insight into the "thing in itself." The modern emphasis on art rather than on our aesthetic experience of natural phenomena can be easily harmonized with the ancient conflation of natural and artistic aesthetics. Indeed, we construct an aesthetic object using our "aesthetic feeling," which cannot be rationalized. The moderns called this "genius," and Plato called it "poetic madness." The connection between art and the aesthetic in "natural" objects is precisely the fact that our "aesthetic feeling," which is used in creating art, comes immediately from our nature. This fact differentiates "art" (in the modern sense of fine art) from other manufactured objects, such as tools or other practical contraptions, which are made by relying merely on conceptual devices and a knowledge base such as manufacturing skills. Indeed, it is common in modern thought to view products of artistic genius as "nature-like."

Let us re-examine the views of two thinkers, Schopenhauer and Schelling, on the role of art objects, keeping two questions in mind: why art is crucial to revelatorics in general, and why it is crucial to the kind of theology (fundamental or systematic) that is based on revelatorics. As was shown above, generally in the German Idealist tradition art enjoys a special position among human activities. Schopenhauer points out the most fundamental reason why. Any scientific or scholarly activity provides us with only a "representation," or an external look at reality and individual things. At the same time, we as individual beings have a very different way of perceiving ourselves or the thing that we are—that is, we perceive ourselves internally, as an active "will." We can never feel either ourselves or things around us by representing them conceptually in an academic or scholarly way. At the same time, this feeling is what seems to be really important to our existence. In fact, it is this feeling that ultimately adds what we call "meaning" or "depth" to all our conceptual processes, which are otherwise perceived as "empty." It is also easy to see how the issue of experiencing ourselves as a "will" as opposed to "representation" or idea is relevant to religion. First of all, at least in the Christian tradition God is a will just like us, or, if we are willing to agree with Schopenhauer, just like any real thing, even an inanimate one. Second, our experience of the divine or transcendent is part of our inner experience of ourselves as a will. According to Schopenhauer, there is only one power that can communicate our own or someone else's experience as a will: art. Art is what ultimately makes us feel as someone, something, or simply differently, instead of giving us an outward description or "representation" of something or someone.

Therefore, art must be important both to our experience as individual wills and to gaining a deeper insight into our religious experience. The way art achieves this, according to Schopenhauer, is precisely through a certain kind of intense "contemplation" that allows us to feel the individual will of someone or something. In the German Idealist tradition, this is mostly possible through the phenomenon of the artistic genius, who can both achieve and communicate effectively an intimate connection with reality, something that borders on divine powers. (Of course, for many German Idealists who espoused the monist point of view, we are ourselves manifestations of the divine will, which makes our inner experience of it through the arts even more important.)

Schelling systematically elucidates another crucial aspect of artistic production that makes it different from anything else and therefore unique in its significance. Our usual phenomenological experience of the "objects of nature" is that the observing self perceives a limit beyond which its powers of perception cannot advance. This phenomenon can be described in terms of the Kantian "things in themselves," the Heideggerian "earthly" nature of things, or the Derridean "trace" character of reality (wherein reality's nature constantly escapes us). Our experience indicates that we are unable to penetrate beyond this perceived limit of things of natural origin. We are usually content to describe what lies beyond this limit by using broad terms such as the "nature" or "matter" of things. The situation, however, is different with produced objects, especially objects of art that often have "nature-like" quality. After they are produced, objects of art acquire an existence of their own that is not unlike the existence of natural objects; something of a more conceptually transparent nature, such as a tool or machine, retains its intelligible structural principles even after it is produced. The unique feature of art objects, however, is that unlike natural objects they have been produced from within the self. While the limits of natural objects that we perceive originate in nature, the limits of art objects that we perceive after their creation originate entirely from within our selves and are contained by our selves. Art is the only phenomenon that both results in a nature-like object and is potentially transparent to phenomenological analysis, since its origin lies within our selves. At the same time, science, which analyzes natural objects, can never get past the "screens" or limits of things. The very process of artistic activity, which results in a creation of a thing-in-itself that nevertheless comes from within the self and is somehow more transparent to the self, is perceived as being a little "miracle" and arouses wonder. Our self feels as if it somehow transcended its limits in creating something "natural" or "unintended" through a conscious and intended process. This way of looking at artistic production in Schelling, first of all, gives us a more precise phenomenological description of why our experience of the arts often leads to an experience of the transcendent. Second, it points out that art is completely unique in its ability to make reality transparent to our phenomenological reflection, thereby providing an unparalleled instrument to theology.

Both observations—that art is crucial to our experience of ourselves as the "will" and that art is a more adequate instrument for breaking through the phenomenological "limits" of things than science or scholarship—explain why art is so important for religion. Incidentally, both also explain why expert or formally elaborate art is more important for religion,[4] and more generally for revelatorics. Any art is potentially capable of functioning in the two ways outlined above, but the more elaborate and formally superior art will achieve better results; either it will create a more powerful perception of things internally as "wills," or it will achieve greater sophistication in analyzing things beyond their perceived "limits." Both observations also suggest that it is the phenomenological analysis of art, or "intellectual contemplation" that is the best method with which to proceed.

This last observation naturally brings us to Husserl, who significantly advances and elaborates the method of phenomenological or eidetic analysis and thus can help us in our analysis of both aesthetic and, generally, revelatory experience. First of all, Husserl also belongs to the ranks of German philosophers who are not primarily interested in art and aesthetics but do end up both recognizing their importance and noticing some connection between art, aesthetics, and our experience of transcendence, which may or may not be interpreted in religious terms. Husserl's model of phenomenological observation is similar to Schelling's. Beyond the realm of eidetically observable phenomena, there is no intelligible reality: things resist our reflection about them and, we can say with Schelling, pose limits. At the same time, our consciousness always "intends beyond itself" without ever completing its

---

4. This issue was recently raised by Brown; see Bychkov and Fodor, eds., *Theological Aesthetics after von Balthasar*.

intentions: thus the phenomena of "beyond" and "transcendent" are explained in terms of intentionality. As a result, phenomenological analysis, with its "transcending" nature, always remains incomplete. The world, or the reality of things, "transcends" consciousness and constitutes a "horizon of unfulfilled anticipations" that are a result of the intentionality of our consciousness. There is never a completely verifiable experience that could be grasped in precise concepts. So how can we possibly comprehend our phenomenological experience of reality? Husserl's answer is that we can still have verifiable experience of external things in the form of "harmonious syntheses." That is, although our eidetic picture can never be complete, it can nevertheless be coherent, with all elements fitting together. Husserl obviously uses aesthetic criteria here. This means that in a realm of conceptual and structural deficiency—such as any experience of reality but particularly in religion—we can be guided only by aesthetic criteria such as "harmony," "elegance," or "coherence." A brief look at the operation of the human mind shows that even scientists apply the same criteria at the stage of hypothesis, that is, when they are dealing with a yet-unknown and unverified reality. In addition to working out, in a more vigorous and systematic way, why aesthetic criteria are indispensable to our dealings with reality—especially in such areas as religion or the transcendent—Husserl is important for another reason. He gives us concrete tools of eidetic analysis of reality, including the arts, that is, he shows us how to go about a precise phenomenological description of the "transcendental constitution" of an object.

The future of eidetic analysis of a Husserlian style probably lies in combining phenomenological reflection with the scientific way of investigating reality, where both procedures can be mutually verified both "from within" and "from without." Such a combination of the two ways of analyzing art objects and aesthetic experience will significantly advance both the broadened field of aesthetics (revelatorics) and the field of theology, both by showing exactly why the arts and aesthetic objects are generally so important to us and by revealing the aesthetic element intrinsic to religion and theology.

BIBLIOGRAPHY

Primary Literature

Albertus Magnus. *Commentarii in I Sententiarum (Dist. XXVI–XLVIII)*. Vol. 26 of *Opera omnia*. Edited by S. Borgnet. Paris: L. Vivès, 1893.

———. *Summa theologica, pars II, qu. 1–67*. Vol. 32 of *Opera omnia*. Edited by S. Borgnet. Paris: L. Vivès, 1895.

———. *De bono*. Vol. 28 of *Opera omnia*. Edited by H. Kühle. Münster: Aschendorff, 1951.

———. *Super Dionysium De Divinis Nominibus*. Vol. 37/1 of *Opera omnia*. Edited by P. Simon. Münster: Aschendorff, 1972.

———. *Summa theologica, pars I*. Vol. 34/1 of *Opera omnia*. Edited by D. Siedler. Cologne: Albertus Magnus Institut, 1978.

Alexander de Hales. *Summa theologica, libri I–III*. 4 vols. Quaracchi: Collegium S. Bonaventurae, 1924, 1928, 1930, 1948.

Alexander de Hales. *Glossa in quatuor libros Sententiarum, libri 1–4*. Bibliotheca Franciscana scholastica Medii Aevi 12–15. Quaracchi/Florence: Collegium S. Bonaventurae, 1951, 1952, 1954, 1957.

Anselmus Cantuariensis. *Opera Omnia*. Edited by F.S. Schmitt. 2 vols. Edinburgh: T. Nelson & Sons, 1946.

Aristotle. *On the Cosmos*. Loeb Classical Library 400. Edited by G. P. Goold. Cambridge: Harvard University Press, 1992.

Arnim, I. von, ed. *Stoicorum veterum fragmenta*. 3 vols. Leipzig: B. G. Teubner, 1921.

Augustinus Hipponensis. *De musica*. Patrologia Latina 32. Edited by J. P. Migne. Paris, 1877.

———. *De vera religione*. Corpus Christianorum Series Latina 32. Edited by K. D. Daur. Turnhout: Brepols, 1962.

———. *De Trinitate*. Corpus Christianorum Series Latina 50. Edited by W. J. Mountain. Turnhout: Brepols, 1968.

———. *Enchiridion*. Corpus Christianorum Series Latina 46. Edited by E. Evans. Turnhout: Brepols, 1969.

———. *De magistro*. Corpus Christianorum Series Latina 29. Edited by K. D. Daur. Turnhout: Brepols, 1970.

———. *De ordine*. Corpus Christianorum Series Latina 29. Edited by W. M. Green. Turnhout: Brepols, 1970.

———. *De libero arbitrio*. Corpus Christianorum Series Latina 29. Edited by W. M. Green. Turnhout: Brepols, 1970.

———. *Confessiones*. Corpus Christianorum Series Latina 27. Edited by L. Verheijen. Turnhout: Brepols, 1981.

———. *De musica liber VI: A Critical Edition with a Translation and an Introduction*. Acta Universitatis Stockholmiensis. Studia Latina Stockholmiensia. Translated and edited by M. Jacobsson. Stockholm: Almqvist & Wiksell International, 2002.

Balthasar, H. U. von. *Herrlichkeit: eine theologische Ästhetik*. 3 vols. Einsiedeln: Johannes Verlag, 1961.

———. *The Glory of the Lord: A Theological Aesthetics*. Translated by E. Leiva-Merikakis et al. Edited by J. Riches et al. Vols. 1–5. San Francisco/Edinburgh: Ignatius Press/T&T Clark, 1982, 1984, 1986, 1989, 1991.

Balthasar, H. U. von. *Apokalypse der deutschen Seele: Studien zu einer Lehre von letzten Haltungen*. Vol. 1. Freiburg: Johannes Verlag, 1998.

Balthasar, H. U. von. *The Truth of the World*. Vol. 1 of *Theo-Logic: Theological Logical Theory*. Translated by A. J. Walker. San Francisco: Ignatius Press, 2000.

Barth, K. *The Doctrine of God*. Vol. 2, Part 1 of *Church Dogmatics*. Edited by G. W. Bromiley and T. F. Torrance. Translated by G. W. Bromiley. Edinburgh: T&T Clark, 1964.

Baumgarten, A. G. *Theoretische Ästhetik: Die grundlegenden Abschnitte aus der "Aesthetica" (1750/58)*. Translated and edited by H. R. Schweizer. Hamburg: F. Meiner, 1983.

Bonaventura. *Opera omnia*. Edited by Collegium S. Bonaventurae. 10 vols. Quaracchi: Collegium S. Bonaventurae, 1882–1902.

Bonaventura. *Libri IV Sententiarum*. Vols. 1–4 of *Opera theologica selecta*. Quaracchi/Florence: Collegium S. Bonaventurae, 1934, 1938, 1941, 1949.

Bonaventura. *Tria opuscula S. Bonaventurae*. Edited by Collegium S. Bonaventurae. Quaracchi: Collegium S. Bonaventurae, 1938.

Chevallier, P., ed. *Dionysiaca: Recueil donnant l'ensemble des traductions latines des ouvrages attribués au Denys de l'Aréopage*. Vol. 1. Paris, Bruges: Desclée de Brouwer & Cie, 1937.

Cicero, M. Tullius. *Scripta quae manserunt omnia*. Vols. 1–3. Edited by R. Klotz. Leipzig: B. G. Teubner, 1864, 1866.

Diels, H., ed. *Die Fragmente der Vorsokratiker*. Vol. 1. Berlin: Weidmann, 1951.

Diogenes Laertius. *Vitae Philosophorum*. Vol. 2. Edited by H. S. Long. Oxford: Clarendon Press, 1964.

Edelstein, L., and I. G. Kidd, eds. *Posidonius. I. The Fragments*. Cambridge: Cambridge University Press, 1972.

Ficino, Marsilio. *Opera Omnia*. Vol. 2. Basel: Heinrich Petri, 1576.

Gadamer, H.-G. *Truth and Method*. Translated by J. Weinsheimer and D. G. Marshall. New York: Continuum, 1999.

Galenus, Claudius. *De placitis*. Vol. 5 of *Opera omnia*. Edited by C. G. Kühn. Leipzig: Cnobloch, 1823.

Guillelmus Altissiodorensis. *Summa aurea, libri 1–4*. Spicilegium Bonaventurianum 16–19. Edited by J. Ribaillier. Paris/Rome: Centre National de la Recherche Scientifique/Collegium S. Bonaventurae, 1980, 1982, 1985, 1986.

Halcour, D. "Tractatus de transcendentalibus entis condicionibus (Assisi, Biblioteca Comunale, Codex 186)." *Franziskanische Studien* 41 (1959): 41–106.

Hegel, G. W. F. *Lectures on the History of Philosophy*. Translated by E. S. Haldane and F. H. Simson. 3 vols. London: Routledge and Kegan Paul, 1955.

———. *On Art, Religion, Philosophy: Introductory Lectures to the Realm of Absolute Spirit*. Edited by J. Glenn Gray. New York/Evanston: Harper & Row, 1970.

———. *Werke*. Edited by E. Moldenhauer and K. Markus Michel. Vols. 19, 20. Frankfurt am Main: Suhrkamp Verlag, 1971.

Heidegger, M. *Being and Time*. Translated by J. Macquarrie and E. Robinson. New York: Harper and Row, 1962.

———. "The Origin of the Work of Art." In *Poetry, Language, Thought*. Translated by A. Hofstadter, pp. 17–87. New York: Harper & Row, 1971.

Hilarius Pictaviensis. *De Trinitate*. Corpus Christianorum Series Latina 62. Edited by P. Smulders. Turnholti: Brepols, 1979.

Husserl, E. *Cartesian Meditations: An Introduction to Phenomenology*. Translated by D. Cairns. The Hague: Martinus Nijhoff, 1960.

Kant, I. *Gesammelte Schriften*. Vol. 5. Berlin: G. Reimer, 1913.

———. *Critique of Judgment*. Hafner Library of Classics 14. Translated by J. H. Bernard. Edited by O. Piest. New York: Hafner Publishing Co., 1951.

———. *Werke*. Edited by W. Weischedel. Vol. 10. Frankfurt am Main: Suhrkamp Verlag, 1957.

Lindbeck, G. A. *The Nature of Doctrine: Religion and Theology in a Postliberal Age*. Philadelphia: Westminster Press, 1984.

Long, A. A., and D. N. Sedley. *The Hellenistic Philosophers*. 2 vols. Cambridge: Cambridge University Press, 1987.

Mansi, J. D. *Sacrorum Conciliorum nova et amplissima collectio*. Florentiae: Expensis Antonii Zatta Veneti, 1759–98.

Nietzsche, F. *Werke*. Edited by G. Colli and M. Montinari. Vol. 3/1. Berlin/New York, 1972.

———. *Basic Writings of Nietzsche*. Edited and translated by W. Kaufmann. New York: Modern Library, 1992.

Petrus Lombardus. *Sententiae in IV libris distinctae*. 2 vols. Spicilegium Bonaventurianum 4–5. Grottaferrata/Rome: Collegium S. Bonaventurae, 1971, 1981.

Philippus Cancellarius Parisiensis. *Summa de bono*. Corpus Philosophorum Medii Aevi 2/1–2. Edited by N. Wicki. Bern: Francke, 1985.

Philodemus. *De musica librorum quae exstant*. Edited by J. Kemke. Leipzig: B. G. Teubner, 1884.

Plato. *Opera*. Edited by I. Burnet. Vols. 1–5. Oxford: Clarendon Press, 1901–1902.

Plotinus. *Opera*. Edited by P. Henry and H.-R. Schwyzer. 3 vols. Paris/Brussels: Descleé de Brouwer/L'Édition Universelle/E. J. Brill, 1951, 1959, 1973.

Plutarchus. *De Stoicorum repugnantiis*. Vol. 6/2 of *Plutarchi Moralia*. Edited by M. Pohlenz. Leipzig: B. G. Teubner, 1952.

Rahner, K. *Final Writings*. Translated by J. F. Donceel and H. M. Riley. Vol. 23 of *Theological Investigations*. New York: Crossroad, 1992.

Schelling, F. W. J. *System of Transcendental Idealism (1800)*. Translated by P. Heath. Charlottesville: University Press of Virginia, 1978.

Schiller, F. *On the Aesthetic Education of Man in a Series of Letters*. Translated and edited by E. M. Wilkinson and L. A. Willoughby. Oxford: Clarendon Press, 1967.

Schopenhauer, A. *The World as Will and Idea.* Translated by R. B. Haldane and J. Kemp. Vol. 1. London: Kegan Paul, 1896.
Sénèque. *Des bienfaits.* Edited by F. Préchac. 2 vols. Paris: Les Belles Lettres, 1961.
Sextus Empiricus. *Opera.* Edited by H. Mutschmann. Vol. 2. Leipzig: B. G. Teubner, 1914.
Stobaeus, Ioannes. *Eclogarum physicarum et ethicarum libri duo.* Edited by A. Meineke. Vol. 2. Leipzig: B. G. Teubner, 1864.
Thomas Aquinas. *Commentum in quatuor libros Sententiarum, libri 1- 2.* Vol. 6 of *Opera omnia.* Parma: P. Fiaccadori, 1856.
Tracy, D. *The Analogical Imagination: Christian Theology and the Culture of Pluralism.* New York: Crossroad, 1981.
Ulrich von Strassburg. *De summo bono, liber II.* Corpus Philosophorum Teutonicorum Medii Aevi 1/2. Edited by A. de Libera. Hamburg: F. Meiner, 1987.
Van Straaten, M., ed. *Panaetii Rhodii Fragmenta.* Leiden: E. J. Brill, 1962.
Wackenroder, W. H., and L. Tieck. *Outpourings of an Art-Loving Friar.* Translated by E. Mornin. New York: Ungar, 1975.
Waszink, J. H., ed. *Timaeus a Calcidio translatus commentarioque instructus.* Plato Latinus 4. London, Leiden: E. J. Brill, 1975.
Wolter, A. *John Duns Scotus: Philosophical Writings.* Indianapolis/Cambridge: Hackett Publishing Company, 1987.
Wolter, A., and O. V. Bychkov, eds. and trans. *John Duns Scotus. The Examined Report of the Paris Lecture (Reportatio I-A): Latin Text and English Translation.* 2 vols. S. Bonaventure, N.Y.: The Franciscan Institute, 2004, 2008.

Secondary Literature

Aertsen, J. A. "Beauty in the Middle Ages: A Forgotten Transcendental?" *Medieval Philosophy and Theology* 1 (1991): 68–97.
———. "Ontology and Henology in Medieval Philosophy (Thomas Aquinas, Master Eckhart and Berthold of Moosburg)." In *On Proclus and His Influence in Medieval Philosophy,* edited by E. P. Bos and P. A. Meijer, 120–40. Leiden/New York/Cologne: E. J. Brill, 1992.
———. "Beauty: Medieval Concepts." In vol. 1 of *Encyclopedia of Aesthetics,* edited by M. Kelly, 249–51. New York/Oxford: Oxford University Press, 1998.
Andreopoulos, A. *Art as Theology: From the Postmodern to the Medieval.* London: Equinox, 2006.
Apel, F. *Himmelssehnsucht. Die Sichtbarkeit der Engel in der romantischen Literatur und Kunst sowie bei Klee, Rilke und Benjamin.* Paderborn: Igel Verlag, 1994.
Ballinger, P. A. *The Poem as Sacrament: The Theological Aesthetic of Gerard Manley Hopkins.* Louvain: Peeters Press, 2000.
Bataille, G. *Theory of Religion.* New York: Zone Books, 1992.
Beare, J. I. *Greek Theories of Elementary Cognition.* Oxford: Clarendon Press, 1906.
Begbie, J. S. *Voicing Creation's Praise: Towards a Theology of the Arts.* Edinburgh: T&T Clark, 1991.
Benediktson, D. T. *Literature and the Visual Arts in Ancient Greece and Rome.* Norman: University of Oklahoma Press, 2000.

Bergmann, S. *God in Context: A Survey of Contextual Theology*. Aldershot: Ashgate, 2003.
Blocker, G. H., and J. M. Jeffers. *Contextualizing Aesthetics: From Plato to Lyotard*. Belmont, Calif.: Wadsworth Publishing Company, 1999.
Boudouris, K., ed. *Greek Philosophy and the Fine Arts*. 2 vols. Athens: International Center for Greek Philosophy and Culture, 2000.
Bowie, A. *Aesthetics and Subjectivity: From Kant to Nietzsche*. Manchester: Manchester University Press, 1990.
Brown, D. *Continental Philosophy and Modern Theology: An Engagement*. Oxford: Blackwell, 1987.
Brown, F. Burch. *Religious Aesthetics: A Theological Study of Making and Meaning*. Princeton: Princeton University Press, 1989.
———. *Good Taste, Bad Taste, and Christian Taste: Aesthetics in Religious Life*. Oxford/New York: Oxford University Press, 2000.
Brucker, J. *Historia critica philosophiae a mundi incunabulis ad nostram usque aetatem deducta*. Leipzig: Weidemann & Reich, 1767.
Bruyne, E. de. *Études d'esthétique médiévale*. 3 vols. Bruges: De Tempel, 1946.
Bürger, P. *Theory of the Avant-garde*. Translated by M. Shaw. Minneapolis: University of Minnesota Press, 1984.
Büttner, S. *Antike Ästhetik: Eine Einführung in die Prinzipien des Schönen*. Munich: C. H. Beck, 2006.
Bychkov, O. V. "The Reflection of Some Traditional Stoic Ideas in the Thirteenth-Century Scholastic Theories of Beauty." *Vivarium* 34, no. 2 (1996): 141–60.
———. "A Propos of Medieval Aesthetics: A Historical Study of Terminology, Sources, and Textual Traditions of Commenting on Beauty in the Thirteenth Century." Ph.D. thesis, University of Toronto, 1999.
———. "ἡ τοῦ κάλλους ἀπορροή: A Note on Achilles Tatius 1.9.4–5, 5.13.4." *Classical Quarterly* 49, no. 1 (1999): 339–41.
———. "*Decor ex praesentia mali*: Aesthetic Explanation of Evil in Thirteenth-Century Franciscan Thought." *Recherches de Théologie et Philosophie médiévales* 68, no. 2 (2001): 245–69.
———. "Image and Meaning: Canonicity in the Eastern Orthodox Tradition." In *Image Makers and Images Breakers*, edited by J. A. Harris, 83–91. New York/Ottawa/Toronto: Legas Press, 2003.
———. "Introduction: The Nature of Theology in Duns Scotus and His Franciscan Predecessors." *Franciscan Studies* 66 (2008): 5–99.
———. "What Does Beauty Have to Do with the Trinity? From Augustine to Duns Scotus." *Franciscan Studies* 66 (2008): 197–212.
Bychkov, O. V., and J. Fodor, eds. *Theological Aesthetics after von Balthasar*. Aldershot: Ashgate, 2008.
Bychkov, O. V., and A. Sheppard. *Greek and Roman Aesthetics*. Cambridge: Cambridge University Press, 2010.
Bychkov, V. V. *Estetika Avrelija Avgustina*. Moscow: Iskusstvo, 1984.
———. *2000 let khristianskoj kul'tury sub specie aesthetica* [2000 years of Christian culture *sub specie aesthetica*]. Vol. 1. Moscow/St. Petersburg: Universitetskaya kniga, 1999.

Bynum, C. W. *The Resurrection of the Body in Western Christianity, 200–1336*. New York: Columbia University Press, 1995.
Chapman, E. *Saint Augustine's Philosophy of Beauty*. New York/London: Sheed & Ward, 1939.
Colish, M. L. *The Stoic Tradition from Antiquity to the Early Middle Ages*. Studies in the History of Christian Thought, vols. 34–35. Leiden: E. J. Brill, 1985.
———. *Peter Lombard*. Brill's Studies in Intellectual History, vols. 41/1–41/2. Leiden: E. J. Brill, 1994.
Costil, P. "L'esthétique stoïcienne." In *Actes du Ier congrès de la Fédération Internationale des Associations d'études classiques. Paris, 28 août—2 septembre 1950*, 360–64. Paris: C. Klincksieck, 1951.
Courcelle, P. *Late Latin Writers and Their Greek Sources*. Cambridge: Harvard University Press, 1969.
Crawford, D. W. *Kant's Aesthetic Theory*. Madison: University of Wisconsin Press, 1974.
Cross, R. *Duns Scotus on God*. Aldershot: Ashgate, 2005.
Dawson, D. *Allegorical Readers and Cultural Revision in Ancient Alexandria*. Berkeley/Los Angeles/Oxford: University of California Press, 1992.
Derrida, J. *Margins of Philosophy*. Translated by Alan Bass. Chicago: University of Chicago Press, 1982.
Desmouliez, A. *Cicéron et son goût: essai sur une définition d'une esthétique Romaine à la fin de la république*. Collection Latomus 50. Brussels: Latomus, 1976.
Dickens, W. T. *Hans Urs von Balthasar's Theological Aesthetics: A Model for Post-Critical Biblical Interpretation*. Notre Dame, Ind.: University of Notre Dame Press, 2003.
Dilthey, W. "The Rise of Hermeneutics." In *W. Dilthey, Hermeneutics and the Study of History*. Vol. 4 of W. Dilthey, *Selected Works*, edited by R. A. Makkreel and F. Rodi, 235–58. Princeton: Princeton University Press, 1996.
Eco, U. *The Aesthetics of Thomas Aquinas*. Translated by H. Bredin. Cambridge: Harvard University Press, 1988.
Faas, E. *The Genealogy of Aesthetics*. Cambridge: Cambridge University Press, 2002.
Felicitas Munzel, G. "'The Beautiful Is the Symbol of the Morally-Good': Kant's Philosophical Basis of Proof for the Idea of the Morally-Good." *Journal of the History of Philosophy* 32, no. 2 (1995): 301–30.
Ferrari, G. R. F. *Listening to the Cicadas: A Study of Plato's Phaedrus*. Cambridge: Cambridge University Press, 1987.
Ferry, L. *Homo Aestheticus: The Invention of Taste in the Democratic Age*. Translated by R. de Loaiza. Chicago/London: University of Chicago Press, 1993.
Fistioc, M. C. *The Beautiful Shape of the Good: Platonic and Pythagorean Themes in Kant's Critique of the Power of Judgment*. New York: Routledge, 2002.
Floratos, C. S. Η αἰσθητικὴ τῶν Στωϊκῶν. Athens: n.p., 1973.
Fontanier, J.-M. "Sur le traité d'Augustin *De pulchro et apto*. Convenance, beauté et adaptation." *Revue des sciences philosophique et théologiques* 73 (1989): 413–21.
Fontanier, J.-M. *La beauté selon saint Augustin*. Rennes: Presses Universitaires de Rennes, 1998.
Fuller, B. A. G. *The Problem of Evil in Plotinus*. Cambridge: Cambridge University Press, 1912.

Fyodorov, N. A. "The Genesis of the Aesthetic Component in the Semantics of the Lexical Group *decus-decorum-decere-dignitas*." *Vestnik Moskovskogo Universiteta (filol. sek.)* 1 (1981): 49–61.
García-Rivera, A. *The Community of the Beautiful: A Theological Aesthetics*. Collegeville, Minn.: Liturgical Press, 1999.
Gardner, L., D. Moss, B. Quash, and G. Ward, eds. *Balthasar at the End of Modernity*. Edinburgh: T&T Clark, 1999.
Gill, C. "Personhood and Personality: The Four-Personae Theory in Cicero, *De officiis* I." *Oxford Studies in Ancient Philosophy* 6 (1988): 169–99.
Graeser, A. *Plotinus and the Stoics: A Preliminary Study*. Leiden: E. J. Brill, 1972.
Guetter, D. "Making Sense of 'The Appropriate' in Plato's *Timaeus*." Ph.D. thesis, University of Toronto, 1997.
Guyer, P. *Kant and the Experience of Freedom: Essays on Aesthetics and Morality*. Cambridge: Cambridge University Press, 1993.
Hadot, P. *Philosophy as a Way of Life: Spiritual Exercises from Socrates to Foucault*. Translated by M. Chase. Edited by A. I. Davidson. Oxford/Cambridge, Mass.: Blackwell, 1995.
Hagendahl, H. *Augustine and the Latin Classics*. Göteborg/Stockholm: Acta Universitatis Gothoburgensis/Almqvist & Wiksell, 1967.
Halliwell, S. *The Aesthetics of Mimesis*. Princeton: Princeton University Press, 2002.
Hammermeister, K. *The German Aesthetic Tradition*. Cambridge: Cambridge University Press, 2002.
Harrison, C. *Beauty and Revelation in the Thought of Saint Augustine*. Oxford: Clarendon Press, 1992.
Hart, D. B. *The Beauty of the Infinite: The Aesthetics of Christian Truth*. Grand Rapids, Mich./Cambridge, UK: W. B. Eerdmans, 2003.
Hartmann, M. *Ästhetik als ein Grundbegriff fundamentaler Theologie: Eine Untersuchung zu Hans Urs von Balthasar*. Dissertationen. Theologische Reihe 5. St. Ottilien: EOS Verlag, 1985.
Hayes, M. J. "Beauty's Resting Place: Unity in St. Augustine's Sensible Aesthetic." Ph.D. thesis, Marquette University, 2003.
Horn, H.-J. "Stoische Symmetrie und Theorie des Schönen in der Kaiserzeit." In *Aufstieg und Niedergang der Römischen Welt. Teil II: Principat*, edited by W. Haase and H. Temporini, 1454–72. Berlin/New York: Walter de Gruyter, 1989.
Janaway, C. *Images of Excellence: Plato's Critique of the Arts*. Oxford: Clarendon Press, 1998.
Jaspers, K. *The Great Philosophers*. Translated by R. Manheim. Edited by H. Arendt. New York: Harcourt, Brace & World, 1957.
Kahn, C. "The Beautiful and the Genuine: A Discussion of Paul Woodruff, Plato, *Hippias Major*." *Oxford Studies in Ancient Philosophy* 3 (1985): 261–87.
Kay, J. A. *Theological Aesthetics: The Role of Aesthetics in the Theological Method of Hans Urs von Balthasar*. European University Papers 23/60. Bern/Frankfurt am Main: Herbert Lang/Peter Lang, 1975.
———. "Hans Urs von Balthasar, a Post-critical Theologian?" *Concilium* 141 (1981): 84–89.

Keller, A. *Aurelius Augustinus und die Musik: Untersuchungen zu "De musica" im Kontext seines Schrifttums.* Würzburg: Augustinus-Verlag, 1993.
Kelly, M., ed. *Encyclopedia of Aesthetics.* 4 vols. New York/Oxford: Oxford University Press, 1998.
Kirby, J. T. "Mimesis and Diegesis: Foundations of Aesthetic Theory in Plato and Aristotle." *Helios: Journal of the Classical Association of the Southwest* 18, no. 2 (1991): 113–28.
Klibansky, R. *The Continuity of the Platonic Tradition during the Middle Ages.* London: The Warburg Institute, 1939.
Koch, J. "Augustinischer und dionysischer Neuplatonismus und das Mittelalter." *Kantstudien* 48, no. 2 (1956–57): 117–33.
Kovach, F. J. "Divine and Human Beauty in Duns Scotus's Philosophy and Theology." In *Scholastic Challenges to Some Medieval and Modern Ideas*, 93–110. Stillwater, Okla.: Western Publications, 1987.
Kuklica, P. "Ciceros ästhetische Ansichten." *Graecolatina et Orientalia* 11–12 (1979–80): 17–29.
Labriolle, P. de. *Histoire de la littérature latine chrétienne.* Paris: Les belles lettres, 1924.
Lafont, C. *Heidegger, Language and World Disclosure.* Cambridge: Cambridge University Press, 2000.
Lehmann, K., and W. Kasper, eds. *Hans Urs von Balthasar: Gestalt und Werk.* Cologne: Communio, 1989.
Liminta, M. T. *Il problema della bellezza in Platone: analisi e interpretazioni dell'Ippia maggiore.* Milan: Vita e pensiero, 1998.
Loessl, J. "*Religio, philosophia* und *pulchritudo*: ihr Zusammenhang nach Augustinus, *De vera religione.*" *Vigiliae Christianae* 47 (1993): 363–73.
Long, A. A. "The Stoic Concept of Evil." *Philosophical Quarterly* 18 (1968): 329–43.
Louth, A. *Discerning the Mystery: An Essay on the Nature of Theology.* Oxford: Clarendon Press, 1983.
Manieri, A. *L'immagine poetica nella teoria degli antichi: phantasia ed enargeia.* Pisa: Istituti editoriali e poligrafici internazionali, 1998.
Matthews, G. B. *The Augustinian Tradition.* Berkeley: University of California Press, 1999.
Maxwell, D. R. "Augustine's *De musica* 6.12.34–6.14.48: An Ontology of Music Which Saves the Soul." M.A. thesis, Concordia Seminary, 1998.
McEvoy, J. "Does Augustinian *Memoria* Depend on Plotinus?" In *The Perennial Tradition of Neoplatonism.* Ancient and Medieval Philosophy 1.24, edited by J. J. Cleary, 383–96. Louvain: Leuven University Press, 1997.
McGregor, B., and T. Norris, eds. *The Beauty of Christ: An Introduction to the Theology of Hans Urs von Balthasar.* Edinburgh: T&T Clark, 1994.
Moda, A. *Hans Urs von Balthasar, un' esposizione critica del suo pensiero.* Bari: Ecumenica Editrice, 1976.
Moravcsik, J. M. E., and P. Temko, eds. *Plato on Beauty, Wisdom and the Arts.* Totowa, N.J.: Rowman and Littlefield, 1982.
Müller, L. "Das 'Schöne' im Denken des Thomas von Aquin." *Theologie und Philosophie* 57 (1982): 413–24.

Nichols, A. *The Word Has Been Abroad: A Guide through Balthasar's Aesthetics.* Washington, D.C.: The Catholic University of America Press, 1998.
North, H. F. "Canons and Hierarchies of the Cardinal Virtues in Greek and Latin Literature." In *The Classical Tradition: Literary and Historical Studies of Harry Caplan*, edited by L. Wallach, 164–83. Ithaca, N.Y.: Cornell University Press, 1966.
O'Connell, R. J. *Art and the Christian Intelligence in St. Augustine.* Cambridge: Harvard University Press, 1978.
O'Donnell, J. *Hans Urs von Balthasar.* Collegeville, Minn.: Liturgical Press, 1992.
O'Donnell, J. J. "Augustine's Classical Readings." *Recherches augustiniennes* 15 (1980): 144–75.
Olejniczak Lobsien, V., and C. Olk, eds. *Neuplatonismus und Ästhetik: Zur Transformationsgeschichte des Schönen.* Transformationen der Antike 2. Berlin/New York: Walter de Gruyter, 2007.
Ouspensky, L., and V. Lossky. *The Meaning of Icons.* Translated by G. E. H. Palmer and E. Kadloubovsky. Crestwood, N.Y.: St. Vladimir's Seminary Press, 1999.
Peter, K. *Die Lehre von der Schönheit nach Bonaventura.* Werl: Dietrich-Coelde-Verlag, 1964.
Pohlenz, M. *Antikes Führertum: Cicero De officiis und das Lebensideal des Panaitios.* Neue Wege zur Antike 2/3. Leipzig/Berlin: B. G. Teubner, 1934.
Pouillon, D. H. "La beauté, propriété transcendantale. Chez les scholastiques (1220–1270)." *Archives d'histoire doctrinale et littéraire du moyen âge* 15 (1946): 263–329.
Pöltner, G. *Schönheit: eine Untersuchung zum Ursprung des Denkens bei Thomas von Aquin.* Vienna/Freiburg/Basel: Herder, 1978.
Ramirez, E. R. J. "Augustine's Proof for God's Existence from the Experience of Beauty: Conf. X.6." *Augustinian Studies* 19 (1988): 121–30.
Rentschler, I., B. Herzberger, and D. Epstein, eds. *Beauty and the Brain.* Basel/Boston/Berlin: Birkhäuser, 1988.
Riches, J., ed. *The Analogy of Beauty: The Theology of Hans Urs von Balthasar.* Edinburgh: T&T Clark, 1986.
Risser, J. *Hermeneutics and the Voice of the Other.* Albany: SUNY Press, 1997.
Roberts, L. *The Theological Aesthetics of Hans Urs von Balthasar.* Washington, D.C.: The Catholic University of America Press, 1987.
Rosemann, P. W. *Understanding Scholastic Thought with Foucault.* New York: St. Martin's Press, 1999.
Saint-Pierre, M. *Beauté, bonté, vérité chez Hans Urs von Balthasar.* Quebec: Les Éditions du Cerf, 1998.
Schanz, M. *Geschichte der römischen Litteratur bis zum Gesetzgebungswerk des Kaisers Justinian.* Vol. 4.2. Munich: C. H. Beck, 1920.
Schmitt, A. "Zahl und Schönheit in Augustins *De musica* VI." *Würzburger Jahrbücher für die Altertumswissenschaft* n.s. 16 (1990): 221–37.
Scola, A. *Hans Urs von Balthasar: A Theological Style.* Grand Rapids, Mich.: William B. Eerdmans, 1995.
Smit, L. A. ""He's all delight": Aesthetic Knowing in the Thought of Bonaventure." Ph.D. thesis, Boston University, 1998.
Sondag, G. "The Conditional Definition of Beauty by Scotus." *Medioevo* 30 (2005): 191–206.

Spanneut, M. *Permanence du Stoïcisme de Zénon à Malraux.* Gembloux: Duculot, 1973.
Spargo, E. J. M. *The Category of the Aesthetic in the Philosophy of Saint Bonaventure.* St. Bonaventure, N.Y.: Franciscan Institute, 1953.
Speer, A. "Aquinas, Thomas." In vol. 1 of *Encyclopedia of Aesthetics*, edited by M. Kelly, 76–79. New York/Oxford: Oxford University Press, 1998.
Steck, C. W. *The Ethical Thought of Hans Urs von Balthasar.* New York: Crossroad, 2001.
Stock, B. *Augustine the Reader: Meditation, Self-knowledge, and the Ethics of Interpretation.* Cambridge: Harvard University Press, 1996.
Svoboda, K. *L'esthétique de Saint Augustin et ses sources.* Brno: Vydava Filosoficka Fakulta, 1933.
———. "Les idées esthétiques de Sénèque." In *Mélanges de philologie, de littérature et d'histoire anciennes offerts à J. Marouzeau par ses collégues et élèves étrangers*, 537–46. Paris: Les Belles Lettres, 1948.
Switalski, B. *Plotinus and the Ethics of St. Augustine.* Polish Institute Series 8. New York: Polish Institute of Arts and Sciences in America, 1946.
Tatarkiewicz, W. *The History of Aesthetics.* 3 vols. Edited by J. Harrell et al. and translated by Adam and Ann Czerniawski et al. The Hague: Mouton, 1970–74.
Testard, M. "Note sur le De Civitate Dei, XXII, 24: Exemple de réminiscences cicéroniennes de saint Augustin." In vol. 1 of *Augustinus Magister: Congrès international augustinien*, 193–200. Paris: Études augustiniennes, 1954.
Testard, M. *Saint Augustin et Cicéron.* 2 vols. Paris: Études augustiniennes, 1958.
Thiessen, G. E., ed. *Theological Aesthetics: A Reader.* Grand Rapids, Mich./Cambridge, UK: W. B. Eerdmans, 2004.
Thomas, H. "Gerard Manley Hopkins and John Duns Scotus." *Religious Studies* 24, no. 3 (1988): 337–64.
Tscholl, J. *Gott und das Schöne beim Hl. Augustinus.* Heverlee-Leuven: Augustijns-Historisch Instituut, 1967.
Verbeke, G. "Augustin et le stoïcisme." *Recherches augustiniennes* 1 (1958): 67–89.
———. *The Presence of Stoicism in Medieval Thought.* Washington, D.C.: The Catholic University of America Press, 1983.
Viladesau, R. *Theological Aesthetics: God in Imagination, Beauty, and Art.* New York/Oxford: Oxford University Press, 1999.
———. *Theology and the Arts: Encountering God through Music, Art and Rhetoric.* New York/Mahwah, N.J.: Paulist Press, 2000.
Wolterstorff, N. *Divine Discourse: Philosophical Reflections on the Claim That God Speaks.* New York: Cambridge University Press, 1995.
Zagdoun, M.-A. *La philosophie stoïcienne de l'art.* Paris: CNRS, 2000.
Zarb, S. "Chronologia operum sancti Augustini secundum ordinem Retractationum digesta." *Angelicum* 11 (1934): 78–91.

INDEX

aesthetic: aesthetic education, 33–34, 165, 171–72; aesthetic vision, 67, 81–82, 89, 91, 93, 99, 116–18, 218; ancient terminology, 145–49, 194–96, 203–5, 220–22; notion of, 15–50; as pointer (*Verweis*) or guide, 27, 67, 137, 151, 155, 159–60, 165–66, 178, 203n75, 209–11, 227n50, 258, 274, 277, 315n136, 321, 325, 328–29; as presentation (*Darstellung*), 22–23, 24n21, 37n58, 38, 42, 44n88, 49, 65, 122, 180, 184, 186, 315n136, 321; purposiveness of, 21–22, 24n21, 25, 30, 53n6, 244–45, 328

aesthetic experience: as disinterested, 22, 25, 27, 34, 73, 158n69, 163, 164n80, 192, 209–10, 243, 324; and morality, 24–25, 33, 49n98, 178, 189n42, 204, 207–10; as revelatory, xiii, 1, 18, 32, 35–38, 41–42, 52, 79, 87, 99, 130, 131n7, 141, 156n62, 160–63, 165, 169, 174–75, 177–79, 197, 198n63, 210–11, 215–16, 223, 227n50, 239–40, 245, 253, 256, 263–65, 286, 309, 315–16, 320–21, 323, 325–30, 333; verification through, 32, 48–49, 53n7, 54–55, 64n32, 65–66, 72–74, 79, 81, 112, 181, 185, 187, 189n41, 191, 193, 202, 259, 284, 286, 334

aesthetics: as autonomous, xi–xii, 18, 27, 34–36, 39, 42, 49–50, 61, 62n28, 79, 131, 158n69, 324; Catholic, xiii, 53, 55–56, 59, 79; Christological, 269, 271, 277, 290, 298; engaged model of, xii, 35–37, 42, 324; Idealist, 37, 57, 130, 207; modern philosophical, 15–50; Protestant, xii–xiv, 52–56, 67, 79; theological, ix–xiv, 1n1, 2n3, 29n36, 31n43, 36, 37, 44n85, 50–101, 104, 109–10, 112, 115–17, 121, 125, 129, 138, 141, 156n56, 162, 180–81, 211–12, 217–18, 223–25, 226n47, 251–52, 257, 268–69, 272–74, 277, 279, 288, 290, 308, 315n136, 318–19, 321, 323–24, 327; transcendental, 19, 62, 119, 123, 138, 216, 240, 249, 256n125, 257n128, 283n42, 323, 326, 328; Trinitarian, 264n139, 268, 270–71, 276–77, 290, 292, 299n91, 320; working definition, 46–50, 119–23

Albert the Great, 114, 124, 144n40, 182, 237, 271, 278n29, 300–301, 307n120

Alexander of Hales, 182, 271, 289, 301; *Summa Halensis*, 301, 302

Ambrose, 143, 181, 205n80, 271n8

analogy, aesthetic, xi, xiii, 19, 24, 26, 45–46, 48–50, 105, 115, 119–23, 130, 323, 327, 330; in ancient thought, 137, 146, 160–62, 165–66, 171, 180–82, 186, 189–90, 193–94, 197, 203–4, 206n85, 207–11; in Augustine, 215n15, 222, 225–26, 228, 235, 265, 267; in Balthasar, 58, 61–62, 64n33, 66–70, 72, 75–76, 87, 90–91; in medieval thought, 268, 270–71, 279, 282, 285n45, 290, 292, 301, 308, 311, 314–20

analogy of being, 56n12, 63n31, 67, 109

Anselm of Canterbury, 78, 114, 121, 125, 140n30, 184n26, 268–69, 278, 280; *Cur Deus homo*, 286–89; *Proslogion*, 257n130, 281–85

Apologists, Christian, 112, 219, 266

Apuleius, 142–43, 144n42

Aristotle, 84, 88n26, 104, 112, 183, 205n82, 250, 295n75; *De anima*, 158, 243n98, 249n113, 250n116; *Poetics*, 185, 204

art: in ancient and medieval thought, 130, 135n19, 169, 173–74, 190–91, 213, 215, 229, 238, 253–54, 256n125, 263, 284; condemnation of, 133, 169, 172–73; and craft, 173–74; in modern aesthetics, 27–46

Augustine: aesthetics of, 212–67; on ascent from beauty, 239–67; *Confessions*, 265–66;

Augustine: *(cont.)*
De civ. Dei, 219–20, 233–34, 235n72, 236; *De lib. arb.,* 258–64; *De magistro,* 239–41; *De musica,* 247–52; *De nat. boni,* 220, 235; *De ordine,* 241–47; *De Trin.,* 264–65; *De vera rel.,* 252–58; *Enchiridion,* 220, 233; on evil and beauty of the whole, 229–38; and Kant, 216, 240, 249–50, 254; proof of existence of God, 231–32; and transcendental aesthetics, 217

Aulus Gellius, 142, 235–36

Balthasar, H. U. von: on Anselm, 280–81; on Augustine, 81–82, 88–89, 91, 217–18; on Bonaventure, 87–88, 98–99, 273–76; and hermeneutics, 78–100; on Plato, 138–41; on Plotinus, 89–90, 91n36, 96n50, 97, 118, 123–24, 141, 223–26, 318; on pseudo-Dionysius, 90n33, 92n38, 97–98, 115, 278–80; on Stoics, 180–81; and theological aesthetics, 37, 44n85, 50–101, 104, 109–10, 112, 115, 117, 125, 129, 138, 141, 181, 211–12, 217–18, 224–25, 257, 272–73, 308, 315n136, 318–19

Barth, K., xiii, 52–59, 62n28, 78–79, 86, 94, 109

Baumgarten, A. G., 15–19, 41, 78, 231, 249

beauty/the beautiful: analogy with health, 193–94, 207; ascent from, 154–57, 161–66, 239–67, 310–16, 318; of Christ, 54, 220, 271, 290, 298–320; of contrast, 220, 231, 233–34; of God, 52–55, 58n17; intellectual, 121–23, 226, 326–27, 330; physical, 132n12, 161–62, 165, 178n10, 190, 193–94, 207–8; as symbol of morality, 25–26, 41, 210; of Trinity, 289–98, 320; of universe, 166–69, 190–93, 229–33

beauty, aesthetic (τὸ κάλλος, *pulchritudo, pulchrum*), 132, 146, 152, 157, 162, 166, 168–69, 171, 182, 190, 194n54, 196–97, 203–4, 205n80, 207–9, 211, 227n51, 257n128, 278, 288, 299, 300, 309, 319

beauty, moral (τὸ καλόν, τὸ πρέπον, *honestum, decorum*), 195–211, 218–20, 271n8, 272

Boethius, 142, 144

Bonaventure: aesthetics of, 268–321; on ascent from beauty, 310–16, 318; on Christ's form *(species Christi),* 298–310, 314–20; *Commentary on the Sentences,* 302–10; *De reductione,* 317n142; *Disputed Questions,* 307–8; on expression, 272, 275–76, 290, 298, 302–3, 305–8; *Hexaemeron,* 275; *Itinerarium,* 310–18; *Legenda major,* 316; *Sermons,* 316; on Trinity, 289–98, 320

Brown, F. B., xv, 47n92, 49n99, 53n6, 56, 71n56, 218, 270n6, 326–27, 329, 333

Calcidius, 142–43, 144n40

catalogy (*Katalogie*), 308

Christ: beauty of, 54, 220, 271, 290, 298–320; Christ's form (*species Christi*), 70–73, 74n68, 75–76, 298–310, 314–20; as image, 272, 276, 298–306, 308–10, 314–15, 317

Cicero, 116, 118, 121, 124, 135, 142–45, 149, 150n54, 155n61, 161, 169, 178, 180, 182–83, 185, 191, 195–96, 203n76, 218–21, 222, 246, 271n8, 277–78; *De divinatione,* 192n48; *De finibus,* 196, 197n62, 198–200, 206n84, 207n88, 208; *De legibus,* 197n62, 207n88; *De natura deorum,* 169, 180, 181–82, 190, 192, 193n50–51, 219, 231–32, 253, 257n130; *De officiis,* 143, 144n41, 171n91, 177n4, 178, 179n14, 180–82, 194n54, 196n58, 60, 197n62, 198, 204–8, 210; *De oratore,* 180n15, 192n46, 48, 234n70; *Orator,* 206n86, 229n52, 235n72; *Part. Orat.,* 186; *Tusc. disp.,* 194, 196n60, 200, 208n89

cognition: and aesthetics, 15–18, 21, 50, 135, 139, 226, 241n94, 244n99, 246, 249, 260, 282–86, 289–90, 302, 306–9, 313–14, 317n142, 324, 328–30; and blindness, 66, 69, 81, 89, 106–7, 311; seeing as, xiii, 47–48, 53n6, 107, 319

cognitive impression (καταληπτικὴ φαντασία), 183–84, 185n30, 187–89, 209, 285n48, 286

coherence, 62n29, 71, 73, 74n68, 108, 111, 112, 231, 334

dance, 263

Dilthey, W., 5, 9n18

Diogenes Laertius, 180n14, 188n40, 198–99, 200n66, 202, 205n82, 206n83, 209

equality: in Augustine, 230n54, 243n98, 250–52, 254–56, 258; in the Trinity, 291–99, 302–5, 309, 313, 314n135, 320

exemplar: in Bonaventure, 272, 276, 305–6, 307–9, 311–12, 317; in Plato, 167, 169, 192

Index — 347

faith, 56, 59–60, 63, 66, 67n42, 68n45, 69, 72–73, 81, 84, 89, 108–10, 114, 250n114, 252–53, 259, 266, 269n4, 270, 274–75, 315n136, 317n142
Fichte, J. G., 27n32, 36n55, 67, 95, 120, 224
Francis, St., 273, 275n21, 316

Gadamer, H.-G., 42, 49n98, 63n31, 64, 66n37, 86n20, 90, 104, 116, 135; and aesthetics, 44–46, 62, 105, 107–8, 132n7, 137–39, 156n62, 180; and hermeneutics, 5–11, 76, 80–82, 85, 88, 92, 93n42, 99, 101, 103, 112–13, 134, 160
Galen, 193–94
genius, 32, 39, 135n19, 153n58, 331–32
Gestalt psychology, 46, 241n94, 265n140
glory, theological concept of, 52, 53n7, 54–55, 58n17, 59–60, 62n28, 63n30, 68, 70n51, 72–73, 87, 91n34, 93, 96, 109, 119, 141, 163n78, 224–26, 228, 270, 275n21, 314, 318–19
God: aesthetic proof of existence, 190–93, 227n27, 231–32, 266n143, 277; as beauty, 52–55

harmony, 21–23, 26, 30–31, 33–34, 42, 45, 63, 71, 72n57, 73–74, 91, 97, 125, 137, 140–41, 151n56, 168, 171n91, 172–73, 188, 191, 192n48, 193, 194n54, 199, 200n66, 201n72, 206, 207–10, 215, 219–21, 227, 237, 238n88, 242–43, 245–50, 252, 254, 257–58, 260, 262–63, 265, 282n40, 283–84, 288–89, 291–92, 298–99, 301, 312n131, 313, 316, 319–21, 326, 329, 334
Hegel, G. W. F., 19n11, 22n19, 29n36, 55, 89, 96n50, 223–24; on aesthetics, 36–38; on Stoics and Kant, 180, 187, 188n38, 189n42
Heidegger, M., 16n3, 17n8, 47, 52, 61–65, 82, 83n13, 104, 110–11, 139, 156n62, 180, 224n44, 280, 332; and aesthetics, 37, 39, 42–44, 46, 49n98, 69n47, 105, 131n7; and hermeneutics, 6, 9n18, 10, 48, 80, 85, 86n20
hermeneutics/hermeneutic approach, 1–11; Balthasar's, 78–100; current aproach, 101–25; as dialogue, 1, 9–11, 15, 52, 92–94, 99, 102, 105, 106n8, 114, 116–17, 123, 135–36, 138, 141–42, 216–18, 240n92, 323; fusion of horizons, 8–11, 85; Gadamer's, 5–11, 76, 80–82, 85, 88, 92, 93n42, 99, 101, 103, 112–13, 134, 160; Romantic, 2, 6n10, 9n18, 82. See also historico-critical method

Hilary of Poitiers, 296, 298, 303–5
historicity, xiv, 4–6, 8, 80, 87, 102–4, 113
historico-critical method/historical school, xii, 2–4, 8–9, 78, 82n12, 83n14, 84, 88, 90n29, 91, 98, 101–3, 114, 116–18, 135, 146
Husserl, E., 6, 19n12, 47–48, 95, 184n26, 224, 240n92, 259; and aesthetics, 333–34

icon, 75, 94, 95n45, 107, 275n21, 328; iconoclasts, 310n125; iconodules, 74, 75n70; iconographic/iconographer, 94–95, 97
intuition/insight, 10, 16, 18–19, 23–24, 27–32, 39, 41, 47–48, 54, 66n39, 78, 84, 99, 103, 119, 135n19, 137, 168, 180–81, 189–90, 201–3, 209, 211, 218, 237, 241, 245–47, 255, 265, 270, 281, 302, 309, 315, 319, 324, 330, 332
Isidore of Seville, 219

John Duns Scotus: on aesthetic proofs, 281–85; on Christ, 303–4; on Trinity, 292–97
joy, of the senses, 53n6, 54, 158, 325, 327–29
judgment, aesthetic, 20–22, 24–26, 68, 178n11, 180n15, 216–17, 231, 237–38, 241, 250, 252–53, 258–67, 284, 285n45; compelling nature of, 244–45, 254–56, 259–61, 265; pleasure as judgment, 243, 248–49, 259, 313, 329
justification, aesthetic, 42, 65, 68, 89, 193, 214–15, 217–19, 220n31, 233, 237–38

Kant, I.: on aesthetics, 18–27; and Augustine, 216–17; and Plato, 135–37; and Stoics, 179–80, 210
Kantians, 18n10, 65–66, 95, 119–20
Kierkegaard, S., 55, 57

Lindbeck, G. A., 107n10, 108, 111
logic, ix, 41, 55, 188, 200–201, 203, 209n93

Macrobius, 142
Manichaeans, 233, 252, 258
manifestation (ἐνάργεια, evidentia), 184–87
Minucius Felix, 191, 266n143
music, xii, 47n92, 71n56, 75, 98, 168, 170–74, 177n8, 190, 191n45, 194n54, 204n79, 221, 227, 230, 237–38, 246–47, 282n40, 284

neo-aesthetics, 53n6, 326–27, 329
Neoplatonists/Neoplatonic, 119n29, 120n32, 143n36, 144, 161, 164n77, 214, 218, 221,

Neoplatonists/Neoplatonic (*cont.*) 223n41, 230, 239, 240, 243, 245, 271, 276, 279–80, 286, 291, 310

Neoscholasticism, 58n17, 67n44, 101

neuroscience/neurobiology, 46–47, 107, 242n97, 256n126

Nietzsche, F., xi, 43, 51, 55, 76n72, 89, 133, 140n29, 217–18, 238, 289n56; and aesthetics, 39–42

number, ancient concept of, 218, 221–22, 243n98, 245–52, 259–60, 262–63, 303n107

ontological difference, 44n85, 60

order, ancient concept of, 125, 133, 138, 140, 143, 145, 152, 166–69, 172n93, 191–92, 198–99, 204n79, 205–9, 218, 230–37, 241–42, 246–51, 286–88, 303n107, 311

painting, 43, 47, 75, 97, 170, 190, 220, 234, 235n72, 237

Peter Lombard, 219, 238, 296, 300–301, 310

Philip the Chancellor, 182, 205n80

Plato: aesthetics of, 129–75; on ascent from beauty, 154–57, 161–66; condemnation of arts, 130–31, 133, 152, 169, 172–74; definitions of beauty, 150–51; *Hippias Major*, 149–51; *Phaedrus*, 152–57; *Republic*, 169–75; *Symposion*, 157–66; *Timaeus*, 166–69

Plotinus, 89, 90n32, 91n36, 96n50, 97, 118–19, 120n32, 123–24, 131n7, 135, 139n27, 141–42, 143n36, 151n55–56, 178n10, 214–15, 218–19, 222–29, 235–37, 242–43, 245n104, 257n129, 267, 278–79, 290, 299n91, 318

Plutarch, 150n53, 197–98, 200–201, 207n87, 211, 236–37

poetry, 8n16, 88n26, 133, 169–70, 171n92, 172–73, 177, 191n45, 247–48, 277n24

postmodern/postmodernity, ix, xi, 40, 47, 76n72, 79, 85n18, 86, 102–5, 108, 117n26, 164n80, 173

proportion, xii, 72n57, 73, 74n68, 75, 168, 180n14, 194n54, 210, 215, 221, 227–28, 242–45, 247–51, 255, 260, 262, 280, 284, 292, 297, 299, 301, 304, 305n112, 307n117, 312–13, 314n135, 320–21

pseudo-Aristotle: *De mundo*, 190

pseudo-Dionysius the Areopagite, 78–85, 90n33, 92n38, 97–98, 115, 120n32, 123–24, 140n30, 142–44, 163n77, 195, 204n78, 223n40, 229, 269, 271, 276–80, 299n91, 300, 307, 310

Quintilian, 185, 235n72

Rahner, K., 57n15, 63, 65, 66n37, 80, 85, 86n20, 95, 120

relations, Trinitarian, 291–98

revelation, theological concept of, xii–xiii, 55–56, 58–59, 60n22, 63, 64n32, 67–73, 74n69, 79, 83, 86n21, 87–88, 90, 96, 98, 109, 115, 119n29, 123, 218, 274–75

revelatorics, 326–27, 329–31, 333–34

rhetoric/rhetorical, xi, 3, 60n22, 76n72, 98, 110, 114–15, 117, 184–85, 186n33, 187, 220, 234, 235n72

Schelling, F. W. J., 15n1, 27–33, 36n55, 39, 42, 224, 331–33

Schiller, F., 32n44, 33–34, 68, 89, 172n94, 209n92, 246, 289n56

Schleiermacher, F., 55

Schopenhauer, A., 34n51, 38–39, 42, 55, 135n19, 331–32

Seneca, 180, 191–92, 193n49, 196, 229n52

sense perception/the senses, x, 19, 47, 64, 69, 72, 132, 165, 178, 270n6, 274n16, 311–15, 317n142, 318, 329; hearing, 56, 107, 151, 242–44, 313n132; vision, 151, 155, 162, 185–86, 208, 217, 242–44, 265, 312–13

Sextus Empiricus, 183, 185n30, 187–88, 199n64, 202, 203n75

Stoics: aesthetics of, 176–211; Chrysippus, 192, 194n54, 235–36, 237n82, 84; Cleanthes, 191n45, 192; criterion of truth, 183–85, 187–89; on moral beauty, 196–209; Panaetius, 179n14, 195n54, 203n76, 204n79, 205n81; on parallels with physical beauty, 193–94, 207; proof of existence of gods, 190–93

sublime/sublimity, x, 33–34, 36, 39n69, 41, 118, 224, 325, 328; in ancient thought, 150, 201, 206, 249–50, 254; in Kant, 20–23, 24n21, 25, 42, 45n88, 61n27, 121–22, 155n62, 210

supersensible ground, 19–21, 23–24, 25n25, 26, 122, 153n59, 256, 283n42

symmetry, 74n68, 178n10, 183, 209n90, 228, 255, 292, 296, 299, 320 taste, aesthetic, 20–21, 26, 62n28, 106, 112n21, 178n11, 210; antinomy of, 21, 245; theories of, 4, 46, 66n37, 146

theology: apologetic or fundamental, 60n23, 68, 70, 76, 107, 110, 116, 212, 216, 252, 253–54, 258–59, 262, 264–69, 271, 280n33, 331; systematic, x, 8, 60n22, 62n29, 70, 76, 80n2, 81–82, 87n24, 88n26, 93n42, 105, 107n10, 108–10, 112–15, 117–18, 264, 268, 289–90, 320, 331

thing-in-itself, 19, 27–29, 38–39, 135n19, 330, 332

Thomas Aquinas, 4n7, 56n13, 57n16, 63n30, 78, 92n41, 98–99, 102n1, 114, 144n41, 182, 271n8, 274, 275n18, 278n29, 300–301, 304

Tillich, P., xiii, 75, 95

Tracy, D., 8n16, 9n19–20, 10n22, 46, 60n22, 62n29, 66n37, 71n56, 76n72, 81–82, 83n14, 86, 87n24, 88, 93n43, 102n2, 104n3, 105, 107n10, 108–10, 116–17, 277n24

transcendence and immanence, 18, 29n36, 36, 120n32, 140n30, 141, 223–24, 226n47, 240, 279, 289n56, 309, 324–25, 330, 333–34

transcendental: aesthetics, 19, 62, 119, 123, 138, 216, 240, 249, 256n125, 257n128, 283n42, 323, 326, 328; philosophy, 18, 30n41, 31, 62n28, 88, 120n32, 217, 239; as transcategorial, 58n16, 148n49

Trinity, beauty of, 289–98, 320

truth, xi–xii, 8, 36–38, 61, 76n72, 81, 102, 116, 121, 139, 231, 237–38, 280n33, 281n37, 284–86, 307, 327; and art and aesthetics, 15–17, 39–42, 69n47, 73, 104, 106, 108, 135n19; criterion of, 48, 183–85, 187–89, 202; as disclosure, 43–46, 62–63, 81–82, 104–5, 110, 137; eternal, immutable, and inner, 241, 246n105, 252, 254, 257, 259–66, 318; and theological aesthetics, 57, 59, 64–65, 97–98, 110; types of, 42, 82, 62n29, 110–12

ugly/ugliness, 16, 146, 152, 158, 171, 173, 194n54, 198, 230, 232–34, 237

Ulrich of Strassburg, 58n16, 182, 300

unity, aesthetic principle of, 17, 214–15, 227, 230n54, 242, 254, 256, 291–92, 303n107

Victorines, 277, 310

Viladesau, R., xv, 1n1, 2n3, 52n2, 55n10, 56n12, 57n15, 58n17, 59n20, 61n25, 66n37, 71n56, 80, 106n8, 110, 174n95, 215n15, 269, 318n143

virtue, 121, 138, 144n42, 158n68, 160, 164, 180n14, 188n40, 194, 196–99, 201–2, 204n79, 205n82, 206n84, 207–8, 210, 236, 258, 265, 316

whole/wholeness, 17–18, 33, 82, 84, 220, 229–38, 248, 313

William of Auxerre, 300

Aesthetic Revelation: Reading Ancient and Medieval Texts after Hans Urs von Balthasar was designed in Adobe Jenson Pro and typeset by Kachergis Book Design of Pittsboro, North Carolina. It was printed on 60-pound Natures Book Natural and bound by Thomson-Shore of Dexter, Michigan.

www.ingramcontent.com/pod-product-compliance
Lightning Source LLC
Chambersburg PA
CBHW020313010526
44107CB00054B/1829